Microsoft®

Windows® CE Programmer's Guide

Microsoft Press

PUBLISHED BY
Microsoft Press
A Division of Microsoft Corporation
One Microsoft Way
Redmond, WA 98052-6399

Library of Congress Cataloging-in-Publication Data
Microsoft Windows CE Programmer's Guide / Microsoft Corporation.
     p.   cm.
  Includes index.
  ISBN 1-57231-643-8
  1. Microsoft Windows (Computer file) 2. Operating systems
(Computers)   I. Microsoft Corporation.
QA76.76.063M524135 1998
005.26'8--dc21   97-43824
                                           CIP

Printed and bound in the United States of America.

2 3 4 5 6 7 8 9 QMQM 3 2 1 0 9 8

Distributed to the book trade in Canada by Macmillan of Canada, a division of Canada Publishing Corporation.

A CIP catalogue record for this book is available from the British Library.

Microsoft Press books are available through booksellers and distributors worldwide. For further information about international editions, contact your local Microsoft Corporation office. Or contact Microsoft Press International directly at fax (425) 936-7329. Visit our Web site at mspress.microsoft.com.

Managing Editor: Ava Chen
Writers: Jason Black, Cheri Christensen, Jon Christiansen, Tom Clark, Kurt Ding, John Dohlen,
     Peggi Goodwin, John Murray, Guy Smith, Waudean Thomas, Nuan Wen
Editors: Laurell Haapanen, Jeanne Hunt
Production: Teresa Atkinson, Troy Gudmundson, Bruce Vanderpool

For Microsoft Press:
Acquisitions Editor: Casey Doyle
Project Editor: Saul Candib

Contents

Part 3   User Interface Services

Part 8   Palm PC

Part 9   Appendix

Preface

The *Windows CE Programmer's Guide* provides all the information you need to write applications for Windows CE-based devices using the Microsoft® Windows® CE application programming interface (API).

The *Windows CE Programmer's Guide* is written for you, if you are one of the following:

- A Win32 developer

  Including a Win32, independent software vendor (ISV), an independent hardware vendor (IHV), a service provider developer, or a corporate MIS developer. You should be proficient in basic Win32 programming. Additionally, you should understand the essentials of the Windows message-driven programming model, and the most widely-used features of the Win32 API.

- An embedded developer

  Including a developer experienced in embedded development and 32-bit embedded operating systems. You should have significant experience using C or C++ and object-oriented methods.

- An internal developer or an original equipment manufacturer (OEM)

  Including an internal developer who is responsible for creating internal build tools, or an OEM who ports Windows CE to hardware platforms.

How This Book Is Organized

The *Windows CE Programmer's Guide* contains the following chapters:

Part 1 Introduction to Windows CE Programming

Chapter 1 through Chapter 3 describe the four primary modules of the Windows CE operating system: the kernel, the file system, the graphics windowing and events subsystem (GWES), and the communications interface. They also discuss what you should consider as you develop an application for Windows CE.

Part 2 Core Services

Chapter 4 and Chapter 5 discuss how Windows CE manages threads, memory, and resources. They also describe the Windows CE communication interface and information processing.

Part 3 User Interface Services

Chapter 6 through Chapter 16 provide the information you need to create a graphical user interface. They discuss windows, controls, dialog boxes, menus, and other resources, and offer tips for designing an effective user interface.

Part 4 Connection Services

Chapter 17 through Chapter 21 describe how Windows CE establishes a serial connection with a Windows-based desktop computer to transfer files, debug remotely, and synchronize databases on the two computers.

Part 5 Web Services

Chapter 22 introduces Mobile Channels technology and describes how to create a mobile channel.

Part 6 Interfaces to Bundled Applications

Chapter 23 through Chapter 25 discuss how to implement Contacts, Inbox, and Mail Transport Service functionality in your applications.

Part 7 Handheld PC

Chapter 26 through Chapter 30 describe programming information specific to the H/PC, such as managing power and sending and receiving data.

Part 8 Palm PC

Chapter 31 through Chapter 33 describe programming information specific to the Palm PC, such as working with the Palm PC shell.

Part 9 Appendix

The Appendix lists functions and interfaces supported by Windows CE.

Glossary

About the CD

The disc contains the following:

- Windows CE Emulation Software Development Kit (SDK), version 2.0
- Online Help version of this book
- Windows CE Programmer's Reference

  Including documentation for all the Windows CE functions, structures, messages, and macros
- Windows CE Device Driver Kit (DDK)
- Online Help version of the documentation for the Windows CE DDK
- Documentation for the Microsoft Platform SDK in online Help format

  Including complete Win32 documentation

▶ **To install the online Help or Windows CE Emulation Platform SDK**

1. Run Setup.exe from the root directory on the CD.
2. Follow the instructions in each dialog box.
3. On the **Setup Type** dialog box, choose **Custom** installation and check only **Online help files** to install just the documentation.

   –Or–

   Install the complete Emulation Platform SDK.

Microsoft Press Support Information

Every effort has been made to ensure the accuracy of this book and the contents of the companion disc. Microsoft Press provides corrections for books through the World Wide Web at http://mspress.microsoft.com/mspress/support/.

If you have comments, questions, or ideas regarding the book or companion disc, send them by e-mail to Microsoft:

MSPINPUT@MICROSOFT.COM

or by postal mail to:

Microsoft Press
Attn: *Windows CE Programmer's Guide* Editor
One Microsoft Way
Redmond, WA 98052-6399

Product support is not offered through these addresses.

Document Conventions

The following typographical conventions are used throughout this book.

Convention	Description
monospace	Indicates source code, structure syntax, examples, user input, and program output. For example, ptbl->SortTable(pSort, TBL_BATCH);
Bold	Indicates an interface, method, function, structure, macro, or other keyword in Windows CE, the Microsoft® Windows® operating system, C, or C++. For example, **CommandBar_Height** is a function. Within discussions of syntax, bold type indicates that the text must be entered exactly as shown.
Italic	Indicates placeholders, most often method or function parameters; these placeholders stand for information that must be supplied by the implementation or the user. For example, *lpButtons* is a function parameter. Also indicates new terms that are defined in the glossary.
UPPERCASE	Indicates flags, return values, messages, and properties. For example, WSAEFAULT is a Windows Sockets error value, MF_CHECKED is a flag, and TB_ADDBUTTONS is a message. In addition, uppercase letters indicate segment names, registers, and terms used at the operating-system command level.
( )	Indicate one or more parameters that you pass to a function, in syntax.

For More Information

- Windows CE development
  http://microsoft.com/windowsce/
- Windows CE logo requirements
  http://microsoft.com/windowsce/logo/
- Windows CE operating system
  Inside Windows CE by John Murray, available in the spring of 1998
- Customizing the Windows CE operating system
  Windows CE Embedded Toolkit for Visual C++ 5.0 documentation
- The Microsoft Windows programming environment
  The Microsoft Platform Software Development Kit and *Programming Windows* by Charles Petzold

Acknowledgments

The Windows CE developer documentation team would like to thank the Windows CE program managers and developers and the Windows CE product support specialists for their support.

PART 1

Introduction to Windows CE Programming

C H A P T E R   1

Overview of the Windows CE Operating System

Microsoft® Windows® CE is a compact, highly efficient, multiplatform operating system. It is not a reduced version of Microsoft® Windows® 95, but was designed from the ground up as a multithreaded, fully preemptive, multitasking operating system for platforms with limited resources. Its modular design allows it to be customized for products ranging from consumer electronic devices to specialized industrial controllers.

General Features of Windows CE

- Provides you with a modular operating system that you can customize for specific products. The basic core of the operating system requires less than 200 KB of ROM.
- Provides interrupt delivery, prioritizing, and servicing.
- Runs on a wide variety of platforms.
- Supports more than 1,000 of the most frequently used Microsoft® Win32® functions, along with familiar development models and tools.
- Supports a variety of user-interface hardware, including touch screen and color displays with up to 32-bits-per-pixel color depth.
- Supports a variety of serial and network communication technologies.
- Supports Mobile Channels to provide Web services for Windows CE users.
- Supports COM/OLE, Automation, and other advanced methods of interprocess communication.

Windows CE has four primary modules or groups of modules.

- The kernel supports basic services, such as process and thread handling and memory management.
- The file system supports persistent storage of information.
- The graphics windowing and events subsystem (GWES) controls graphics and window-related features.
- The communications interface supports the exchange of information with other devices.

The Windows CE operating system also contains a number of additional modules that support such tasks as managing installable device drivers and supporting COM/OLE. The following illustration describes how these features fit into the overall structure of the Windows CE operating system.

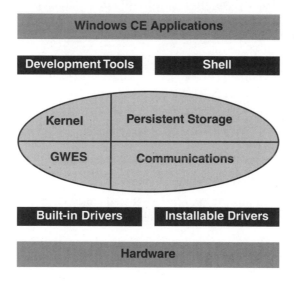

Windows CE operating system structure

Summary of the Windows CE Operating System

The following section outlines the major features of Windows CE. The features mentioned are discussed in more detail throughout the chapter.

Kernel

The Kernel—the core of the operating system—provides system services for managing threads, memory, and resources. It includes:

- Preemptive, priority-based thread scheduling based on the Win32 process and thread model. Priority inversion is prevented with a system of priority inheritance that dynamically adjusts thread priorities.

- Predictable thread synchronization mechanisms, including wait objects. Examples of these mechanisms are named mutexes, critical sections, and named and unnamed event objects.

- Efficient memory management based on dynamic-link libraries (DLLs), which link user applications at run-time.

- A flat, virtual address space, with 32 MB of memory reserved for each process. Process memory is protected by altering page protections.

- On-demand paging for both read-only memory (ROM) and random access memory (RAM).

- Heap size that is limited only by available memory.

- Control of interrupt handling. You can map interrupt requests (IRQs) to hardware interrupts and implement your own interrupt service routines and interrupt service threads.

- Extensive debugging support, such as including just-in-time debugging.

Persistent Storage

The file system supports persistent storage of information. It includes:

- Support for FAT file systems with up to nine FAT volumes.

- Transactioned file handling to protect against data loss.

- Demand paging for devices that support paging.

- FAT file system mirroring to allow preservation of the file system if power is lost or cold reset is needed.

- Installable block device drivers.

Communications Interface

The communications interface supports a wide range of technologies. It includes:

- Support for serial communications, including infrared links.
- Support for Internet client applications, including Hypertext Transfer Protocol (HTTP) and File Transfer Protocol (FTP) protocols.
- A Common Internet File System (CIFS) redirector for access to remote file systems by means of the Internet.
- A subset of Windows Sockets (Winsock) version 1.1, plus support for Secure Sockets.
- A Transmission Control Protocol/Internet Protocol (TCP/IP) transport layer configurable for wireless networking.
- An Infrared Data Association (IrDA) transport layer for robust infrared communication.
- Both Point-to-Point Protocol (PPP) and Serial Line Internet Protocol (SLIP) for serial-link networking.
- Support for local area networking through the network driver interface specification (NDIS).
- Support for managing phone connections with the Telephony API (TAPI).
- A Remote Access Service (RAS) client for connections to remote file systems by modem.

Graphics, Windowing, and Events Subsystem (GWES)

The GWES module supports the graphics and windowing functionality needed to display text and images and to receive user input. It includes:

- Support for a broad range of window styles, including overlapping windows.
- A large selection of customizable controls.
- Support for keyboard and stylus input.
- A command bar combining the functionality of a toolbar and a menu bar.
- An **Out of Memory** dialog box that requests user action when the system is low on memory.

- Full UNICODE support.
- A multiplatform graphics device interface (GDI) that supports the following features:
  - Both color and grayscale displays, with color depths of up to 32 bits per pixel.
  - Palette management.
  - TrueType and raster fonts.
  - Printer, memory, and display device contexts (DCs).
  - Advanced shape drawing and bit block transfer capabilities.

Kernel

The Windows CE kernel contains the core operating system functionality that must be present on all Windows CE-based platforms. It includes support for memory management, process management, exception handling, multitasking, and multithreading.

The Windows CE kernel borrows much of what is best from Windows-based desktop platforms. For example, all Windows CE-based applications run in a fully preemptive, multitasking environment, in protected memory spaces. Windows CE supports native Unicode strings, allowing you to internationalize applications.

Unlike the kernels found on Windows-based desktop platforms, the Windows CE kernel uses DLLs to maximize available memory. The DLLs are written as reentrant code, which allows applications to simultaneously share common routines. This approach minimizes the amount of memory-resident code required to execute applications.

Processes and Threads

As a multitasking operating system, Windows CE can support up to 32 simultaneous processes, each process being a single instance of an application. In addition, multithreading support allows each process to create multiple threads of execution. A thread is a part of a process that runs concurrently with other parts. Threads operate independently, but each one belongs to a particular process and shares the same memory space. The total number of threads is limited only by available physical memory.

Processes rely on Win32 messages to initiate processing, control system resources, and communicate with the operating system and the user. Each process has its own message queue. For multithreaded applications, each thread also has its own separate message queue. When there are no messages in the queue and the thread is not engaged in any other activity, the system suspends the thread, saving CPU resources.

Although a thread can operate independently, it often needs to be managed by the process. For example, one thread may depend on another for information. Thread synchronization suspends a thread's execution until the thread receives notification to proceed. Windows CE supports thread synchronization by providing a set of *wait objects*, which stops a thread until a change in the wait object signals the thread to proceed. Supported wait objects include critical sections, named and unnamed events, and named mutex objects. For more information, see Chapter 3, "Working with Processes and Threads."

Windows CE implements thread synchronization with minimum processor resources—an important feature for many battery-powered devices. And, unlike many operating systems, Windows CE uses the kernel to handle thread-related tasks, such as scheduling, synchronization, and resource management. Consequently, an application need not poll for process or thread completion or perform other thread-management functions.

Because Windows CE is preemptive, it allows the execution of a process or thread to be preempted by one with higher priority. It uses a priority-based, time-slice algorithm, with eight levels of thread priority, for thread scheduling.

Interrupt Handling

To provide efficient processing of interrupts, Windows CE splits interrupt handling into two distinct parts: an interrupt service routine (ISR) and an interrupt service thread (IST). When triggered, the ISR does little more than launch the IST that is responsible for handling the event. Once the IST has been launched, the ISR returns and the system can respond to the next interrupt.

Dividing interrupt handling this way allows the ISR to be very small and fast. This minimizes interrupt latencies and speeds interrupt processing. The Windows CE Embedded Toolkit for Visual C++ makes it possible for you to specify interrupt timing and priorities for a specific platform.

Memory Architecture

The Windows CE kernel supports a single, flat, or unsegmented, virtual address space that all processes share. Instead of assigning each process a different address space, Windows CE protects process memory by altering page protections. Because it maps virtual addresses onto physical memory using the kernel, you do not need to be concerned with the physical layout of the target system's memory.

Approximately 1 GB of virtual memory is available to processes. It is divided into 33 *slots*, each 32 MB in size. The kernel protects each process by assigning it to a unique slot with one slot reserved for the currently running process. Thus, the number of processes is limited to 32, but there is no limit, aside from physical memory, on the total number of threads.

The kernel prevents an application from accessing memory outside of its allocated slot by generating an exception. Applications can check for, and handle, such exceptions by using the try-except statement.

Windows CE allows memory mapping, which permits multiple processes to share the same physical memory. Memory mapping results in very fast data transfer between cooperating processes, or between a driver and an application. Approximately 1 GB of virtual address space, distinct from that used for the slots, is allocated for memory mapping.

Windows CE always allocates memory to applications one page at a time. The system designer specifies page size when the operating system is built for the target hardware platform. On a Handheld PC (H/PC), for example, the page size is typically either 1 KB or 4 KB.

Physical Memory Usage

Windows CE-based platforms usually have no disk drive. Therefore, physical memory, typically consisting of a combination of ROM and RAM, plays a substantially different role on a Windows CE-based platform than it does on a desktop computer.

Because ROM cannot be modified by the user, it is used for permanent storage. The contents of ROM, determined by the original equipment manufacturer (OEM), includes the operating system and any built-in applications that the manufacturer provides, for example, Microsoft® Pocket Word and Microsoft® Pocket Excel on an H/PC. Depending on your product requirements, you can also place application code in ROM.

Because on most Windows CE systems, RAM is maintained continuously, it is effectively nonvolatile. This feature allows your application to use RAM for persistent storage as well as program execution, compensating for the lack of a disk drive. To serve these two purposes, RAM is divided into storage, also known as the *object store*, and program memory. Program memory is used for program execution, while the object store is used for persistent storage of data and any executable code not stored in ROM.

To minimize RAM requirements on Windows CE-based devices, executable code stored in ROM usually executes in-place, not in RAM. Because of this, the operating system needs only a small amount of RAM for such purposes as stack and heap storage.

Applications are commonly stored and executed in RAM. This approach is used primarily by third-party applications that are added by the user. Because RAM-based applications are stored in compressed form, they must be uncompressed and loaded into program memory for execution. To increase the performance of application software and reduce RAM use, Windows CE supports on-demand paging. With it, the operating system needs to uncompress and load only the memory page containing the portion of the application that is currently executing. When execution is finished, the page can be swapped out, and the next page can be loaded.

Like RAM-based applications, ROM-based executable code, including DLLs, can be compressed. When compressed, the code does not execute in place, but is handled much like its RAM-based counterpart. The code is uncompressed and loaded a page at a time into RAM program memory, and then is swapped out when no longer needed.

Persistent Storage

The storage memory portion of RAM is referred to as the object store. It includes three types of data storage:

- The Windows CE file system, which contains application and data files.
- The Windows CE database, which provides structured storage. It offers an alternative to storing user data and application data in files or in the registry.
- The Windows CE system registry, which is used to store the system configuration and any other information that an application must access quickly.

The Windows CE file system holds executable files and data files that the user installs or creates. It supports up to nine FAT volumes. Each volume is treated as a *storage card*. If a storage card has multiple partitions, then each partition is treated as a separate volume. It is possible to support other types of file systems by writing block device drivers. For more information on block device drivers, see the documentation for the Windows CE Device Driver Kit (DDK). Files are typically stored in compressed form. Applications access the file system with standard Win32 file system functions. For more information about Windows file management, see Chapter 4, "Accessing Persistent Storage."

To reduce the data loss during a critical failure, such as loss of power, the Windows CE file system is transactioned. In addition, the file system implements a transactioned *mirroring* scheme to track FAT file system operations that are not transactioned. The mirroring scheme restores the FAT volume if power is lost while a critical operation is performed.

The Windows CE database provides general-purpose, structured storage of data, but it is not a full-fledged database. In particular, Windows CE databases have only one level of hierarchy. Records cannot contain other records, nor can they be shared between databases. For more information about storage, see Chapter 4, "Accessing Persistent Storage."

Platforms that implement the Windows CE operating system commonly ship with one or more built-in databases. For example, the H/PC comes with calendar and contacts applications that use databases to store their information. Windows CE provides an API that allows users and applications to create and use additional databases as needed.

The system registry is used to store a variety of information, such as system or application configuration data. It is similar to the registry found on Windows-based desktop platforms. Applications running on a Windows CE-based device can access and modify information in the registry with standard Win32 functions.

It is also possible to access the Windows CE object store from an attached desktop computer using one of the following approaches:

- The Windows CE Remote API (RAPI) includes a set of functions that you can use to manipulate the file system and the registry. An application running on the desktop computer invokes RAPI functions, which act on the object store of the linked Windows CE-based device. For more information, see Chapter 17, "Invoking Functions from a Desktop Computer."

- Windows CE offers an extensive and sophisticated set of tools for transferring data between a desktop computer and an attached Windows CE-based device. For example, you can use these tools to synchronize data between a Windows CE-based device and an attached desktop computer when you update a list of contacts. For more information, see Chapter 20, "Synchronizing Data."

- The object store can also be modified when installing an application. For more information, see Chapter 21, "Installing and Managing Applications."

Communications Interface

Windows CE-based platforms support a variety of communications hardware and data protocols, including serial input/output (I/O) support, such as infrared transceiver support; a subset of the TAPI; and networking, which includes support for the following:

- Internet clients, including HTTP and FTP, and Internet security protocols.
- Access to remote file systems through a CIFS redirector.
- Internet Control Message Protocol (ICMP) messaging support.
- A subset of Winsock version 1.1, including support for security protocols.
- A RAS client.
- TCP/IP and IrDA.
- NDIS for local area networking.
- PPP and SLIP for serial link and modem networking.

Serial Communications

Serial I/O is the simplest form of communication supported by Windows CE. It is used when there is a direct, one-to-one connection between two devices. It can take place over a variety of hardware connections, but most Windows CE-based devices use simple serial cables or infrared transceivers. Transferring information over a serial cable connection is similar to reading from or writing to a file, and it uses some of the same functions. Windows CE also includes a set of functions used to manage the connection itself.

Windows CE allows direct serial I/O over an infrared link using the same serial communication functions that are used for wired connections. When using an infrared link, the I/O is "raw," which means that the bit stream is not processed in any way. For example, there is no collision detection in Windows CE.

The IrDA protocols provide more robust communication than raw infrared (IR). The IrDA protocols are available through Infrared Sockets (IrSock), which is an extension of Winsock. As an alternative to using IrSock directly, IrComm uses the same function calls as standard serial communication, but uses IrSock and the IrDA protocols internally.

Network Communications

Windows CE supports a network stack with a number of options. Network communications can take place over a variety of hardware, including infrared, serial, Ethernet, and wireless links. Although the network stack is accessible only through the Winsock interface, Windows CE also provides several high-level APIs that use Winsock internally, and handle the details of setting up and managing socket connections:

- The WinINET API provides support for Internet browsing protocols, including FTP and HTTP 1.0. It also provides access to three Internet security protocols, Secure Sockets Layer (SSL) 2.0, Secure Sockets Layer 3.0, and Private Communication Technology (PCT) 1.0.

- The WNet API provides access to remote file systems through a Common Internet File System (CIFS) redirector. Currently, operating system connections are supported only for Microsoft® Windows® 95 and Microsoft® Windows NT®. The redirector supports UNC names, such as //serverXX/shareXX, but not drive letters.

- ICMP requests, commonly referred to as pings, are used to determine whether or not a host is available.

The Winsock interface provides direct access to the network stack. Windows CE supports a subset of Winsock 1.1, as well as the three Internet security protocols mentioned earlier. For infrared communication, Windows CE supports the IrSock extension of Winsock, which enables socket-based infrared communication using the industry-standard IrDA protocols.

Windows CE supports a RAS client at the same level in the network stack as Winsock, but this client serves a different purpose. RAS is a multi-protocol router used to connect remote devices. The Windows CE RAS client is identical to the Win32 RAS, except it supports only one point-to-point connection at a time.

The TCP/IP suite, developed for the Internet, is arguably the most flexible and widely implemented network protocol. It is supported by a wide variety of systems and forms the core of the Windows CE network stack. Many Windows CE-based mobile devices have wireless communication capabilities. However, conventional TCP/IP stacks may work poorly with wireless technology because they were intended to function efficiently on wired networks. The Windows CE TCP/IP stack is designed to be configured for wireless networking.

At the base of the network stack, Windows CE supports data-link layers for serial-link networks and local area networks (LANs). Many Windows CE-based devices connect to a network using a serial communication link, such as a modem. To support serial-link networking, Windows CE implements the widely used serial line Internet (SLIP) and Point-to-Point Protocol (PPP). Three protocols are available for authentication in serial-link communication: Password Authentication Protocol (PAP), Challenge Handshake Authentication Protocol (CHAP), and Microsoft CHAP.

To support connections to LANs, Windows CE implements NDIS 4.0, but supports only Ethernet miniport drivers. Windows CE does not support wide area networks (WANs). For more information on NDIS support, see the documentation for the Windows CE DDK.

Telephony Application Programming Interface

Using a modem involves making and managing a telephone connection, tasks which fall outside most standard communication protocols. To facilitate the use of a telephone connection, Windows CE includes a TAPI service provider for an AT command-based modem, knows as a Unimodem. TAPI is a collection of utilities that allows applications to take advantage of a variety of telephone and communications services without needing detailed knowledge of the particular technology. You can use the TAPI service provider with internal or PC Card modems.

The Windows CE implementation of TAPI focuses on outgoing calls and provides outbound dialing and address translation services. Windows CE does not support inbound calls. To provide flexibility in the choice of hardware, TAPI supports installable service providers.

Graphics, Windowing, and Event Subsystem

The Graphics Windowing and Event Subsystem (GWES) is the graphical user interface between the user, your application, and the operating system. GWES handles user input by translating keystrokes, stylus movements, and control selections into messages that convey information to applications and the operating system. GWES handles output to the user by creating and managing the windows, graphics, and text that are displayed on display devices and printers.

GWES supports all the windows, dialog boxes, controls, menus, and resources that make up Windows CE user interface. This interface allows users to control applications by choosing menu commands, pushing buttons, checking and unchecking boxes, and manipulating a variety of other controls. GWES provides information to the user in the form of bitmaps, carets, cursors, text, and icons.

Even Windows CE-based platforms that lack a graphical user interface use GWES basic windowing and messaging capabilities. These provide the means for communication between the user, the application, and the operating system.

As part of GWES, Windows CE provides support for active power management to extend the limited lifetime of battery-operated devices. The operating system automatically determines a power consumption level to match the state of operation of the device.

The following illustration describes the basic GWES structure.

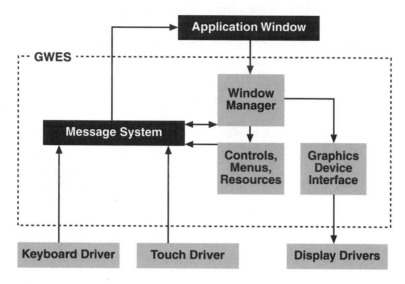

GWES structure

Window Management

The most central feature of GWES is the window. In Windows CE-based platforms with traditional graphical displays, the window is the rectangular area of the screen where an application displays output and receives input from the user. However, all applications need windows in order to receive messages from the operating system, even those created for devices that lack graphical displays.

When you create a window, Windows CE creates a message queue for the window. The operating system translates the information it receives from the user into messages which it places into the message queue of the active window. The application processes most of these messages, and passes the rest back to Windows CE for processing.

Windows CE does not send applications any messages dealing with the nonclient area of the window. A window's nonclient area is the area of the window where an application is not allowed to draw, such as the title bar and scroll bars. The window manager controls the nonclient area.

Windows CE does not support the **Maximize** and **Minimize** buttons. A user can send the window to the back of the Z order by tapping the window's button on the taskbar. The user restores the window by tapping its taskbar button again.

The taskbar is always visible on Windows CE. You cannot hide the taskbar or use the full screen to display a window.

Controls, Menus, Dialog Boxes, and Resources

GWES provides controls, menus, dialog boxes, and resources to provide the user with a standard way to make selections, carry out commands, and perform input and output tasks.

Controls and dialog boxes are child windows that allow users to view and organize information and to set or change attributes. A dialog box is a window that contains controls.

All menus in Windows CE are implemented as top-level, pop-up windows. Windows CE supports scrolling menus that automatically add scroll arrows when a menu does not fit on the screen.

Windows CE does not support menu bars, but it does support command bars, which combine the functionality of a menu bar and tool bar in one control. Command bars make efficient use of the limited space available on many Windows CE-based devices.

Windows CE supports the following types of controls, menus, dialog boxes, and resources:

Application-defined dialog boxes	Bitmaps
Carets	Check boxes
Combo boxes	Command band
Command bars	Common dialog boxes
Cursors	Custom draw service
Date and time picker controls	Edit control
Group boxes	Header controls
Icons	Image lists
Images	Keyboard accelerators
List boxes	List views
Menus	Message boxes
Month calendar controls	Progress bars
Property sheets	Push buttons
Radio buttons	Rebars
Scroll bars	Static controls
Status bars	Strings
Tab controls	Toolbars
ToolTips	Track bars
Tree views	Up-down controls

In addition to the controls listed in the previous table, Windows CE supports the HTML viewer control, which makes it easier for you to add HTML support to your applications.

Graphics Device Interface

The graphics device interface (GDI) is the GWES subsystem that controls the display of text and graphics. You use GDI to draw lines, curves, closed figures, text, and bitmapped images.

GDI uses a device context (DC) to store the information it needs to display text and graphics on a specified device. The graphic objects stored in a DC include a pen for line drawing, a brush for painting and filling, a font for text output, a bitmap for copying or scrolling, a palette for defining the available colors, and a region for clipping. Windows CE supports printer DCs for drawing on printers, display DCs for drawing on video displays, and memory displays for drawing in memory.

GDI features supported by Windows CE are described in the following table.

GDI feature	Description
Raster and TrueType fonts	Allows only one of these to be used on a specified system. TrueType fonts generate superior text output because they are scalable and rotatable.
Custom color palettes, and both palettized and nonpalettized color display devices	Supports color formats of 1, 2, 4, 8, 16, 24, and 32 bits per pixel (bpp). The first two are unique to Windows CE.
Bit block transfer functions and raster operation codes	Allows you to transform and combine bitmaps in a wide variety of ways.
Pens and brushes	Supports dashed, wide, and solid pens, and patterned brushes.
Printing	Supports full graphical printing.
Shape drawing functions	Supports the ellipse, polygon, rectangle, and round rectangle shapes.

User Input

You can configure Windows CE to meet the user input requirements of a variety of different platforms. Currently, the keyboard, input panel, voice, and the stylus are the usual input method on Windows CE-based devices.

Keyboard functionality in Windows CE is similar to that of Windows-based desktop platforms. And, like those platforms, Windows CE supports hot keys. A hot key gives the user high-priority system access for specific purposes, such as canceling a time-consuming file transfer operation.

A unique feature of Windows CE is that it supports the use of a stylus and a touch screen in place of a mouse. Touching the screen with the stylus mimics the left-button mouse click.

Additional Support for Applications

Windows CE allows you to add several modules to facilitate program development or add additional programming capabilities.

The Microsoft Component Object Model (COM) is a powerful tool for object-oriented development. Windows CE provides a set of functions and structures designed to support application development based on COM. They can be divided into two groups:

- COM

  A simple protocol that defines COM objects along with a library that offers object management services.

- Automation

  A more sophisticated set of object management services that allows applications to coordinate their interactions with each other.

Both services are derived from a subset of the Windows NT object services. For more information on the use of COM/OLE, see the documentation for the Microsoft Windows Platform SDK.

For Windows CE-based platforms intended to perform as adjuncts to a desktop computer, Windows CE provides the following tools to allow a user to manage and transfer data between a desktop computer and an attached Windows CE-based device. These services include:

- A connection manager for establishing and maintaining the connection. For more information, see Chapter 18, "Receiving Connection Notification."

- A data synchronization interface to allow synchronization of shared data. For more information, see Chapter 20, "Synchronizing Data."

- File filters for importing and exporting files. For more information, see Chapter 19, "Transferring Files."

- RAPI for enabling a client on a desktop computer to request services, such as file manipulation, from a server on an attached Windows CE-based device. For more information, see Chapter 17, "Invoking Functions from a Desktop Computer."

- Application installation and management services for installing and uninstalling Windows CE-based applications from an attached desktop computer or other sources. For more information, see Chapter 21, "Installing and Managing Applications."

Windows CE-based devices may have one or more applications included on ROM. The Contacts and Inbox applications are of particular interest because they are open, general-purpose applications. If you have unique requirements, you can use these applications as processing engines inside proprietary code.

To aid you in implementing compatible applications, the Windows CE SDK provides a set of functions and structures that a custom application can use to interface with the built-in Contacts and Inbox applications. They are:

- The Contacts Database API, which supports functions and structures for querying and manipulating the records in a Contacts database. For more information, see Chapter 23, "Contacts Database."

- The Mail Interface API, which supports functions and structures that allow an application to be compatible with the Windows CE Inbox mail client. This API also provides services for mail transport and storage. For more information, see Chapter 24, "Inbox."

- The Mail Transport API, which allows applications to connect to the mail server and transmit and receive messages. For more information, see Chapter 25, "Mail Transport Service."

Most Windows CE-based devices have a shell to manage the user interface (UI) and handle such tasks as launching applications and switching between tasks. Because of the variety of Windows CE-based platforms, the operating system contains no standard shell; each platform has a shell designed for its particular needs. Refer to OEM documentation for information on the shell available for a particular platform. The shells implemented for a Palm PC and an H/PC are discussed in their respective platform-specific sections of this book.

Devices that are integral to a Windows CE-based platform, such as a wired serial port, have built-in drivers that are provided by the OEM. You can install other devices by means of the built-in serial port, PC Card slot, or USB port. Examples of installable devices include modems, printers, digital cameras, and bar code readers. Because these are added by the user, they require installable drivers.

The Win32 API provides a rich set of interface methods that make device drivers easier to write and more adaptable. You use the same functions whether you are dealing with a disk file, serial port, parallel port, pipe, or other type of device. Devices and files that must be accessed by multiple processes or threads simultaneously can be locked on a region-by-region basis. The Win32 API supports both synchronous and asynchronous methods of device access, and is designed with complex device interfaces in mind.

For more information on Windows CE support for installable device drivers, see the documentation for the Windows CE DDK.

To support development of devices and applications for a variety of locales, Windows CE includes national language support (NLS). The national language support API allows you to specify information about the system and the user locale. Support for localization of applications includes built-in support for French, German, Italian, Spanish, Brazilian Portuguese, and Japanese.

C H A P T E R   2

Programming Considerations

Windows CE is an operating system (OS) based on the Win32 application programming interface (API). Because of this relationship, you must understand the Win32 programming environment to develop Windows CE-based applications. If you are a Windows 95 or Windows NT programmer, you already know how to write code for Windows CE and how to use an integrated development environment (IDE). However, if you have never written an event-driven application, you must become familiar with the fundamentals of Windows programming.

Whether you are an experienced Windows software programmer or a beginner, you must first determine the unique configuration of the hardware platform and shell for which you are developing. Because Windows CE is a modular operating system, an original equipment manufacturer (OEM) chooses specific modules and components to configure Windows CE-based devices. For example, if you are programming for a Handheld PC (H/PC), you must know how much RAM the manufacturer has included.

Once you are familiar with your target platform, your next consideration is what programming environment to use. For your programming environment, you can choose among Microsoft® Visual C++®, Microsoft® Visual Basic® or Microsoft® Visual J++™. For your Windows CE toolkit, you can choose among the following:

- Windows CE Toolkit for Visual C++ 5.0
- Windows CE Toolkit for Visual Basic 5.0
- Windows CE Toolkit for Visual J++ 1.1
- Windows CE Embedded Toolkit for Visual C++ 5.0

In addition to choosing a programming environment and toolkit, you must determine whether or not to use other available programming tools, such as the Microsoft Foundation Class (MFC) libraries or the Active Template Library (ATL).

If you plan to port Windows-based desktop applications to Windows CE, you need to consider how the hardware design of your target device affects ported applications. As you will learn later in this chapter, memory, power, user-interaction devices, and the broad range of CPU and communications options are all critical concerns when porting. For example, hardware design determines whether the user interacts with the device by typing on a keyboard, giving voice commands, or writing on the screen with a stylus.

Other porting considerations include which Win32 APIs are supported by Windows CE, how the interfaces of the two systems are similar and different, and whether the desktop application uses the native language format used by Windows CE. Though these issues require solutions specific to your application and development needs, the guidelines in this chapter can help you write applications that port smoothly.

To debug and test your code, the Windows CE IDE provides an emulator for supported platforms, such as the H/PC. For unsupported platforms, such as a platform with no user interface, Windows CE provides a debugging interface that you can use to write your own tools.

The following sections discuss the programming considerations just mentioned and direct you to additional information. For information on Windows CE programming considerations, see http://www.microsoft.com/windowsce/.

Introduction to Win32 Programming

If you are an embedded software programmer, you may be unfamiliar with the general techniques of event-driven programming in Windows. The purpose of this section is to outline the fundamentals of the Windows programming model and the related Win32 API. If you are an experienced Windows programmer, you may want to skip this section.

Windows is an event-driven operating system. An event may be a keystroke, a tap on the screen, or a command for a window to repaint itself. Every time an event takes place, the operating system sends a message to the relevant process. Essentially, a Windows-based program receives messages, interprets those messages, and takes an appropriate action.

A basic Windows-based program has three primary elements: a window, a message pump, which is also called a message loop, and a message processor. This section describes how these work together.

Although windows are commonly thought of in terms of visual display, they can be defined as non-visible. For example, if you are programming an application with no user interface, you will need a non-visible window to process messages. Each window has a window handle, or *hwnd*, associated with a message processor that handles messages for the window. Additionally, a window handle is used any time you need to call a function that requires *hwnd* as a parameter.

A message pump is a simple loop that runs continuously while the application runs, receiving messages and dispatching them to the appropriate message processor. When events occur that generate messages, the operating system places the messages in a message queue. Each queue has a message pump that takes the messages one at a time and dispatches them to the appropriate message processor for handling. Although a simple application will have a single queue, a multithreaded application may have a queue for each thread. The message pump continues running until it receives a message to terminate the application.

A simple Windows-based program has two primary functions: a message processor, usually called a **WndProc**, and **WinMain**, which provides an entry point to the program. The **WndProc** function processes messages for a particular window. Although there are many Windows messages, only a few, such as WM_PAINT and WM_CREATE, must be processed by the application. In general, an application processes those messages that are relevant to its operation and passes the remaining messages back to the operating system for default processing. The primary purpose of **WinMain** is to host the principal message pump for the application. It can also handle application initialization and shutdown procedures.

Win32 Application Programming Interface

The term *Win32* describes an API that is common to all of the Microsoft 32-bit Windows-based platforms—Windows 95, Windows NT, and Windows CE.

The Win32 API is a library of functions and related data types that provide applications with access to the features supported by Windows-based platforms. A common API allows you to port applications easily, leverage what you already know, and draw upon a library of existing programming knowledge, examples, and third-party resources.

Although the Win32 API provides you with a common set of interfaces for Windows 95, Windows NT, and Windows CE, you must be aware of differences among the platforms. For example, Windows CE is designed for embedded platforms and therefore does not need to support all the Win32 functions. Conversely, Windows CE includes functions specifically designed for embedded platforms that are not supported by Windows-based desktop platforms.

For easy reference, the Win32 components are grouped by functionality into categories, such as graphics device interface (GDI), multimedia, windows management, remote procedure calls (RPC), and system services. Within the GDI category, you will find such components as drawing functions, mouse manipulation functions, and clipboard functions.

As a programmer, you will find three categories of Win32 components of particular interest: processes and threads, memory management, and exception handling. The first two are discussed in separate chapters in this guide. For more information, see Chapter 3, "Working with Processes and Threads," and Chapter 29, "Writing Memory-Efficient Applications." Because Windows CE does not support C++ exception handling, you must use the exception handling features built into the Win32 API. For information on the exception handling macros supported by Win32, see the appropriate Windows CE toolkit reference.

If you would like to know more about Windows programming, see *Programming Windows 95* by Charles Petzold, which is available from Microsoft Press. Although this book does not specifically address Windows CE, it adequately describes event-driven programming. You may also be interested in the sample code included with the Windows CE SDK.

Windows CE Platform and Shell Considerations

The configuration of your target platform dictates what kind of user interface (UI) and shell you need. Unlike Windows-based desktop platforms, Windows CE does not have a standard UI. Rather, the target hardware determines UI components. Although most platforms require some kind of UI, the interface may not resemble the one on a Windows-based desktop computer, and platforms incorporated into larger systems or computers may have no UI.

If you need a UI similar to that found on a Windows-based desktop computer, Windows CE provides a shell component for that purpose. However, if you need a different UI than the shell and the device manufacturer does not provide one, you must build your own using the Windows CE Shell API. For example, you can use this API to develop an application that allows the user to write directly on the device's screen with a stylus. Such capability is not included in the API for Windows-based desktop platforms.

Programming Tools

To write an application for Windows CE, you must assemble and use a set of development tools based on one of the programming languages that Windows CE supports. This tool set is your development system. Your language choices are Visual C++, Visual Basic, or Visual J++. If you choose to program in C++, you must then decide which of the C++ toolkits is appropriate for your application. Finally, you can choose to use any of the specialized tools that are supported by Windows CE: Component Object Model (COM), Microsoft Foundation Classes (MFC), Active Template Library (ATL), and National Language Support (NLS). These can aid you in writing your application.

Windows CE Toolkits

After you have chosen and installed a programming language, install one of the following Windows CE toolkits:

- Windows CE Toolkit for Visual C++ 5.0
- Windows CE Toolkit for Visual Basic 5.0
- Windows CE Toolkit for Visual J++ 1.1
- Windows CE Embedded Toolkit for Visual C++ 5.0

The toolkit you choose becomes part of your existing IDE and supplies tools for debugging and testing Windows CE-based applications. For example, the Windows CE Toolkit for Visual C++ 5.0 is equipped with an emulator that allows you to observe how your application functions without downloading your program to a target device. Also, the Windows CE Toolkit for Visual C++ 5.0 and the Windows CE Toolkit for Visual Basic 5.0 have tools that allow you to access a remote device from a desktop computer and perform Windows CE-specific tasks on the remote device.

The next sections discuss the specialized development tools that are supported by Windows CE.

Component Object Model

COM allows you to develop independent, reusable software components that connect together to form applications. COM components are binary bits of executable code that function like mini-applications. They can be disconnected and replaced at run time without relinking or recompiling the application. Because COM is language-independent, you can write your components in any programming language you choose.

The benefit of using COM is that you can upgrade application components independently of each other. This allows you to change or add application features without having to upgrade the entire application. You can plug and unplug components from your application, as well as interchange them with other components. In order to achieve this flexibility, COM components must be able to dynamically link together. Dynamic linking is accomplished through encapsulation, the process of hiding the details of how a component is implemented. You can do this by creating an *interface* through which a component or a client can connect. A client is a program or component that uses another component. All COM components must interact through an interface. Additionally, all COM components must inherit from, and implement, the **IUnknown** interface.

COM maintains the COM library, which contains a small number of functions and data structures used to create interfaces and coordinate object services. To use the libraries in Windows CE, call the **CoInitializeEx** function before you call any other functions, except for the memory allocation functions. Similarly, to close the libraries, call the **CoUnitialize** function.

COM objects operate according to the client/server model. A COM server is a COM object that exports and implements interfaces in order to provide services to clients. The server is responsible for implementing an interface and helping a client navigate among various interfaces. A COM client creates an instance of a server object and retrieves a pointer to it. Clients use the services provided by a server object by calling an interface's methods. A client need not have any knowledge of the implementation details of the server. The underlying COM libraries facilitate communication between a server and a client.

Windows supports two types of COM servers: an *in-process* (Inproc) server, which resides as a dynamic-link library (DLL) in the client's process, and an *out-of-process* server, which resides as an executable file (.exe) on either the local or a remote computer. Windows CE supports only in-process servers. A COM server implements the **QueryInterface** method of the **IUnknown** interface to make its services available to clients. This method receives an interface identifier (IID) and returns a pointer to that interface if it is implemented within the server component. A client can call methods only on an object that is an instance of the server class. Thus, the client must instantiate the class before it invokes methods of a COM object.

COM Threading Model

Windows CE supports only a free-threading model in which a component may be called by any thread at any time. When you develop your application, ensure that the component synchronizes itself to prevent simultaneous accesses by different free threads. To register the threading model of a COM object, which is the named value, you can add *ThreadingModel* to the object's **InprocServer32** key. Use the string "Free" to present the information in a user-readable form.

Structured Storage

Structured storage is a file system within a file. COM uses it to efficiently store multiple types of objects in one document. COM defines structured storage as a collection of two types of COM objects, *storage* and *stream*. The former behaves as a directory and the latter as a file. A storage object must implement the **IStorage** interface and a stream object must implement the **IStream** interface. Just as a directory in a file system can contain subdirectories and files, a storage object can contain other storage objects and stream objects. A storage object keeps track of the locations and sizes of the contained storage and stream objects. A stream object stores data as a consecutive sequence of bytes.

Structured storage helps to reduce the performance penalties and overhead for storing separate objects in a flat file. Other benefits include incremental access and multiple uses of data in a transacted process, as well as providing facilities for saving files in low-memory situations. Windows CE provides a default implementation, currently for the H/PC platform, of the interfaces, functions, and enumeration required for structured storage services. This default implementation includes the following:

- **IStorage**, **IStream**, and **IRootStorage**

  These interfaces provide methods for opening storage, committing and reverting changes, copying and moving elements, and reading and writing streams.

- **IPersist** and **IPersistStorage**

  These interfaces provide methods for reading data formats of individual objects and are capable of executing persistent storage.

- **ILockBytes**

  This interface provides methods for writing files to specific types of physical storage media, such as hard disks or tape drives. Objects implementing this interface are known as *LockBytes* objects. Windows CE does not provide any *LockBytes* objects when implementing default structured storage.

- **StgCreateDocfile, StgCreateDocfileOnILockBytes, StgOpenStorage, StgOpenStorageOnILockBytes**

  These functions allow clients to create a new compound file or to open an existing one on a default or custom *LockBytes* object.

- **STGM** enumeration

  The flags listed in **STGM** permit clients to specify the access modes for regulating access to compound files.

Persistent Object State

Persistent object state refers to information about an object that must be preserved beyond the object's lifetime. Persistent states are typically stored in nonvolatile memory, such as hard disks or battery-backed RAM. To make a persistent object in COM, the object must support a *persistent object interface*. COM uses the persistent object interface to coordinate operations for initializing, loading, and saving persistent objects. To conform to the COM persistent object protocol, client applications determine when and where an object should store its state and the object determines the format for data storage. A persistent object must also implement the **IPersist** interface because all persistent object interfaces inherit from it. In Windows CE, only structured storage can be made persistent.

Automation Through ActiveX Objects

Just as a user interface helps a user communicate with a software application, automation enables applications or scripting tools to interact with other applications or tools. Automation is a COM-based technology that enables interoperability among Microsoft® ActiveX™ components, including OLE components. To make their services available, applications or tools define COM objects to expose their unique features in terms of *methods*, *properties*, and *events*. Other applications and tools interact with the exposed objects to use these services. The exposed COM objects are known as ActiveX objects and the applications or tools calling ActiveX objects are known as ActiveX clients.

ActiveX clients invoke the **IDispatch** interface, or they call member functions directly in the object's virtual function table (**VTBL**). The table lists the addresses of all the properties and methods of an object, including the member functions of the interface it supports. The first three members of **VTBL** are the members of the **IUnknown** interface. ActiveX objects implementing a **VTBL** interface are standard COM objects. Clients must support pointers to access these objects. However, the object implementing the **IDispatch** interface offers additional features that makes the object accessible to a client without any pointer support. Clients written in Visual Basic use **IDispatch**, whereas those written in C++ may use both **VBTL** and **IDispatch**. The ActiveX objects in your applications should support both interfaces.

ActiveX objects publish themselves by means of *Type Libraries*, which are used by clients to determine the characteristics of an object, such as the supported interfaces and the names and addresses of the members of each interface. The developer of an ActiveX object should create the type library. Windows CE offers full support of the four type-building interfaces: **ICreateTypeInfo**, **ICreateTypeInfo2**, **ICreateTypeLib** and **ICreateTypeLib2**.

For a complete discussion of COM-based object services, see the documentation for the Microsoft Platform SDK.

Microsoft Foundation Classes

MFC is a Windows class library and a complete, object-oriented application framework. MFC for Windows CE includes additional classes unique to Windows CE, such as the command bar control. Though you can write your own Windows CE class libraries, you will find that using the ones provided in MFC saves you time and effort. By organizing related and reusable Windows CE functions into logical classes, MFC encapsulates much of the Windows CE API.

As mentioned, MFC is an object-oriented application framework. An application framework provides both a structural foundation and a set of fundamental components that you can use to expand on the structure and adapt to different purposes. An example of this is the MFC message mapping architecture. In non-MFC applications, the window procedure is a large switch statement that determines what kind of message the window has received. The switch then processes the message appropriately. The MFC framework manages messages more efficiently than this by providing a message pump for every derived class. The class uses message maps, rather than switch statements, to route messages to the appropriate message handler function. A message map is a simple set of macros defined in the MFC library. If you are using the Windows CE MFC Class Wizard, the Wizard inserts the macros into your code for you when you select the messages you want your class to handle.

Active Template Library

ATL for Windows CE is a template library specifically designed for creating ActiveX controls and other COM components. Because your ATL components implement only the specific interfaces that your project requires, the code you create is smaller and faster than the code you would create by using MFC for the same project.

One important use of ATL is to help you create ActiveX servers. An ActiveX server is a DLL or .exe that contains one or more COM components. The components may include simple objects, dialog boxes, and property sheets that belong to a full ActiveX control. A server also provides the class factories that instantiate the components when they are requested by clients. It contains code to enter and remove itself from the registry and notify COM when it can safely be unloaded from memory. Windows CE supports only in-process servers, which are DLLs that are loaded directly into the address space of the calling process. Because an in-process server runs in the same address space as its host, it does not incur the overhead associated with cross-process marshalling on every call.

National Language Support

If you plan to release your application in the international market, you must keep language and cultural differences in mind when you develop specifications for the user interface and feature set. Consider the following potential trouble spots:

- Text expansion. English text often grows when translated. In most cases, text increases by 10 or 15 percent; in some languages, localized text can be as much as 30 to 35 percent longer than the source text.

- Use of abbreviations. In some languages, abbreviations are not commonly used, for example, in Georgian, days of the week are not abbreviated.

- Use of symbols, metaphors, and colors. Most have specific cultural meaning. Some common symbols in the United States may not be recognized or may be misunderstood in other countries—for example, a mailbox.

- Use of bidirectional text. Text may be written and read from left to right, right to left, or top to bottom.

- Unique keyboard layout. Languages that use diacritical marks, such as Spanish and French, must have keyboards that support dead keys.

- Use of an Input Method Editor. Some languages, such as Japanese, have thousands of glyphs; therefore, the standard keyboard input is not sufficient to represent all the characters.

- Word order and punctuation. Of particular concern are differences in the punctuation of currency and other numbers, and the word order of dates. Though in English, word order is critical to meaning, in highly inflected languages, such as Spanish, word endings may have more significance.

The time to address these concerns is in the design phase of your project. For example, you will be disappointed to discover—after your program is completed—that the Spanish word *aceptar* will not fit onto your application's **OK** button. The following list provides tips for making your program easier to translate or localize:

- Put all text strings that have to be translated in one location, such as a resource or text file.

- Declare string buffers of a variable size.

- Use the correct sorting method, date, time, and currency representation for that locale.

- Design controls, buttons, and the taskbar to accommodate different text length.

Windows CE makes your globalization efforts easier in two ways. Because Windows CE is a Unicode environment, all characters are double-byte; therefore, you do not have to be concerned with manipulating both single-byte and double-byte characters. In addition, Windows CE includes NLS, which provides NLS API as well as some font and keyboard functions. For a list of the NLS functions supported by Windows CE, see the appendix "Lists of Functions and Interfaces."

You must consider the constraints of the device on which your application will run when you globalize your application. The following list describes some of the complex interactions between your application, a Windows CE-based device, and the needs of users in different countries:

- The manufacturer of the device, not the application programmer, determines what countries or locales to support.

- Because a user does not log into the device, the user locale and the default system locale are the same. For example, if you call the function **GetSystemDefaultLangID** or the function **GetUserDefaultLangID**, you obtain the same information.

- The Windows CE operating system loads only one keyboard driver. Although it is possible to load a different keyboard driver than the one installed, you would generally not do this because the device has a built-in keyboard.

- The locale can be changed by the programmer or by the user through an application such as the Control Panel. Changing the locale often requires changing the font, because the code page and character set change with the locale change.

- Because RAM is limited on most Windows CE-based devices, it is not practical to install multiple fonts. Therefore, using a different font requires installing a new one, which can be time-consuming.

For more information on NLS, see *Developing International Software* by Nadine Kano, Microsoft Press.

Porting Win32-Based Applications to Windows CE

Because Windows CE is a Win32-based operating system, you may be able to re-use code developed for Windows-based desktop platforms with little modification. Though porting existing code can be quicker and easier than writing it from scratch, keep the following differences between Windows CE and desktop platforms in mind:

- Hardware design and function. For example, limited memory will influence how you manipulate graphics.
- User interface. The conventional desktop computer model of a user interface that features a keyboard, mouse, and screen may not be appropriate for a Windows CE-based platform.
- Win32 API and related development tools. Windows CE supports a subset of what is available for desktop platforms.
- Extensions to the Win32 API. Some unique features of Windows CE may have no Win32 counterparts, for example, the Notification API. Other Windows CE features may replace comparable Win32 functionality, for example, the Command Bar API.

Hardware Considerations

When you port code between platforms, remember that the hardware configuration of most Windows CE-based platforms differs from that of a desktop computer. In some cases, a Windows CE-based platform might not be recognizable as a computer, though the functionality might be typical for a desktop computer. In addition, a Windows CE-based device may have hardware that has no counterpart on a conventional desktop computer, such as a Global Positioning System (GPS) chip. The most important hardware considerations for Windows CE-based devices are memory, power, user-interaction devices, and the broad range of CPU and communications options. Just recompiling your code with the appropriate Windows CE header files is not sufficient. You must examine the code to be ported while keeping in mind memory, power use, and user input devices.

Windows CE is designed to run on devices that have much less available memory than desktop computers. They may have no disk drive or other mass-storage device, or may support PC Cards that can be used as an alternative to a disk. Even if mass storage is available on the device, RAM is used to store data and applications and to execute programs. In general, you should limit the RAM requirements of your application and associated data and resources.

Windows CE supports functions, structures, and messages that are not supported in Win32, but that may be useful to you when you port code across platforms. Many of these elements will help you manage limited resources. For example, if memory resources become tight during operation, Windows CE has a procedure to reduce memory use and restore available memory to acceptable levels. The key to this procedure is the WM_HIBERNATE message, which notifies applications of low memory. Because this message is not part of Win32, you must implement a handler for it and cooperate when the message is received.

A Windows CE-based platform that operates on batteries has a limited energy supply. If you develop an application for such a platform and must port it, follow these guidelines to make the most of limited power resources:

- Avoid cycling the CPU unnecessarily. An active CPU, and the **PeekMessage** function in particular, consume significant energy.
- Limit your use of common desktop computer hardware that drains batteries rapidly, such as a modem.
- Do not exceed available battery resources. Windows CE displays a warning message to users when batteries start to run low, but it does not send a message to running applications. Therefore, if your application places substantial demands on the batteries, you will need to poll the system with the **GetPowerStatusEx** function to determine battery status.

Applications for desktop computers assume that the user will get information from a relatively large screen and will communicate with the computer using a keyboard and a pointing device. Windows CE-based platforms may use very different hardware than this. The screen is generally smaller or absent, and the platform may have no keyboard or pointing device at all. On the other hand, a Windows CE-based platform may provide user-interaction hardware that is not commonly found on a desktop computer, such as a microphone for speech recognition or a stylus and screen for handwriting recognition. For more information about user-interface considerations, see "User Interface Considerations" later in this chapter.

In addition, Windows CE offers a variety of communications hardware options, including infrared (IrDA) and radio transceivers, that require special consideration. Windows CE supports most standard communication methods, including serial communication, TCP/IP, and IrDA stacks, through WinSockIt. It also supports output by means of modems, infrared transceivers, and local-area networks. For more information about different communications hardware and communications programming, see Chapter 5, "Using Communications."

API Considerations

When porting code from one platform to another, an important consideration is the difference in the APIs supported by the two operating systems. As stated earlier, Windows CE does not support any 16-bit functions and some Win32 functions are not implemented completely, for example, a full range of styles or flags. Also be aware that Windows CE supports and extends an essential subset of the Win32 API, while excluding functions that are not needed, or are redundant, for Windows CE-based devices. For example, the Windows CE graphical device interface provides a powerful, full-color graphical display system by supporting many of the shape, bit-block transfer, palette, font, and color functions. However, to remain compact, some of the Win32 special graphic functions, such as **MoveTo** and **LineTo**, are eliminated.

In addition to supporting a subset of the Win32 API, Windows CE extends it in a number of ways. Most of these extensions support the unique capabilities of Windows CE-based platforms. Some, such as the command bar API, replace a set of Win32 functions and work in a way that is more suitable for Windows CE-based devices.

When you port an application from Win32 to Windows CE, remove unsupported functions and modify your code to use supported functions. Then, thoroughly review your code, keeping in mind the limitations and potentials of your platform. For more information, see "Example Program for H/PC" in the online Help.

You can reuse any Visual C++, Visual Basic, or Visual J++ code in your Windows CE-based application. If your application was developed using a Microsoft IDE, such as Visual C++, Visual Basic, or Visual J++, you can continue to use that IDE with Windows CE by installing the appropriate toolkit.

As discussed earlier, many Win32 applications are developed using MFC and ATL. Windows CE supports subsets of both of these tools. In addition, Windows CE supports a subset of COM/OLE, a powerful and flexible approach to object-oriented programming that is used by many applications. You may be able to port an application that uses COM/OLE, MFC, or ATL with only minor revisions.

Character Set Considerations

As stated earlier, Windows CE is a Unicode environment. While it supports ASCII functionality to allow the exchange of text files, the native text format is Unicode. The following list provides guidelines for converting ASCII-based code to Unicode:

- Include Tchar.h. It has all the necessary conversions.
- Use the Win32 string functions, rather than the C run-time library equivalents.
- Use TCHAR or LPTSTR for declarations. Declaring character variables as TCHAR allows the code to be compiled as either Unicode or ASCII.
- Use the **TEXT** macro for string literals, such as Text("a string"). The **TEXT** macro identifies a string as Unicode when the UNICODE compile flag is used or as an ANSI string when Unicode is not defined.

Use the size of (TCHAR) operator to ensure that your code is valid for both Unicode and ASCII. When you increment pointers, remember that an ASCII character is one byte, but that a Unicode character is two bytes.

User Interface Considerations

Some of the greatest differences between a Windows CE-based platform and a standard desktop computer are in the UI. Though some Windows CE-based platforms, such as the H/PC, may be similar to a conventional desktop computer, others may modify or eliminate altogether the familiar screen, keyboard, and mouse of a desktop computer.

For Windows CE-based platforms, the screen is not as powerful and flexible a way to communicate information to the user as it is with a desktop computer because the screen is typically much smaller, with lower resolution. Though some devices have color screens, many support only grayscale or monochrome graphics. For devices that dispense with the screen entirely, you may need to develop alternative ways to communicate information.

A key element of a graphical UI is a pointing device, which enables a user to interact with the various graphical elements of the UI. Though a mouse may not be appropriate, some Windows CE-based devices, such as an H/PC, have a touch screen and stylus that work much the same way as a mouse. Others may have no pointing device at all, and must depend on other navigation techniques, such as arrow keys, or may use an entirely different approach to interaction, such as speech recognition.

Keyboards on Windows CE-based devices are generally more difficult to use and are less flexible than they are on desktop computers. Because they may be too small to support a full set of alphanumeric characters, they may provide only a collection of special-purpose keys for users to communicate with the application. Text-entry, if supported, may be through an input panel, which enables a user to type characters by way of a touch screen, rather than a physical keyboard. Because this method of text entry is more difficult for users, rely on other forms of communication over text entry whenever possible.

Debugging and Testing Windows CE-Based Applications

An effective set of debugging tools can speed up the time-consuming process of debugging an application and make it easier to determine the source of problems. The Windows CE IDE provides a set of tools for such tasks as emulation and remote debugging on H/PCs, and special tools for debugging other Windows CE-based platforms.

Desktop Emulation Debugging and Testing

The desktop emulation tool included with Windows CE allows you to write and debug an H/PC application on any computer running Windows NT. With emulation, you can test and debug your application without downloading your software to a device. You can even use emulation to write a Windows CE-based application without having a device. Though you can determine a great deal about the functionality and appearance of your application with emulation, once your application is running correctly in the emulation environment, you must download it to a target device for final testing and evaluation. In addition to testing for defects and reliability, testing for usability is critical, because most Windows CE-based platforms have a small desktop area that can present access problems.

Remote Debugging and Testing

In addition to desktop emulation, Windows CE contains several tools that enable you to examine your application as it runs. These remote tools are described in the following table.

Tool	Purpose
Remote Connection Server	Creates a network connection between a desktop computer and an H/PC. Remote Connection Server will not synchronize a remote device and a desktop computer.
Remote Zoomin	Enlarges a section of an H/PC screen.
Remote Registry Editor	Edits the Windows CE registry. Because there is no tool like RegEdit on an H/PC, you view and edit the H/PC registry using this desktop tool.
Remote Object Viewer	Allows you to view the object store on a remote H/PC device and on a desktop computer.
Remote Spy	Displays a graphical view, on a desktop computer, of the system processes, threads, windows, and window messages that are running on a remote H/PC.

In order to use the remote tools, you must connect your desktop computer to your remote device with a standard serial cable connection. For information on how to physically connect your desktop computer and a remote device, see the user's guide that came with your device.

Non-Standard Debugging and Testing

If you are developing software for a Windows CE-based platform, such as an H/PC, you can use the Windows CE emulation environment and remote tools to debug and test your application. However, if you are developing applications for other Windows CE-based platforms, such as embedded systems, you will have to devise your own debugging and testing tools.

The Windows CE API includes the interfaces necessary to create a full-featured debugger application, such as the one provided with Visual C++ or WinDbg. Although the creation tools exist, the limited size of the Windows CE environment makes such a debugger unrealistic. If you decide to write a debugger application, the best approach is to create a debug client using Windows CE debug functions and to communicate the relevant events to a desktop computer-based debugger. When writing a debugging application, choose one of the following ways to start the debugging session:

- Launch a process with **CreateProcess** and specify DEBUG_PROCESS or DEBUG_ONLY_THIS_PROCESS in the **dwCreateFlags** member. In addition to the DEBUG_PROCESS flag, use CREATE_SUSPENDED to prevent the application from running after it is initialized. Once suspended, a debugger can initialize and add any appropriate break points.

  –Or–

- Attach to an already running application. To attach to a process, you must obtain permission to access the process by calling **OpenProcess** and passing in the identifier of the process you want to debug. If a valid handle is returned, call **DebugActiveProcess** to start debugging. After attaching to the process, the CREATE_PROCESS_DEBUG_EVENT returns the primary thread handle and the multiple CREATE_THREAD_DEBUG_EVENTs return the secondary thread handles. After attaching to the process and receiving the initial events, the process's thread is resumed. Unlike Windows NT, Windows CE has no EXCEPTION_DEBUG_EVENT. All thread handles must be closed with **CloseHandle** when you stop debugging.

Windows CE has built-in support for just-in-time (JIT) debugging. JIT debugging enables you to run an application outside of the development environment. When an error occurs, the application calls the installed debugger. You register your JIT debugger by placing the name of your debugger in the registry located at HKEY_LOCAL_MACHINE\Debug. To enable JIT, you must warm-boot the device after the JITDebugger value is added to the registry.

If you choose not to write a debugging application, you must create some debugging tools inside your Windows CE-based application. Windows CE provides both functions and structures to do this. For a list of supported debugging functions, see the appendix "Lists of Functions and Interfaces."

No matter what tools you use, you must thoroughly test your application on every kind of device that will run your application.

PART 2

Core Services

C H A P T E R   3

Working with Processes and Threads

When you start a Windows CE-based application, the operating system automatically creates a process and a primary thread for that process. A process is a single instance of a running application and a thread is the basic unit of execution. Windows CE-based applications can incorporate multiple processes and each process can contain multiple threads.

Every process has at least one thread. You create additional threads by calling the **CreateThread** function. You call the **ExitThread** function to free up the resources used by a thread when it is no longer needed. Calling **Exit Thread** for an application's primary thread causes the application to terminate.

Note Unlike processes on Windows-based desktop platforms, a Windows CE process will terminate if its primary thread is terminated, even if there are other active threads in existence for the process.

When the Windows CE operating system initializes, it creates a single 4 GB virtual address space. It is divided into 33 *slots*, each 32 MB. The address space is shared by all processes. When a process initializes, Windows CE selects an open slot for the process in the system's address space. Slot zero is reserved for the currently running process. In addition to assigning a slot for each process, Windows CE creates a stack and a message queue for each thread in the process. Each stack has an initial size of at least 1 KB. Because the stack size is CPU-dependent; the system allocates 4 KB for each stack on some devices. The maximum number of threads is dependent upon the amount of available memory.

When a process initializes, the operating system stores in the slot assigned to the process all dynamic-link libraries (DLLs), the stack, the heap, the application code, and the data section for each process. DLLs are loaded at the top of the slot, followed by the stack, the heap, and the executable file (.exe). The bottom 64 KB is always left free.

For an overview of processes and threads, see Chapter 1, "Overview of the Windows CE Operating System." For a list of the functions that support manipulating processes and threads, see the appendix "Lists of Functions and Interfaces."

Creating and Terminating a Process

When you initiate a program from within a running application, the application calls the **CreateProcess** function to load the new application into memory and to create a new process with at least one new thread.

▶ **To create and terminate a process**

- Call the **CreateProcess** function to create a process.

  The *lpApplicationName* parameter must specify the name of the module to execute. Windows CE does not support passing NULL for *lpApplicationName*.

- Call the **TerminateProcess** function to terminate a process.

  Windows CE processes do not have exit codes and cannot terminate themselves. You cannot use **TerminateProcess** to terminate a Protected Server Library (PSL) for processes contained therein.

Scheduling Threads

When the operating system creates a new process, it also creates at least one thread and assigns that thread a priority level. Processes running under Windows CE are not assigned a priority class, so preemption is based solely on the thread's priority. Threads with a higher priority are scheduled to run first. Threads with the same priority level run in a round-robin fashion, with each receiving a slice of execution time. Threads at a lower priority do not run until all threads with a higher priority have finished. All threads are created with a default priority of THREAD_PRIORITY_NORMAL.

▶ **To change the priority level of a thread**

- Call the **SetThreadPriority** function passing in one of eight priority level values. The values are described in the following table.

Priority	Description
THREAD_PRIORITY_TIME_CRITICAL	Indicates 3 points above normal priority.
THREAD_PRIORITY_HIGHEST	Indicates 2 points above normal priority.
THREAD_PRIORITY_ABOVE_NORMAL	Indicates 1 point above normal priority.
THREAD_PRIORITY_NORMAL	Indicates normal priority.
THREAD_PRIORITY_BELOW_NORMAL	Indicates 1 point below normal priority.
THREAD_PRIORITY_LOWEST	Indicates 2 points below normal priority.
THREAD_PRIORITY_ABOVE_IDLE	Indicates 3 points below normal priority.
THREAD_PRIORITY_IDLE	Indicates 4 points below normal priority.

Synchronizing Processes and Threads

Windows CE supports preemptive multitasking. Multitasking operating systems must ensure that processes and threads are synchronized. Windows CE provides many ways to coordinate multiple threads of execution. For example, you can use *wait functions* and *synchronization objects*. You pass a synchronization object as a parameter to a wait function. The wait function does not return until its specified criteria has been met. The type of wait function determines the set of criteria used. When a wait function is called, it checks whether the wait criteria has been met. If the criteria has not been met, the calling thread enters an efficient wait state, consuming very little processor time.

Using Wait Functions

Windows CE supports two types of wait functions, single-object and multiple-objects. The single object function is **WaitForSingleObject**. The multiple object functions are **WaitForMultipleObjects** and **MsgWaitForMultipleObjects**.

The **WaitForSingleObject** function requires a handle of one synchronization object. This function returns when one of the following occurs:

- The specified object is in the signaled state.
- The time-out interval elapses. You can set the time-out interval to INFINITE to specify that the wait will not time out.

The **WaitForMultipleObjects** and **MsgWaitForMultipleObjects** functions enable the calling thread to specify an array containing one or more synchronization object handles. These functions return when one of the following occurs:

- The state of any one of the specified objects is set to signaled or the states of all objects have been set to signaled. You control whether one or all of the states will be used in the function call.

- The time-out interval elapses. You can set the time-out interval to INFINITE to specify that the wait will not time out.

The following code example shows how to use the **CreateEvent** function to create two event objects. It then uses the two created objects as parameters in the function call to **WaitForMultipleObjects**. The **WaitForMultipleObjects** function does not return until one of the objects is set to signaled.

```
HANDLE hEvents[2];
DWORD i, dwEvent;

for (i = 0; i < 2; i++)
{
   hEvents[i] = CreateEvent(
      NULL,               // no security attributes
      FALSE,              // auto-reset event object
      FALSE,              // initial state is nonsignaled
      NULL);              // unnamed object
   if (hEvents[i] == NULL)
   {
      printf("CreateEvent error: %d\n", GetLastError() );
      ExitProcess(0);
   }
}

dwEvent = WaitForMultipleObjects(
   2,                     // number of objects in array
   hEvents,               // array of objects
   FALSE,                 // wait for any
   INFINITE);             // indefinite wait

switch (dwEvent)
{
   case WAIT_OBJECT_0 + 0:
      break;

   case WAIT_OBJECT_0 + 1:
      break;

   default:
      printf("Wait error: %d\n", GetLastError());
      ExitProcess(0);
}
```

MsgWaitForMultipleObjects is similar to **WaitForMultipleObjects**, except that it allows you to specify input event objects in the object handle array. You select the type of input event to wait for in the *dwWakeMask* parameter. **MsgWaitForMultipleObjects** does not return if there is unread input of the specified type in the queue. It returns only when new input arrives.

For example, a thread can use **MsgWaitForMultipleObjects** with its *dwWakeMask* parameter set to QS_KEY. This blocks its execution until the state of a specified object has been set to signaled and there is keyboard input available in the thread's input queue. The thread can use the **GetMessage** or **PeekMessage** function to retrieve the input.

When waiting for the states of all objects to be set to signaled, the multiple-object functions do not modify the states of the specified objects until the states of all objects have been set to signaled. For example, the state of a mutex object can be signaled, but the calling thread does not get ownership until the states of the other objects specified in the array have also been set to signaled. In the meantime, some other thread may get ownership of the mutex object, thereby setting its state to nonsignaled.

The following code example shows the use of the **MsgWaitForMultipleObjects** function in a message loop. The loop continues until a WM_QUIT message appears in the queue. The *dwWakeMask* parameter is set to QS_ALLINPUT so all messages are checked.

```
int MessageLoop
   (
     HANDLE* lphObjects,          // handles that need to be waited on
     int     cObjects             // number of handles to wait on
   )
{
     while (TRUE)
     {
        // block-local variable
        DWORD result ;
        MSG msg ;

        while (PeekMessage(&msg, NULL, 0, 0, PM_REMOVE))
        {
           if (msg.message == WM_QUIT)
              return 1;
           DispatchMessage(&msg);
        }

        result = MsgWaitForMultipleObjects(cObjects, lphObjects,
                 FALSE, INFINITE, QS_ALLINPUT);
```

```
        if (result == (WAIT_OBJECT_0 + cObjects))
        {
            continue;
        }
        else
        {
            Other Code (result - WAIT_OBJECT_0) ;
        }
    }
}
```

Be careful when using the wait functions and code that directly or indirectly create windows. If a thread creates any windows, it must process messages. Message broadcasts are sent to all windows in the system. If you have a thread that uses a wait function with no time-out interval, the system will deadlock. Two examples of code that indirectly create windows are DDE and COM **CoInitialize**. If you have a thread that creates windows, use **MsgWaitForMultipleObjects** rather than the other wait functions.

Using Synchronization Objects

A *synchronization object* is an object whose handle can be specified in one of the wait functions. Windows CE uses event, mutex, and critical section objects only for synchronization. Although it uses process and thread objects for synchronization as well, they are available for other uses.

Event Objects

An *event object* is a synchronization object that allows one thread to notify another that an event has occurred. A thread uses **CreateEvent** to create an event object. The creating thread specifies the initial state of the object and whether it is a manual-reset or auto-reset event object. The creating thread can also specify a name for the event object. Threads in other processes can open a handle of an existing event object by specifying its name in a call to **CreateEvent**. For additional information about names for mutex and event objects, see "Interprocess Synchronization" later in this chapter. Windows CE uses event objects to tell a thread when to perform its task or to indicate that a particular event has occurred. For example, a thread that writes to a buffer resets the event object to signaled when it has finished writing. By using an event object to notify the thread that its task is finished, the thread can immediately start performing other tasks.

A single thread can specify different event objects in several simultaneous overlapped operations. If this is the case, use one of the multiple-object wait functions to wait for the state of any one of the event objects to be signaled. You can also use event objects in a number of situations to notify a waiting thread of the occurrence of an event. For example, overlapped input/output (I/O) operations on files, named pipes, and communications devices use an event object to signal their completion. For more information about the use of event objects in overlapped I/O operations, see "Synchronization and Device I/O" later in the chapter.

In the following code example, an application uses event objects to prevent several threads from reading from a shared memory buffer while a master thread is writing to that buffer. The master thread uses the **CreateEvent** function to create a manual-reset event object. It sets the event object to nonsignaled when it is writing to the buffer and then resets the object to signaled when it has finished writing. The master thread then creates several reader threads and an auto-reset event object for each thread. Each reader thread sets its event object to signaled when it is not reading from the buffer.

```
#define NUMTHREADS 4

HANDLE hGlobalWriteEvent;

void CreateEventsAndThreads(void)
{
    HANDLE hReadEvents[NUMTHREADS], hThread;
    DWORD i, IDThread;

    hGlobalWriteEvent = CreateEvent
        (
        NULL,                    // no security attributes
        TRUE,                    // manual-reset event
        TRUE,                    // initial state is signaled
        "WriteEvent"             // object name
        );

    if (hGlobalWriteEvent == NULL)
    {
                                 // error exit
    }
```

```
for(i = 1; i <= NUMTHREADS; i++)
{
   hReadEvents[i] = CreateEvent
      (
      NULL,                        // no security attributes
      FALSE,                       // auto-reset event
      TRUE,                        // initial state is signaled
      NULL);                       // object not named

   if (hReadEvents[i] == NULL)
   {
                                   // error exit
   }

   hThread = CreateThread(NULL, 0,
      (LPTHREAD_START_ROUTINE) ThreadFunction,
      &hReadEvents[i],             // pass event handle
      0, &IDThread);
   if (hThread == NULL)
   {
                                   // error exit
   }
}
}
```

In the following code example, before the master thread writes to the shared buffer, it uses the **ResetEvent** function to set the state of *hGlobalWriteEvent*, an application-defined global variable, to nonsignaled. This blocks the reader threads from starting a read operation. The master thread then uses the **WaitForMultipleObjects** function to wait for all reader threads to finish any current read operations. When **WaitForMultipleObjects** returns, the master thread can safely write to the buffer. After it has finished writing, it sets *hGlobalWriteEvent* and all the reader-thread events to signaled, which enables the reader threads to resume their read operations.

```
VOID WriteToBuffer(VOID)
{
     DWORD dwWaitResult, i;


     if (! ResetEvent(hGlobalWriteEvent) )
     {
                                   // error exit
     }
```

```
dwWaitResult = WaitForMultipleObjects
   (
   NUMTHREADS,                        // number of handles in array
   hReadEvents,                       // array of read-event handles
   TRUE,                              // wait until all are signaled
   INFINITE);                         // indefinite wait

switch (dwWaitResult)
{
   case WAIT_OBJECT_0:
                                      // Write to the shared buffer.
      break;

                                      // An error occurred.
   default:
      printf("Wait error: %d\n", GetLastError());
      ExitProcess(0);
}

if (! SetEvent(hGlobalWriteEvent) )
{
                                      // error exit
}

for(i = 1; i <= NUMTHREADS; i++)
   if (! SetEvent(hReadEvents[i]) )
   {
                                      // error exit
   }
}
```

In the following code example, before starting a read operation, each reader thread uses **WaitForMultipleObjects** to wait for the application-defined global variable, *hGlobalWriteEvent*, and its own read event to be signaled. When **WaitForMultipleObjects** returns, the reader thread's auto-reset event has been reset to nonsignaled. This blocks the master thread from writing to the buffer until the reader thread uses the **SetEvent** function to set the event's state back to signaled.

```
VOID ThreadFunction(LPVOID lpParam)
{
    DWORD dwWaitResult, i;
    HANDLE hEvents[2];

    hEvents[0] = (HANDLE) *lpParam;    // thread's read event
    hEvents[1] = hGlobalWriteEvent;

    dwWaitResult = WaitForMultipleObjects
        (
        2,                             // number of handles in array
        hEvents,                       // array of event handles
        TRUE,                          // wait till all are signaled
        INFINITE);                     // indefinite wait

    switch (dwWaitResult)
    {

      case WAIT_OBJECT_0:
          break;

                                       // An error occurred.
      default:
         printf("Wait error: %d\n", GetLastError());
         ExitThread(0);
    }


    if (! SetEvent(hEvents[0]) )
    {
                                       // error exit
    }
}
```

Mutex Objects

A *mutex object* is a synchronization object whose state is set to signaled when it is not owned by any thread, and nonsignaled when it is owned. Its name comes from its usefulness in coordinating mutually-exclusive access to a shared resource. Only one thread at a time can own a mutex object. For example, to prevent two threads from writing to shared memory at the same time, each thread waits for ownership of a mutex object before executing the code that accesses the memory. After writing to the shared memory, the thread releases the mutex object.

A thread uses the **CreateMutex** function to create a mutex object. The creating thread can request immediate ownership of the mutex object and can also specify a name for the mutex object. Threads in other processes can open a handle to an existing mutex object by specifying its name in a call to **CreateMutex**. For additional information about names for mutex and event objects, see "Interprocess Synchronization" later in this chapter.

Any thread with a handle of a mutex object can use one of the wait functions to request ownership of the mutex object. If the mutex object is owned by another thread, the wait function blocks the requesting thread until the owning thread releases the mutex object using the **ReleaseMutex** function. The return value of the wait function indicates whether the function returned for some reason other than the state of the mutex being set to signaled.

Once a thread owns a mutex, it can specify the same mutex in repeated calls to one of the wait functions without blocking its execution. This prevents a thread from deadlocking itself while waiting for a mutex that it already owns. To release its ownership under such circumstances, the thread must call **ReleaseMutex** once for each time that the mutex satisfied the conditions of a wait function.

If a thread terminates without releasing its ownership of a mutex object, the mutex object is considered to be abandoned. A waiting thread can acquire ownership of an abandoned mutex object, but the wait function's return value indicates that the mutex object is abandoned. To be safe, assume that an abandoned mutex object indicates that an error has occurred and that any shared resource being protected by the mutex object is in an undefined state. If the thread proceeds as though the mutex object had not been abandoned, the object's abandoned flag is cleared when the thread releases its ownership. This restores typical behavior, if a handle to the mutex object is subsequently specified in a wait function.

In the following code examples, a process uses the **CreateMutex** function first to create a named mutex object, and in the second piece of code, to open a handle of an existing mutex object. Additionally, it uses structured exception-handling to ensure that the thread properly releases the mutex object.

```
HANDLE hMutex;


hMutex = CreateMutex
    (
    NULL,                          // no security attributes
    FALSE,                         // initially not owned
    "MutexToProtectDatabase");     // name of mutex

if (hMutex == NULL)
{
                                   // Check for error.

}
```

When a thread of this process writes to the database, it first requests ownership of the mutex. If it gets ownership, the thread writes to the database and then releases its ownership.

The example uses the **try-finally** structured exception-handling syntax to ensure that the thread properly releases the mutex object. To prevent the mutex object from being abandoned inadvertently, the **finally** block of code is executed no matter how the **try** block terminates—unless the **try** block includes a call to the **TerminateThread** function.

```
BOOL FunctionToWriteToDatabase(HANDLE hMutex)
{
    DWORD dwWaitResult;


    dwWaitResult = WaitForSingleObject(
        hMutex,         // handle of mutex
        5000L);         // five-second time-out interval

    switch (dwWaitResult)
    {
        case WAIT_OBJECT_0:
          try
          {
                  // Write to the database.
          }

          finally
          {
             if (! ReleaseMutex(hMutex))
             {
                  // Deal with error.
             }

          break;
          }
```

```
                               // Cannot get mutex ownership due to time-out.
        case WAIT_TIMEOUT:
            return FALSE;

                               // Got ownership of the abandoned mutex object.
        case WAIT_ABANDONED:
            return FALSE;
    }

    return TRUE;
}
```

Critical Section Objects

A *critical section object* is a synchronization object that provides synchronization similar to that provided by mutex objects, except that critical section objects can be used only by the threads of a single process. Like a mutex object, a critical section object can be owned by only one thread at a time, which makes it useful for protecting a shared resource from simultaneous access. There is no guarantee about the order in which threads obtain ownership of the critical section; however, Windows CE processes all threads equally.

A process is responsible for allocating the memory used by a critical section. Typically, this is done by declaring a variable of the type CRITICAL_SECTION. Before the threads of the process can use it, you must initialize the critical section by using the **InitializeCriticalSection** function.

A thread uses **EnterCriticalSection** to request ownership of a critical section and it uses the **LeaveCriticalSection** function to release ownership. If the critical section object is currently owned by another thread, **EnterCriticalSection** waits indefinitely for ownership. In contrast, when a mutex object is used for mutual exclusion, the wait functions accept a specified time-out interval.

Once a thread owns a critical section, it can make additional calls to **EnterCriticalSection** without blocking its execution. This prevents a thread from deadlocking itself while waiting for a critical section that it already owns. To release its ownership, the thread must call **LeaveCriticalSection** once for each time that it entered the critical section.

Any thread of the process can use the **DeleteCriticalSection** function to release the system resources that were allocated when the critical section object was initialized. After this function has been called, the critical section object can no longer be used for synchronization.

When a critical section object is owned, the only other threads affected are those waiting for ownership in a call to **EnterCriticalSection**. Threads that are not waiting are free to continue running.

The following code example shows how a thread initializes, enters, and leaves a critical section. As with the mutex example described earlier, this example uses the **try-finally** structured exception-handling syntax to ensure that the thread calls the **LeaveCriticalSection** function to release its ownership of the critical section object.

```
CRITICAL_SECTION GlobalCriticalSection;

InitializeCriticalSection(&GlobalCriticalSection);


{
    EnterCriticalSection(&GlobalCriticalSection);
                    // Access the shared resource.
}
finally
{
                        // Release ownership of the critical section.
    LeaveCriticalSection(&GlobalCriticalSection);
}
```

Interprocess Synchronization

Because multiple processes can have handles to the same event or mutex object, these objects can be used to accomplish interprocess synchronization. The process that creates an object can use the handle returned by the creation function, **CreateEvent** or **CreateMutex**. Other processes can open a handle to the object by using its name in another call to the appropriate creation function.

Named objects provide an easy way for processes to share object handles. The name specified by the creating process is limited to the number of characters defined by MAX_PATH. It can include any character except the backslash path-separator character (\). Once a process has created a named event or mutex object, other processes can use the name to call the appropriate function, either **CreateEvent** or **CreateMutex**, to open a handle to the object. Name comparison is case-sensitive.

The names of event and mutex objects share the same name space. If you specify a name that is in use by an object of another type when you create an object, the function succeeds, but **GetLastError** returns ERROR_ALREADY_EXISTS. To avoid this error, use unique names and be sure to check function-return values for duplicate-name errors.

If the name specified in a call to **CreateEvent** matches the name of an existing event object, the function returns the handle of the existing object. When using this technique for event objects, however, none of the calling processes should request immediate ownership of the event. If multiple processes do request immediate ownership, you may have difficulty predicting which process will get the initial ownership.

The following code examples illustrate the use of object names by creating and opening named objects. The first process uses the **CreateMutex** function to create the mutex object. Note that the function succeeds even if there is an existing object with the same name.

```
HANDLE hMutex;
DWORD dwErr;

hMutex = CreateMutex
    (
    NULL,                           // no security descriptor
    FALSE,                          // mutex not owned
    "NameOfMutexObject");           // object name

if (hMutex == NULL)
    printf("CreateMutex error: %d\n", GetLastError() );
else
    if ( GetLastError() == ERROR_ALREADY_EXISTS )
        printf("CreateMutex opened existing mutex\n");
    else
        printf("CreateMutex created new mutex\n");
```

The second process uses the **CreateMutex** function to open a handle of the existing mutex.

```
HANDLE hMutex;

hMutex = OpenMutex
    (
    MUTEX_ALL_ACCESS,               // request full access
    FALSE,                          // handle not inheritable
    "NameOfMutexObject");           // object name

if (hMutex == NULL)
    printf("OpenMutex error: %d\n", GetLastError() );
```

Synchronization and Device I/O

Windows CE supports both synchronous and asynchronous I/O operations on files and serial communications devices. The **WriteFile**, **ReadFile**, and **WaitCommEvent** functions can be performed either synchronously or asynchronously.

When a function is executed synchronously, it does not return until the operation has been completed. This means that the execution of the calling thread can be blocked for an indefinite period while it waits for a time-consuming operation to finish. Functions called for overlapped operation can return immediately, even though the operation has not been completed. This enables a time-consuming I/O operation to be executed in the background while the calling thread is free to perform other tasks. For example, a single thread can perform simultaneous I/O operations on different handles, or even simultaneous read-and-write operations on the same handle.

Windows CE does not support the overlapped I/O features of Windows NT. The *lpOverlapped* parameter to **ReadFile** or **WriteFile** must be NULL. Therefore, Windows CE cannot signal the event passed in when the I/O operation is completed. However, Windows CE does support simultaneous synchronous or asynchronous calls to **ReadFile** or **WriteFile** made by separate threads that are overlapped in time; this is not supported in Windows NT.

Synchronizing Access to a Shared Variable

The functions **InterlockedDecrement**, **InterlockedExchange**, and **InterlockedIncrement** provide a simple mechanism for synchronizing access to a variable that is shared by multiple threads. The threads of different processes can use this mechanism, if the variable is in shared memory.

The **InterlockedIncrement** and **InterlockedDecrement** functions combine the operations of incrementing or decrementing the shared variable and checking the resulting value. This atomic operation is useful in a multitasking operating system, in which the system can interrupt one thread's execution to grant a slice of processor time to another thread. Without such synchronization, one thread could increment a variable, but be interrupted by the system before it can check the resulting value of the variable. A second thread could then increment the same variable. In this scenario, when the first thread receives its next time slice, it checks the value of the variable, which has now been incremented not once, but twice. The interlocked variable-access functions of Windows CE protect against this kind of error. The **InterlockedExchange** function atomically exchanges the values of the specified variables.

C H A P T E R   4

Accessing Persistent Storage

The persistent storage that Windows CE makes available to applications is called the *object store*. This is the part of memory that is not used for the operating system.

The object store is used for the following purposes:

- Registry entries

  The registry is a hierarchical database in which Windows CE stores information necessary to configure the operating system. It contains information on user profiles, applications, hardware, ports in use, and so on. The registry replaces most of the text-based initialization (.ini) files used in MS-DOS and Windows 3.x configuration files, such as AUTOEXEC.BAT and CONFIG.SYS.

  Specific registry locations are described in various chapters of the *Windows CE Programmer's Guide*. An example of a registry location used for synchronization is HKEY_LOCAL_MACHINE\Software\Microsoft\Windows CE Services\ Services\Synchronization\Objects.

  Windows CE supports a subset of the Win32 registry functions. The differences between the Windows CE functions and their Win32 counterparts are minimal. The main difference is that Windows CE assigns a default security descriptor to keys, so the parameter for security attributes in **RegCreateKeyEx** should be set to NULL. For a list of the supported functions, see the appendix "Lists of Functions and Interfaces."

- Files

  The file system functions available to Windows CE-based applications are those supported by the Windows CE kernel. Note that the C Runtime library does not include any file access functions, such as **fopen**, **fread**, and **fprintf**. The following discussion highlights specific points concerning the Windows CE file system functions. For a list of the file system functions, see the appendix "Lists of Functions and Interfaces."

CreateFile opens existing files as well as creates new files. Windows CE does not support simultaneous read/write operations; thus, files cannot be created with the overlapped attribute set. To write to a file in the equivalent of append mode, call **CreateFile** and **SetFilePointer**. To overwrite the contents of a file, call **CreateFile** and **SetEndOfFile**. **ReadFile** does not support asynchronous reads nor does it support reads through a socket. **WriteFile** does not support asynchronous writes, and, unlike MS-DOS, Windows CE interprets zero bytes as a null write. To truncate or extend files, use **SetEndOfFile**.

A ROM file is a file stored on a device as read-only memory, for example, flash memory or PC Cards. A ROM file is an option for dealing with the memory limitations of a Windows CE-based platform. The **GetFileAttributes** function has additional return values for files stored in ROM. The FILE_ATTRIBUTE_INROM value identifies the file as read-only. The FILE_ATTRIBUTE_ROMMODULE value indicates that the file is designed to be executed in place, without first being copied to RAM. The **CreateFile** function cannot be used to access this type of file; the **LoadLibrary** and **CreateProcess** functions must be used instead.

- Windows CE databases

The rest of this chapter discusses Windows CE databases and the functions which relate to them. For a list of the Windows CE database functions, see the appendix "Lists of Functions and Interfaces."

Object Identifiers

Each object in the object store—whether a directory, file, database, or database record—is associated with a unique object identifier. The system generates an object identifier for each object when it is created. The most common use of object identifiers is accessing databases and their records.

Object type	Where to obtain the object identifier
Directory or file	The **dwOID** member of WIN32_FIND_DATAW from **FindFirstFile** or **FindNextFile**.
	The **dwOID** member of BY_HANDLE_FILE_INFORMATION from **GetFileInformationByHandle**.
Database	Return value of **CeCreateDatabase** or **CeFindNextDatabase**.
Database record	Return value of **CeSeekDatabase**, **CeReadRecordProps**, or **CeWriteRecordProps**.

Another important use of object identifiers is to obtain information on any object in the store. To accomplish this, a Windows CE-based application calls the **CeOidGetInfo** function and supplies the object identifier in the parameter of type **CEOID**. **CeOidGetInfo** returns the object data in a **CEOIDINFO** structure. This structure's **wObjType** member contains a flag that indicates the object type. The data in the structure depends on the type of object. For example, if the object is a database record, the **CEOIDINFO** structure's **wObjType** member contains the flag OBJTYPE_RECORD, indicating that the data for the object consists of a **CERECORDINFO** structure. If there is no valid object for the object identifier the return value of **CeOidGetInfo** is FALSE.

The following code example shows how to use the object identifier to obtain the object type of any object in the object store.

```
CEOID WceObjID;              // object identifier
CEOIDINFO WceObjInfo;        // structure that contains object info
TCHAR szMsg[MAX_STRING];     // string to display with object info
...
if (CeOidGetInfo(WceObjID, &WceObjInfo))
{
   switch (WceObjInfo.wObjType)
   {
      case OBJTYPE_FILE:
         wsprintf(szMsg, TEXT("Object is a file: %s"),
                        WceObjInfo.infFile.szFileName);
         break;
      case OBJTYPE_RECORD:
         wsprintf(szMsg, TEXT("Object is a record"));
         break;
      case OBJTYPE_DATABASE:
         wsprintf(szMsg, TEXT("Object is a database: %s"),
                        WceObjInfo.infDatabase.szDbaseName);
         break;
      case OBJTYPE_DIRECTORY:
         wsprintf(szMsg, TEXT("Object is a directory: %s"),
                        WceObjInfo.infDirectory.szDirName);
         break;
      default:
         // handle error ...
         break;
   }
}
```

Working with Windows CE Databases

A Windows CE database is simply a general-purpose, flexible, structured collection of data. A Windows CE database consists of *records*, where each record consists of one or more *properties*. A *property* refers to a data item that consists of a property identifer, a data type identifier, and the data value. For example, an application could use a database of address records, where the properties of each record include a name, street address, city, state, zip code, and telephone number. Windows CE supports integer, string, time, and byte array, or BLOB, data types.

Devices that run the Windows CE operating system usually ship with several built-in databases and allow users and applications to create additional databases. For example, the Handheld PC (H/PC) comes with calendar and task list applications that have databases for user data.

Note that databases allow only one level of hierarchy. That is, records cannot contain other records. Nor can records be shared by databases—each record is unique, has a unique object identifier, and is present in only one database. The recommended maximum size of a record in bytes is given by the constant **CEDB_MAXRECORDSIZE**. The recommended maximum property size is given by **CEDB_MAXPROPDATASIZE**. Both of these constants are defined in Rapi.h and Windbase.h.

Unlike traditional databases, opening and closing a Windows CE database does not imply that any transactioning has occurred. The database is not committed at closing, but rather it is committed after each individual call.

It is not possible to lock a Windows CE database to restrict access. Thus, several applications can have open handles to the same database at the same time. However, Windows CE supports several notification messages that can tell an application when another application creates, modifies, or deletes database records. The messages are sent to the specified window when you call **CeOpenDatabase** and supply a non-null window handle.

Windows CE supports the following messages:

Message	Description
DB_CEOID_CHANGED	Another thread modified an object in the object store. The message supplies the object identifier.
DB_CEOID_CREATED	Another thread created an object in the object store. The message supplies the object identifier.
DB_CEOID_RECORD_DELETED	Another thread deleted a record. The message supplies the record's object identifier.

Each database includes information about the database as a whole, such as its name, an optional *database type identifier* that you can use to group similar databases, and up to four sort keys that describe how the records in the database will be sorted.

Creating and Deleting Databases

The **CeCreateDatabase** function creates a database. When calling the function, specify the name, an optional database type identifier, and optional sort order specifications. **CeCreateDatabase** returns the object identifier of the newly created database.

The database type identifier is an optional, application-defined value that allows you to differentiate individual databases. For example, you can have a different type of database for an address book than for a to-do list. The type identifier allows you to group related databases for searching, record management, and enumeration of databases.

For a discussion of sorting and sort orders, see "Sorting Records" later in this chapter.

To delete a database, the application passes the database's object identifier to **CeDeleteDatabase**.

The following code example shows how to open a database of addresses by calling the **CeOpenDatabase** function. If the database does not exist, call the **CeCreateDatabase** function to create a new address database with three different sort orders. After creating the database, try again to open the database.

```
// Global variables:
//    g_oidAddressDatabase - Object identifier of address database
//    g_hAddressDatabase - Open handle to the address database

BOOL OpenAddressDatabase (HWND hwndNotify, CEPROPID cepidSortProperty)
{
    CEOID oidAddressDatabase;   // Object identifier of address database
    SORTORDERSPEC sort[MAX_MSG_PROPERTIES]; // Sort order descriptions

    g_hAddressDatabase = CeOpenDatabase(&oidAddressDatabase,
        TEXT("Addresses"),  cepidSortProperty, 0, hwndNotify);

    if (g_hAddressDatabase == INVALID_HANDLE_VALUE)
    {
```

```
            sort[0].propid = HHPR_LAST_NAME;
            sort[0].dwFlags = 0;                    // sort in ascending order
            sort[1].propid = HHPR_CITY;
            sort[1].dwFlags = 0;                    // sort in ascending order
            sort[2].propid = HHPR_STATE;
            sort[2].dwFlags = 0;                    // sort in ascending order

        g_oidDatabase = CeCreateDatabase(TEXT("Addresses"), 0,
            MAX_MSG_PROPERTIES, sort);

        g_hAddressDatabase = CeOpenDatabase(&oidAddressDatabase, NULL,
cepidSortProperty, 0,
            NULL);
    }

    if (!g_hAddressDatabase)
        return FALSE;

    return TRUE;
}
```

Getting Information About a Database

Each database in the object store contains information about that database
as a whole, including its name, type identifier, and sort order specifications.
This information is defined in the **CEDBASEINFO** structure through the
CeCreateDatabase and **CeSetDatabaseInfo** functions. As discussed earlier,
this information can be accessed using **CeOidGetInfo**.

The database name is a null-terminated string that contains up to 32 characters.
The type identifier is a double-word value that can be used for any application-
defined purpose, typically to differentiate one type of database from another while
enumerating them. The sort order specification determines the order in which the
database seek functions examine the records in a database.

Enumerating Databases

Enumerating databases is the process of sequentially accessing each database in a
group. The group can either include all databases in the object store or only those
of a specified type. Enumeration can be used when a change needs to be made to
all databases of a certain type, or when synchronizing data between the desktop
computer and the Windows CE-based device.

To enumerate databases, call the **CeFindFirstDatabase** and
CeFindNextDatabase functions.

CeFindFirstDatabase establishes and returns a handle to the enumeration context
for the type identifier specified. If the type identifier was zero, the context will
include all the databases. Note that **CeFindFirstDatabase** does not give the
object identifier for the first database. Use the handle to the enumeration
context to call **CeFindNextDatabase** repeatedly to obtain the object identifiers
for each database in turn. When there are no more databases of that type,
CeFindNextDatabase returns the value zero. To ensure that there was no
problem with the enumeration, call **GetLastError** and check for the
ERROR_NO_MORE_ITEMS value.

When the application is finished enumerating databases, it must close the handle
to the enumeration context by using the **CloseHandle** function.

The following code example enumerates all databases in the object store and adds
their names to a combo box.

```
HANDLE hEnumDB;          // handle to a database enumerator
TCHAR szBuf[MAX_BUF];    // tmp string for combobox or message box
HWND hCB1;               // combo box; value set by calling GetDlgItem
...
hEnumDB = CeFindFirstDatabase(0);
if (INVALID_HANDLE_VALUE == hEnumDB)
{
                         // error handling omitted...uses GetLastError()
    return;              // continue only if FindFirst succeeds
}
while( (WceObjID = CeFindNextDatabase(hEnumDB)) != 0)
{
    if (!CeOidGetInfo(WceObjID, &WceObjInfo) )
    {
        CloseHandle(hEnumDB);
                         // error handling omitted...uses GetLastError()
        return;          // continue only if FindNext succeeds
    }
    else
    {
        wsprintf(szBuf, WceObjInfo.infDatabase.szDbaseName);
        SendMessage(hCB1, CB_ADDSTRING, 0, LPARAM(szBuf));
    }
}
CloseHandle(hEnumDB);
```

Opening a Database

Before accessing records or properties in a database, you must obtain a handle to the database by calling the **CeOpenDatabase** function. Specify either the database name or its object identifier. The **CeOpenDatabase** function returns an open database handle that you can use in subsequent calls for reading or modifying the database. When you finish using the database, close the handle by calling the **CloseHandle** function.

Use the CEDB_AUTOINCREMENT flag when calling **CeOpenDatabase** to increase performance when reading many properties. This flag directs the system to automatically increment the seek pointer every time you access a database property with the **CeReadRecordProps** function. The seek pointer marks the record that will be read by the next read operation.

When calling **CeOpenDatabase**, you can specify the identifier of a property to use as the sort order for the database. The system uses the sort order to increment the seek pointer after each subsequent call to **CeReadRecordProps**, if the CEDB_AUTOINCREMENT flag is specified. The sort order also determines the property that the **CeSeekDatabase** function uses to traverse the database.

The following code example demonstrates the call to **CeOpenDatabase**.

```
CEOID objId;                          // database ID
TCHAR szDbName[MAX_SIZE];             // contains the database name
HANDLE hDb;                           // handle to the database
...
hDb = CeOpenDatabase(&objId,          // tmp location for the database id
                     szDbName,        // database name
                     0,               // sort order; 0 indicates ignore
                     CEDB_AUTOINCREMENT, // flags
                     NULL);           // window handle for notifications
// perform error checking on hDb handle before continuing...
// perform other operations on the database, then close it
CloseHandle(hDb);
```

For more information about sort order, see "Sorting Records" later in this chapter. For more information about moving the seek pointer, see "Searching for Records" later in this chapter.

Working with Database Records

You use several functions to work with database records. These functions allow you to create, modify, and delete records and their properties.

You can create new records or modify existing records using the **CeWriteRecordProps** function. The function parameters include the handle to the database and the object identifier of the record to add. If the object identifier is zero, **CeWriteRecordProps** creates a new record.

To write properties to a record, fill an array of **CEPROPVAL** structures and pass the address of the array to **CeWriteRecordProps** along with the database handle and the record's object identifier. Each structure contains a property identifier and the data value for that property. To specify the data value, fill the **val** member, which is defined as a **CEVALUNION** union. The **CEPROPVAL** structure also includes a flag member that you can set to CEDB_PROPDELETE in order to delete the specified property or properties. If the **CeWriteRecordProps** function succeeds, the object identifier of the new or modified record is returned.

Use the **CeDeleteRecord** function to delete a record from a database, supplying the object identifier of the record and the handle to the open database that contains the record.

The following code example creates and writes a new property that is a byte array, or BLOB.

```
CEPROPVAL NewProp;       // the new property contains a BLOB
CEBLOB blob;             // the BLOB contains a byte array
BYTE * pBuf = NULL;      // the actual BLOB data
UINT cbBuf;              // count of bytes needed in BLOB
...
                         // figure out the size needed, then allocate it
pBuf = (BYTE *) LocalAlloc(LMEM_FIXED, cbBuf);
                         // put the actual data into pBuf here...

                         // now set up to write the new BLOB property
NewProp.propid = CEVT_BLOB;
NewProp.wFlags = 0;
blob.dwCount = cbBuf;    // count of bytes in the buffer
blob.lpb = pBuf;         // set CEBLOB field to point to buffer
NewProp.val.blob = blob; // BLOB itself points to the buffer
oid = CeWriteRecordProps(hDb,
    0,                   // new record
    1,                   // one property
    &NewProp);           // pointer to the BLOB property
                         // perform error handling by checking oid...
```

Write a record into a database by filling an array of **CEPROPVAL** structures and passing the array to the **CeWriteRecordProps** function, along with an open handle to the database in which to add the record. The following code example shows how to add a record to a database.

```
// SetAddressData - Adds a name and address to an address database in
//    the object store.
// Returns the object identifier of the record in which the name and
//    address are written.
// pAddressData - Pointer to a structure that contains the name and
//    address to add

// Global variable:
//    g_hAddressDatabase - Open handle to the address database

CEOID SetAddressData(PADDRESSDATA pAddressData)
{
   CEPROPVAL rgPropVal[ADDRESS_PROP_COUNT];
   WORD wCurrent = 0;

// Use a C runtime function to zero-fill the array of property
// values.
   memset(&rgPropVal, 0, sizeof(CEPROPVAL) * ADDRESS_PROP_COUNT);

   rgPropVal[wCurrent].propid = HHPR_NAME;
   rgPropVal[wCurrent++].val.lpwstr = pAddressData->pwszName;

   rgPropVal[wCurrent].propid = HHPR_STREET;
   rgPropVal[wCurrent++].val.lpwstr = pAddressData->pwszStreet;

   rgPropVal[wCurrent].propid = HHPR_CITY;
   rgPropVal[wCurrent++].val.lpwstr = pAddressData->pwszCity;

   rgPropVal[wCurrent].propid = HHPR_STATE;
   rgPropVal[wCurrent++].val.lpwstr = pAddressData->pwszState;

   rgPropVal[wCurrent].propid = HHPR_ZIP_CODE;
   rgPropVal[wCurrent++].val.ulVal = pAddressData->dwZip;

   oid = CeWriteRecordProps(g_hAddressDatabase, 0, wCurrent,
      rgPropVal);

   return oid;
}
```

Reading Records and Properties

After opening a Windows CE database, the seek pointer is positioned at the first record according to the selected sort order.

The **CeReadRecordProps** function reads properties from the record where the seek pointer is currently positioned. When calling **CeReadRecordProps**, indicate the properties to be read by specifying an array of property identifiers. Also specify the buffer into which the function is to write the property information, and a value indicating the size of the buffer. If you specify the CEDB_ALLOWREALLOC flag, the system will reallocate the buffer if it is too small to hold the property information. Note that the system stores records in compressed format and must decompress records as they are read. For efficiency, you should read all of the desired properties in a single call rather than in several separate calls.

When the property is read successfully, the property information is copied into the specified buffer as an array of **CEPROPVAL** structures, and the function returns the record's object identifier.

If the system cannot find a requested property in the specified record, the **CEPROPVAL** structure for that property receives the CEDB_PROPNOTFOUND flag. All of the variable size data, such as strings and BLOBs, are copied to the end of the buffer. The **CEPROPVAL** structures contain pointers to this data.

If you specified the CEDB_AUTOINCREMENT flag when opening the database, **CeReadRecordProps** increments the seek pointer.

The following code example demonstrates how to read properties from the database using the autoincrement and reallocation flags.

```
CEOID objId;         // object identifier; use for db, each record
HANDLE hDb;          // handle to the database
WORD cProps;         // count of properties returned by Read operation
LPBYTE pBuf = NULL;  // no init size; let CeReadRecordProps realloc
DWORD cbBuf;         // count of bytes in buffer
...
hDb = CeOpenDatabase(&objId,     // tmp location for the database id
                szDbName,        // database name
                0,               // sort order; 0 indicates ignore
                CEDB_AUTOINCREMENT,
                NULL);           // window handle for notifications
// perform error checking on hDb handle before continuing...
while (objId = CeReadRecordProps(hDb,
                CEDB_ALLOWREALLOC,
                &cProps,         // return count of properties
                NULL,            // retrieve all properties
                &pBuf,           // buffer to return prop data
                &cbBuf))         // count of bytes in pBuf1
    {                            // record is now available in pBuf1
    // add code here to manipulate the props in this record
    }
```

```
// at this point, all records have been read from the database
CloseHandle(hDb);
```

Sorting Records

When creating a new database, you can specify up to four sort order descriptions to associate with the database. A *sort order description* is a **SORTORDERSPEC** structure that contains the identifier of a property on which the database records are to be sorted. The structure also includes a combination of flags that indicate whether to sort the records in ascending or descending order, whether the sort is case-sensitive, and whether to place records that do not contain the specified property before or after all other records. By default, sorting is done in descending order and is case-sensitive. Records not containing a specified property are placed at the end of all other records.

Note Sorts on binary properties are not allowed.

Because sort orders increase the amount of time and system resources needed to perform each insertion or deletion, it is best to use the minimum number of sort orders for an application. However, do not use too few. While it is possible to use **CeSetDataBaseInfo** to reorder the database, this process is even more expensive in terms of time and system resources. It could take several minutes to reorder a large database.

Typically, each record in a database contains a similar set of properties, and each type of property shares the same property identifier. For example, each record in a Contacts database might contain a name, street address, city, state, zip code, and telephone number. Each name property would have the same property identifier, each street address property would have the same property identifier, and so on. You can select one of these properties and direct the system to sort the records based on it. The order in which the records are sorted affects the order in which the database-seeking function **CeSeekDatabase** finds records in the database.

You specify the sort order when you call the **CeOpenDatabase** function. Only one sort order can be active for each open handle. However, by opening multiple handles to the same database, you can use more than one sort order.

Note Multiple sort orders cannot be specified for a single property.

Searching for Records

Use the **CeSeekDatabase** function to search for a record in a database. The **CeSeekDatabase** function always uses the current sort order as specified in the call to **CeOpenDatabase**. If the CEDB_AUTOINCREMENT flag was specified, each read operation on the database will automatically increment the seek pointer from the current position to the next position.

The **CeSeekDatabase** function can perform different types of seek operations. When calling the function, you specify a flag that indicates the type of seek operation, and a value whose meaning depends on the specified flag. For example, to find a particular record, you specify the CEDB_SEEK_CEOID flag and the object identifier of the desired record. When **CeSeekDatabase** finds a record, the seek pointer is positioned at that record. Any subsequent read operation takes place at the location of the seek pointer.

Note A seek can only be performed on a sorted property value.

Seek operations are affected by the sort order associated with the open database handle. For example, suppose the Contacts database was opened using a sort on the name property. If you specify the CEDB_SEEK_VALUEFIRSTEQUAL flag and a value of "Joe Smith," the **CeSeekDatabase** function will search from the beginning of the database looking only at the name property of each record, stopping when, and if, a matching property is found.

You can change the sort order that was set when the database was created by using the **CeSetDatabaseInfo** function, but this is not usually advised. The system maintains a set of indexes and other information that it uses to optimize database searches for the specified sort orders. When new sort orders are specified, the system must revise all of that internal information, which can take several minutes for large databases. The following code example demonstrates a call to **CeSeekDatabase**.

```
CEOID oid, oidSeek;        // Object identifier of record sought/returned
DWORD dwIndex;             // Index of record seeked to

// set value of oidSeek appropriately...
// actual set operation omitted from this fragment
// Perform the seek
oid = CeSeekDatabase(hDb,
                CEDB_SEEK_CEOID, // request a seek operation
                oidSeek, // specifies the record to seek
                &dwIndex); // on success, index to the record
if (!oid)
     // error handling goes here; omitted from this fragment...
// Continues at this point only if record found
// After finding the record, read it and get its data
oid = CeReadRecordProps(hDb, CEDB_ALLOWREALLOC,
            &wCount, NULL, &lpBuffer, &wSize);
```

The following code example shows how to find a record in a database and read its properties into a buffer. The function **GetAddressData** takes two parameters: the object identifier of a record and a pointer to an application-defined **ADDRESSDATA** structure that receives the record's property data. First, the **GetAddressData** function allocates a temporary buffer for the property data, and then it calls the **CeSeekDatabase** function to find the record that has the specified object identifier. If the record is found, the **CeReadRecordProps** function reads the property data into the temporary buffer. Finally, the property data is copied from the temporary buffer into the application-defined **ADDRESSDATA** structure.

```
// GetAddressData - Retrieves the contents of an address record
// Returns a code that indicates the result of the function
// pAddressData - Pointer to an application-defined ADDRESSDATA
//     structure that receives the data from the address record
//
// Global variable:
//     g_hAddressDatabase - Open handle to the address database

ECODE GetAddressData(CEOID oidSeek, PADDRESSDATA pAddressData)
{
    LPBYTE lpBuffer;           // Buffer for address record
    WORD wSize = 1024;         // Size of buffer
    CEOID oid;                 // Object identifier of record found or read
    DWORD dwIndex;             // Index of record seeked to
    WORD wCount;               // Number of properties in record
    int i;                     // Loop counter
    CEPROPID propid;           // Property identifier
    WORD wLength;              // String length
    ECODE ec = EC_SUCCESS;     // Error/success code
```

```
lpBuffer = (LPBYTE) LocalAlloc(LMEM_FIXED, wSize);
if (!lpBuffer)
   return EC_OUTOFMEMORY;

oid = CeSeekDatabase(g_hAddressDatabase, CEDB_SEEK_CEOID,
   oidSeek, &dwIndex);
if (!oid)
   return EC_SEEK_FAILURE;

oid = CeReadRecordProps(g_hAddressDatabase, CEDB_ALLOWREALLOC,
   &wCount, NULL, &lpBuffer, &wSize);
if (!oid)
   return EC_READ_FAILURE;

for (i = 0; i < wCount; i++ )
   {
   propid = ((CEPROPVAL*) lpBuffer)[i].propid;

   switch (propid)
      {
      case HHPR_NAME:
      {
                          // Copy the addressee's name.
         TCHAR* pData;

         wLength =
            lstrlen(((CEPROPVAL*) lpBuffer)[i].val.lpwstr);
         pData = (TCHAR*) LocalAlloc(LMEM_FIXED,
            wLength * sizeof(TCHAR) + 1);
         If (pData)
         {
            lstrcpy(pData,
               ((CEPROPVAL*) lpBuffer)[i].val.lpwstr);
            pAddressData->pwszName = pData;
         }
         else
         {
            ec = EC_OUTOFMEMORY;
         }
      }
      break;

      case HHPR_STREET:
      {
```

```
                                    // Copy the addressee's street address.
                        TCHAR* pData;

                        wLength =
                           lstrlen(((CEPROPVAL*)lpBuffer)[i].val.lpwstr);
                        pData = (TCHAR*) LocalAlloc(LMEM_FIXED,
                           wLength * sizeof(TCHAR) + 1, FALSE);
                        if (pData)
                        {
                           lstrcpy(pData,
                              ((CEPROPVAL*) lpBuffer)[i].val.lpwstr);
                           pTaskData->pwszDescription = pData;
                        }
                        else
                        {
                           ec = EC_OUTOFMEMORY;
                        }
                     }
                     break;

                        .
                        .                    // Copy the remaining record properties to
                        .                    // the ADDRESSDATA structure.


                  default:
                     break;
               }

            if (ec != EC_SUCCESS)
               break;
         }

      if (lpBuffer)
         LocalFree(lpBuffer);

      return ec;
   }
```

CHAPTER 5

Using Communications

Windows CE supports a wide range of communications options for transmitting and receiving data. You can use communications for a variety of tasks, including:

- Downloading files from a desktop computer or network
- Exchanging information with another Windows CE-based device
- Sending and receiving e-mail
- Sending data to a server
- Browsing the Internet
- Reading bar codes

To support the many different types of communication, Windows CE-based devices can include a variety of hardware. Some hardware may be an integral part of the device. For example, many Windows CE-based devices include a connector for a serial cable or an infrared (IR) transceiver. If a PC Card slot is available, users can also extend the built-in capabilities of the device with third-party communications hardware, such as a modem or a bar code reader. Available communications hardware includes:

- Serial cables
- IR transceivers
- Wireless transceivers
- Modems
- Bar code readers

Windows CE supports two basic types of communications technology: serial and network. While some hardware can support only one type, the same hardware is often used for both. Which type of communication is appropriate is governed in large part by how the communicating devices are connected.

You can use serial communications when two devices have a one-to-one connection. Each sender has only one possible receiver, and vice versa. A common example is two devices connected by a serial cable. Because there is no ambiguity about where the data is from and where it is going, it can be streamed from one device to the other with little or no processing. Examples of serial communications include:

- Transferring information from a desktop computer to a Windows CE-based device by means of a serial cable

- Sending text to a printer using an IR transceiver

With networks, every transmission is usually seen by many receivers, whether or not they are the intended recipient. For one-to-one communication to take place over a network, simply streaming the information will not work. Each transmission must also include addresses that identify the sender and the intended recipient. A receiver can thus monitor the network and pick out only those transmissions that are addressed to it. It can then use the senders address to respond. The Windows CE *network stack* handles addressing and related tasks. You use a network for such tasks as:

- Downloading a file from a corporate local area network to a Windows CE-based device

- Browsing the Internet using a modem connection to an independent service provider

- Sending e-mail when you are away from home using a wireless service

Serial Communications

Serial communication requires a one-to-one connection between transmitter and receiver, typically by way of a serial cable. IR transceiver modems are also used for serial communications.

From the standpoint of software, each serial device is identified by its COM port name, for example, "COM1:" and "COM2:." The COM-port assignments are stored in the registry under \HKEY_LOCAL_MACHINE\Drivers. Because they may be installable, check \HKEY_LOCAL_MACHINE\Active to see which drivers are loaded.

Serial communication over a COM port is similar to reading from, or writing to, a file, and it uses some of the same functions. Regardless of the hardware, the basic procedure works as described in the next section, "Implementing Serial Communications."

Using IR transceivers is more complex. Windows CE supports two ways to use an IR transceiver for serial communications. One approach supported by some Windows CE-based devices treats the IR transceiver like a serial cable. The data is not processed by the system in any way. The sending and receiving applications are responsible for dealing with collision-detection and other potential problems. This approach is referred to as *raw infrared,* or *raw IR.*

The COM port assigned to raw IR is determined by the original equipment manufacturer (OEM) and is listed in the registry. Because it may share a port assignment with a wired serial connector, you should check the registry. If the port is shared, you must use **EscapeCommFunction** to set the port to IR mode.

A second approach to serial IR communications uses the Infrared Data Association (IrDA) protocols. These protocols are part of the network stack, and are discussed in "Infrared Sockets" later in this chapter. To simplify their use for serial communications, Windows CE provides an emulator (IrComm), that enables an application to communicate using the IrDA protocols in much the same way it does with raw IR.

From a programming standpoint, the main difference between raw IR and IrComm is that they have different COM-port assignments. With IrComm, there is also no need to explicitly configure the port for IR by calling **EscapeCommFunction**.

Implementing Serial Communications

This procedure outlines how to implement serial communications in an application. With the exception of step 3, the procedure is identical for all three approaches.

▶ **To use serial communications**

1. Determine which COM port you need to open.

   Port numbers are stored in the \HKEY_LOCAL_MACHINE\Drivers registry key. Active drivers are listed in the \HKEY_LOCAL_MACHINE\Active registry key.

2. Call **CreateFile** with *lpFileName* set to the COM-port name, for example,"COM1:."

   The colon (:) is part of the port name and must be included. Set the *lpSecurityAttributes* parameter to NULL and the *dwFlagsAndAttributes* parameter to zero.

3. For raw IR transmission, place the port in IR mode by calling. **EscapeCommFunction** with *hFile* set to the handle returned by **CreateFile** and *dwFunc* set to SETIR.

4. Call **SetCommTimeouts** to set the communication timeouts.

5. Call the **ReadFile** and **WriteFile** functions to transmit and receive serial data.

When one thread is waiting for a **ReadFile** function to return, **ReadFile** calls issued by other threads are blocked until the initial **ReadFile** call returns. The same is true for the **WriteFile** function.

6. Call **CloseHandle** to close the serial port.

Using a Modem

An application that uses a modem must be able to handle such tasks as dialing the appropriate phone number and breaking the connection when the session is over. To simplify the process of using a modem, Windows CE supports a subset of the Microsoft telephony application programming interface (TAPI), which handles only outbound calls. TAPI provides a set of functions that applications can use to handle the process of making and managing a modem connection, but not the actual transfer of data.

▶ **To make a modem connection using TAPI**

1. Call **lineInitialize** to initialize TAPI.

This function returns the number of line devices available. You must provide the name of the callback function that TAPI should use to return data. For more information, see "TAPI Callback Function" later in this chapter.

2. Call **lineOpen** to open the line.

3. Call **lineMakeCall**.

When the call is set up, TAPI returns a LINE_REPLY message through the callback function. This message indicates only that the call has been established at the local end, perhaps indicated by a dial tone.

As the connection process proceeds, TAPI returns a series of LINE_CALLSTATE messages through the callback function indicating the progress of the connection, for example, dialtone and ringing. When the connection is completed, TAPI returns a LINECALLSTATE_CONNECTED message.

During information transfer, TAPI continues to manage the connection, but the application handles data transmission and reception. When transmission is finished, TAPI returns a LINE_CALLSTATE message, such as one indicating that a remote disconnect has occurred.

4. Call **lineClose** to close the line.

5. Call **lineShutdown** to terminate the session.

TAPI Callback Function

TAPI sends messages to an application through a callback function implemented by the application. Implement the callback function according to the following definition.

```
void CALLBACK LineCallbackFunc (DWORD hDevice, DWORD dwMsg, DWORD
wCallbackInstance, DWORD dwParam1, DWORD dwParam2, DWORD dwParam3);
```

hDevice

A handle to the line device associated with the callback. Do not use the **HANDLE** type for this parameter.

dwMsg

The line device message. Line device messages are described in the following table.

Message	Description
LINE_ADDRESSSTATE	Indicates that the status of an address on a currently open line has changed
LINE_CALLINFO	Indicates that call information has changed
LINE_CALLSTATE	Indicates that the status of the call has changed
LINE_CLOSE	Indicates that the line device has been forcibly closed
LINE_CREATE	Indicates that a new line device has been created
LINE_DEVSPECIFIC	Indicates that a device-specific event has occurred
LINE_LINEDEVSTATE	Indicates that the state of a line device has changed
LINE_REMOVE	Indicates that a device has been removed, usually for good
LINE_REPLY	Reports the results of function calls that completed asynchronously
LINE_REQUEST	Reports the arrival of a new request from another application

dwCallbackInstance
>   The callback instance data.

dwParam1
>   A message parameter, used as needed to send additional information.

dwParam2
>   A message parameter, used as needed to send additional information.

dwParam3
>   A message parameter, used as needed to send additional information.

Windows CE Networking

Windows CE supports a variety of networking options that range from serial link networking over a modem to wireless communications. Networking capabilities include:

- Sending an ICMP request, also known as a ping
- Communicating over the Internet with the Windows CE Internet API, known as WinInet
- Accessing remote file systems
- Using Windows Sockets
- Using network security features
- Accessing an IR transceiver using the IrDA protocols

There are several types of networking that are supported:

- Local area networking
- Wired serial-link networking using serial cables or modems
- Infrared networking
- Wireless networking

Windows CE network support is organized in layers. The network stack is responsible for taking data from applications, breaking it into one or more *packets*, and adding whatever header information is necessary to ensure that the packet arrives at its destination. The following illustration describes the schematics of the network stack.

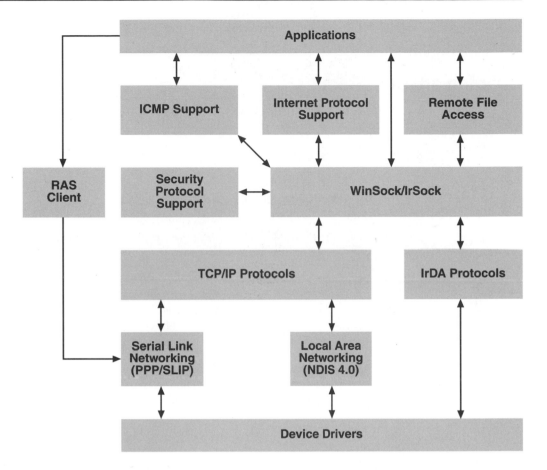

Network stack schematics

There are several ways to access the network stack:

- The Windows Sockets (Winsock) API provides applications with the means to exchange packets with a remote site. It handles all the details of creating the needed header information, but leaves the format of the data up to the application. All network communication on Windows CE uses Winsock directly or indirectly.

- The WinInet API supports high-level data protocols, such as Hypertext Transmission Protocol (HTTP) or File Transfer Protocol (FTP). These APIs ensure that the data is properly structured and relieve applications of the need to use Winsock directly.

- A Common Internet File System (CIFS) redirector gives applications access to remote file systems. Windows CE also provides support for a Remote Access Service (RAS) client, which allows a Windows CE-based device to connect to a remote host.

The following sections describe the Windows CE network stack from the top to the bottom.

Sending an ICMP Request

Send an Internet Control Message Protocol (ICMP) request, or ping, to determine whether or not a particular host is available.

▶ **To send an ICMP request**

1. Call **ICMPCreateFile** to create a handle on which requests can be issued.
2. Call **ICMPSendEcho** to send an ICMP echo request. It returns the status of the host.
3. Call **ICMPCloseHandle** to close the handle created by **ICMPCreateFile**.

Communicating over the Internet

Much of the communication that takes place over the Internet involves the use of high-level protocols, such as HTTP. These protocols specify how the data contained in the packets must be structured.

WinInet provides a set of tools for developing Internet client applications, such as browsers, that use the FTP and HTTP Internet protocols. WinInet also simplifies the details of making and using socket connections. Use WinInet to:

- Connect to remote sites.
- Download HTML pages.
- Send FTP requests to upload or download files, or to get directory listings.

The Windows CE version of WinInet is similar to WinInet for Windows-based desktop platforms, with two significant differences:

- Most callback functions are handled synchronously in Windows CE. Only **InternetReadFile** and **InternetQueryDataAvailable** operate in both synchronous and asynchronous modes.
- Windows CE supports Unicode by default.

WinInet uses Internet handles that are passed to functions that offer specific Internet services, such as making an HTTP request. These handles are generally organized in a tree. The following illustration describes a hierarchy that you might use for HTTP communications.

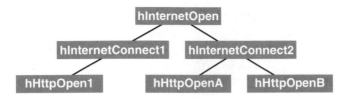

Hierarchy of HTTP communications

The *hInternetOpen* handle is the root of the tree and is used by all HTTP sessions. The *hInternetConnect* handle identifies a particular site. It is used to open a connection to the site that is then represented by an *hHttpOpen* handle. This handle can then be used to send an HTTP request.

When a parent node handle is closed, all its child handles will be closed recursively. In the previous example, closing *hInternetConnect2* also closes *hHttpOpenA* and *hHttpOpenB*.

For more information about how to use WinInet, see the Microsoft Platform SDK.

Using WinInet to Access HTTP

This procedure outlines how to use WinInet to access an internet site using the HTTP protocol.

▶ **To use the HTTP protocol**

1. Call **InternetOpen** to get an Internet handle.

2. Call **InternetConnect** to create a session handle for the site.

3. Call **HttpOpenRequest** to open the site and prepare it for the HTTP request.

4. Call **HttpSendRequest** to send the request.

5. Call **InternetReadFile** or **InternetQueryDataAvailable** to download information.

6. Call **InternetCloseHandle** to close open handles.

Accessing Remote File Systems

For access to remote file systems, Windows CE supports a CIFS redirector. The CIFS protocol is also referred to as the Server Message Block (SMB) protocol. A redirector is a module through which one computer gains access to another. The redirector has two purposes: to reestablish disrupted connections and to handle remote file system requests by packaging them and then sending them to the target host for processing. The target host returns the results to the originating computer.

The Windows CE redirector allows connections to computers running Windows NT, Windows 95, or any other server that is compliant with the NT LM 0.12 dialect of the CIFS specification. Applications gain access to the redirector either through the Windows CE WNet API or the Universal Name Convention (UNC). Drive letters are not supported.

To use the WNet functions under Windows CE, the redirector dynamic-link library (DLL), known as Redir.dll, and the NetBios DLL, known as Netbios.dll, must be installed on the system. If these DLLs are not installed, the WNet functions return ERROR_NO_NETWORK.

Note The NetBios DLL contains only what is necessary to support the CIFS redirector. The NETBIOS applications interface is not supported by Windows CE.

Managing Network Connections with WNet

Use one of following functions to establish a network connection:

- **WNetAddConnection3**, if you know the information needed to identify the network resource.

  –Or–

- **WNetConnectDialog1**, if you need feedback from the user. This function prompts the user to choose a local name or UNC in a dialog box.

You can terminate a connection using any of these functions:

- Use **WNetCancelConnection2** to break the connection and remove the folder from the \NETWORK directory.

  –Or–

- Use **WNetDisconnectDialog** to start a general browsing dialog box that allows the user to manage the disconnection.

  –Or–

- Use **WNetDisconnectDialog1** to disconnect from a network resource. If the underlying network returns WN_OPEN_FILES, the function prompts the user for confirmation. If an error occurs, it informs the user.

Determining Available Network Resources

The WNet API includes a set of functions to enumerate the available network resources.

▶ **To create a network resource list**

1. Call **WNetOpenEnum**, which returns an enumeration handle used in step 2.

2. Call **WNetEnumResource** to package the information about the resources in the form of an array of **NETRESOURCE** structures.

3. Call **WNetOpenEnum** to enumerate a container's resources. A container is a network resource that contains other resources.

4. Call **WNetCloseEnum** to close the enumeration handle.

Windows Sockets

Sockets are a general purpose, connection-oriented networking interface supported by most operating systems. The Windows implementation of sockets, commonly called Winsock, is designed to run efficiently on Windows while maintaining compatibility with the Berkeley Software Distribution standard, known as Berkeley Sockets. The Winsock API is the only way for an application to access the TCP/IP or IrDA protocols on a Windows CE-based device. High-level APIs, such as WinInet, use Winsock internally, but it can also be used directly.

Windows CE supports all of the standard Winsock 1.1 calls. It also implements **WSAIoctl**, which is provided to allow applications to set and query secure socket options.

Each socket that is created has an associated **SOCKADDR** structure that identifies the underlying transport protocol. Because the length of a network address is protocol-dependent, each supported protocol has its own **SOCKADDR** structure. The Windows CE implementation of Winsock supports two transport protocols, TCP/IP and IrDA. Their associated **SOCKADDR** structures are SOCKADDR_IN for TCP/IP protocol and SOCKADDR_IRDA for IrDA protocol.

For more information on Winsock, see the documentation for the Microsoft Platform SDK.

Infrared Sockets

Winsock is typically used with the TCP/IP protocols. Infrared Sockets (IrSock), is an extension to Winsock that allows it to be used also for IR communication using the IrDA protocol. Each endpoint must support an IrDA-compliant device and an IrDA-compliant protocol stack.

Some Winsock functions work differently with IrDA than they do with TCP/IP. The principal differences are:

- Name service

  Conventional Winsock name service is best suited to fixed networks in which the group of devices that can accept a socket connection is relatively static. Conversely, IrDA is designed to handle browsing for whatever resources are within range. It works in an ad hoc manner, and devices come and go frequently as they move in and out of range.

  Because of these differences, IrSock does not use the conventional Winsock name service functions. Instead, name service is incorporated into the communication stream.

- Method of addressing

  Addressing is based on Logical Service Access Point Selectors (LSAP-SELs), numbered from 1 through 127. Because of the small range of values available, it is usually better not to bind sockets directly to an LSAP-SEL. Instead, the Information Access Service (IAS) provides a means for dynamic binding of sockets to LSAP-SELs.

  To use IAS, a server application binds a socket to an IAS service name. The client application uses the service name when using **Connect**. Neither application knows, or needs to know, the LSAP-SEL that is assigned by the IAS. This procedure is outlined in the following sections.

- Enhanced socket options

  Windows CE includes two socket options to access the unique features of the IrDA protocol:

  - IRLMP_IAS_SET allows an application to set a single class in the local IAS. The application specifies the class to set, the attribute, and the attribute type. The application must allocate a buffer of the necessary size for the passed parameters.

  - IRLMP_RAW_MODE allows an application to switch between the reliable TinyTP mode, which is the default setting, and the less reliable IrLMP mode. This option is only available after calling **socket** to obtain a socket handle and before calling **bind** and **connect**.

Using Infrared Sockets

The basic procedure for using IrSock is similar to that for Winsock. Server applications and client applications have somewhat different procedures.

▶ **To create and use a socket with a server application**

1. Allocate a stream socket with **socket**. Use AF_IRDA for the address format parameter and SOCK_STREAM for the type.
2. Bind the service name to the socket with **bind**. Pass a SOCKADDR_IRDA structure for the *address* parameter.
3. Listen for an incoming connection with **listen**.
4. Accept an incoming client with **accept**.
5. Use **send** and **recv** to communicate with the client.
6. Close the socket with **closesocket**.

▶ **To create and use a socket with a client application**

1. Allocate a stream socket with **socket**, as with the server application.
2. Search for the server, and retrieve its ID with **getsockopt**.
3. Connect to the server with **connect**, using SOCKADDR_IRDA for the *name* parameter.
4. Use **send** and **recv** to communicate with the server.
5. Close the socket with **closesocket**.

The code examples in the following two sections demonstrate these procedures, using IAS. You could run these samples on a pair of Handheld PCs (H/PCs) or Palm PCs, for example.

Sample Infrared Socket Server

This sample IrSock server allocates a socket and binds it to the IAS name, "MyServer." It then allocates a single connection object and prepares the server to listen for incoming connections. When the client contacts the server, the server accepts the connection. It then receives a string from the client, passes one back, and closes the connection.

```
#include <windows.h>
#include <af_irda.h>

int WINAPI WinMain(HINSTANCE hInstance, HINSTANCE hPrevInstance,
                   LPTSTR lpCmdLine, int nCmdShow )
{
    SOCKET          ServerSock,
                    ClientSock;

    SOCKADDR_IRDA   address = {AF_IRDA, 0, 0, 0, 0, "MyServer"};

    char            helloServer[25];              // ASCII String
    TCHAR           helloText[25];                // UNICODE String
    int             idx = 0;

    ServerSock = socket(AF_IRDA, SOCK_STREAM, 0);

    bind(ServerSock, (struct sockaddr *)&address, sizeof(address));

    listen(ServerSock, 1);

    ClientSock = accept(ServerSock, 0, 0);

    recv(ClientSock, helloServer, sizeof(helloServer), 0);

    for (idx = 0; idx <= sizeof(helloServer); idx++)
         helloText[idx] = helloServer[idx];

    MessageBox (NULL, helloText, TEXT("IR Server"), MB_OK);

    send(ClientSock, "Hello Client!", strlen("Hello Client!")+1, 0);

    closesocket(ClientSock);
    closesocket(ServerSock);

return 0;
}
```

Sample Infrared Socket Client

This sample IrSock client opens a socket and makes five attempts to locate a server. If none is found, it displays a message box to inform the user of the failure. When a server is detected, the client queries the server for its device identifier and sends a greeting to the service named "My Server." It then waits for the server to respond, displays a message box with the response, and closes the socket.

```
#include <windows.h>
#include <af_irda.h>

#define NumRetries   5

int WINAPI WinMain(HINSTANCE hInstance, HINSTANCE hPrevInstance,
                   LPTSTR lpCmdLine, int nCmdShow )
{
   SOCKET         sock;
   SOCKADDR_IRDA  address = {AF_IRDA, 0,0,0,0, "MyServer"};
    EVICELIST     devList;
   int            devListLen = sizeof(devList),
                  cnt = 0,
                  idx = 0;
   char           helloClient[25];
   TCHAR          helloText[25];

   sock = socket(AF_IRDA, SOCK_STREAM, 0);
   devList.numDevice = 0;       // initialize number of devices to zero

   while ((devList.numDevice == 0) && (cnt <= NumRetries))
   {
        getsockopt(sock, SOL_IRLMP, IRLMP_ENUMDEVICES,
                 (char *)&devList, &devListLen);
        cnt++;
        Sleep(1000);           // Wait one second before retrying
   }
   if  (cnt > NumRetries)
   {
        MessageBox (NULL, TEXT("Server could not be located"),
                 TEXT("IR Client"), MB_OK);
   }
   else
    {
                             // Get socket address of server
        for (idx = 0; idx <= 3; idx++)
           address.irdaDeviceID[idx] =
           devList.Device[0].irdaDeviceID[idx];

        connect(sock, (struct sockaddr *)&address,
                sizeof(SOCKADDR_IRDA));

        send(sock, "Hello Server!", strlen("Hello Server!")+1, 0);

        recv(sock, helloClient, sizeof(helloClient), 0);

        for (idx = 0; idx <= sizeof(helloClient); idx++)
             helloText[idx] = helloClient[idx];
```

```
                    MessageBox (NULL, helloText, TEXT("IR Client"), MB_OK);

                    closesocket(sock);
            }
        return 0;
        }
```

Network Security Features

Windows CE supports program comprehension tool (PCT) 1.0 and Secure Sockets Layer (SSL) versions 2.0 and 3.0 security protocols. These protocols are available either through WinInet or directly from Winsock.

The simplest approach to using the security protocols is to use WinInet.

▶ **To access security protocols with WinInet**

1. Connect with **InternetConnect**, using the INTERNET_FLAG_SECURE flag. For HTTP, invoke **HttpOpenRequest**, with the desired security flags set.

2. Proceed with the remainder of the session as described in "Using WinInet to Access HTTP" earlier in this chapter.

Certificate Authentication

Authentication is the process of determining whether or not a remote host can be trusted. To establish its trustworthiness, the remote host must provide an acceptable authentication certificate based on public-key cryptography. Windows CE supports X.509-style certificates.

Remote hosts establish their trustworthiness by obtaining a certificate from a Certificate Authority (CA). The CA may, in turn, have certification from a higher authority, and so on, creating a chain of trust. To determine whether a certificate is trustworthy, an application must determine the identity of the root CA, and then decide if it can be trusted.

Windows CE maintains a database of trusted CAs. When a secure connection is attempted by an application, Windows CE extracts the root certificate from the certification chain and checks it against the CA database. It delivers the root certificate to the application through a certificate validation callback function, along with the results of the comparison against the CA database.

Applications bear ultimate responsibility for deciding whether or not the certificate is acceptable. They are free to accept or reject any certificate, based on whatever criteria are appropriate. If the certificate is rejected, the connection is not completed. At a minimum, a certificate should meet the following two requirements: It should be current, and the identity contained within the certificate should match the identity of the root CA.

The certificate validation callback function must be implemented by all client applications that use secure sockets. The value it returns determines whether or not the connection will be completed by Winsock. It must have the following syntax:

```
int SslValidate (
        DWORD       dwType
        LPVOID      pvArg
        DWORD       dwChainLen
        LPBLOB      pCertChain
        DWORD       dwFlags
);
```

The parameters contain the following information:

- The *dwType* parameter specifies the type of data pointed to by *pCertChain*. This must be SSL_CERT_X.509, specifying that *pCertChain* is a pointer to an X509 style certificate.

- The *pvArg* parameter is the application-defined context, passed by the SSLVALIDATECERTHOOK structure.

- The *dwChainLen* parameter is the number of certificates pointed to by *pCertChain*. It will always be equal to one.

- The *pCertChain* parameter is a pointer to the root certificate.

- If the root issuer of the certificate could not be found in the CA database, the *dwFlags* parameter will contain SSL_CERT_FLAG_ISSUER_UNKNOWN. The application can either attempt to verify the issuer itself, or return SSL_ERR_CERT_UNKNOWN.

The values returned by the callback function are described in the following table.

Return value	Description
SSL_ERR_BAD_DATA	The certificate is not properly formatted.
SSL_ERR_BAD_SIG	The signature check failed.
SSL_ERR_CERT_EXPIRED	The certificate has expired.
SSL_ERR_CERT_REVOKED	The certificate has been revoked by its issuer.
SSL_ERR_CERT_UNKNOWN	The issuer is unknown, or some unspecified problem arose in the processing of the certificate, rendering it unacceptable.
SSL_ERR_OKAY	The certificate is acceptable.

Implementing a Secure Socket

The following procedure outlines how to establish a secure socket connection.

▶ **To implement a secure socket**

1. Create a socket with **socket**.

2. Set the socket in secure mode with **setsockopt**. Set the *level* parameter to SO_SOCKET, *optname* to SO_SECURE, and set *optval* to a DWORD set to SO_SEC_SSL.

3. Specify the certificate validation callback function by invoking **WSAIoctl** with the SO_SSL_SET_VALIDATE_CERT_HOOK control code.

4. To specify a particular security protocol, invoke **WSAIoctl** with the SO_SSL_GET_PROTOCOLS control code to determine the default protocols. Then call **WSAIoctl** with the SO_SSL_SET_PROTOCOLS control code to select the protocols to be enabled. Otherwise, Windows CE will select the protocol to be used.

5. Make a connection with **connect**.

   The certificate callback function is automatically invoked. The connection can be completed only if the callback function verifies the acceptability of the certificate by returning SSL_ERR_OKAY.

6. Transmit and send as usual.

   The **send** and **recv** functions automatically encrypt and decrypt the data.

7. When finished, close the socket with **closesocket**.

Using a Deferred Handshake

A deferred handshake allows an application to create an unsecured connection and then later convert it to a secure connection.

▶ **To implement secure sockets with a deferred handshake**

1. Create a socket with **socket**.

2. Set the socket in secure mode with **setsockopt**.

   The *level* parameter should be set to SO_SOCKET, *optname* should be set to SO_SECURE, and *optval* should be a DWORD set to SO_SEC_SSL.

3. Specify the certificate validation callback function by invoking **WSAIoctl** with the SO_SSL_SET_VALIDATE_CERT_HOOK control code.

4. Set the socket in deferred handshake mode with **WSAIoctl**. The control code should be set to SO_SSL_SET_FLAGS and the flag set to SSL_FLAG_DEFER_HANDSHAKE.

5. Establish a non-secure connection with the remote party using **connect**.

6. Transmit and receive unencrypted data as usual.

7. To switch to secure mode, invoke **WSAIoctl** with the SO_SSL_PERFORM_HANDSHAKE control code.

    The certificate callback function is automatically invoked. The handshake is successful only if the callback function verifies the acceptability of the certificate by returning SSL_ERR_OKAY.

8. Transmit and receive as usual.

    The **send** and **recv** functions encrypt and decrypt the data automatically.

9. When finished, close the socket with **closesocket**.

TCP/IP

TCP/IP stacks are designed to work efficiently on wired networks. They may perform differently on wireless networks. For example, settings that are appropriate to a 10 Mbps Ethernet connection may consume more bandwidth than necessary on a wireless network by generating unneeded retransmission requests.

To use wireless networking efficiently, some TCP/IP parameters may need to be tuned to the characteristics of the supporting network. Because network parameters are maintained on a per adapter basis, applications must determine the appropriate adapter and change the associated registry settings. For more information about modifying the registry, see Chapter 4, "Accessing Persistent Storage." The parameters most likely to need modification are:

- Receive window size. The registry key for this parameter is <Adapter Name>\tcpip\parms\TcpWindowSize. In general, larger receive windows work better with high-delay, high-bandwidth networks. For greatest efficiency, the receive window should be an even multiple of the TCP Maximum Segment Size (MSS). It should not exceed the system maximum. The registry key for this parameter is tcpip\parms\GlobalMaxTcpWindowSize.

- Initial roundtrip time. The registry key for this parameter is <Adapter Name>\tcpip\parms\TcpInitialRTT. Roundtrip times are generally longer for wireless networks than for wired networks.

- Delayed acknowledgment timer. The registry key for this parameter is <Adapter Name>\tcpip\parms\TcpDelAckTicks.

Data Link Protocols

Windows CE provides data-link layer support for both serial input/output (I/O) and local area networks (LANS). It supports the following:

- Point-to-Point Protocol (PPP) and serial line Internet protocol (SLIP) for serial- and modem-based networking.
- Dynamic Host Configuration Protocol (DHCP) and Address Resolution Protocol (ARP) for LANs.
- A subset of NDIS 4.0:
  - Only Ethernets are supported.
  - Only Miniport drivers are supported, not intermediate or legacy drivers.

NDIS 4.0 does not expose an API to applications. For information related to device drivers, see the documentation for the Windows CE DDK.

NDIS 4.0 for Windows CE is packaged as a DLL, rather than a .sys file. This feature permits the ARP and NDIS modules to be partially installed. If an OEM chooses this option, the network stack will be configured for them but the DLLs will not be added to ROM. If the modules are needed for an application, the DLLs can be added to RAM.

Remote Access Service

RAS is a software-based multiprotocol router that is used to connect a remote device, known as a RAS client, to a host desktop computer, known as an RAS server. RAS applications are usually executed on the client device and connect to the server using PPP/SLIP.

Windows CE provides support for an RAS client. While most of the standard Win32 RAS functions are supported, only one point-to-point connection at a time is allowed. The connection can be a wired serial connection or a dial-up modem connection.

Entries in the RAS phone book contain the information necessary to establish an RAS connection. Windows CE stores these entries in the registry. The RAS phone book information includes:

- The phone number to dial, along with country code and area code.
- The IP addresses to use while the connection is active.
- The network protocols.
- The type of device being used to make the connection.

Windows CE-based applications that use RAS while running under emulation can link to Coredll.lib to resolve the RAS API entry points. This is the proper method for device builds, or use the NT RAS API set, that is, link to NT Rasapi32.lib. The NT Remote Access Service needs to be installed on the desktop computer with at least one port configured for dial out. A modem is also required to use RAS.

Using RAS

This procedure outlines how to connect with a RAS server.

▶ **To use RAS**

1. Determine which phone number to call.

    If the number is in the phone book, you can retrieve it with **RasEnumEntries**.

2. Establish a connection with **RasDial**.

    - Ignore the *dialExtensions* parameter, and set it to NULL.

    - Set the *lpszPhoneBook* parameter to NULL.

      Phone book entries are stored in the registry.

    - Set the *dwNotifierType* parameter to 0xFFFFFFFF.

      If the application needs to receive messages from RAS, the messages must be sent to an HWND. There is no support for callback functions.

3. When the session is complete, terminate it with **RasHangup**.

If an HWND was specified in the **RasDial** call, it receives a WM_RASDIALEVENT message every time a change-of-state event occurs. The *wParam* and *lParam* values carry the following information:

- *wParam*: *RASCONNSTATE* indicates the state that the RasDial remote access connection process is about to enter.

- *lParam:* A non-zero value for *dwError* indicates which error has occurred.

User Interface Services

CHAPTER 6

Designing a User Interface for Windows CE

An application's user interface serves two main purposes: to receive user input and provide user output. How well your application handles these tasks depends on your hardware capability, your operating system configuration, and the input and output requirements of your target platform.

Before designing your application, you need to ask some important questions about its interface: Will it be graphical or non-graphical? How will your application receive user input? Will users type commands with a keyboard, with a touch screen, with voice commands, or with buttons on a console? How will you provide feedback to the user? Will your device support an LCD screen or audio feedback?

Windows CE supports a range of device platforms, from handheld computers to industrial embedded systems. Its modular design allows you to use only the features you need to create applications for the specific platform you have chosen. Because user interface requirements vary from one platform to another, this chapter describes general design considerations for a graphical user interface. Platform-specific design considerations, such as those pertaining to a Handheld PC (H/PC) or Palm PC, are discussed in later chapters.

A well-designed user interface focuses on users and their tasks. Good user-interface design considers general design principles as well as how graphics, color, and layout influence the usability of an application. Apply the following design concepts when creating an interface focused on the needs of the user.

- Give the user control

   Allow the user, not the computer or software, to initiate actions. Remember, the goal of the user is not to use the application, but to accomplish a task.

- Use familiar concepts

  To increase familiarity with the interface, allow users to manipulate representations of the tasks they perform. For example, if you provide a desktop-like interface, allow users to drag icons depicting documents to an icon depicting a trash bin when deleting a file. For other types of interfaces, be sure buttons and icons relate to the tasks they perform. One example of this would be to display a wrench icon to start an automotive maintenance application.

  Another way to increase your user's familiarity with the interface is to avoid using modes whenever possible. Modes, which occur when identical commands or keystrokes perform different actions in different situations, force users to think about how the application works instead the tasks at hand. Though modes are best avoided, warning boxes and message boxes are two types of modes that are necessary and appropriate.

- Be consistent

  Consistency makes the interface familiar and predictable, which reduces user errors and improves performance. Consistency is enhanced with components that have a similar appearance and behavior and with actions that have the same result regardless of context. For example, in a desktop environment, scroll bars operate the same way, regardless of whether the scroll bar is in a list box or window. To achieve consistency, reuse standard commands across tasks and present commands in the same way in each task.

- Allow interactive discovery

  Let the user explore the interface through trial and error, while warning him or her about potential damage to the system or data. To minimize user problems, provide clear error messages and indicate appropriate actions for the user to take to recover from an error or correct the problem that caused it. If possible, make actions reversible or recoverable.

- Provide feedback

  Present the user with timely visual and audio cues to confirm that the software is responding to input.

- Focus on aesthetics

  Effective visual design is aesthetically pleasing. An attractive interface helps the user select appropriate competing information and suggests a high-quality application.

- Design with simplicity

  Simple interfaces, with an uncluttered display, are easy to learn and easy to use. Show only the most important controls directly on the interface and hide the rest in menus. Reduce the number of different tasks presented in a single window or screen and group related tasks together. Simplicity is especially important in Windows CE-based devices with small displays.

- Support multiple input methods

  Whenever possible, provide multiple methods for performing an operation. To accomplish this, support different types of input devices if possible, and provide keyboard shortcuts or accelerators for specific tasks, if your device supports a keyboard.

Designing Windows and Dialog Boxes

Many graphical user interfaces use a desktop metaphor, which simplifies common file operations by presenting them in a familiar context. Depicting files as paper documents, directories as folders, and deleted items within a trash can are examples of the desktop metaphor. Though appropriate for most applications running on an HPC or similar device, this metaphor may not be appropriate for some embedded systems, such as a car navigation application or a point-of-sale device. If the desktop metaphor is not appropriate for your application, use another familiar metaphor that seems suitable. Virtual reality applications commonly use a room metaphor.

Whatever metaphor you choose, it is important to provide a context or point of reference for your application. When using the desktop metaphor, you can accomplish this by presenting objects in standard windows and dialog boxes. If using a different metaphor, you may choose to forgo using windows entirely, and present objects only in dialog boxes. If you do use windows in your application, they should occupy the full screen, unless your application will be used in conjunction with another application. An online Help system is one example of an application whose windows do not take up the full screen because the user benefits from seeing its windows displayed with another application. If you are creating an application whose windows do not take up the full screen, design the window to be a fixed size, because Windows CE does not support the resizing of windows by users.

Windows CE supports several window styles. Some contain borders, while others contain scroll bars. One common window style is WS_OVERLAPPED. This window style displays a window button on the taskbar. This is important because users navigate from one open window to another by tapping an application's window button on the taskbar and restore a window by tapping its taskbar button again. An application displays a button on the taskbar only if its primary window contains the WS_OVERLAPPED style. Additionally, when the system is running low on power, it sends the WM_HIBERNATE message to all windows that have a button on the taskbar. If an application does not have a button on the taskbar it cannot receive and respond to this message.

Dialog boxes are secondary windows that contain controls and provide information to a user about actions. Windows CE supports three types of dialog boxes: application-defined dialog boxes, message boxes, and property sheets.

An application-defined dialog box helps users perform tasks specific to an application. It provides a great deal of flexibility by allowing you to place controls directly onto the body of the dialog box. This is especially useful when designing interfaces that do not use a desktop metaphor, because you can design an entire application interface using only application-defined dialog boxes to house controls. When using an application-defined dialog box, include only as many controls as are necessary for your application and space them adequately.

An application-defined dialog box can be modal or modeless. A modal dialog box requires the user to supply information or cancel the dialog box before allowing the application to continue. A modeless dialog box allows the user to supply information and return to a previous task without closing the dialog box.

A message box is a modal dialog box that displays a message and prompts for user input. It typically contains a text message and one or more predefined buttons.

A property sheet is a collection of tabbed dialog boxes that enables a user to view and modify the properties of an object.

In a desktop metaphor, a dialog box typically contains **OK** and **Cancel** commands, which initiate a user's request or dismiss the window, respectively. In Windows CE, the **X** button represents both the **Close** and **Cancel** commands. Follow these guidelines for using the **X** and **OK** buttons in dialog boxes:

- If the only buttons in a dialog box are the **OK** and **Cancel (X)** buttons, place them in the top right corner of the command bar, as they appear in a standard Windows CE dialog box.

- If a dialog box does not have an **OK** or **Cancel (X)** button, place the **Close (X)** button in the command bar. Place all other buttons in the body of the dialog box.

- When the **OK** and **X** buttons perform the same function, use the **OK** button, because users are more comfortable clicking the **OK** button than the **X** button to confirm an action.

- Never place an **OK** button both in the command bar and in the body of a dialog box, because many users find this confusing. However, you can place a **Cancel** button in the body of a dialog box and an **X** button on the command bar, if you like.

Developing Menus

Menus are collections of commands, attribute selections, separators, and other selectable elements. All menus in Windows CE are implemented as top-level, pop-up windows that do not support buttons. Although Windows CE supports owner-drawn menu items, it handles them as it would other menu items.

Windows CE does not support menu bars. Instead, it combines the functionality of a menu bar and a toolbar into one control, called a command bar, which makes efficient use of the screen space available on many Windows CE-based devices.

Windows CE supports the following four types of menus:

- Pop-up

   A pop-up menu is a floating menu that displays commands specific to the object selected by the user, or to the object's immediate context. A pop-up menu appears at the location on the screen where the user accessed it. It is typically used for common commands that rarely change in content and for items that require a small amount of screen space. Restrict the number of items in a pop-up menu to less than 10.

- Scrolling

   Scrolling menus are unique to Windows CE. With scrolling menus, you do not have to limit the size of a menu to the number of items that fit on the screen. If a menu is taller than the height of the display area, Windows CE adds scrolling arrows so the user can scroll the menu up and down. If a menu has too many columns to fit within the width of the display area, Windows CE ignores all column breaks and makes the menu a single-column scrolling menu.

- Cascading

   A cascading menu is a secondary menu or submenu that appears when a certain option is selected in the parent menu. A triangular arrow next to the parent item in a menu indicates a cascading menu. Windows CE displays cascading menus in alphabetical order. If the height of a cascading menu exceeds the maximum screen height of 240 pixels, the menu adopts a multiple-column mode, which shows the remaining menu items in an adjacent column. Use a cascading menu to group related menu items or when a choice leads to a short list of related options.

- Pull-down

  A pull-down menu contains commands accessed from a command or menu bar. It is commonly used to display text, but can also contain graphics, colors, and shading. When creating a pull-down menu, display all possible command choices on the menu. Items that cannot be chosen due to the state of the application should be dimmed. Use a pull-down menu to provide access to a small number of items whose content rarely changes.

Working with Command Bars

One of the challenges you may encounter when creating a Windows CE-based application is having to design for a small screen. To maximize the screen real estate available for applications in the client area, the operating system supports a new type of control, the command bar. Command bars are unique to Windows CE because they combine a menu bar, toolbar, and address bar. Windows CE supports multiple command bars, each containing gripper controls that enable users to hide buttons and menus. Command bars can contain combo boxes, edit boxes, and buttons, as well as other types of controls. They also can include the **Close** (**X**) button, the **Help** (**?**) button, and the **OK** button, usually found on the title bar of Windows-based desktop applications.

Command bars vary from 480 pixels to 640 pixels in length depending on the screen resolution. Microsoft recommends that you always display a command bar in Windows CE-based applications when using the desktop metaphor. Because Windows CE does not allow you to place an application's title or icon on the command bar, users identify an application by the label and icon on its taskbar button.

Command bars are composed of bands, separated by gripper controls. Each band can contain up to one child window, which can be a toolbar or any other control. The default is to display a toolbar. Additionally, each band can have its own bitmap, which is displayed as a background for the toolbar on that band. A user can resize or reposition a band by dragging its gripper bar. If a band has a text label next to its gripper bar, a user can maximize the band and restore it to its previous size by tapping the label with the stylus. For more information, see Chapter 11, "Foundation Controls."

A command bar menu is a list of commands that drops down when a user taps the menu's caption on the command bar with the stylus. Menu titles on a command bar appear in bold text. If you include a menu bar, always position it as the first (leftmost) element on the command bar. If you provide **File**, **Edit**, **View**, **Insert**, **Format**, **Tools**, and **Window** menus, always place them in this order, from left to right. The menu titles appear as bold text surrounded by a rectangular frame.

Windows CE supports ToolTips for command bar and toolbar buttons, but not for menus or combo boxes on a command bar. ToolTips usually display only the title of a button command, but they can also display the shortcut key for the command. If you include a shortcut key, follow these guidelines:

- Place the shortcut key two spaces after the text, in parentheses.
- Capitalize only the first letter of the control key abbreviation.
- Capitalize the command identifier.
- Use a plus sign, with no spaces, between the control key and the letter, for example, CTRL+B.

You can place check boxes or radio buttons on the command bar to enable users to toggle between different views. Moving between views can make windows more readable by eliminating unnecessary scrolling. A command bar button can display both text and images. This allows you to include text as part of a button label to provide descriptions, which eliminates the need for ToolTips.

If you choose to place a label next to your edit control on a command bar, you have two choices. You can insert a static text field above or to the left of the control. Alternatively, you can include an edit control label inside the text field as the default text. In this case, you would enclose the label between angle brackets, for example, <name>. Because the user can no longer see the control's label when he or she types text in the field, using a static text field is preferable. The default system font for applications based on Windows CE version 2.0 is Tahoma, 9 point. Windows CE version 1.0 used MS Sans Serif, 8 point, which is a smaller raster font. If your device has a small screen size and a low-contrast LCD, you should use a non-bold typeface when displaying control labels, unless the labels appear on a light gray background.

If you provide individual **New**, **Open**, **Save**, and **Print** buttons on a command bar, you must position them in this order, from left to right. If you provide individual **Bold**, **Italic**, and **Underline** buttons, you must also place them in this order, from left to right. Always make buttons at least 23 pixels high and 23 pixels wide. Leave at least 2 pixels between adjacent controls and at least 4 pixels between a control and the edge of the screen. If you plan to support touch interaction in which users use a finger rather than a stylus, make all buttons at least 38 x 38 pixels. However, to conserve space, consider creating a combo box button instead of three or four separate buttons. You can also create a TAB and ARROW KEY navigation order for command bar buttons. When a command bar button has the input focus, the button activates if the user presses the SPACEBAR or the ENTER key. The user must be able to select either option.

Choosing Controls

Windows CE supplies a set of pre-constructed elements, known as controls, that you can use to build an application. Controls, objects that users interact with to enter or manipulate data, commonly appear in dialog boxes, but can also appear on toolbars and command bars. Windows CE supports many predefined controls, which can be divided into two categories: window controls and common controls. Window controls send the WM_COMMAND message and include buttons, combo boxes, edit controls, list boxes, scroll bars, and static controls. Common controls send the WM_NOTIFY message and include all other controls. They are divided into the following sub-categories: foundation controls, file controls, scale controls, informational controls, and miscellaneous controls that are used for specific Windows CE-based platform functionality.

Due to the large number of controls available in Windows CE, determining which control to use in a specified situation is often difficult. When choosing a control, you must consider the type of input you are trying to capture, the abilities and limitations of the control, and the characteristics of your platform's screen. To assist you in this task, all predefined Windows CE controls and their uses are described in the following tables.

Windows CE Window Controls

Control	Description	Use
Check box	A two-part control consisting of a square box and text options. Each option acts as a switch that can be turned on — selected — or off — deselected. When an item is turned on, a check appears within the square box; otherwise, the square box is empty. Users can select more than one option.	When setting properties, attributes, or values. When more than one choice can be selected. When ample screen space is available. When options do not change.
Radio button	A two-part control consisting of a small circle and text options. When an option is selected, the circle appears highlighted or filled. Only one option can be selected at one time.	When setting properties, attributes, or values. When only one choice can be selected. When ample screen space is available. When options do not change.

Control	Description	Use
Push button (Command button)	A square or rectangle with a text or graphic label inside. When selected, an application immediately performs the associated action or command.	To perform an action. To display a menu or window. To set a condition or property value. When ample screen space is available.
Group box	A rectangular frame that surrounds a group of controls.	To visually relate a group of related controls. To visually relate elements within a control.
Combination box	A control possessing the characteristics of both an edit control and a list box or drop-down list box. Information may either be typed into the edit control field or selected from items displayed in the list box.	When options are large in number and not frequently selected. When the list of options may change. When only one choice can be selected. When screen space is limited; use with a drop-down list box combination only. To capture unlisted data. When users prefer to type information rather than select it from a list. When a keyboard is present.
Edit control	A rectangular box in which information can be typed by the user or in which information is displayed for read-only purposes. Edit controls typically contain captions and can be designated as either single-line or multiple-line.	When options are difficult to categorize and vary in length. When screen space is limited. When a keyboard is present. When providing a list of options is not feasible.

Control	Description	Use
List box	A rectangular box containing a list of items from which either a single selection is made, or multiple selections are made. Lists can contain either text or graphics. If the list exceeds the boundaries of the box, scroll bars appear, enabling users to view the remaining items.	When options are large in number and not frequently selected. When screen space makes radio buttons or check boxes impractical. When the list of options may change. When ample screen space is available.
Drop-down list box	A rectangular box with an arrow button on the side. When the arrow button is selected, the box displays a hidden list of items which seems to drop-down from a single item. If the list exceeds the boundaries of the box, scroll bars appear, enabling users to view the remaining list.	When only one choice can be selected. When screen space is limited. When options are large in number and not frequently selected.
Scroll bar	A rectangular container consisting of a scroll area, a slider box, and arrows. Scroll bars are typically found on primary and secondary windows.	To view information that uses more than the allotted space.
Static control	A text field that displays read-only information.	To display a caption. To provide instructional information. To display descriptive information.

Foundation controls, used to contain or manage other controls, are described in the following table.

Windows CE Foundation Controls

Control	Description	Use
Command band	A special kind of rebar control. It has a fixed band at the top containing a toolbar with a **Close** (**X**) button, and optionally, a **Help** (**?**) button and **OK** button, in the right corner. By default, each band in the command bands control contains a command bar. You can override this if you want a band to contain some other type of child window.	To provide easy access to frequently used commands or options. When screen space is limited.
Command bar	A toolbar that combines a menu bar as well as the **Close** (**X**) button, the **Help** (**?**) button, and the **OK** button. A command bar can contain menus, combo boxes, buttons, and separators. A separator is a blank space you can use to divide other elements into groups or to reserve space in a command bar.	To provide easy access to frequently used commands or options. When screen space is limited.
Toolbar	A panel that contains a set of controls.	To provide easy access to frequently used commands or options.
Property sheet	A control to define property sheets. It accepts dialog box layout specifications and automatically creates tabbed property pages.	When creating property sheets.
Tab control	A tab control resembles a divider in a notebook and is used to define sections of information within the same window.	To present repetitive, related information. To present options or settings that can be applied to one object.

Control	Description	Use
Rebar	A control that acts as a container for a child window. It contains one or more bands; each band can contain one child window, which can be a toolbar or any other control. Each band can have its own bitmap, which is displayed as a background for the toolbar on that band. A user can resize or reposition a band by dragging its gripper bar. If a band has a text label next to its gripper bar, a user can maximize the band and restore it to its previous size.	When screen space is limited. To hide and show portions of a command bar.

File controls, used to display files, are described in the following table.

Windows CE File Controls

Control	Description	Use
Header control	A heading above a column of text or numbers that can be divided into two or more parts for multiple columns. Each part can operate like a command button to support a different function.	To display text and graphics. To aid the user in sorting or sizing columns of information.
Image list	A special list box that contains a collection of images that are all the same size, such as bitmaps or icons. Image lists manage images, but do not display them. They are designed to be used with list view and tree view controls.	To display a relationship between a set of containers. When ample screen space is available. When the displaying of icons or images is appropriate.
Tree view	A special list box that displays a hierarchical set of labeled items as an indented outline. It includes buttons that allow the outline to be expanded and contracted.	To display a relationship between a set of containers. When ample screen space is available.

Control	Description	Use
List view	A special list box that displays a collection of files or folders consisting of an icon and a label. Selection and navigation in this control work similarly to that in a folder window.	When the displaying of icons is appropriate. When ample screen space is available.

Scale controls, used to increment scaled values, are described in the following table.

Windows CE Scale Controls

Control	Description	Use
Spin box	An edit control with an associated spin button control. A spin box allows the user to select an option by scrolling through a small list or by typing an item in the edit control field.	When options are infrequently selected and small in number. When screen space is limited. To capture unlisted data. When users prefer to type information rather than select it from a list. When only one choice can be selected.
Trackbar control (Slider)	A bar with tick marks on it and a slider or thumb. The tick marks represent a range of values. When a user drags the slider arm, it moves in the appropriate direction, tick by tick.	To set an attribute. When only one choice can be selected. When a limited range of possible settings exist. When options are incremented. When ample screen space is available.

Informational controls, used to provide information about tools, processes, or time, are described in the following table.

Windows CE Informational Controls

Control	Description	Use
Progress bar	A display-only control that consists of a rectangular bar that fills from left to right.	To provide visual feedback concerning completion of a process. When ample screen space is available.

Control	Description	Use
Date and time picker	A control that provides users with an easy a way to modify date and time information. Each field in the control displays a time element, such as month, day, hour, or minutes.	To modify date and time information. When screen space is limited.
Status bar	An area within a window, typically at the bottom, that displays information. It can contain display-only controls.	To provide information about the current state of what is being viewed in the window. To provide a descriptive message about a selected menu or toolbar.
Month calendar control	A child window that displays a monthly calendar. The calendar can display one or more months at a time.	To select date information. When screen space is limited.
ToolTip	A small pop-up window containing information about a control. A ToolTip appears when a pointer is moved over a control not possessing a label.	To identify a control that has no caption. To reduce screen clutter caused by control captions.

Miscellaneous controls, used for specific Windows CE-based platform functionality, are described in the following table.

Windows CE Miscellaneous Controls

Control	Description	Use
HTML viewer control	A control that provides the functionality required to implement the Windows CE Pocket Internet Explorer.	To view HTML text and embedded images. For more information about the HTML viewer control, see Chapter 10, "Overview of Controls."

Control	Description	Use
Rich Ink control	A control that captures stylus motions in order to emulate the act of writing or drawing on paper. The control's document view, under the touch screen, serves as electronic paper. In addition to capturing images, Active Ink also has editing and formatting capabilities.	To accept user input without using a keyboard. For more information about the Rich Ink control, see Chapter 7, "User Input."

In addition to predefined controls, Windows CE supports a new custom draw service. The custom draw service is not a predefined control; it is a service that makes it easy to customize a common control's appearance. You can use the custom draw service to change a common control's color or font, or to partially or completely draw the control. This is useful when your interface uses several text boxes, because you can draw the borders of the text box before the user inserts text, and then hide borders when displaying text. This enables you to place text closer together, making your interface appear less cluttered.

Besides using the controls included in Windows CE, you can also create your own custom controls. When designing custom controls, avoid the following pitfalls common to many designs:

- Controls are difficult to use.

  Make controls easy to use. For example, make controls larger; use colors that contrast with the screen background; remove nearby controls and unnecessary images; and place controls in a central location. Additionally, when you design a control, have a variety of people test its usability. Also consider differences in the capabilities of the people that need to use the control.

- Controls are too close together.

  They should be spaced far enough apart so that users do not accidentally select one control while intending to select another.

- Controls are hard to interpret.

  A control should in some way resemble or depict its corresponding function so that users can determine how to use it. For example, it is common to place an image of scissors on a button control that is used to "cut" or remove text.

- Controls are hard to distinguish.

  Controls should have easily recognizable differences. When you have several similar controls close together and lined up, people confuse them with each other. Distinguish controls by size, position, shape, and color, and always distinguish a control by more than a single feature.

- Controls are hidden.

  Controls should be obvious so that users do not overlook them. If you want to remove a control from view, place it where users expect to find it, such as in a menu.

- Controls are not predictable.

  Controls that have the same function should operate the same way. Controls should also function the same regardless of where they are placed. Also, controls should follow a consistent rule. If a control uses a different operating principle, design the control so that it will not be confused with controls that operate under different operating principles. Additionally, users expect a control to behave in ways consistent with previous experiences or cultural norms. For example, moving a slider control to the right represents an increase whereas moving the slider to the left represents a decrease.

Using Color and Grayscale Palettes

Designers often rely on color to make an application aesthetically pleasing. However, using color randomly or excessively can affect usability. To use color effectively, keep the following guidelines in mind when designing your interface:

- Display no more than four colors on a single screen at one time and limit the colors for your entire application to fewer than eight. The more colors you use, the more confusing the screen will appear to the user.

- Use color in combination with other emphasis techniques to discriminate areas on the interface and identify crucial features. Never use color alone to distinguish elements, because users may have difficulty distinguishing colors in inadequate lighting. Use fonts, icons, screen placement, or patterns in addition to color to distinguish screen elements.

- Avoid spectrally extreme color combinations, such as red and blue or yellow and purple, because they can make images seem blurred.

- Design applications for a grayscale display whenever possible because many users may not have color displays. Then, when the application is finished, you can add color.

- Use bright colors for extended viewing, because dim colors may not be legible once a user's eyes adapt to the color.

- Avoid colors lacking contrast as well as colors of equal brightness, because they are not easily distinguished.

- Use black, gray, and white to improve resolution in fine detail.

- Use common color associations, such as red for stop, or green for go, to avoid confusion.

The color design model for Windows CE uses a 16-color Windows palette, based on the Windows 95 color scheme, and is measured in bits per pixel (bpp). Windows CE supports pixel formats of 1, 2, 4, 8, 16, 24, and 32 bbp. Your application should determine the color format supported by a display device, and then adopt a complimentary display strategy.

Note An 8-bpp display driver can display a 32-bpp device independent bitmap (DIB) by mapping each color in the DIB color table to a specific color on the device. The palette available in the application displaying the bitmap determines what mapping is used. The application can lose color information if it does not use an appropriate palette or if a bitmap uses more colors than the palette can hold.

Standard Windows CE 16-Color Palette

Color:	Red	Green	Blue		Color:	Red	Green	Blue	
White	255	255	255		Dark Blue	0	0	128	
Teal	0	255	255		Yellow	255	255	0	
Purple	255	0	255		Green	0	255	0	
Blue	0	0	255		Dark Yellow	128	128	0	
Light Gray	192	192	192		Dark Green	0	128	0	
Dark Gray	128	128	128		Red	255	0	0	
Dark Teal	0	128	128		Dark Red	128	0	0	
Dark Purple	128	0	128		Black	0	0	0	

Standard Windows CE 16-color palette

Some Windows CE-based devices support only a 2-bpp palette, with four gray-scale colors: black, white, light gray, and dark gray. On a grayscale display, a single-pixel graphical element, such as a dot or a line, can be difficult to distinguish without a strong, contrasting color adjacent to it. For example, white and light gray elements can be hard to see unless presented against a black or dark gray background.

Likewise, light colors may be difficult to distinguish. When using light colors, you may need to double the thickness of pixels or lines to strengthen them. Light gray works well for creating a shadow effect around large controls on a white background and for anti-aliasing, which adds colored pixels to a graphic to smooth jagged edges. If you use light gray as a background color for your screen, use a white line to visually separate key areas, such a command bar or owner-drawn menu, from other areas of the screen.

Windows CE does not arbitrate between the palettes of the background and foreground applications. Because of this, you should use only the first ten and last ten colors included in the stock palette of a display device, which are generally the standard Windows VGA colors.

Creating Icons and Bitmaps

In a graphical user interface, icons convey attributes or tasks. An effective icon clearly represents its function and is easy to remember; an ineffective icon reduces the usability of an application by making it appear obscure and unapproachable.

Icons are used in different ways. They can either resemble what they represent— for example, a book used to represent a dictionary—or they can represent a characteristic of something, such as a gas pump to represent a gas station. Icons can also be symbolic representations, which may or may not be clear to the user. An example of this type of icon is the light bulb icon found in many Windows-based applications, which turns on and off the TipWizard.

Icons are most often used on buttons, but they can be used for progress indicators as well. When a Windows CE color icon has a Windows 95 equivalent, both icons use the same design and color. However, you must create a 16-color version and a grayscale version of the icon to ensure that it displays correctly on both color and 2-bpp devices.

Note The icon editor in the Windows CE Toolkit for Visual C++ 5.0 can create icon (.ico) files that retain both 16-color and 2-bpp gray versions of an icon.

In addition to using Windows 95 icon equivalents, you can create your own icons using the standard Windows 16-color palette. To add dimensionality to an icon, use highlights and shadows, but remember, the icons you create must translate correctly to 2-bpp gray if your device supports both grayscale and color displays. The following table shows how the 16-color palette translates to four grays.

Color	Red	Green	Blue	Gray conversion
Black	0	0	0	Black
White	255	255	255	White
Dark gray	128	128	128	Dark gray
Light gray	192	192	192	Light gray
Dark red	128	0	0	Black
Red	255	0	0	Dark gray
Dark yellow	128	128	0	Dark gray
Yellow	255	255	0	Light gray
Dark green	0	128	0	Black
Green	0	255	0	Dark gray
Dark cyan	0	128	128	Dark gray
Cyan	0	255	255	Light gray
Dark blue	0	0	128	Black
Blue	0	0	255	Dark gray
Dark magenta	128	0	128	Dark gray
Magenta	255	0	255	Light gray

Receiving User Input

User input devices allow users to interact with the user interface. Windows CE supports several types of user input devices, such as a keyboard, a touch screen, a stylus, ink input, and voice recognition, though the types of user input devices available on your hardware platform may vary. For general design considerations for user input devices, see *Windows Interface Guidelines for Software Design*.

Providing User Feedback

In addition to receiving user input, a user interface provides feedback to the user by displaying messages. Messages are communications to the user that are displayed on the screen. They either inform the user of the system's activities or status, or they prompt the user to complete some action. To be effective, messages should be clear, concise, and understandable to the user. To assist you in creating effective messages, use the following guidelines when writing message text:

- Write using active voice, which is easier to understand than passive voice.
- Always state the problem, cause, and solution in your message text, no matter how obvious the solution may be.

- Place important information at the beginning of your text. It is easier to remember than items placed in the middle.

- Keep messages brief and simple, with sentences that target a fifth-grade reading level. This will ensure that your message is communicated effectively to users of varying verbal abilities.

- Avoid using unnecessary technical terminology in your messages. Most users do not enjoy searching through reference material in order to translate a message.

- Avoid blaming the user for errors. Threatening remarks that blame the user for problems can heighten anxiety and increase the chance of more errors.

- Avoid patronizing or condescending messages. They are annoying and often offensive.

- Avoid relying on default system-supplied messages, because they are often cryptic and can be frustrating to the user.

You can also include an identification number in your message text in order to identify the message for support purposes. If you include an identification number, place it at the end of the message text and not in the title bar or at the beginning of the text where it may curtail the user's ability to quickly read the message.

C H A P T E R   7

User Input

User input is the means by which a user communicates with an interactive device, such as a Windows CE-based device. An original equipment manufacturer (OEM) can configure Windows CE to meet the user input requirements of a variety of different hardware platforms. Windows CE supports keyboard, mouse, and stylus input devices.

Different Windows CE-based platforms support different combinations of input devices. For example, some platforms, such as the Palm PC, support a touch screen, rather than a keyboard, for text entry. Other platforms may include handwriting recognition software in place of, or in addition to, a keyboard. Keep your target platform in mind when you design an application.

Keyboard Input

The keyboard is an important means of user input on many Windows CE-based devices. Windows CE maintains a device-independent keyboard model that enables it to support a variety of keyboards. Because most Windows CE-based devices have built-in keyboards, the OEM usually determines the keyboard layout for a specified Windows CE-based device.

At the lowest level, each key on the keyboard generates a *scan code* when it is pressed and released. The scan code is a hardware-dependent number that identifies the key. Unlike Windows-based desktop platforms, Windows CE has no standard set of window keyboard scan codes. For this reason, you should not depend on scan code values unless your application will only run on platforms for which you know the scan code values.

The keyboard driver maps each scan code to a *virtual key code*. The virtual key code is a hardware-independent number that identifies the key. Because keyboard layouts vary from language to language, Windows CE offers only the core set of virtual key codes that are found on all keyboards. This core set includes the Latin letters, numbers, and a few other critical keys, such as the function and arrow keys. Keys not included in the core set also have virtual key code assignments, but their values vary from one keyboard layout to the next. Therefore, you should only depend on the virtual key codes that are in the core set.

In addition to mapping, the keyboard driver determines which characters the virtual key generates. A single virtual key generates different characters depending on the state of other keys, such as the SHIFT and CAPS LOCK keys. Do not confuse virtual key codes with characters. Although many of the virtual key codes have the same numerical value as one of the characters that the key generates, the virtual key code and the character are two different things. For example, the same virtual key generates the uppercase "A" character and the lowercase "a" character.

User Input System

The user input system delivers keyboard messages containing scan code, virtual key code, and character information to the appropriate window. To understand how this system works, you need to understand the relationship between the *active window*, the *focus window*, and the *foreground window*.

Each thread maintains its own active window and focus window. The active window is a *top-level window*. The focus window is either the active window or one of its descendents. At any one time, there is one thread in the system that is considered the foreground thread. The active window of this thread is the foreground window. The user-input system places keyboard messages in the message queue of the foreground thread. The thread's message loop pulls the message from the queue and sends it to the thread's focus window. If the focus window is NULL, the active window receives the message.

To summarize the relationship between these window types:

- The active window is always a top-level window or NULL.
- The focus window is always the active window, a descendent of the active window, or NULL.
- The foreground window is always the active window of the foreground thread.

There are a number of ways that a thread can become the foreground thread. If an application calls the **SetForegroundWindow** function and specifies a top-level window, the thread that owns the window becomes the foreground thread and the window becomes its active window. This function also moves the window to the top of the Z order. You can use **SetForegroundWindow** on any top-level window. For more information on Z order, see Chapter 9, "Windows."

In most cases, if the user taps on a window, the system will bring that window to the foreground. The thread that created the window becomes the foreground thread. If the foreground window is hidden or destroyed, the system designates another window as the foreground window. In that case, the new foreground window's thread becomes the foreground thread. You can use the **GetForegroundWindow** function to get the current foreground window.

In general, an application thread does not need to set the foreground window explicitly. This is usually done by the system as the user selects and closes windows with the stylus. Use the **SetActiveWindow** function to activate a window. If the calling thread is the foreground thread, then the new active window automatically becomes the foreground window. When the activation changes, the system sends a WM_ACTIVATE message to the window that is being deactivated and to the window that is being activated. A thread can use the **GetActiveWindow** function to access its active window.

An application thread uses the **SetFocus** function to move the focus between its windows. When the focus changes, the system sends a WM_KILLFOCUS message to the window that is losing the focus. It sends a WM_SETFOCUS message to the window that is gaining the focus.

The system ensures that the focus window is always the active window or a descendent of the active window. If the focus is changed to a window with a different top-level ancestor, the system first changes the activation, and then it changes the focus.

Key and Character Messages

Windows CE includes two kinds of messages for keyboard events: keystroke messages, which control a windows behavior, and character messages, which determine the text that is displayed in the window.

Windows CE generates a keystroke message whenever the user presses or releases a key. When the user presses a key, the system generates either a WM_KEYDOWN or WM_SYSKEYDOWN message. If the user holds a key down long enough to start the keyboard's automatic repeat feature, the system generates repeated WM_KEYDOWN or WM_SYSKEYDOWN messages. When the user releases a key, a WM_KEYUP or WM_SYSKEYUP message is generated.

System keystroke messages are generated when the user types a key in combination with the ALT key or when the user types a key and the focus is NULL. If the focus is NULL, the keyboard event is delivered to the active window. These messages have the WM_SYS prefix in the message name.

Windows CE does not automatically generate character messages. An application's message loop calls **TranslateMessage** to generate character messages. **TranslateMessage** translates the keyboard message into the appropriate character message. Not all keystroke messages generate character messages.

Windows CE includes four character messages: WM_CHAR, WM_SYSCHAR, WM_DEADCHAR and WM_SYSDEADCHAR. The WM_CHAR message contains the character and flags that provide other information. Applications that display characters that the user types from a keyboard process the WM_CHAR message.

Some non-English keyboards provide keys that enable the user to add diacritic marks to characters produced by subsequent keystrokes. In these cases, the system generates a WM_DEADCHAR message when the diacritic key is pressed. When the user presses a subsequent key, Windows CE generates a single WM_CHAR message if the diacritic and character can be combined, or two WM_CHAR messages if they cannot be combined. Applications typically do not process WM_DEADCHAR messages.

If the keystroke is a WM_SYSKEY style message, the system generates corresponding WM_SYSCHAR and WM_SYSDEADCHAR messages. Applications usually do not process these messages.

Checking Other Keys

While processing a keyboard message, an application sometimes needs to determine the status of a different key than the one that generated the current message. You can use the **GetKeyState** function to determine the state of certain keys. This function returns the key's state at the time the current message was generated. The **GetAsyncKeyState** function returns the state of the key at the time of the call.

The Windows CE version of these functions differ slightly from their desktop counterparts. Unlike the equivalent functions in Windows-based desktop platforms, **GetKeyState** supports only a limited number of keys, and **GetAsyncKeyState** returns the current key state even if a window in another thread has the keyboard focus.

Hot Key Support

A *hot key* is a key combination that generates a WM_HOTKEY message. The message is routed to a particular window, regardless of whether or not that window is the current foreground window or focus window.

You define a hot key by calling the **RegisterHotKey** function and specifying the combination of keys that generates the WM_HOTKEY message, the handle of the window to receive the message, and the hot key identifier. When the user presses the hot key, the system places a WM_HOTKEY message in the message queue of the thread that created the specified window. The *wParam* parameter of the message contains the hot key identifier. Before the application terminates, it should use the **UnregisterHotKey** function to destroy the hot key.

Processing Keyboard Messages

The window procedure of the window that has the keyboard focus receives keystroke messages when the user types on the keyboard. An application that responds to keyboard input typically processes WM_KEYDOWN messages only.

In general, you should use the **TranslateMessage** function in your message loop to translate every message, not just keystroke messages. Although **TranslateMessage** has no effect on other types of messages, using it ensures that keyboard input is translated correctly.

When a window procedure receives the WM_CHAR message, it should examine the character code that accompanies the message to determine how to process the character.

If a window procedure processes system keyboard messages, it should pass the message to the **DefWindowProc** function. Otherwise, all system operations involving the ALT key will be disabled whenever that window has the keyboard focus. Windows CE uses the WM_SYSCHAR message to implement menu mnemonics.

The *lParam* parameter of a keystroke message contains the following additional information about the keystroke that generated the message.

Information type	Explanation
Repeat count	Specifies the number of times the keystroke was repeated as a result of the user holding down the key.
Scan code	Gives the hardware-dependent scan code of the key.

Information type	Explanation
Context code	Has a value of one, if the ALT key was pressed, and of zero, if it was released.
Previous key state	Has a value of one, if the pressed key was previously down, and zero, if it was previously up. It has a value of one for WM_KEYDOWN and WM_SYSKEYDOWN keystroke messages generated by the automatic repeat feature.
Transition state	Has a value of one, if the key was released, or of zero, if it was pressed.

Using the Caret

A window that receives keyboard input displays the characters the user types in the window's client area. A window should use a caret to indicate the position in the client area where the next character will appear. The window should create and display the caret when it receives the keyboard focus and it should hide and destroy the caret when it loses the focus. A window can perform these operations when the WM_SETFOCUS and WM_KILLFOCUS messages are processed.

Use the **CreateCaret**, **ShowCaret**, **DestroyCaret**, and **HideCaret** functions to control the visibility of the caret. Use the **SetCaretPosition** function to change the position of the caret as the user types.

Stylus Input

In many Windows CE environments, users interact with applications by using a stylus and a screen. The stylus and screen provide a direct and intuitive alternative to mouse interaction.

The stylus generates an input event whenever the user touches the screen with a stylus or moves the stylus when the tip is touching the screen. To an application, stylus input is a subset of mouse input. When a user presses and releases a stylus on a screen, the application processes these events clicks with the left mouse button. When a user moves the stylus across the screen, the application processes this as a mouse move event.

Stylus input events in a window are posted to the message queue of the thread that created the window.

Stylus Messages

A window receives a stylus message whenever a stylus event occurs within the window's client area. When the user presses the stylus to the screen, the window receives a WM_LBUTTONDOWN message. When the stylus is lifted from the screen, the window receives a WM_LBUTTONUP message. A window will receive a WM_LBUTTONDBLCLK instead of a WM_LBUTTONDOWN under the following conditions:

- The window class was registered with the CS_DBLCLKS class style.
- The stylus touches the screen within a certain distance of the last stylus location.
- The stylus touches the screen within a certain time limit after the stylus touched the screen.

If the user moves the stylus while pressing it to the screen, Windows CE generates a WM_MOUSEMOVE message.

Styles input messages supported by Windows CE are described in the following table.

Message	Meaning
WM_LBUTTONDBLCLK	The user double-tapped the screen.
WM_LBUTTONDOWN	The user pressed the screen.
WM_LBUTTONUP	The user released the stylus from the screen.
WM_MOUSEMOVE	The user moved the stylus while the tip was pressed to the screen.

The *lParam* parameter of a stylus message indicates the position of the stylus tip. The low-order word is the x-coordinate and the high-order word is the y-coordinate. The coordinates are specified in *client coordinates*. In the client-coordinate system, all points are specified relative to the upper-left corner of the client area.

The *wParam* parameter contains flags that indicate the status of the other stylus buttons and the CTRL and SHIFT keys at the time of the stylus event. Check for these flags when the way you process a stylus event depends on the state of another stylus button or on the CTRL key or SHIFT key. The *wParam* parameter can be a combination of the following flags.

Value	Meaning
MK_CONTROL	The CTRL key is down.
MK_LBUTTON	The stylus is touching the screen.
MK_SHIFT	The SHIFT key is down.

Inking Input

The Rich Ink control allows you to capture stylus motions with little effort. It provides a convenient means for applications to accept input from a user without using a keyboard. For a user, taking notes or drawing sketches with the Rich Ink control is very much like writing or drawing on paper.

In addition to capturing images, Rich Ink has powerful editing and formatting capabilities. For example, when the user deletes a word from handwritten notes on the screen, the control automatically closes the resultant word gap. Some examples of how Rich Ink can be used include:

- An electronic form application that accepts a user's handwritten signature.
- A calendar application with an embedded Rich Ink control that allows a user to jot down a "To-Do" list for a selected date.

▶   **To embed the Rich Ink control in your application**

1. Call **InitCommonControls** to load the common control dynamics-link library (DLL).
2. Call **InitInkX** to load and initialize the Rich Ink control.
3. Call **CreateDialog** to instantiate a dialog box with a custom ink control.

    –Or–

1. Call **InitCommonControls** to load the common control DLL.
2. Call **InitInkX** to load and initialize the Rich Ink control.
3. Call **CreateWindow** and specify the class name as WC_INKX.

The EReceipt and InkControl sample codes provide two examples of the implementation.

After initialization, the Rich Ink control communicates with the calling application using the standard Windows CE messaging system. It sends the IM_SHOWCMDBAR message to the ink control to show or hide the command bar. It sends the IM_GETDATALEN, IM_GETDATA, and IM_SETDATA messages between the ink control and the application to transmit inking data, such as a note or sketch. It sends the IM_REINIT message to the ink control to erase all the content from the control. It sends the standard EM_GETMODIFY and EM_SETMODIFY messages to the ink control to determine if its content has been modified and to set the modification flag in the control, respectively.

As an example of using the ink control, consider a calendar application with a Rich Ink control, named as *InkX*, embedded in a dialog box. The control's command bar can be toggled by using **SendDlgItemMessage** to send an IM_SHOWCMDBAR message. The state of the command bar is specified in the accompanying *wParam*:

```
SendDlgItemMessage(hInk, IM_SHOWCMDBAR, (WPARAM)m_bCmdBar, 0L);
```

Here *hInk* is a handle to the *InkX* control and *m_bCmdBar* is set to either TRUE or FALSE to specify whether or not the command bar is visible.

To save an edited or a newly created note, you must get the data length by sending:

```
InkDataLen=SendDlgItemMessage(hInkX, IM_GETDATALEN, 0, 0L);
```

For each date entry, the application keeps an ink note, *pInkData*, of the **BYTE** pointer type. The application should first allocate sufficient memory to store the ink note, and then pass the *pInkData* pointer to the control through the messages *lParam* parameter:

```
InkDatalen=SendDlgItemMessage(hInkX, IM_GETDATA, InkDataLen,
(LPARAM)pInkData);
```

When the user taps a calendar date, the application should retrieve any previously saved ink data and bring up the ink control. It then sends the following message to refresh the document view with the retrieved ink data:

```
SendDlgItemMessage(hInkX, IM_SETDATA, dwInkDataLen, (LPARAM)pInkData);
```

The *dwInkDataLen* parameter gives the length of the ink data; *pInkData* is a pointer to the data itself. You should release the ink data, *pInkData*, once it has been passed to the ink control.

C H A P T E R 8

Graphics Device Interface

In Windows CE, as in Windows-based desktop platforms, the graphics device interface (GDI) controls the display of text and graphics. You use GDI to draw lines, curves, closed figures, text, and bit images.

The principle features of the Windows CE GDI are listed in the following table.

GDI feature	Supported attributes
Filled Shapes and lines	Ellipse, polygon, polyline, rectangle, rounded rectangle
Pens and brushes	Dashed, wide, and solid pens; pattern brushes
Bit block transfer functions	**PatBlt, BitBlt, MaskBlt, StretchBlt, TransparentImage**
ROP Codes	All ROP2, ROP3, and ROP4 codes
Colors	Pixel depths of 1, 2, 4, 8, 16, 24, and 32 bits per pixel (bpp)
Fonts	TrueType and raster fonts
Printing	Full graphical printing
Palettes	Functions that create, change, query, and realize palettes

The Windows CE GDI is designed for devices with limited system resources. Therefore, it does not include many of the special graphic functions found in Windows-based desktop platforms. As a consequence, the Windows CE GDI is a powerful, full color graphical display system with a relatively small footprint.

For more information about GDI in Windows-based desktop platforms, see the documentation for the Microsoft Platform SDK. For an introduction to the GDI in 32-bit Windows programming, see *Programming Windows 95*, by Charles Petzold (Microsoft Press).

Unique Features of the Windows CE GDI

The following GDI features are available only in Windows CE, not in Windows-based desktop platforms.

GDI feature	Windows CE supports
Bit block transfer	The new **TransparentImage** function, which transfers all portions of a bitmap except for those drawn in a specified "transparent" color.
Colors and palettes	All of the pixel formats supported in Windows-based desktop platforms, as well as a 2-bits-per-pixel (bpp) format.

Windows CE does not support the following GDI features found in Windows-based desktop platforms.

GDI feature	Windows CE does not support
Bitmaps	Compressed bitmap formats.
Colors and palettes	Dithering or a standard palette. If there is no color table associated with an image, the color palette selected in the device context (DC) becomes the default color table.
	Windows CE does not arbitrate between the palettes of the background and foreground applications. The application running in the foreground has complete control over the system palette.
Device contexts	Information DCs.
	Streching or polygon-fill graphic modes.
	Class or private type device contexts.
	Multiple mapping modes. It supports only the text-mapping mode, which maps the logical coordinate systems to the physical coordinate system in a 1:1 ratio.
Fonts	Multiple font styles. Windows CE allows either raster or TrueType fonts to be used on a specified system, but not both.
Graphics objects	Paths or metafiles.
Pens and brushes	Dotted pens, inside frame pens, pen endcap styles, hatched brushes, or wide, dashed pens, though it does support wide pens and dashed pens.

GDI feature	Windows CE does not support
Printing	Print spooling or the printing of multiple copies. Windows CE has no print manager.
	Windows CE does not send graphical information directly to output devices. Instead, it passes all graphical operations to device drivers that, in turn, send the information to display devices and printers. One of the reasons Windows CE has a small footprint is because it does not need to maintain hardcoded routines for interfacing with multiple output devices.
Regions	Non-rectangular regions. Like Windows 95, but unlike Windows NT, Windows CE represents regions using 16-bit values.
Shape and line drawing	Functions necessary to draw an arc, a beizer curve, a chord, a pie, a polypolygon, or a polypolyline.

Device Contexts

A *device context* (DC) is a GDI structure containing information that governs the display of text and graphics on a particular output device. You use a DC to store, retrieve, and modify the attributes of graphic objects and to specify graphic modes. The graphic objects stored in a DC include a pen for line drawing, a brush for painting and filling, a font for text output, a bitmap for copying or scrolling, a palette for defining the available colors, and a region for clipping.

DCs supported by Windows CE are described in the following table.

Device context type	Description
Display	Supports drawing operations on display devices.
Printer	Supports drawing operations on printers.
Memory	Supports drawing operations on device-dependent bitmaps or DIB sections.

The graphics modes control general display characteristics, such as how colors are mixed. Graphics modes supported by Windows CE are described in the following table.

Graphics mode type	Description
Background mode	Defines how background colors are mixed with window or screen colors for text and bitmap operations.
Drawing mode	Defines how foreground colors are mixed with window or screen colors for pen, brush, bitmap, and text operations.

Note Windows CE does not support multiple mapping modes. The only mapping mode is MM_TEXT, which maps logical coordinates to the physical coordinates in a 1:1 ratio from left to right and top to bottom.

Using Device Contexts

You cannot directly modify a device context (DC). You obtain access to a DC indirectly by using functions that return a handle to a DC.

Display Device Contexts

You create a display device context to draw in the client area of a display device. To do so, call the **BeginPaint** or **GetDC** function and supply a handle to a window. Windows CE will return a handle to a display device context with default objects, attributes, and graphic modes. You can begin drawing using these defaults, or you can choose a new object, change the attributes of an existing object, or choose a new mode. When you have finished drawing in the display area, you must release the device context by calling the **EndPaint** or **ReleaseDC** function. Use **BeginPaint** and **EndPaint** together, and use **GetDC** and **ReleaseDC** together. You use **BeginPaint** and **EndPaint** when you are processing WM_PAINT messages in your window procedure. The rest of the time, you generally use **GetDC** and **ReleaseDC** to obtain and release a DC.

Note Windows CE supports only common DCs.

Printer Device Contexts

You obtain a handle to a printer DC by calling the **CreateDC** function. Call the **DeleteDC** function to delete the printer DC when you are finished printing.

Note You must delete, rather than release, a printer device context; the
ReleaseDC function fails if you try to use it to free a printer device context.

Memory Device Contexts

You use a memory device context to store bit images in memory rather than
sending them to an output device. A memory DC allows Windows CE to treat
a portion of memory as a virtual device. You can create a memory DC for a
particular device by calling the **CreateCompatibleDC** function and supplying a
handle to the device's DC. Memory DCs are also called compatible DCs because
they are created to be compatible with a particular device. Windows CE will
create a temporary 1 pixel x 1 pixel, monochrome bitmap and select it into the DC
after calling **CreateCompatibleDC**. Before you can begin drawing with this DC,
you must use the **SelectObject** function to select a bitmap with the appropriate
width and height into the DC. Once the new bitmap is selected into the memory
DC, you can use the DC to store images. For more information on image storage,
see the "Bitmaps" section later in this chapter.

Graphic Objects

All newly created DCs start with a default brush, palette, font, pen, and region.
You can examine a default object's attributes by calling the **GetCurrentObject**
and **GetObject** functions. The **GetCurrentObject** function returns a handle
identifying the current pen, brush, palette, bitmap, or font, and the **GetObject**
function initializes a structure containing that object's attributes.

To replace a default object, call one of the following object-specific
creation functions.

Graphic object	Creation functions
Bitmap	**CreateBitmap**, **CreateCompatibleBitmap**, **CreateDIBSection**
Brush	**CreateDIBPatternBrushPt**, **CreatePatternBrush**, **CreateSolidBrush**
Palette	**CreatePalette**
Font	**CreateFontIndirect**
Pen	**CreatePen**, **CreatePenIndirect**

Each of these functions returns a handle identifying the new object. After you
retrieve a handle, you can call the **SelectObject** function to select the new object
into the DC. However, you should save the handle to the default object. When
you finish using the new object, use **SelectObject** to restore the default object,
and delete the new object with the **DeleteObject** function.

> **Note** Failure to delete objects that are no longer in use can cause serious performance problems.

Saving and Restoring Device Contexts

Use the **GetDeviceCaps** function to retrieve device data using a device context for any of the following types of devices:

- Raster displays
- Dot-matrix printers
- Ink-jet printers
- Laser printers

GetDeviceCaps can provide information about a device's color format and raster capabilities, as well as its shape, text, and line drawing capibilites. You supply **GetDeviceCaps** with a handle to a device context and an index specifying the type of data to be retrieved.

The **SaveDC** function records the condition of your device context's graphic objects and graphic modes on a special GDI stack. You can call this function to save your application's original state, providing you with a "clean slate" for later drawing. Call **RestoreDC** to return the DC to this original state.

Graphic Modes

Windows CE initializes a device context with default graphic modes. You can get the current background mix mode with the **GetBkMode** function and set it with the **SetBkMode** function. In Windows CE, the background mix mode effects the appearence of text and dashed pens. You can set the foreground mix mode with the **SetROP2** function. The foreground mix mode controls how the brush or pen colors and the image colors are combined. **SetROP2** returns the mix mode for the last foreground mix mode.

You can change the viewport origin from its default starting point of the upper-left corner of the screen with the **SetViewportOrgEx** function.

Bitmaps

A *bitmap* is an array of bits that, when mapped to a rectangular pixel array on an output device, creates an image. You use bitmaps to create, modify, and store images.

There are two types of bitmaps: device-dependent bitmaps (DDBs) and device-independent bitmaps (DIBs). A DDB does not have its own color table and can therefore only be properly displayed by a device with the same display memory organization as the one on which it was created. A DIB, on the other hand, generally has its own color table, and therefore can be displayed on a variety of devices.

Virtually all graphs information in Windows CE is stored in DIB format. Windows CE supports DDBs only to remain compatible with applications written for early versions of Windows. You should use DIBs in all applications you write for, or port to, Windows CE.

The **BITMAP** structure contains all of the height, width, and color data needed to draw a DDB. The data needed to draw a DIB is stored in a **BITMAPINFO** structure which consists of a **BITMAPINFOHEADER** structure and two or more **RGBQUAD** structures. The **BITMAPINFOHEADER** structure contains information about the dimensions and color format of a DIB. Each **RGBQUAD** structure defines one of the bitmap's colors.

Windows CE supports bitmaps with pixel depths of 1, 2, 4, 8, 16, 24, and 32 bits per pixel (bpp). For more information on colors in Windows CE, see Chapter 6, "Designing a User Interface for Windows CE."

Windows CE does not support compressed bitmap formats, such as run-length encoded bitmaps.

Using Bitmaps

You can create a DIB with the **CreateDIBSection** function, and then select it into a device context with the **SelectObject** function. You use the **DeleteObject** function to delete the DIB.

In order to store a DDB in memory, you must first create a memory DC with the **CreateCompatibleDC** function. This function creates a DC that is compatible with the specified device. The DC contains a single-bit array that serves as a placeholder for a bitmap. You can use the **CreateBitmap** or **CreateCompatibleBitmap** function to create a bitmap of the desired size, and then select it into the DC with the **SelectObject** function. Windows CE then replaces the single-bit array with an array large enough to store color information for the specified rectangle of pixels.

When you draw using the handle returned by **CreateCompatibleDC**, the output does not appear on a device's drawing surface; instead, it is stored in memory. To copy the image stored in memory to a display device, call the **BitBlt** function. **BitBlt** copies the bitmap data from the bitmap in the source DC into the bitmap in the target DC. In this case, the source DC is the memory DC, and the target DC is the display DC. Thus, when **BitBlt** completes the transfer, the image will appear on the screen. By reversing the source and target DCs, you can use **BitBlt** to transfer images from the screen into memory.

BLT functions, such as **BitBlt,** can be used to modify as well as transfer bitmaps. These functions modify a destination bitmap by combining it with a pen, a brush, and, in some cases, a source bitmap, in a format specified by a raster operation (ROP) code. Each ROP code specifies a unique logical pattern for combining graphic objects. For example, the **SRCCOPY** ROP simply copies a source bitmap to a destination bitmap while the **MERGECOPY** ROP merges the colors of a source rectangle with a specified pattern.

The ROP code types are described in the following table.

ROP type	Description
ROP2	Combines a pen or brush with a destination bitmap in one of 16 possible combinations.
ROP3	Combines a brush, a source bitmap, and a destination bitmap in one of 256 possible combinations.
ROP4	Uses a monochrome "mask" bitmap to combine a foreground ROP3 and a background ROP3. The mask uses zeros and ones to indicate the areas where each ROP3 will be used.

When the source and destination bitmaps are different sizes, you can use the **StrechBlt** function to perform a BLT between the two bitmaps. **StrechBlt** copies a bitmap from a source rectangle into a destination rectangle, stretching or compressing the bitmap to fit the destination rectangle.

You can use the **PatBlt** function to paint a selected rectangle using a selected brush and an ROP3 code.

You can use the **TransparentImage** to transfer all portions of a bitmap except for those drawn in a specified transparent color. This function is especially useful for transferring non-rectangular images, such as icons.

Note Windows CE supports arbitrary bit pixel formats, which allow you to use blt functions between bitmaps with different pixel depths.

The **BITMAPINFO** structure defines the dimensions and color information for a DIB. The **BITMAPINFO** structure must include a color table if the images are palettized, usually with formats of 1, 2, 4, and 8 bbp. For non-palettized images with 16 bpp or 32 bpp, the color table must be three entries long; the entries must specify the value of the red, green, and blue bitmasks. Because GDI ignores the color table for 24-bpp bitmaps, you should store the image's pixels in blue-green-red (BGR) format.

Colors and Palettes

Some display devices and printers display only monochrome images; others use hundreds, thousands, or even millions of colors. You should design your applications to display properly on devices with a variety of color capabilities.

The color range available to a display device is determined primarily by the pixel depth that it supports. Pixel depth is measured in bits per pixel (bpp). Each bit can have a value of 1 or 0. A pixel depth of 1 bpp allows only two values, black and white. A pixel depth of 2 bpp has four possible color values or all possible combinations of 0s and 1s with two bits. In general, the number of possible colors is equal to 2 raised to the power of the pixel depth. Windows CE supports pixel depths of 1, 2, 4, 8, 16, 24, and 32 bpp.

Note Windows CE supports a pixel depth of 2 bpp, which is not supported in Windows-based desktop platforms.

A color palette is an array that contains the color values that can be displayed or drawn on a output device. Color palettes are used by devices that can only display a subset of their potential colors at any specified time.

Each time you create a device context, Windows CE creates a default palette for that device context. Windows CE has no standard color palette. It assigns colors to a bitmap based on the bitmap's associated color table. If an image has no color table, Windows CE uses the color palette in the currently selected DC.

The default palette typically has 256 entries (colors), though the exact number varies. The device determines which colors are in the default palette. Display devices, for example, often use the 16 standard VGA colors and four other Windows-defined colors. Printer devices may use other default colors.

If you specify a pen or text color that is not in the default palette, Windows CE will approximate the color with the closest color in the palette.

You cannot change the entries in the default palette. However, you can create your own logical palette and select the palette into a DC in place of the default palette. You can use logical palettes to define and use colors that meet your specific needs. Windows CE enables you to create multiple logical palettes. You can attach each logical palette to a unique DC or you can switch between multiple logical palettes in a single DC.

Windows CE supports both palettized and non-palettized color display devices. Palettized devices have a color palette coded directly into their display card. Non-palettized devices use the pixels' bit values in the frame buffer to directly define colors in terms of their red, green, and blue values. You can use the **GetDeviceCaps** function to determine whether or not a device supports color palettes.

Using Colors

You can use the **GetDeviceCaps** function, which specifies the NUMCOLORS value, to discover the number of colors a device supports. Usually, this count corresponds to a physical property of the output device, such as the number of inks in the printer or the number of distinct color signals the display adapter can transmit to the monitor.

Windows and applications use parameters and variables having the **COLORREF** type to pass and store color values. You can extract the individual values of the red, green, and blue components of a color value by using the **GetRValue**, **GetGValue**, and **GetBValue** macros, respectively. Use the **RGB** macro to create a color value from individual red, green, and blue component values.

If you request a color that the display device cannot generate, Windows CE will approximate it with a color that the device can generate. For example, if you attempt to create a red pen for a black and white printer, you will receive a black pen instead—Windows CE uses black as the approximation for red.

You can discover how Windows CE will approximate a specified color by using the **GetNearestColor** function. The function takes a color value and returns the color value of the closest matching color the device can generate.

Note Windows CE does not support dithering.

Windows CE handles colors in bitmaps differently than colors in pens, brushes, and text. Compatible bitmaps, created by using the **CreateBitmap** or **CreateCompatibleBitmap** function, retain color information in a device-dependent format. No color values are used, and the colors are not approximated.

DIBs retain color information either as color values or color palette indexes. If color values are used, the colors may be approximated as necessary. Color palette indexes can only be used with devices that support color palettes. Although Windows does not approximate colors identified by indexes, the colors in the bitmap could change if the palette changes.

Note An offscreen DIB section should have the same color table as the screen, otherwise GDI will have to perform a time-consuming, color-translating BLT when the DIB section is transferred to the screen. For grayscale devices, the color table should be 0x000000, 0x808080, 0xc0c0c0, and 0xffffff. For color devices, the application should first query the stock palette to determine its color display capabilities, and then build a matching color table.

Creating and Using Palettes

To create a logical palette, you should assign values to the members of a **LOGPALETTE** structure and pass a pointer to the structure to the **CreatePalette** function. The function returns a handle to a logical palette with the values specified in the **LOGPALETE** structure.

To gain access to the colors in the logical palette, use the **SelectPalette** function to select the palette into the current device context, and then use the **RealizePalette** function to make the system palette the same as the palette in the current device context. You can use the colors in the palette as soon as the logical palette has been realized.

Note The **GetSystemPaletteEntries** and **RealizePalette** functions will fail if the device associated with the selected device index does not have a settable palette. You can use **GetDeviceCaps** to find out if the device has a settable palette.

Your logical palette should have just enough entries to represent the colors you need. You can use the **GetDeviceCaps** function to retrieve the maximum palette size associated with a device, or the **SIZEPALETTE** member.

You can use the **SetPaletteEntries** function to change the colors in an existing logical palette. After you have updated the colors, use **RealizePalette** to update the display. If you select a logical palette into more than one DC, any changes you make to the logical palette will affect all the DCs to which it is attached.

You can use the **GetPaletteEntries** function to retrieve the color values for a logical palette. Use the **GetNearestPaletteIndex** function to retrieve the value in a specified logical palette that most closely matches a specified color value.

Use the **DeleteObject** function to delete a logical palette. Be sure that the logical palette is not selected into a device context when you delete it.

Windows CE does not arbitrate between the palettes of the background and foreground applications. The application running in the foreground has complete control over the system palette. Because of this, you should generally use only the first ten and last ten colors included in the stock palette of a display device, which are generally the standard Windows VGA colors. Applications that use other colors may not display properly when they run in the background. Because Windows CE does not perform any color matching operations between the foreground and background applications, background applications cannot call **RealizePalette**.

Pens

In Windows CE, a *pen* is a graphic object for drawing lines. Drawing applications use pens to draw freehand lines and straight lines. Computer-aided design (CAD) applications use pens to draw visible lines, section lines, center lines, and so on. Word processing and desktop publishing applications use pens to draw borders and rules. Spreadsheet applications use pens to designate trends in graphs and to outline bar graphs and pie charts.

Windows CE stock pens include the **BLACK_PEN** and the **WHITE_PEN**, which each draw a solid, 1-pixel-wide line in their respective color, and the **NULL_PEN** which does not draw. You obtain the stock pens with the **GetStockObject** function.

You use the **CreatePen** or **CreatePenIndirect** functions to create a custom pen with a unique color, width, or pen style.

The pen styles supported by Windows CE are described in the following table.

Pen style	Description
PS_SOLID	Draws a solid line
PS_DASH	Draws a dashed line
PS_NULL	Does not draw a line

Windows CE supports wide pens and dashed pens, but it does not support wide, dashed pens, dotted pens, inside frame pens, geometric pens or pen endcap styles. All Windows CE pens are cosmetic.

You can create a pen with a unique color by storing the red, green, blue (RGB) triplet that specifies the desired color in a **COLORREF** structure and passing this structure's address to the **CreatePen** or **CreatePenIndirect** function. In the case of **CreatePenIndirect**, the **COLORREF** pointer is actually incorporated into the **LOGPEN** structure, which is used by **CreatePenIndirect**.

> **Note** The wide pen requires a lot of GDI computation. To improve the performance of a handwriting application, use a standard-sized pen whenever possible.

Brushes

In Windows CE, a *brush* is a graphic object for painting the interior of closed shapes. Drawing applications use brushes to paint shapes; word processing applications use brushes to paint rules; CAD applications use brushes to paint the interiors of cross-section views; and spreadsheet applications use brushes to paint graphs.

When you call a function that creates a brush, such as **CreatePatternBrush**, it returns a handle to a logical brush. When you select the logical brush into the DC with the **SelectObject** function, the device driver for the corresponding device creates the physical brush that will be used for painting.

When you call a painting function, GDI maps a pixel in the brush bitmap to the window origin of the client area. The window origin is the upper-left corner of the window's client area. The coordinates of the mapped pixel are called the brush origin. The default brush origin is the upper-left corner of the brush bitmap, at the coordinates (0, 0). You can use the **SetBrushOrgEx** function to change the location of the brush origin by a specified number of pixels. To make the changes effective, you must use the **SelectObject** function to select the modified brush.

Windows CE supports three types of logical brushes: stock brushes, solid brushes, and pattern brushes.

The seven types of stock brushes consist of the white brush, black brush, gray brush, light gray brush, dark gray brush, the null brush (which does not paint), and the hollow brush. You can use the **GetStockObject** function to select one of the stock brushes.

Windows CE maintains 21 stock brushes whose colors are used in window elements such as menus, scroll bars, and buttons. You can obtain a handle to a system stock brush with the **GetSysColorBrush** function. Furthermore, you can retrieve the color window element with the **GetSysColor** function, and set a color corresponding to a window element with the **SetSysColors** function.

A solid brush contains 64 pixels of the same color in a square that is 8 x 8 pixels. You can call the **CreateSolidBrush** function to create a solid brush of a specified color. To paint with your solid brush, use **SelectObject** to select it into a specified DC.

You can create a pattern brush from an application-defined bitmap or a DIB. To create a logical pattern brush, you must create a bitmap, and then call the **CreatePatternBrush** or **CreateDIBPatternBrushPt** function, supplying a handle that identifies the bitmap or DIB.

Windows CE does not support hatched brushes. However, you can achieve the effect of a hatched brush by creating a pattern brush with the desired hatch pattern using the **CreateDIBPatternBrushPt** function. You can create bitmaps of multiple sizes as well.

Printing

Windows CE does not send printing commands directly to output devices. Instead, it passes all output information to device drivers, which, in turn, send the information to display devices and printers. Windows CE has a small footprint in part because it does not need to maintain hardcoded routines for interfacing with multiple output devices.

Most applications strive for what you see is what you get (WYSIWYG) output. Ideally, WYSIWYG would mean that text drawn with a specified font and size on the screen would have a similar appearance when it is printed. However, it is almost impossible to obtain true WYSIWYG output, partly because of differences between video and printer technologies.

To obtain a WYSIWYG effect when drawing text, call the **CreateFont** function and specify the typeface name and logical size of the font you would like to draw with, and then call the **SelectObject** function to select the font into a printer DC. Windows CE will select a physical font that is the closest possible match to the specified logical font.

Before you start a print job, you should use **SetAbortProc** to establish an abort procedure. Your abort procedure should include a modeless dialog box that allows a user to cancel a print job. Once you have initialized the necessary variables, registered your **AbortProc** function, and displayed your modeless **Cancel** dialog box, you can start the print job by calling the **StartDoc** function.

Once you have started the print job, you can define individual pages in the document by calling the **StartPage** and **EndPage** functions and embedding the appropriate calls to GDI drawing functions within this bracket. After you have defined the last page, you can close the document and end the print job with the **EndDoc** function.

As previously stated, Windows CE does not have a print manager. It will not spool or print more than a single copy of a document at a time.

> **Note** The display driver does all the rendering in Windows CE and scales the output to the printer resolution. If you intend to print text, you should use a system with TrueType fonts because raster fonts cannot be scaled to different printer resolutions without severely compromising the quality of the text.

Regions

In Windows CE, a *region* is a rectangle that can be filled, painted, inverted, framed, and tested to see if it contains a particular point.

You create a region by calling **CreateRectRgn** or **CreateRectRgnIndirect**. These functions return a handle identifying the new region. Once you have a handle to a region, you can select the region into a DC with the **SelectObject** function. You can perform a variety of operations on a region: You can combine or compare it with another region, paint or invert its interior, draw a frame around it, retrieve its dimensions, and test whether or not a particular point lies within it.

> **Note** When using the **CreateRectRgn** and **CreateRectRgnIndirect** functions, use values for regions that can be represented by 16-bit integers because that is how region data is stored in Windows CE.

The following table describes in which ways you can use the **CombineRgn** function to combine two regions together.

Value	Meaning
RGN_AND	The intersecting parts of two original regions define a new region.
RGN_COPY	A copy of the first of the two original regions defines a new region.
RGN_DIFF	The part of the first region that does not intersect the second defines a new region.
RGN_OR	The two original regions define a new region.
RGN_XOR	Those parts of the two original regions that do not overlap define a new region.

You can use the **EqualRgn** function to determine whether or not two regions are equal in size and shape. You can use the **FillRgn** function to paint the interior of a region with a specified brush.

Windows CE does not support the **InvertRgn** or **InvertRect** functions. You can achieve the effect of **InvertRect** by using the **PatBlt** function with an ROP code of DSTINVERT.

You can retrieve the dimensions of a region's bounding rectangle by calling the **GetRgnBox** function. The bounding rectangle is the smallest rectangle that can be drawn around a region. Use the **OffsetRgn** function to move a region a specified number of logical units. Use **GetRegionData** to retrieve data describing a region.

Note The **GetRegionData** function returns a different number of rectangles for a specified region than its Windows equivalent.

The **PtInRegion** function determines if a point is inside a specified rectangle. To determine if the point is in a region, you must pass the location of the point along with a region's handle to **PtInRegion**.

Clipping Regions

You can use clipping regions to restrict your output to a specified subregion of the client area. To use a clipping region, you must select it into the DC associated with the display device.

Clipping is used in Windows CE in a variety of ways. Word processing and spreadsheet applications clip keyboard input to keep it from appearing in the margins of a page or spreadsheet. CAD and drawing applications clip graphics output to keep it from overwriting the edges of a drawing or picture.

Some DCs provide a predefined or default clipping region. For example, the device context created by the **BeginPaint** contains a predefined rectangular clipping region that corresponds to the invalid rectangle that needs to be repainted. However, the DCs created by the **CreateDC** and **GetDC** functions contain empty clipping regions; clipping is only done to keep graphics output in the window's client area.

You can perform a variety of operations on clipping regions. Some of these operations require a handle identifying the region and some do not. For example, you can perform the following operations directly on a DC's clipping region.

- Determine whether part of the client area intersects a region by calling the **RectVisible** function.

- Exclude a rectangular part of the client area from the current clipping region by calling the **ExcludeClipRect** function.

- Combine a rectangular part of the client area with the current clipping region by calling the **IntersectClipRect** function.

After obtaining a handle identifying the clipping region, you can perform any operation that is common with regions, such as:

- Combine a copy of the current clipping region with a second region by calling the **CombineRgn** function.

- Compare a copy of the current clipping region to a second region by calling the **EqualRgn** function.

- Determine whether a point lies within the interior of a copy of the current clipping region by calling the **PtInRegion** function.

Shapes and Lines

Windows CE allows you to draw lines and a variety of filled shapes including an ellipse, a polygon, a rectangle, and a rounded rectangle.

A line is a set of highlighted pixels on a raster display or a set of dots on a printed page identified by two points: a starting point and an ending point. In Windows CE, the pixel located at the starting point is always included in the line, and the pixel located at the ending point is always excluded.

You can draw a series of connected line segments by calling the **Polyline** function and supplying an array of points that specify the ending point of each line segment.

Note Windows CE does not support the **LineTo** or the **MoveToEx** functions. However, you can use the **Polyline** function in Windows CE to achieve the same results that you would get in Windows-based desktop platforms if you called the **MoveToEx** function and then made repeated calls to the **LineTo** function.

Filled shapes are geometric shapes that Windows CE outlines with the current pen and fills with the current brush. Windows CE supports four filled shapes: ellipse, polygon, rectangle, and round rectangle, which is a rectangle with rounded corners.

An application written for Windows uses filled shapes in a variety of ways. Spreadsheet applications, for example, use filled shapes to construct charts and graphs; drawing applications allow users to draw figures and illustrations using filled shapes.

An ellipse is a closed curve defined by two fixed points—*f1* and *f2*—such that the sum of the distances—*d1* + *d2*—from any point on the curve to the two fixed points is constant. The following illustration describes an ellipse drawn by using the **Ellipse** function.

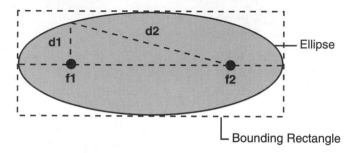

Result of the Ellipse function

When calling **Ellipse**, you supply the coordinates of the upper-left and lower-right corners of the ellipse's bounding rectangle. A bounding rectangle is the smallest rectangle that completely surrounds the ellipse.

A polygon is a filled shape with straight sides. Windows CE uses the currently selected pen to draw the sides of the polygon, and the current brush to fill it. Windows CE fills all enclosed regions within the polygon with the current brush.

Note Windows CE does not support multiple fill modes. When it fills a polygon, it fills all subareas created by intersecting lines within the polygon. This manner of filling is equivalent to the Winding fill mode used on Windows-based desktop platforms.

A rectangle is a four-sided polygon whose opposing sides are parallel and equal in length, and whose interior angles are 90 degrees. Although you can use the **Polygon** function to draw a rectangle if you supply it with all four sides, it is easier to use the **Rectangle** function. This function requires only the coordinates of the upper-left and the lower-right corners.

You can use the **RoundRect** function to draw a rectangle with rounded corners. Supply this function with the coordinates of the lower-left and upper-right corners of the rectangle, and the width and height of the ellipse used to round each corner.

You can use the **FillRect** function to paint the interior of a rectangle. You can use the **FillRgn** function to fill a region using the specified brush.

Because Windows CE does not support paths, many line-drawing functions that are available in the Windows-based desktop platforms are not available in Windows CE. Windows CE does not support functions to draw an arc, a beizer curve, a chord, a pie, a polypolygon, or a polypolyline. However, you can approximate these shapes using existing Windows CE drawing functions. For example, you can create an arc using the **Ellipse** function with an appropriately defined clipping region.

Note The **Ellipse** and **RoundRect** functions require a lot of GDI computation. To increase your application's performance, use these functions sparingly.

Text and Fonts

In Windows CE, a font is a collection of glyphs that share a common design. A font is characterized by its typeface, style, and size.

A font's typeface determines the specific characteristics of the glyphs, such as the relative width of the thick and thin strokes used in any specified character. The style determines a font's weight and slant. Font weights can range from thin to black. Slants can be roman (upright) and italic. The size of a font is the distance from the bottom of a lowercase "g" to the top of an adjacent uppercase "M," measured in points. A point is approximately 1/72 of an inch.

In Windows CE, fonts are grouped into families that share common stoke-width characteristics. Fonts within a family are distinguished by size and style. The font families are described in the following table.

Font family name	Description
Decorative	Specifies a novelty font, for example, Old English.
Dontcare	Specifies a generic family name. This name is used when information about a font does not exist or does not matter.
Modern	Specifies a monospace font with or without serifs. Monospace fonts are usually modern; examples include Pica, Elite, and Courier New.
Roman	Specifies a proportional font with serifs, for example, Times New Roman.
Script	Specifies a font that is designed to look like handwriting; examples include Script and Cursive.
Swiss	Specifies a proportional font without serifs, for example, Arial.

These family names correspond to constants found in the WINGDI.H header file: FF_DECORATIVE, FF_DONTCARE, FF_MODERN, FF_ROMAN, FF_SCRIPT, and FF_SWISS. Use these constants when you create, select, or retrieve information about a font.

TrueType and Raster Fonts

Windows CE supports raster and TrueType font technologies but allows only one type to be used on a specified system. The choice of TrueType or raster font types is made when the system is designed and cannot be changed afterwards by an application.

The differences between raster and TrueType fonts have to do with the way the glyph for each character or symbol is stored in the respective font-resource file. A raster font glpyh is a tiny bitmap that represents a single character's size. Because the bitmaps for each glyph in a raster font are designed for a specific resolution on a particular device, raster fonts are generally considered to be device-dependent.

A TrueType font glyph contains outlines and hints. Windows CE uses these hints to adjust the outlines used to draw the glyphs. These hints and the respective adjustments are based on the amount of scaling used to reduce or increase the size of the glyph. Because TrueType characters can be scaled up or down and still retain their original appearance, they are considered to be device-independent.

A font's glyphs are stored in a font-resource file. A font-resource file for a raster font is stored in a .fon file. TrueType fonts have two files, a short .fot header file and a .ttf file that contains the actual data.

Using Fonts

Use the **AddFontResource** function to load a font from a font-resource file. When you finish using an installed font, use the **RemoveFontResource** function to remove it. Whenever you add or delete a font resource, you should use the **SendMessage** function to send a **WM_FONTCHANGE** message to all top-level windows in the system. This message notifies other applications that the application has added or removed a font to the internal font table. You do not need to use **AddFontResources** to create or realize system fonts.

There are two stages to selecting a font. In the first stage, you specify the ideal font you would like to use. This theoretical font is called a logical font. In the second stage, an internal algorithm finds the physical font that is the closest match to your specified logical font. A physical font is a font stored on the device or in the operating system. The process of finding the physical font that most closely matches a specified logical font is called font mapping.

▶ **To use a font**

1. Use the **EnumFontFamilies** function to list the available fonts.

   This is especially useful when you want to determine which fonts are available from a specified font family or typeface.

2. Use the values returned by the font enumeration function to initialize the members of a **LOGFONT** structure.

3. Create the logical font by calling the **CreateFontIndirect** function and passing it a pointer to the initialized **LOGFONT** structure.

4. Select the logical font into the current device context with the **SelectObject** function.

When you call **SelectObject**, Windows CE loads the physical font that most closely matches the logical font specified in the **LOGFONT** structure.

When initializing the members of the **LOGFONT** structure, be sure that the **lfCharSet** member specifies a specific character set. This member is used in the font mapping process and the results will be inconsistent if this member is not initialized correctly. If you specify a typeface name in the **lfFaceName** member of the **LOGFONT** structure, be sure that the **lfCharSet** value contains a matching value.

Windows CE keeps a table containing all the fonts available for application use. When you call **CreateFontIndirect**, Windows CE chooses a font from this table.

Windows CE provides six stock logical fonts. You can use the **GetStockObject** function to obtain a stock font. The stock font values are described in the following table.

Value	Meaning
ANSI_FIXED_FONT	Specifies a monospace font based on the Windows character set, usually represented by a Courier font.
ANSI_VAR_FONT	Specifies a proportional font based on the Windows character set, usually represented by the MS Sans Serif font.
DEVICE_DEFAULT_FONT	Specifies the preferred font for the specified device, usually represented by the System font for display devices.
OEM_FIXED_FONT	Specifies a monospace font based on an OEM character set. For IBM computers and compatibles, the OEM font is based on the IBM desktop computer character set.

Value	Meaning
SYSTEM_FONT	Specifies the System font. This is a proportional font based on the Windows character set, and is used by the operating system to display window titles, menu names, and text in dialog boxes. The System font is always available. Other fonts are available only if they have been installed.
SYSTEM_FIXED_FONT	Specifies a monospace font compatible with the System font in Windows versions earlier than 3.0.

Enumerating Fonts

You can enumerate the available fonts by calling the **EnumFonts** or **EnumFontFamilies** function. These functions send information about the available fonts to a callback function that the application supplies. The callback function stores the information in the **LOGFONT** structure and in either the **NEWTEXTMETRIC** structure for TrueType fonts or the **TEXTMETRIC** structure for raster fonts. By using the information returned from these functions, you can limit the user's choices to available fonts only.

The **EnumFontFamilies** function is similar to the **EnumFonts** function but includes some extra functionality for use with TrueType fonts. The **EnumFontFamilies** function enumerates all the styles associated with a specified typeface, not simply the bold and italic attributes. For example, when the system includes a TrueType font called Courier New Extra-Bold, **EnumFontFamilies** lists it with the other Courier New fonts.

Note Despite its name, **EnumFontFamilies** actually enumerates the styles associated with a specified typeface—for example, Arial—rather than a font family, such as Roman.

If you do not supply a typeface name, the **EnumFonts** and **EnumFontFamilies** functions supply information about one font in each available family. To enumerate all the fonts in a DC, you can specify NULL for the typeface name, compile a list of the available typefaces, and then enumerate each font in each typeface.

A font resource is a group of individual fonts in a specified character set that has various combinations of heights, widths, and pitches. You can load font resources and add the fonts in each resource to the operating system font table by using the **AddFontResource** function. To remove a font resource from the font table, you can use the **RemoveFontResource** function.

Formatting Text

Windows CE provides a complete set of functions to format and draw text in an application's client area and on a printed page.

The default text color for a display DC is black; the default background color is white; and the default background mode is OPAQUE. Use the **SetTextColor** and **GetTextColor** functions to respectively set and retrieve the color of text drawn in the client-area of a window or printed by a color printer. Use the **SetBkColor** and **GetBkColor** functions to respectively set or retrieve the background color. Use the **SetBkMode** and the **GetBkMode** functions to respectively set or retrieve the background mode. The background mode specifies the logical method for combining the selected background color with the current colors on the video display.

You can use the **GetTextExtentPoint32** function to compute the width and height of a string of text. You can use the **GetTextMetrics** function to retrieve a font's logical dimensions. You can call the **GetDeviceCaps** function to determine the dimensions of an output device.

Drawing Text

After you have selected a font, set your text-formatting options, and computed the necessary character width and height values for a string of text, you can draw characters and symbols using either the **DrawText** or **ExtTextOut** function. When you call one of these functions, the operating system passes the call to the graphics engine, which in turn passes the call to the appropriate device driver.

In most cases **ExtTextOut** is faster than **DrawText**. However, there are some instances when **DrawText** is more efficient, as in the case where you need to draw multiple lines of text within the borders of a rectangular region. **DrawText** does not work with rotated text.

C H A P T E R   9

Windows

A message is the means by which the user communicates with Windows CE and your application. A window object, which is usually referred to as a window, is the means by which an application receives messages from the user and the operating system.

In Windows CE-based systems with graphical displays, windows are the primary input and output devices. Applications use the graphics device interface (GDI) to display output in a window. The messaging system passes user input to a window in the form of messages. Unlike Windows-based desktop platforms, not all Windows CE-based devices have a graphical display. However, because all applications need to process messages, all applications must have windows, even those that do not have a graphical display.

Every window is a member of a window class. A window class is a template for creating window objects. When you write an application, you register at least one window class that you use to create a window or windows.

Note Windows CE does not support dynamic data exchange (DDE), multiple-document interface (MDI), or window properties.

For specific information about designing windows, see Chapter 6, "Designing a User Interface for Windows CE."

Sample Windows-Based Application

Every Windows CE-based application must have **WinMain** as its entry point function. **WinMain** performs a number of tasks, including registering the window class for the main window and creating the main window. **WinMain** registers the main window class by calling the **RegisterClass** function and it creates the main window by calling the **CreateWindowEx** function. **WinMain** does not need to do these things itself; it can call other functions to perform any or all of these tasks.

The system does not automatically display the main window after creating it. Rather, the application's **WinMain** function uses the **ShowWindow** function to display the window.

Even the simplest Windows-based application has a message loop and a window procedure. The message loop, typically part of an application's **WinMain** function, enables your application to receive messages and to dispatch them to the appropriate window procedure. The window procedure is a function that processes the messages that the system sends to your window. The system calls your window procedure as a result of the messages that your message loop receives and dispatches. You usually do not call your window procedure directly from your application. Each window class specifies an initial window procedure.

This section contains a code example that is used to create a simple Windows-based application. This sample application demonstrates the basic framework common to all Windows-based applications, and begins executing with the **WinMain** function that performs the following tasks:

1. **WinMain** stashes the application-instance handle in a global variable. Because this handle is used in various places throughout a program, it is common to put it in a global variable that is accessible to all functions. The smallest possible interval a timer can measure is the system-tick interval.

2. **WinMain** calls the application-defined **InitApplication** function that calls the **RegisterClass** function to register the application's main window class. More complicated applications may need to register more window classes and to determine whether other instances of the application are running.

3. **WinMain** calls the application-defined **InitInstance** function that calls the **CreateWindow** function to create a window. **CreateWindow** returns a window handle identifying the new window. This handle is used to refer to the window in subsequent function calls.

4. **WinMain** creates the message loop by calling the **GetMessage**, **TranslateMessage**, and **DispatchMessage** functions in the format displayed in the sample application. This loop receives messages and dispatches them to the window procedures.

Note that the application does not directly call the window procedure, **MainWndProc**. The system calls this function as the message loop receives and dispatches messages. In this application, **MainWndProc** processes only the WM_CLOSE message that tells the window to close. When the window receives a WM_CLOSE message, it calls the **PostQuitMessage** function that causes the next call to **GetMessage** to return FALSE. This, in turn, causes the message loop to terminate and the application to exit.

Windows CE sends many other messages to the window besides WM_CLOSE. **MainWndProc** passes all other messages to the **DefWindowProc** function, which is the default window procedure provided by the system. You should pass all messages to **DefWindowProc** that you do not process yourself; otherwise, your window may not function correctly.

```c
#include <windows.h>
#define ZeroVar(v) \ memset(&v, 0, sizeof(v))

HINSTANCE g_hInstance;

const TCHAR* const pszMainWndClassName = TEXT("MainWndClass");

//Here is the application's window procedure.
LRESULT CALLBACK MainWndProc(
  HWND hwnd,
  UINT message,
  WPARAM wParam,
  LPARAM lParam
  )
{
  switch ( message )
   {
   case WM_CLOSE:
      DestroyWindow(hwnd);
      PostQuitMessage(0);
      return 0;
   }
   return DefWindowProc(hwnd, message, wParam, lParam);
}
```

```
BOOL InitInstance(void)
{
   BOOL bRet = FALSE;
   HWND hwndMain;

   hwndMain = CreateWindow(
         pszMainWndClassName,
         TEXT("Main"),
         WS_OVERLAPPED|WS_SYSMENU,
         CW_USEDEFAULT, CW_USEDEFAULT,
         CW_USEDEFAULT, CW_USEDEFAULT,
         NULL,
         NULL,
         g_hInstance,
         NULL
         );

   ShowWindow(hwndMain, SW_SHOW);
   UpdateWindow(hwndMain);

   bRet = TRUE;

   return bRet;
}

BOOL InitApplication(void)
{
   BOOL bRet = FALSE;
   WNDCLASS wc;

   ZeroVar(wc);

   //   Set up information about the class.
   wc.style              = 0;
   wc.lpfnWndProc        = MainWndProc;
   wc.cbClsExtra         = 0;
   wc.cbWndExtra         = 0;
   wc.hInstance          = g_hInstance;
   wc.hIcon              = 0;
   wc.hCursor            = 0;
   wc.hbrBackground      = (HBRUSH)GetStockObject(WHITE_BRUSH);
   wc.lpszMenuName       = NULL;
   wc.lpszClassName      = pszMainWndClassName;

   bRet = RegisterClass(&wc);
   return bRet;
}
```

```
int WINAPI WinMain (
    HINSTANCE hInstance,
    HINSTANCE hPrevInstance,
    LPTSTR    lpCmdLine,
    int nCmdShow
    )
{
    MSG msg;
    g_hInstance = hInstance;

    if ( !InitApplication() )
        {
        goto leave;
        }

    if ( !InitInstance() )
        {
        goto leave;
        }


    while ( GetMessage(&msg, NULL, 0, 0) )
        {
        TranslateMessage(&msg);
        DispatchMessage(&msg);
        }

leave:
    return 0;
}
```

Window Fundamentals

The appearance and behavior of a window is largely determined by its inherent attributes and its relationship to other windows. You assign attributes to a window by setting window styles and extended styles, and by calling functions that alter window attributes.

Windows are always rectangular. They are placed above and below each other along an imaginary line that runs perpendicular to the screen. This stack of windows is called the Z order. Each window has a unique position in the Z order. Windows that appear first in the Z order are considered to be in front of, or on top of, windows that appear later in the Z order. A window's position in the Z order affects its screen appearance. Windows may partially or totally obscure each other depending on their location, size, and position in the Z order.

A window is divided into a *nonclient area*, which is occupied by borders, scroll bars, and various other controls, and a *client area,* which is everything else. You are free to draw in the client area, but not in the nonclient area. In Windows CE, the nonclient area of a window is controlled exclusively by the window manager. Windows CE does not send applications any messages dealing with the nonclient area.

A window may be visible or hidden, depending on whether or not its WS_VISIBLE style is turned on or off. A window that has the WS_VISIBLE style turned off will not be visible on the screen. A window that has the WS_VISIBLE style turned on may or may not be visible on the screen, depending on whether it is obscured by other windows. Covering or uncovering a window with another window does not change the WS_VISIBLE style.

Every window has a unique identifier called a window handle. When you create a window, you receive a window handle, which you can then use to call functions that use the window. Handles are especially useful in applications that create multiple child windows. Applications can change the window's handle by calling the **SetWindowLong** function and retrieve the handle by calling the **GetWindowLong** function.

Window Relationship Fundamentals

When you create a window, you can designate it as a child of another window. A window that has a child is referred to as a parent window. Windows CE has rules governing the display and behavior of parent and child windows. For example, a child window always appears in front of its parent window and can only draw inside its parent window.

Child windows can have their own child windows. A child window that can trace a relationship to a parent window through a chain of parent-child window relationships, however long, is said to be a descendent of the parent window. Likewise, a parent window that can trace a relationship to a child window through a chain of parent-child windows is said to be an ancestor window of that child window. For example, if Window A is the child window of one of Window B's child windows, Window A is a descendent of Window B, and Window B is an ancestor of Window A.

A window that has no parent is called a *top-level window*. Windows that have the same parent are referred to as sibling windows. Even though they may be in different applications, all top-level windows are considered siblings.

A window can be defined as another window's owner. Top-level windows may own other top-level windows. Unlike a window in the parent-child relationship, an owned window is allowed to draw outside of its owner's window.

System-Defined Window Classes

Windows CE includes several system-defined windows classes. Because Windows CE registers these classes, you do not need to; you can immediately create windows with them.

The simplest group of these built-in classes are the controls. Controls provide simple display and user interaction. You generally create controls as child windows of a more complicated window.

Dialog boxes are windows that manage a number of controls. You create them with a template that specifies which controls are to be included in the dialog box. The dialog box then manages the user interaction between the controls and the rest of the program.

Message boxes are specialized dialog boxes. They generally have minimal text and a few buttons. Because the system handles the details of creating and interacting with the dialog box, message boxes are easy to use.

Creating Windows

You create windows with the **CreateWindow** or **CreateWindowEx** function. The only difference between these functions is that **CreateWindowEx** supports the extended style parameter, *dwExStyle*, while **CreateWindow** does not. These functions take a number of parameters that specify the attributes of the window being created.

Note In Windows CE, **CreateWindow** is implemented as a macro which calls **CreateWindowEx**.

Windows CE includes additional functions, including **DialogBox**, **CreateDialog**, and **MessageBox**, for creating special-purpose windows such as dialog boxes and message boxes.

The **CreateWindowEx** function has the following prototype.

```
HWND
CreateWindowEx(
    DWORD       dwExStyle,        //Extended style parameter
    LPCWSTR     lpClassName,      //Class name parameter
    LPCWSTR     lpWindowName,     //Window name parameter
    DWORD       dwStyle,          //Style parameter
    int         X,                //Horizontal parameter
    int         Y,                //Vertical parameter
    int         nWidth,           //Width parameter
    int         nHeight,          //Height parameter
    HWND        hwndParent,       //Parent parameter
    HMENU       hMenu,            //Menu parameter
    HINSTANCE   hInstance,        //Instance handle parameter
    LPVOID      lpParam);         //Creation data parameter
```

The window attributes in **CreateWindowEx** are described in the following table.

Window attributes	Description
Extended style	The dw*ExStyle* parameter specifies one or more window extended styles. These have their own set of WS_EX_* flags and should not be confused with the WS_* flags.
Class name	Every window belongs to a window class. Except for built-in classes, like controls, an application must register a window class before creating any windows of that class. The *lpClassName* parameter specifies the name of the class that is used as a template for creating the window.
Window name	The window name, which is also called window text, is a text string that is associated with a window. The *lpWindowName* parameter specifies the window text for the newly created window. Windows use this text in different ways. A main window, dialog box, or message box typically displays its window text in its title bar. A button control, edit control, or static control displays its window text within the rectangle occupied by the control. A list box, combo box, or scroll bar control does not display its window name. All windows have the text attribute, even if they do not display the text.

Window attributes	Description
Style	The dw*Style* parameter specifies one or more window styles. A window style is a named constant that defines an aspect of the window's appearance and behavior. For example, a window with the WS_BORDER style has a border around it. Some window styles apply to all windows; others apply only to windows of specific window classes. For more information about windows styles, see the "Window Styles" section later in this chapter.
Horizontal and vertical coordinates	The *X* and *Y* parameters specify the horizontal and vertical screen coordinates, respectively, of the window's upper-left corner.
Width and height coordinates	The *nWidth* and *nHeight* parameters determine the width and height of the window in device units.
Parent	The *hwndParent* parameter specifies the parent or the owner of a window, depending on the style flags passed in.
	If neither WS_POPUP nor WS_CHILD is specified, the *hwndParent* parameter may be a valid window handle or NULL. If the parameter is NULL, the new window is a top-level window without a parent or owner. If it is non-NULL, the new window is created as a child of the specified parent window.
	If WS_CHILD is specified, the *hwndParent* parameter must be a valid window handle. The new window is created as a child of the parent window.
	If the WS_POPUP style is specified, the new window is created as a top-level window and the *hwndParent* parameter specifies the owner window. If WS_POPUP is specified, and the parameter is NULL, the new window is partially owned by Windows CE. The WS_POPUP style overrides the WS_CHILD style.
Menu	Windows CE does not support menu bars. In Windows CE, you can use the *hMenu* parameter to identify only a child window. Otherwise, it must be NULL.
Instance handle	The *hInstance* parameter identifies the handle of the specific instance of the application that creates the window.
Creation data	Every window receives a WM_CREATE message when it is created. The *lpParm* parameter is passed as one of the message parameters. Although it can be any value, it is most commonly a pointer to a structure that contains data that may be needed to create a particular window.

The class name for a new window class has to be a Unicode string. You can use the **TEXT** macro to cast a string as Unicode, for example, **TEXT**("classname").

An application uses the **SetWindowText** function to change the window text after it creates the window. It uses the **GetWindowTextLength** and **GetWindowText** functions to retrieve the window text from a window.

Application Windows

An *overlapped window* is a top-level window that is meant to serve as an application's main window. It can also have a command bar, task bars, and scroll bars. An overlapped window used as a main window typically includes all of these components. An application creates an overlapped window by specifying the WS_OVERLAPPED or WS_OVERLAPPEDWINDOW style in the **CreateWindowEx** function.

Because many Windows CE-based devices have small screens, you should use the full screen for your primary window. To accommodate different screen sizes, use either the dimensions returned by the **GetSystemMetrics** function to define the size of your primary window or specify CW_USEDEFAULT in the *nWidth* and *nHeight* parameters that you send to **CreateWindow** or **CreateWindowEx**.

The qualities of an application window depend on the platform for which it was designed. For Windows CE-based platforms that support graphical user interfaces, a typical application window may include a command bar, a client area, and a vertical scroll bar.

The *command bar* is a Windows CE toolbar that can contain menus, controls, and separators. An application's command bar typically contains a menu bar as well as a **Close** (**X**) button, a **Help** (**?**) button, and an **OK** button. Windows CE does not support the **Maximize** or **Minimize** buttons found in Windows-based desktop platforms.

Items on the menu bar represent the main categories of commands. Choosing an item on the menu bar typically opens a pop-up menu whose items correspond to the tasks within a specified category. By choosing a command, the user directs the application to carry out a task. In Windows CE, menu bars are always contained within command bars; Windows CE does not support stand-alone menu bars.

Note In Windows CE, the command bar is considered part of the client area.

A *pop-up window* is a special type of overlapped window used for dialog boxes, message boxes, and other temporary windows that appear outside an application's main window. Title bars are optional for pop-up windows; otherwise, pop-up windows are the same as overlapped windows of the WS_OVERLAPPED style.

You create a pop-up window by specifying the WS_POPUP style in **CreateWindowEx**. To include a title bar, specify the WS_CAPTION style.

Destroying Windows

In general, an application must destroy all the windows it creates. Use the **DestroyWindow** function to destroy a window. When a window is destroyed, the system hides the window, sends a WM_DESTROY message to the window procedure of the window being destroyed, and removes any internal data associated with the window. The window handle becomes invalid and can no longer be used by the application.

Destroying a window automatically destroys the window's descendant windows. The **DestroyWindow** function sends a WM_DESTROY message to the initial window being destroyed and then to its descendant windows. Any windows owned by the window are also automatically destroyed.

You should destroy any window that is no longer needed. Before destroying a window, you should save or remove any data associated with the window and release any system resources allocated for the window. Windows CE releases any resources that you do not release.

Destroying a window does not affect the window class from which the window is created. You can still create new windows by using the class, and any existing windows of that class continue to operate.

Window Styles

Window styles are attributes that are controlled by specific window style flags. There are also extended window styles that have their own set of flags. For this discussion, "window style" refers to the basic window styles, as well as the extended window styles. However, when you write code, you must distinguish between the two. The basic window styles have a prefix of WS_*; the extended styles have a prefix of WS_EX_*.

Most window styles are set when you create a window. There are a few, however, which are sometimes useful to change while a program is running. Use the **SetWindowLong** function to change a window style.

General window styles supported by Windows CE are described in the following table.

Style	Description
WS_CHILD	Specifies a child window. This should not be changed after the window is created.
WS_POPUP	Specifies a pop-up window. This style should not be changed after the window is created.
WS_VISIBLE	Specifies a window that is initially visible. This style can be turned on and off to change window visibility.
WS_DISABLED	Specifies a window that is initially disabled. A disabled window cannot receive input from the user.
WS_CLIPCHILDREN	Excludes the area occupied by child windows when drawing occurs within the parent window. This style is used on the parent window. Windows CE windows always have the WS_CLIPCHILDREN style.
WS_CLIPSIBLINGS	Excludes the area occupied by sibling windows that are above a window.
WS_GROUP	Specifies the first control of a group of controls. This style is used primarily when creating dialog boxes. The group consists of this first control and all controls defined after it, up to the next control for which the WS_GROUP style is specified. Because the first control in each group often has the WS_TABSTOP style, a user can move from group to group.
WS_TABSTOP	Specifies a control that can receive the keyboard focus when the user presses the TAB key. This style is used primarily when creating controls in a dialog box. Pressing the TAB key changes the keyboard focus to the next control with the WS_TABSTOP style.
WS_EX_NOACTIVATE	Specifies that a window cannot be activated. If a child window has this style, tapping it does not cause its top-level parent to activate. Although a window that has this style will still receive stylus events, neither it nor its child windows can get the focus.
WS_EX_NODRAG	Specifies a stationary window that cannot be dragged by its title bar.

Style	Description
WS_EX_NOANIMATION	Prevents a window from showing animated exploding and imploding rectangles and from having a button on the taskbar.
WS_EX_TOPMOST	Creates a window that will be placed and remain above all non-topmost windows. To add or remove this style, use the **SetWindowPos** function.

Note Windows-based desktop platforms do not support the WS_EX_NODRAG, WS_EX_NOACTIVATE, and WS_EX_NOANIMATION styles. These styles are only available in Windows CE.

Nonclient Area Styles

Styles that affect the appearance of the nonclient area of a window are described in the following table.

Style	Description
WS_BORDER	Specifies a window with a thin-line border.
WS_CAPTION	Specifies a window with a title bar and border.
WS_DLGFRAME	Specifies a window with a dialog box border style. A window with this style cannot have a title bar.
WS_HSCROLL	Specifies a window with a horizontal scroll bar.
WS_VSCROLL	Specifies a window with a vertical scroll bar.
WS_OVERLAPPED	Specifies a window with the WS_BORDER and WS_CAPTION styles.
WS_SYSMENU	Specifies a window with a window menu on its title bar. Use in conjunction with the WS_CAPTION style.
WS_EX_CAPTIONOKBTN	Includes an **OK** button in the title bar.
WS_EX_CLIENTEDGE	Specifies a window with a border with a sunken edge.
WS_EX_CONTEXTHELP	Includes a **Help** button (**?**) in the title bar of the window.

Style	Meaning
WS_EX_DLGMODALFRAME	Specifies a window with a double border.
WS_EX_OVERLAPPEDWINDOW	Combines the WS_EX_CLIENTEDGE and WS_EX_WINDOWEDGE styles.
WS_EX_STATICEDGE	Specifies a window with a three-dimensional border style. This style should be used for items that do not accept user input.
WS_EX_WINDOWEDGE	Specifies a window with a border with a raised edge.

Note Windows CE does not have a system menu, but you can use the WS_SYSMENU style to add the standard **Close (X)** button to a window's title bar.

Window Size and Position

A window's size and position are expressed as a bounding rectangle, given in coordinates relative to the screen or to the parent window. The coordinates of a top-level window are relative to the upper-left corner of the screen; the coordinates of a child window are relative to the upper-left corner of the parent window.

For example, a top-level window having the coordinates (10, 10) is placed 10 pixels to the right of the upper-left corner of the screen and 10 pixels down from it. A child window having the coordinates (10, 10) is placed 10 pixels to the right of the upper-left corner of its parent window's client area and 10 pixels down from the upper-left corner of that client area.

When you create a window, you can set the initial size and position of the window directly or direct the system to calculate the initial size and position by specifying CW_USEDEFAULT in the **CreateWindow** or **CreateWindowEx** function. After creating a window, set the window's size or position by calling the **MoveWindow** or **SetWindowPos** function.

If you need to create a window with a client area of a particular size, use the **AdjustWindowRectEx** function to calculate the required size of a window based on the desired size of the client area. Pass the resulting size values to the **CreateWindowEx** function.

Though you can create a window of any size, you should not create one that is larger than the screen on your target device. Before setting a window's size, check the width and height of the screen by using **GetSystemMetrics** with the SM_CXSCREEN and SM_CYSCREEN flags.

You can use the **GetWindowRect** function to retrieve the coordinates of a window's bounding rectangle. **GetWindowRect** fills a **RECT** structure with the coordinates of the window's upper-left and lower-right corners. The coordinates are relative to the upper-left corner of the screen, even for a child window. The **ScreenToClient** or **MapWindowPoints** function maps the screen coordinates of a child window's bounding rectangle to coordinates relative to the parent window's client area.

The **GetClientRect** function retrieves the position and size of a window's client area. Because the coordinates are relative to the client area itself, the client area's upper-left corner is always at location (0, 0) and the coordinates of the lower-right corner are the width and height of the client area. Because the command bar is part of the client area in Windows CE, it is included in the dimensions returned by the **GetClientRect** function.

Use the **WindowFromPoint** function to retrieve the handle to the window that occupies a particular point on the screen. Use the **ChildWindowFromPoint** function to retrieve the handle to the child window that occupies a particular point in the parent window's client area. Use the **ClientToScreen** function to convert the client coordinates of a specified point to screen coordinates. Conversely, use the **ScreentoClient** function to convert the screen coordinates of a specified point into client coordinates.

Use the **SetWindowPos** function to change a window's position in the Z order. This function can place a window at the top of the Z order, at the bottom of the Z order, or behind a specific sibling window. **SetWindowPos** is the primary function for positioning windows. This function can change all aspects of a window's position and visibility.

Topmost Windows

A *topmost window* is a window that has the WS_EX_TOPMOST style. Topmost windows are above all non-topmost sibling windows in the Z order. You can create a topmost window by specifying the WS_EX_TOPMOST style when you create the window. You can also make a window a topmost window by calling the **SetWindowPos** function and setting the *hWndInsertAfter* parameter to HWND_TOPMOST.

A window may lose its topmost style by calling **SetWindowPos** and setting the *hWndInsertAfter* parameter to HWND_NOTOPMOST. If a window is positioned directly after a non-topmost window, then that window loses its WS_EX_TOPMOST style.

Do not confuse topmost with top-level. Top-level refers to whether or not a window has a parent, whereas topmost refers to a specific style that controls the Z order for the window.

You can set the **SetWindowLong** function to give a the window the WS_EX_TOPMOST style. However, this function does not change the window's Z order.

Window Visibility

You can control a window's visibility by using the **ShowWindow** or **SetWindowPos** functions to turn its WS_VISIBLE style on or off. Think of the WS_VISIBLE style as a way to hide a window. If this style is turned off, neither the window nor any of its descendants will be drawn on the screen. In other words, hiding a window hides the window itself, as well as all of its children, all of their children, and so on. Even though a child window is hidden when its parent is hidden, the child window's WS_VISIBLE style is not changed when its parent's style is changed. A child window may have the WS_VISIBLE style turned on and still not be visible, if it has a parent or ancestor window with a WS_VISIBLE style turned off.

You can use the **IsWindowVisible** function to determine whether or not a window is visible. This function checks the window and its ancestors to determine if the window is visible. A window may be considered visible, but may not appear on the screen, if it is covered by other windows.

By default, the **CreateWindowEx** function creates a hidden window, unless you specify the WS_VISIBLE style. Typically, an application sets the WS_VISIBLE style after it has created a window to keep details of the creation process hidden from the user. For example, an application may keep a new window hidden while it customizes the window's appearance.

Changing the visibility of a window does not automatically change the visibility of any windows it owns. Also, if you create a dialog box whose parent window is not visible, the dialog box will be visible. To avoid this inconsistency, do not create a dialog box that is owned by an invisible window.

Window Relationships

The thread and process that create a window own it. Most functions that modify a window will only work if they are called by the thread that created the window. This ownership by a thread or process is not related to the owner-owned relationship between windows.

When a thread or process terminates, Windows CE removes all windows that are owned by that thread or process. Windows that are removed when a thread or process terminates do not always receive WM_DESTROY messages. For this reason, it is a good idea for you to destroy your windows explicitly, rather than depending on the system to do it.

Parent and Child Windows

As previously mentioned, when you create a window, you can designate it as a child of another window by specifying the WS_CHILD style when you call the **CreateWindowEx** function. A child window has only one parent window. A parent can have any number of child windows and these, in turn, can have their own child windows. Use the **IsChild** function to determine whether a window is a descendant window of a specified parent window.

You can change the parent window of an existing child window by calling the **SetParent** function. When you do, the system removes the child window from the client area of the old parent window and moves it to the client area of the new parent window. The **GetParent** function retrieves the handle to a window's parent window.

A child window is always kept directly in front of its parent window. You cannot place a child window behind its parent or other ancestor window. When the Z order or screen position of a window is changed, its children automatically move along with it. A child window is positioned relative to the upper-left corner of its parent's client rectangle.

Although you can place or size a child window outside of a parent window, Windows CE does not allow a child window to draw any part of itself outside of its parent's client rectangle. In Windows CE, a parent window cannot draw on its children, and a window cannot draw on siblings that are in front of it. In other words, all windows behave as if they have the WS_CLIPCHILDREN and WS_CLIPSIBLING styles. You can avoid some of these restrictions by using the **GetDCEx** function.

When you use **DestroyWindow** to destroy a window, its children are destroyed as well.

Owner-Owned Windows

As previously mentioned, one window can own another. In such cases, the window that owns another window is called the owner window, and the window that is owned is called the owned window. Although the relationship between an owner window and an owned window is similar to the relationship between a parent and child window there are some differences. For example, unlike child windows, owned windows can draw outside of their owners.

You can create an owner-owned relationship between top-level windows when you create a window with the WS_POPUP style. Because top-level windows do not have parents, the window that you specify as the parent when you call the **CreateWindow** function becomes the owner of the new window. Owned windows can in turn own other windows. You can use the **GetParent** function to return the owner of a specified window. When a window is destroyed, any windows that it owns are also destroyed.

Owner-owned windows move as a group. If you move a window forward in the Z order, its owner window and owned windows move forward with it. Windows CE keeps owned windows in front of their owners. Although Windows CE does not prevent you from inserting a top-level window between an owner window and an owned window, it does keep owned groups of windows together when one is moved in the Z order. This means that when you change a window's Z order, Windows CE displaces any windows that are between the window and its owned or owner windows. Moving or sizing a window does not affect the location or size of its owner or owned windows.

You can create a WS_POPUP window with a NULL owner. When you do, the window becomes partially owned by the desktop. If Windows CE moves the desktop to the top of the Z order, these windows will remain on top of the desktop. However, if you move the window to the top of the Z order, it does not pull the desktop with it. Threads in the system that do not usually have any kind of window interface use this style when they need to display a message to the user.

Messages and Message Queues

Both Windows CE and applications use messages to communicate with windows. Although messages are generally used to notify a window of particular events, some messages cause the window to perform an action.

Messages consist of a *message identifier* and optional parameters. The term "message" is used to mean either the message identifier or the identifier and the parameters together. The specific meaning is usually clear from the context.

A message identifier is a named constant that identifies a message. When a window procedure receives a message, it uses a message identifier to determine how to process the message. For example:

WM_CREATE is sent to a window when it is created.

WM_DESTROY is sent to a window when it is destroyed.

WM_PAINT is sent to a window when the window's client area has changed and must be repainted.

Message parameters contain data or the location of data that a window procedure will use to process the message. The meaning and value of the message parameters depend on the message identifier. A message parameter can contain an integer, packed bit flags, a pointer to a structure containing additional data, or other information. A window must check the message identifier to determine how to interpret the message parameters.

Message Queues

The message queue coordinates the transmission of messages for a specified thread. Every thread can have only one message queue. When a message is passed to a window, it is placed on the message queue of the window's thread. The thread receives and dispatches the message.

There are two ways to pass a message to a window. The first is called posting a message; the second is called sending a message. In this section, the term "receiver's message queue" refers to the message queue of the thread that created the receiver window.

Posting Messages

Use the **PostMessage** function to post a message to a window. **PostMessage** combines the message identifier and parameters into a message and places it on the receiver's message queue. Eventually, the receiver's message loop removes the message from the message queue and dispatches it to the appropriate window procedure.

PostMessage is an asynchronous function. Windows CE does not synchronize between the sending thread and the receiving thread for posted messages. When the call to **PostMessage** returns, there is no guarantee that the window procedure for the receiver window has processed the message. In fact, if the message was posted to the same thread, the window procedure definitely has not processed the message.

You can post a message without specifying a window. If you supply a NULL window handle when you call the **PostMessage** function, the message is posted to the queue associated with the current thread. Because no window handle is specified, you must process the message directly from the message loop. This is one way to create a message that applies to the entire application, instead of to a specific window.

Sending Messages

Use the **SendMessage** function to send messages to a window. Unlike **PostMessage**, **SendMessage** is a synchronous function. It does not return until the window procedure of the receiver window has processed the message.

You typically send a message when you want a window procedure to perform a task immediately. The **SendMessage** function sends the message directly to the window procedure of the receiver window. The **SendMessage** function waits until the window procedure completes processing and then returns the message result. Parent and child windows often communicate by sending messages to each other. For example, a parent window that has an edit control as its child window can set the text of the control by sending a message to it. The control can notify the parent window of user-initiated changes to the text by sending messages back to the parent.

If the receiving thread is the same as the sending thread, **SendMessage** calls the window procedure directly. If the receiving thread is a different thread from the sending thread, the two message queues synchronize the message passing. The sending thread does not continue executing until the receiving thread processes the message. The receiving thread does not process the message, if it is not executing a message loop. Consequently, if you send a message to a window in a thread that is not executing a message loop, the sending thread stops responding.

Receiving and Dispatching Messages

A message loop that receives and dispatches messages is the heart of every Windows CE-based application. Every thread that creates a window is continuously receiving messages and dispatching messages to window procedures.

You can use the **GetMessage** function to receive messages. When a thread calls **GetMessage**, Windows CE examines the thread's message queue for incoming messages. Windows CE processes messages in the following order:

1. Windows CE-based checks for messages that were placed on the queue by the **SendMessage** function. After the system removes the message from the queue, it dispatches the message to the appropriate window procedure from within the **GetMessage** function. This is done to guarantee that the sender and receiver message queue remain synchronized. The receiver must call **GetMessage** for the sent messages to be processed.

2. If no sent message is found, Windows CE checks the queue for messages that were placed on the queue by a call to **PostMessage**.

3. If no posted message is found, Windows CE checks the queue for messages that were posted by the user input system.

   By processing user input messages at a lower priority, the system guarantees that each input message and any posted messages that result from it are processed completely before moving on to the next input message.

4. If no posted input messages are found, Windows CE checks the queue for WM_QUIT messages that were placed on the queue by a call to **PostQuitMessage**.

5. If no posted quit messages are found, Windows CE checks the queue for WM_PAINT messages that were placed on the queue by the windowing system.

6. If no paint messages are found, Windows CE checks the queue for WM_TIMER messages that were placed on the queue by the timer system.

When **GetMessage** receives any of the previous messages, it returns the message content. It is then the responsibility of the thread to call **DispatchMessage** to dispatch the message to the correct window procedure. If the message is a WM_QUIT message, the return value of **GetMessage** is zero, which causes the thread to end its message loop.

The system dispatches messages in the **GetMessage** call of the message loop, and the application dispatches messages by using the **DispatchMessage** function in the message loop. Windows CE handles the details of finding the window procedure of the receiver window.

Processing Intermediate Messages

You may need to process some of the messages you receive from **GetMessage** before you send them out using **DispatchMessage**. The most common processing routines are **TranslateMessage**, **TranslateAccelerator**, and **IsDialogMessage**. Some of these routines can dispatch messages internally because the application no longer needs to call **DispatchMessage** in the main message loop.

You usually call **TranslateMessage** before you call **DispatchMessage**. **TranslateMessage** determines which characters go with keyboard messages. **TranslateMessage** posts the characters to the message queue to be picked up on the next pass of the message loop.

Use the **TranslateAccelerator** function to intercept keyboard messages and generate menu commands. Use the **IsDialogMessage** function to ensure the proper operation of modeless dialog boxes.

You can remove a message from its queue with the **GetMessage** function. Use the **PeekMessage** function to examine a message without removing it from its queue. This function fills an **MSG** structure with information about the message. However, you should use the **PeekMessage** function carefully. Because the **PeekMessage** function does not block waiting for a message, it is commonly used in loops in Windows-based desktop platforms. This allows an application to continue processing whether or not there are any messages in its queue. In a Windows CE-based application, if an application does not block waiting for a message or some other event, the kernel cannot put the CPU into low-power mode, which can quickly drain the device's batteries. Also, in Windows CE, **PeekMessage** does not remove WM_PAINT messages.

Messages and the Window Procedure

A window procedure is a function that receives and processes all messages sent to the window. The window procedure in the sample program at the beginning of this chapter was called the **MainWndProc**. Every window class has a window procedure, and every window created with that class initially uses the same window procedure to respond to messages. Although you can set the window procedure for an individual window after the window is created, this is a more advanced programming technique.

The system sends a message to a window procedure by passing the message data as arguments to the procedure. The window procedure then performs an appropriate action for the message; it checks the message identifier and, while processing the message, uses the information specified by the message parameters.

A window procedure rarely ignores a message. If it does not process a message, it should pass the message along for default processing. The window procedure does this by calling the **DefWindowProc** function, which performs a default action and returns a message result. The window procedure must then return this value as its own message result. Most window procedures process just a few messages and pass the others on to **DefWindowProc**.

Window procedures can be, and often are, shared by more than one window. The handle of the specific window receiving the message is available as an argument of the window procedure.

Message Types

Windows CE supports both system-defined messages and application-defined messages. System-defined messages have message identifiers ranging from 0 to 0x3ff. Messages with message identifiers ranging from 0x400 to 0x7fff are available for application-defined messages.

There are two types of system-defined messages: general window messages, which are used for all windows, and special purpose messages, which apply to a particular class of windows. General window messages cover a wide range of information and requests, including messages for stylus and keyboard input and window creation and management.

The prefix of the symbolic constant for the message generally identifies the category to which the message belongs. For example, general window messages all start with WM, whereas messages that apply only to button controls start with BM.

Message types supported by Windows CE are described in the following table.

Message prefix	Description
BM	Button message
BN	Button notification
CB	Combo box message
CBN	Combo box notification
CDM	Common dialog box message
CDN	Common dialog box notification
CPL	Control panel message
DB	Object store message
DM	Dialog box default push button message
DTM	Date time picker and HTML viewer messages
DTN	Date time picker notification
EM	Edit control message
EN	Edit control notification
HDM	Header control message
HDN	Header control notification
IMN	Input context message
LB	List box control message
LBN	List box notification
LINE	Line device message
LVM	List view message
LVN	List view notification
MCM	Month calender message
MCN	Month calendar notification
NM	Messages sent by a variety of controls
PBM	Progress bar message
PSM	Property sheet message
PSN	Property sheet notification
RB	Rebar message
RBN	Rebar notification
SB	Status bar window message
SBM	Scroll bar message
STM	Static bar message
STN	Static bar notification
TB	Toolbar message

Message prefix	Description
TBM	Trackbar message
TBN	Trackbar notification
TCM	Tab control message
TCN	Tab control notification
TVM	Tree view message
TVN	Tree view notification
UDM	Up-down control message
UDN	Up-down control notification
WM	General window messages

You can define your own messages for use by your own windows. If you create your own messages, be sure that the window procedure that receives them interprets and processes them correctly. The operating system makes no attempt to interpret application-defined messages.

In some situations, you need to use messages to communicate with windows that are controlled by other processes. In this situation, call the **RegisterWindowMessage** function to register a message identifier. The message number returned by this function is guaranteed to be unique throughout the system. By using this function, you prevent the conflicts that can arise if different applications use the same message identifier for different purposes.

Windows CE defines a WM_HIBERNATE message to notify an application when system resources are running low. When an application receives this message, it should attempt to release as many resources as possible. Every Windows CE-based application that uses even moderate amounts of system resources should implement a handler for the WM_HIBERNATE message.

Note If an application's window is not visible, it cannot receive a WM_HIBERNATE message. This is because the WM_HIBERNATE message is only sent to applications that have a button on the taskbar, which only visible windows do. A window that is hidden will not get this message, even if it is a top-level, overlapped window.

Windows CE does not support hooking messages because the extra processing required by hooks could seriously degrade the performance of Windows CE-based devices.

Timers

A timer is a system resource that can notify an application at regular intervals. An application associates a timer with a window and sets the timer for a specific time-out period. Each time the specified interval, or *time-out value*, for a specified timer elapses, the system uses a WM_TIMER message to notify the window associated with the timer. Because the accuracy of a timer depends on the system clock rate and how often the application retrieves messages from the message queue, the time-out value is only approximate. The smallest possible interval a timer can measure is the system tick interval.

Use the **SetTimer** function to create a timer. The timer can be associated with a particular window or with just the thread. If you associate the timer with a window, then message loop processing will cause the WM_TIMER message to be dispatched to the window's window procedure. If you do not associate the timer with a window, you must design the message loop to recognize and handle the WM_TIMER message.

If the call to **SetTimer** includes a **TimerProc** callback function, the procedure is called when the timer expires. This call is done inside the **GetMessage** or **PeekMessage** function. This means that a thread must be executing a message loop to service a timer, even if you are using a timer callback procedure.

A new timer starts timing its interval as soon as it is created. An application can change a timer's time-out value by using the **SetTimer** function, and it can destroy a timer by using the **KillTimer** function. To use system resources efficiently, applications should destroy timers that are no longer necessary.

You can use the timer and window identifiers to identify timers associated with a window. You can identify timers that are not associated with a particular window by using the identifier returned by the **SetTimer** call.

Timer messages have a low priority in the message queue. Although you know that the window associated with a timer is notified sometime after the timer interval expires, you cannot know the exact time it will receive the notification.

Timers expire at regular intervals, but a timer that expires multiple times before being serviced does not generate multiple WM_TIMER messages.

Rectangles

Windows CE uses rectangles to specify clipping regions, identify portions of the client area that need to be repainted, and define areas for displaying text and graphics among other things. Use a **RECT** structure to define a rectangle. The structure specifies the coordinates of two points: the upper-left and lower-right corners of the rectangle. The sides of the rectangle extend from these two points and are parallel to the x-axis and the y-axis.

Because applications can use rectangles for many different purposes, the Windows rectangle functions do not use an explicit unit of measure. Instead, all rectangle coordinates and dimensions are given in signed, logical values. The function in which the rectangle is used determines the unit of measure.

The **SetRect** function creates a rectangle, the **CopyRect** function makes a copy of a specified rectangle, and the **SetRectEmpty** function creates an empty rectangle. An empty rectangle is any rectangle that has zero width, zero height, or both. The **IsRectEmpty** function determines whether a specified rectangle is empty. The **EqualRect** function determines whether two rectangles are identical — that is, whether they have the same coordinates.

The **InflateRect** function increases or decreases the width or height of a rectangle or both. The **OffsetRect** function moves a rectangle by a specified amount. The **PtInRect** function determines whether a specified point lies within a specified rectangle. The point is in the rectangle if it lies on the left or top edge of the rectangle or is completely within the rectangle. The point is not in the rectangle if it lies on the right or bottom edge. The **IntersectRect** function creates a new rectangle that is the intersection of two existing rectangles. The **UnionRect** function creates a new rectangle that is the union of two existing rectangles.

C H A P T E R   1 0

Overview of Controls

In Windows CE, a *control* is a child window that an application uses in conjunction with another window to perform simple input and output (I/O) tasks. Controls are most often used within dialog boxes, but they can also be used in other windows. Controls offer users a familiar interface, making applications easier to use and learn.

Windows CE defines two basic kinds of controls: *windows controls* and *common controls*. Windows controls, which include buttons, combo boxes, edit controls, list boxes, scroll bars, and static controls, all send WM_COMMAND messages. Common controls, which include most other controls, generally send a WM_NOTIFY message, though a few send WM_COMMAND messages as well.

To use windows controls, you must include either the Windows.h or the Winuser.h header file in your application (Windows.h includes Winuser.h). To use most of the common controls, you must include the Commctrl.h header file in your application. To use property sheets, which are a type of common control, you must include the Prsht.h header file.

You can use macros to send messages for both common and windows controls. For more information about message-related macros, see the appendix "Lists of Functions and Interfaces."

Windows CE currently supports the *HTML viewer control*, which is neither a standard windows control nor a common control. The HTML viewer control provides a simple interface for rendering HTML text, displaying embedded images, and notifying the application of user events.

Overview of Windows Controls

A windows control is a predefined child window that enables a user to make selections, carry out commands, and perform input and output tasks. When Windows creates controls for a dialog box, each control is the child of the dialog box. When an application creates a control, the control is the child of a window identified by the application. A control sends messages, called *notification messages*, to its parent window when the control is manipulated by the user. The application relies on these notification messages to determine what action the user wants the application to take.

Controls are most often used within dialog boxes, but they can also be used in other windows. Controls within dialog boxes provide the user with the means to type text, select options, and direct a dialog box to complete its action. Controls in other windows provide a variety of services, such as letting the user choose commands, scroll down the screen, and view and edit text.

Windows CE supports the following windows controls:

Check Boxes

Combo Boxes

Edit Controls

Group Boxes

List Boxes

Push Buttons

Radio Buttons

Scroll Bars

Static Controls

You can create windows controls individually by specifying the name of the window class when calling the **CreateWindowEx** function.

Because controls are windows, you can manipulate them by using the window-management functions, such as **ShowWindow** and **EnableWindow**. If the window class for a control supports control messages, you can also manipulate a control of that class by using the **SendMessage** function to send these messages to the control.

For guidelines on using controls in user interface design, see Chapter 6, "Designing a User Interface for Windows CE."

Predefined Controls

Windows provides several predefined window classes for controls. Controls belonging to these window classes are called *predefined controls*. An application creates a predefined control of a particular type by specifying the appropriate window class name in either the **CreateWindowEx** function or the dialog box template. Predefined window classes are described in the following table.

Window class	Description
BUTTON	Creates a button control, which notifies the parent window when the user clicks the control.
COMBOBOX	Creates a combo box —a combination of list box and edit control — that lets the user select and edit items.
EDIT	Creates an edit control, which lets the user view and edit text.
LISTBOX	Creates a list box, which displays a list from which the user can select one or more items.
SCROLLBAR	Creates a scroll bar control, which lets the user choose scroll direction and distance in a related window.
STATIC	Creates a static control, which often acts as a label for another control. Static controls can display both text and images, such as icons.

Each predefined window class has a corresponding set of *control styles* that enable an application to vary the appearance and behavior of the controls it creates. For example, the BUTTON class supports styles to create push buttons, radio buttons, check boxes, and group boxes. You specify the style when you create the control.

In addition to control styles, each predefined window class has a corresponding set of notification and control messages. Applications rely on the notification messages to determine when the user has provided input to the controls. For example, a push button sends a BN_CLICKED message to the parent window when the user clicks the button. Applications use the control messages to retrieve information from the controls and to manipulate the appearance and behavior of the controls. For example, an application can send a BM_GETCHECK message to a check box to determine whether it currently contains a check mark.

Most programmers make extensive use of predefined controls in dialog boxes and other windows. Because predefined controls offer many capabilities, a full discussion of each is beyond the scope of this chapter.

Custom Controls

You can create custom controls to perform tasks not supported by predefined controls. Windows CE provides the following ways to create custom controls:

- Use owner-drawn buttons, list boxes, and combo boxes.
- Use the subclass procedure to produce a custom control.
- Register and implement an application-defined window class.

Buttons, list boxes, and combo boxes have owner-drawn styles available that direct the control to send a message to the parent window whenever the control must be drawn. This feature enables you to alter the appearance of a control. For buttons, the owner-drawn style affects how the system draws the entire control. For list boxes and combo boxes, the parent window draws the items within the control, and the control draws its own outline.

You can designate list boxes, combo boxes, and buttons as owner-drawn controls by creating them with the appropriate style. When a control has the owner-drawn style, Windows CE handles the user's interaction with the control as usual, performing such tasks as detecting when a user has chosen a button and then notifying the button's owner of the event. However, because the control is owner-drawn, the parent window of the control is responsible for the visual appearance of the control.

You can use the subclass procedure to create a custom control. The subclass procedure alters selected behaviors of the control by processing those messages that affect the selected behaviors. All other messages pass to the original window procedure for the control.

You can create custom controls by registering an application-defined window class and specifying the name of the window class in the **CreateWindowEx** function or in the dialog box template. The process for registering an application-defined window class for a custom control is the same as for registering a class for an ordinary window. Each class must have a unique name, a corresponding window procedure, and other information.

At a minimum, the window procedure draws the control. If an application uses the control to let the user type information, the window procedure also processes input messages from the keyboard and stylus and sends notification messages to the parent window. In addition, if the control supports control messages, the window procedure processes messages sent to it by the parent window or other windows. For example, controls often process the WM_GETDLGCODE message sent by dialog boxes to direct a dialog box to process keyboard input in a specified way.

Control Notification Messages

A control sends a notification message to its parent window to notify the parent about user input or changes to the control. The notification message is a WM_COMMAND message that includes a control identifier and a notification code identifying the nature of the event. A *control identifier* is a unique number that the application uses to identify the control sending the message. In Windows CE, control identifiers are only valid for child windows.

The application sets the identifier for a control when it creates the control. The application specifies the identifier either in the *hMenu* parameter of the **CreateWindowEx** function or in the **id** member of the dialog box template, which is the **DLGITEMTEMPATE** structure.

A control must retrieve its identifier before it can send notification messages. A control can use the **GetDlgCtrlID** function to retrieve its control identifier.

Control Messages

A parent window or other windows send control messages to direct a control to perform specific tasks. The window procedure processes these messages and carries out the requested action.

Control messages can be predefined or application-defined. Windows has several predefined messages, such as WM_GETTEXT and WM_GETDLGCODE, that it sends to controls. These messages typically correspond to window-management functions that carry out actions on windows. The window procedure for an application-defined control processes any predefined control message that affects the operation of the control. Such messages are described in the following table.

Message	Recommendation
WM_GETDLGCODE	Process if the control uses the ENTER, ESC, TAB, or arrow keys. The **IsDialogMessage** function sends this message to controls in a dialog box to determine whether to process the keys or pass them to the control.
WM_GETFONT	Process if the WM_SETFONT message is also processed.
WM_GETTEXT	Process if the control text is not the same as the title specified by the **CreateWindowEx** function.
WM_GETTEXTLENGTH	Process if the control text is not the same as the title specified by the **CreateWindowEx** function.
WM_KILLFOCUS	Process if the control displays a caret, a focus rectangle, or another item to indicate that it has the input focus.

Message	Recommendation
WM_SETFOCUS	Process if the control displays a caret, a focus rectangle, or another item to indicate that it has the input focus.
WM_SETTEXT	Process if the control text is not the same as the title specified by the **CreateWindowEx** function.
WM_SETFONT	Process if the control displays text. Windows CE sends this message when creating a dialog box that has the DS_SETFONT style.

Because an application-defined control message is specific to the designated control, you must explicitly send it to the control by using the **SendMessage** or **SendDlgItemMessage** function. The numeric value for each message must be unique and must not conflict with the values of other window messages.

Overview of Common Controls

Common controls are a set of windows that are supported by the common control library, which is a dynamic-link library (DLL) included with the Windows operating system. Like other control windows, a common control is a child window that an application uses in conjunction with another window to perform I/O tasks.

Common controls offer users a familiar interface for performing common tasks, which makes applications easier to use and learn. Most common controls send the WM_NOTIFY message instead of the WM_COMMAND message sent by Windows Controls.

To use most of the common controls, you must include the Commctrl.h header file in your application. To use property sheets, you must include the Prsht.h header file.

Before you can create or use any common controls, you have to register them. You can do this in either of two ways. You can call the **InitCommonControls** function, which registers all the common controls at once, except for the rebar, month calendar, and date and time picker controls. Or, you can call the **InitCommonControlsEx** function, which registers a specific common control class. Calling either of these functions ensures that the common DLL is loaded.

Windows CE supports the following common controls:

Command bands

Command bars

Date and time picker

Header controls

Image lists

List views

Month calendar controls

Progress bars

Property sheets

Rebars

Status bars

Tab controls

Toolbars

ToolTips

Trackbars

Tree views

Up-down controls

Windows CE does not support the following controls commonly used on Windows-based desktop platforms: animation controls, ComboBoxEx controls, drag lists, flat scroll bars, hot keys, Internet Protocol (IP) address controls, or rich edit controls. Windows CE supports ToolTips only for toolbar and command bar buttons.

For general guidelines on using common controls in user interface design, see Chapter 6, "Designing a User Interface for Windows CE."

Common Control Styles

Though Windows CE supports some styles that apply to a broad spectrum of common controls, each of the common controls also has a set of styles that are unique to that control. Unless noted otherwise, these unique styles apply to header controls, toolbar controls, rebars, and status windows.

Common control styles supported by Windows CE are described in the following table.

Style	Description
CCS_ADJUSTABLE	Enables a toolbar's built-in customization features, which allow the user to drag a button to a new position or to remove a button by dragging it off the toolbar. In addition, the user can double-click the toolbar to display the **Customize Toolbar** dialog box, which allows the user to add, delete, and rearrange toolbar buttons.
CCS_BOTTOM	Causes the control to position itself at the bottom of the parent window's client area and sets the width of the control to be the same as the parent window's width. Status windows have this style by default.
CCS_NODIVIDER	Prevents a 2-pixel highlight from being drawn at the top of the control.
CCS_NOMOVEY	Causes the control to resize and move itself horizontally, but not vertically, in response to a WM_SIZE message. Header windows have this style by default. This style does not apply if your control has the CCS_NORESIZE style.
CCS_NOPARENTALIGN	Prevents the control from automatically moving to the top or bottom of the parent window. Instead, the control keeps its position within the parent window despite changes to the size of the parent. If the application also uses the CCS_TOP or CCS_BOTTOM styles, it adjusts the height to the default, but does not change the position and width of the control.
CCS_NORESIZE	Prevents the control from using the default width and height when setting its initial size or a new size. Instead, the control uses the width and height specified in the request for creation or sizing.
CCS_TOP	Causes the control to position itself at the top of the parent window's client area and matches the width of the control to the width of the parent window. Toolbars have this style by default.
CCS_LEFT	Causes the control to display vertically on the left side of the parent window.
CCS_RIGHT	Causes the control to display vertically on the right side of the parent window.

Style	Description
CCS_NOMOVEX	Causes the control to resize and move itself vertically, but not horizontally, in response to a WM_SIZE message. This message does not apply if your control has the CCS_NORESIZE style.
CCS_VERT	Causes the control to display vertically.

Custom Draw Services

Windows CE supports the custom draw service. The custom draw service is not a common control; it is a service that makes it easy to customize a common control's appearance. You can use it to change a common control's color or font, or to partially or completely draw the control.

A common control that supports the custom draw service provides this service by sending an NM_CUSTOMDRAW notification at specific times during drawing operations. The *lParam* of the NM_CUSTOMDRAW notification is a reference to an **NMCUSTOMDRAW** structure. If the control is a list view, it uses the **NMLVCUSTOMDRAW** structure; if it's a tree view, it uses the **NMTVCUSTOMDRAW** structure. This structure contains information that the application can use to determine how to draw the control. The following common controls can provide the custom draw service:

  Command bands

  Header controls

  List views

  Toolbars

  Trackbars

  Tree views

For information about custom draw services for common controls, see the "Paint Cycles, Drawing Stages, and Notification Messages" and "Using Custom Draw Services" sections later in this chapter.

Paint Cycles, Drawing Stages, and Notification Messages

Like all Windows-based applications, common controls paint and erase themselves based on messages received from the system or other applications. The process of a control painting or erasing itself is called a paint cycle. Controls that support custom draw send NM_CUSTOMDRAW notification messages periodically throughout each paint cycle. This notification message is accompanied by an **NMCUSTOMDRAW** structure or another structure that contains an **NMCUSTOMDRAW** structure as its first member.

In addition to other information, the **NMCUSTOMDRAW** structure informs the parent window about what stage of the paint cycle the control is in. This is referred to as the draw stage, and is represented by the value in the structure's **dwDrawStage** member. A control informs its parent about four basic, or global, draw stages. The flag values, defined in Commctrl.h, that represent these stages in the structure are described in the following table.

Global draw stage value	Description
CDDS_PREPAINT	Before the paint cycle begins.
CDDS_POSTPAINT	After the paint cycle is complete.
CDDS_PREERASE	Before the erase cycle begins.
CDDS_POSTERASE	After the erase cycle is complete.

Each of the preceding values can be combined with the CDDS_ITEM flag to specify draw stages for items. Item-specific values contained in Commctrl.h are described in the following table.

Item-specific draw stage value	Description
CDDS_ITEMPREPAINT	Before an item is drawn.
CDDS_ITEMPOSTPAINT	After an item has been drawn.
CDDS_ITEMPREERASE	Before an item is erased.
CDDS_ITEMPOSTERASE	After an item has been erased.

You must process the **NM_CUSTOMDRAW** notification message and then return a specific value that informs the control what it must do.

Using Custom Draw Services

The key to harnessing custom draw functionality is in responding to the NM_CUSTOMDRAW notification messages that a control sends. The return values your application sends in response to these notifications determine the control's behavior for that paint cycle.

This section contains information about how your application can use NM_CUSTOMDRAW notification return values to determine the control's behavior. Use the NM_CUSTOMDRAW notification message for:

- Responding to the prepaint notification
- Requesting item-specific notifications
- Drawing the item yourself
- Changing fonts and colors

Responding to the Prepaint Notification

At the beginning of each paint cycle, the control sends the NM_CUSTOMDRAW notification message, which specifies the CDDS_PREPAINT value in the **dwDrawStage** member of the accompanying **NMCUSTOMDRAW** structure. The value that your application returns to this first notification dictates how and when the control sends subsequent Custom Draw notifications for the rest of that paint cycle. In response to the first notification, your application can return a combination of flags, as described in the following table.

Return value	Effect
CDRF_DODEFAULT	The control draws itself. It does not send additional NM_CUSTOMDRAW messages for this paint cycle. This flag cannot be used with any other flag.
CDRF_NOTIFYITEDRAW	The control notifies the parent of any item-specific drawing operations. It sends NM_CUSTOMDRAW notification messages before and after it draws items.

Requesting Item-Specific Notifications

If your application returns CDRF_NOTIFYITEMDRAW to the initial prepaint custom draw notification, the control sends notifications for each item it draws during that paint cycle. These item-specific notifications have the CDDS_ITEMPREPAINT value in the **dwDrawStage** member of the accompanying **NMCUSTOMDRAW** structure. Your application can request that the control send another notification when it is done drawing the item by returning CDRF_NOTIFYPOSTPAINT to these item-specific notifications. Otherwise, your application can return CDRF_DODEFAULT and the control will not notify the parent window until it starts to draw the next item.

Drawing the Item

If your application draws the item, it should return CDRF_SKIPDEFAULT. This allows the control to skip items that it need not draw, which conserves system resources. Keep in mind that returning this value means that the control will not draw any portion of the item, so your application must draw any item images.

Changing Fonts and Colors

Your application can use custom draw to change an item's font. To do this, select the HFONT you want into the device context specified by the **hdc** member of the **NMCUSTOMDRAW** structure associated with that notification. Because the font you select might have different metrics than the default font, be sure that you include the CDRF_NEWFONT bit in the return value for the notification message. For more information on using this functionality, see the sample code in the "Sample Custom Draw Function" section later in this chapter.

The font that your application specifies is used to display that item when it is not selected. Custom draw does not allow you to change the font attributes for selected items.

Sample Custom Draw Function

The following code example shows how an application-defined function processes custom draw notification messages sent by a child list view control. Upon receiving the prepaint notification CDDS_PREPAINT, the function requests item-specific notifications by returning CDRF_NOTIFYITEMDRAW. When it receives the subsequent item-specific notifications, it selects a previously created font into the provided device context and specifies new colors before returning CDRF_NEWFONT.

```
LRESULT DoNotify(HWND hwnd, UINT msg, WPARAM wParam, LPARAM lParam)
{
    LPNMLISTVIEW  pnm    = (LPNMLISTVIEW)lParam;

    switch (pnm->hdr.code){
        case NM_CUSTOMDRAW:{
            LPNMLVCUSTOMDRAW  lplvcd = (LPNMLVCUSTOMDRAW)lParam;

            if(lplvcd->nmcd.dwDrawStage == CDDS_PREPAINT)
                return CDRF_NOTIFYITEMDRAW;

            if(lplvcd->nmcd.dwDrawStage == CDDS_ITEMPREPAINT){
                if(!(lplvcd->nmcd.dwItemSpec % 3))
                    SelectObject(lplvcd->nmcd.hdc, g_hNewFont);
                else
                    return(CDRF_DODEFAULT);

                lplvcd->clrText = RGB(150, 75, 150);
                lplvcd->clrTextBk = RGB(255,255,255);

                return CDRF_NEWFONT;
                }
            }

        default:
            break;
    }

    return 0;
}
```

HTML Viewer Control

The Hypertext Markup Language (HTML) viewer control provides a viewer for displaying HTML text and embedded images. The HTML viewer provides the functionality required to implement Microsoft® Pocket Internet Explorer and the Help engine.

You can also create other viewers based on the HTML viewer control. An HTML source can include references to other sources, which may provide different types of data. If the application determines that some of the data it retrieves is of a type other than HTML, it can invoke another type of viewer to display that data.

To use the HTML viewer control, you must include the Htmlctrl.h header file and either link your application with the Htmlview.dll dynamic link, or load the HTML viewer DLL by calling the **LoadLibrary** function. When you call **LoadLibrary**, pass "Htmlview.dll" as the *lpLibFileName* parameter.

Before you can create or use the HTML viewer control, you have to register it by calling the **InitHTMLControl** function. You create an HTML viewer control by specifying DISPLAYNAME in the *lpClassName* parameter to the **CreateWindow** function.

▶ **To create the HTML viewer control**

1. Load the HTML viewer DLL by calling the **LoadLibrary** function, specifying "Htmlview.dll" in the *lpLibFileName* parameter.

2. Register the HTML viewer control class by calling the **InitHTMLControl** function.

3. Create a window for the HTML viewer control by calling the **CreateWindow** function, specifying DISPLAYNAME in the *lpClassName* parameter.

▶ **To display an HTML document**

1. Clear the current contents of the HTML viewer control by sending it a WM_SETTEXT message.

2. Load an HTML document and copy the document's text to the control by sending the control a series of DTM_ADDTEXT messages for ASCII or DTM_ADDTEXTW messages for Unicode.

3. When the document processing is complete, send the control a DTM_ENDOFSOURCE message.

4. Process any NM_HOTSPOT notifications sent by the control when the user taps a link or submits a form.

5. For each NM_INLINE_IMAGE notification received from the control, load the image so that the HTML viewer control will display the image-loading icon.

6. After the image has loaded successfully, send the control a DTM_SETIMAGE message containing the bitmap handle (HBITMAP) of the image to display.

   If the image does not load successfully, send a DTM_IMAGEFAIL message, which indicates to the control that it should display the broken image icon.

7. For each NM_INLINE_SOUND notification received from the control, load the sound, and then play it the number of times indicated in the *dwLoopCount* parameter.

The following code example shows how to create an HTML viewer control.

```
#define DISPLAYCLASS  TEXT("DISPLAYCLASS")

BOOL g_bMakeFit = TRUE;           // DTM_ENABLESHRINK Shrink-enable flag
TCHAR const c_szHTMLControlLibrary[] = TEXT("htmlview.dll");

HINSTANCE g_hInstHTMLCtrl;        // HTML Control Viewer instance
HINSTANCE hInstance;              // Application instance
HWND m_hwndHtml;                  // Handle to HTML DISPLAYCLASS window

g_hInstHTMLCtrl = LoadLibrary(c_szHTMLControlLibrary);

InitHTMLControl(hInstance);

LRESULT WndProc (HWND hwnd, UINT msg, WPARAM wp, LPARAM lp)
{
   switch (message)
   {
     case WM_CREATE:
     {
        m_hwndHtml = CreateWindow(DISPLAYCLASS, NULL,
           WS_CHILD | WS_VISIBLE | WS_VSCROLL | WS_CLIPSIBLINGS,
           rc.left, rc.top, rc.right - rc.left, rc.bottom - rc.top,
           hWnd, (HMENU)IDC_HTMLVIEW, g_hInst, NULL);
        SetFocus(m_hwndHtml);
        PostMessage(m_hwndHtml, DTM_ENABLESHRINK, 0, g_bMakeFit);
        break;
     }
        .
        .
        .
   }
}
```

Note When calling the **LoadLibrary** and **CreateWindow** functions, the library or class name has to be a Unicode string. Use the **TEXT** macro to cast a string as Unicode, for example, **TEXT**("Htmlview.dll").

Pocket Internet Explorer is an example of an application that uses the HTML viewer control. The application (Webview.exe) links with the dynamic-link library that provides the HTML viewer control (Htmlview.dll). The application provides the user interface, retrieves the data from the Uniform Resource Locators (URL), and interprets the data.

The following illustration describes how the application interacts with the HTML viewer control.

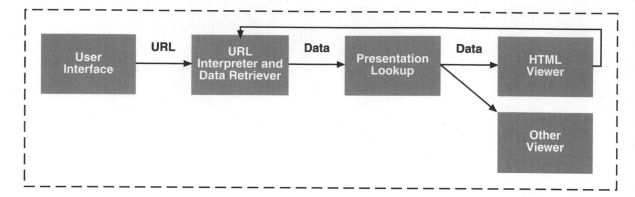

Interaction between the application and HTML viewer control

Note The HTML viewer control interface is not an ActiveX control, and does not expose any COM interfaces.

CHAPTER 11

Foundation Controls

The controls described in this chapter are all common controls that contain or manage other controls. For example, a command bar can contain menus, combo boxes, and buttons. A command band can contain a variety of controls including command bands. All of the controls described in this chapter are designed as containers for other controls.

The following controls are described in this chapter:

- Command bars
- Property sheets
- Rebars
- Command bands
- Tab controls
- Toolbars

Command Bars

A command bar is a toolbar that can include a menu bar as well as the **Close** (**X**) button, the **Help** (**?**) button, and the **OK** button, usually found on the title bar of Windows-based desktop applications. A command bar can contain menus, combo boxes, buttons, and separators. A separator is a blank space you can use to divide other elements into groups or to reserve space in a command bar.

You create a command bar by using the **CommandBar_Create** function. Windows CE registers this class when it loads the common control dynamic-link library (DLL). You can use the **InitCommonControls** function to ensure that this DLL is loaded.

Windows CE command bar

Using Command Bars

You can create a command bar to organize your application's menus and buttons.

▶ **To create a command bar**

1. Initialize an **INITCOMMONCONTROLSEX** structure with ICC_BAR_CLASSES in the **dwICC** member.

2. Register the command bar class by calling the **InitCommonControlsEx** function, and then passing in the **INITCOMMONCONTROLSEX** structure.

3. Create the commands bands control by calling the **CommandBar_Create** function.

4. Add controls to the command bar by calling the **CommandBar_InsertMenubar**, **CommandBar_AddBitmap**, **CommandBar_AddButtons**, and **CommandBar_InsertComboBox** functions.

5. Add the **Close** and **Help** buttons by calling the **CommandBanr_AddAdornments** function and passing CMDBAR_HELP in the *dwFlags* parameter. Windows CE automatically adds the **Close** button.

In addition to creating and registering command bars, you can use command bar functions to perform the following procedures:

- Destroy a command bar.
- Determine a command bar's height.
- Add bitmaps, buttons, and ToolTips to a command bar.
- Insert combo boxes and menu bars into a command bar.
- Determine whether or not a command bar is visible.
- Obtain a handle to a command bar menu or submenu.
- Show or hide a command bar.
- Redraw a command bar.

The window procedure for a command bar automatically sets the size of the command bar and positions it along the top of the parent window's client area. It also destroys the command bar when its parent window is destroyed. Use the **CommandBar_Destroy** function to destroy the command bar without destroying the parent window.

Unlike a scroll bar and a status bar, the command bar is part of the client area of your application. To determine the useable portion of the application window, use the **CommandBar_Height** function to retrieve the command bar's height in pixels, and then subtract the height of the command bar from the size of the client rectangle, which you obtain by calling **GetClientRect**.

Use the **CommandBar_AddAdornments** function to add the **Close** button (**X**), the **Help** button (**?**), and the **OK** button to a command bar. Though every command bar must have a **Close** button, the **OK** button and the **Help** button are optional. Do not call the **CommandBar_AddAdornments** function until after you have added all the other elements to the command bar.

A command bar stores the information needed to draw the button images in an internal list, which is empty when the command bar is created. Each image has a zero-based index that you use to associate the image with a button. Use the **CommandBar_AddBitmap** function to add an array of images to the end of the list. This function returns the index of the first new image that was added. The system includes a set of predefined command bar buttons with header files that define constant values for their indexes.

You can add both buttons and ToolTips to your command bar. Use the **CommandBar_InsertButton** function to add a single button or separator to a command bar. Use the **CommandBar_AddButtons** function to add several command bar buttons or separators at once to a command bar. To create a separator, specify TBSTYLE_SEP as the **fsStyle** member of the **TBBUTTON** structure you pass in the *lpButton* parameter. Use the **CommandBar_AddTooltips** function to add ToolTips describing the command bar buttons.

Use the **CommandBar_InsertComboBox** function to create a combo box and insert it into a command bar. This function always creates a combo box with the WS_CHILD and WS_VISIBLE styles. You can specify other supported combo box styles as well.

To insert a menu bar into a command bar, you can use either the **CommandBar_InsertMenubar** or **CommandBar_InsertMenubarEx** function. **CommandBar_InsertMenubar** inserts a menu bar identified by a resource identifier. **CommandBar_InsertMenubarEx** inserts a menu bar identified by either a resource name or menu handle.

Note Each element in a command bar has a zero-based index by which command bar functions can identify it. The leftmost element has an index of zero, the element immediately to its right has an index of one, and so on. When you use any of the **CommandBar_Insert** functions, the menu bar, button, or combo box is inserted to the left of the button whose index you specify in the *iButton* parameter.

Although Microsoft style guidelines recommend that you always have either a command bar or a command bands control in Windows CE-based applications, you can provide users with the option to hide the command bar, as long they can retrieve it. Use the **CommandBar_Show** function to show or hide the command bar. Use the **CommandBar_IsVisible** function to determine whether a command bar is visible.

Use the **CommandBar_GetMenu** function to obtain the handle of a menu bar in a command bar. To obtain the handle of a submenu on the menu bar, use the **GetSubMenu** function.

Call **CommandBar_DrawMenuBar** to redraw the command bar after modifying a menu bar on the command bar. Do not use the **DrawMenuBar** function for menu bars on the command bar.

Note Do not use 0xFFFFFFFF as the command identifier of a command bar control. This identifier is reserved for use by the command bar.

The following code example shows how to create a command bar.

```
INITCOMMONCONTROLSEX icex;
icex.dwSize = sizeof(icex);
icex.dwICC  = ICC_BAR_CLASSES;
InitCommonControlsEx(&icex);

HWND hwndCB, hwnd;

hwndCB = CommandBar_Create(g_hInst, hwndParent, ID_COMMANDBAR);

CommandBar_InsertMenubar(hwndCB, g_hInst, IDM_MAINMENU, 0);

CommandBar_AddBitmap(hwndCB, HINST_COMMCTRL, IDB_STD_SMALL_COLOR, 15,
16, 16);

CommandBar_AddButtons(hwndCB, sizeof(tbButtons)/sizeof(TBBUTTON),
tbButtons);

hwndCombo = CommandBar_InsertComboBox(hwndCB, g_hInst, COMBO_WIDTH,
    CBS_DROPDOWNLIST | WS_VSCROLL, ID_COMBOBOX, 16);

CommandBar_AddAdornments(hwndCB, CMDBAR_HELP, 0);
```

For an example of how to use a command bar in an application, see the Cmdbar sample application described in "Windows CE Sample Applications" in the online Help.

Property Sheets

A property sheet is a system-defined dialog box that you use to view or modify the attributes, or properties, of an object. A property sheet includes a frame, a title bar, and three buttons: **OK**, **Cancel** (**X**), and **Help** (**?**), which are located at the top of the window. To use property sheets, you must include the Prsht.h header file in your application.

A property sheet contains and manages one or more related dialog boxes, called property pages. Each property page has a tab, similar to a tab on a file folder or in a notebook. A user selects a property page by tapping its tab with a stylus. The dialog box procedures for each property page receive notification messages when the user clicks the buttons on that page.

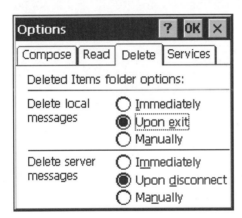

Windows CE property sheet

Property Sheet Pages

Each page in a property sheet is an application-defined modeless dialog box that manages the controls that allow a user to view and edit the properties of an object. A property sheet must contain at least one property page, but cannot contain more than the value of MAXPROPPAGES as defined in the header files.

A property sheet sends notification messages to the dialog box procedure for a page when the page becomes active or inactive and when the user clicks the **OK**, **Cancel** (**X**), or **Help** (**?**) button. The notifications are sent in the form of WM_NOTIFY messages. The *lParam* parameter of the WM_NOTIFY messages points to an **NMHDR** structure, which includes the window handle of the property sheet dialog box.

Some notification messages require that a property sheet page return either TRUE or FALSE in response to the WM_NOTIFY message. To respond, the page must use the **SetWindowLong** function to set the DWL_MSGRESULT value for the page dialog box to either TRUE or FALSE.

Note The dialog box procedure for a page must not call the **EndDialog** function. Doing so will destroy the entire property sheet, not just the page.

Each page has a corresponding label, which the property sheet displays in the tab that it creates for the page. Because all property sheet pages expect you to use a Roman font, not bold, you must ensure that the font is not bold by specifying the DS_3DLOOK style in the dialog box template.

Note Users access property sheets by using an ALT+Tap action. In Windows CE, use ALT+Tap for any operation for which you would use a right-click mouse event on a Windows-based desktop platform.

Using Property Sheets

Before creating a property sheet, you must define one or more pages.

▶ **To define a property sheet page**

1. Create a **PROPSHEETPAGE** structure that contains information about a property sheet's icon, label, dialog box template, dialog box procedure, and other attributes.

2. Call the **CreatePropertySheet** function and pass it a pointer to the **PROPSHEETPAGE** structure. The function returns a **HPROPSHEETPAGE** handle to the property page.

Once you have defined one or more property sheet pages, you can create a property sheet. One way to create a property sheet is to specify the address of a **PROPSHEETHEADER** structure in a call to the **PropertySheet** function. The structure defines the icon and title for the property sheet and also includes a pointer to an array of **HPROPSHEETPAGE** handles. When **PropertySheet** creates the property sheet, it includes the pages identified in the array. The order of the array determines the order of the pages in the property sheet.

Another method to create a property sheet is to specify an array of **PROPSHEETHEADER** structures instead of an array of **HPROPSHEETPAGE** handles. In this case, **PropertySheet** creates handles for the pages before adding them to the property sheet.

The **PropertySheet** function automatically sets the size and initial position of a property sheet. The position is based on the position of the owner window, and the size is based on the largest page specified in the array of pages when the property sheet is created.

After creating a property sheet, you can add and remove pages by using the PSM_ADDPAGE message. Note that the size of the property sheet cannot change after it has been created, so the new page must be no larger than the largest page currently in the property sheet. To remove a page, use the PSM_REMOVEPAGE message. When you define a page, you can specify the address of the **PropSheetPageProc** callback function that the property sheet calls when it creates or removes the page. Using **PropSheetPageProc** allows you to initialize and cleanup individual property sheet pages.

To destroy a page that was created by the **CreatePropertySheetPage** function but was not added to the property sheet, use the **DestroyPropertySheetPage** function. Destroying a property sheet automatically destroys all of the pages that have been added to it. The system destroys the pages in reverse order from that specified in the array used to create the pages.

You specify the title of a property sheet in the **PROPSHEETHEADER** structure that you used to create the property sheet. If the **dwFlags** member includes the PSH_PROPTITLE value, the property sheet adds the prefix "Properties" to the specified title string. Use the PSM_SETTITLE message to change the title after a property sheet has been created.

By default, a property sheet uses the name string specified in the dialog box template as the label for the property page sheet page. You can override the name string by including the PSP_USETITLE value as the **dwFlags** member of the **PROPSHEETPAGE** structure that defines the page. When PSP_USETITLE is specified, the **pszTitle** member must contain the address of the label string for the page.

Active and Inactive Property Sheet Pages

A property sheet can have only one active page at a time. The active sheet is at the top of the overlapping stack of pages. The user activates a page by selecting its tab; an application uses the PSM_SETCURSEL message to activate a page. Before the page that will become the active page is visible, the property sheet sends it the PSN_SETACTIVE notification message. The page should respond by initializing its control windows.

The property sheet determines whether to enable or disable the **Help** button for an active page by checking for the PSP_HASHELP style. If the page has this style, it supports the **Help** button. If the PSP_HASHELP style is not present, it disables the button. When the user clicks the **Help** button, the active page receives the PSN_HELP notification message. The page should respond by displaying help information.

When the user clicks **OK**, the property sheet sends the PSN_KILLACTIVE notification message to the active page, giving it an opportunity to validate the user's changes. If the page determines that the changes are valid, it should call the **SetWindowLong** function to set the DWL_MSGRESULT value for the page to FALSE. In this case, the property sheet sends the PSN_APPLY notification message to each page, directing it to apply the new properties to the corresponding item. If the page determines that the user's changes are not valid, it should set DWL_MSGRESULT to TRUE and display a dialog box informing the user of the problem. The page remains active until it sets DWL_MSGRESULT to FALSE in response to a PSN_KILLACTIVE message.

The property sheet sends the PSN_RESET notification message to all pages when the user clicks the **Cancel** button, indicating that it is about to destroy the property sheet. A page should use the notification to perform cleanup operations.

Note To set the position of a property sheet window in an application, use the **SetWindowPos** function rather than the **MoveWindow** function. Call **SetWindowPos** in the dialog box procedure of the property page that will open first when the user activates a property sheet.

Rebars

A rebar control, which has one or more bands, is a container for child windows. Each band can contain one child window, which can be a toolbar or any other control. Each band can have its own bitmap, which is displayed as a background for the toolbar on that band. A user can resize or reposition a band by dragging its *gripper bar*. If a band has a text label next to its gripper bar, a user can maximize the band and restore it to its previous size by tapping the label with the stylus.

Windows CE rebar

Like other common controls, a rebar control sends WM_NOTIFY messages to its parent window. A rebar control also forwards to its parent window all messages it receives from the child windows assigned to its bands.

You create a rebar control by specifying REBARCLASSNAME in the *lpClassName* parameter to the **CreateWindowEx** function. This class is registered when the common control dynamic-link library (DLL) is loaded. You can use the **InitCommonControlsEx** function to ensure that this DLL is loaded. To register the rebar control class using the **InitCommonControlsEx** function, specify the ICC_COOL_CLASSES flag as the **dwICC** member of the **INITCOMMONCONTROLSEX** structure you pass in the *lpInitCtrls* parameter.

Rebar controls support the Windows CE custom draw service, which makes it easy to customize a rebar control's appearance. For more information on custom draw service, see Chapter 10, "Overview of Controls."

Rebar Styles

Rebar styles supported by Windows CE are described in the following table.

Style	Description
CCS_VERT	Causes the control to appear vertically at the left side of the parent window.
RBS_AUTOSIZE	Specifies that the layout of a band will automatically change when the size or position of its control changes. When the layout changes, the control sends an RBN_AUTOSIZE notification.
RBS_BANDBORDERS	Displays narrow lines to separate adjacent bands.
RBS_FIXEDORDER	Displays multiple bands in the same order at all times. A user can move bands to different rows, but the band order is static.
RBS_SMARTLABELS	Displays the icon for a band that has one only when the band is minimized. If a band has a text label, the label is displayed only when the band is in its restored state or in its maximized state.
RBS_VARHEIGHT	Displays a band at the minimum required height, when possible. Without this style, the command bands control displays all bands at the same height, using the height of the tallest visible band to determine the height of other bands.
RBS_VERTICALGRIPPER	Displays the size grip vertically, instead of horizontally, in a vertical command bands control. This style is ignored for command bands controls that do not have the CCS_VERT style.

Note Windows CE is the only Windows-based platform that supports the RBS_SMARTLABELS style for rebar controls.

Windows CE also supports a rebar band style, called RBBS_NOGRIPPER. When you assign this style to a band in a rebar, the band does not have a gripper. This style applies to individual bands, not to the entire rebar.

Command Bands

The command bands control is a special kind of rebar control. It has a fixed band at the top containing a toolbar with a **Close** (**X**) button, and optionally, a **Help** (**?**) button and an **OK** button, in the right corner. By default, each band in the command bands control contains a command bar. You can override this, however, if you want a band to contain some other type of child window.

Windows CE command band

▶ **To create a command band control**

1. Initialize an **INITCOMMONCONTROLSEX** structure with (ICC_BAR_CLASSES | ICC_COOL_CLASSES) as the **dwICC** member.

2. Register the command bands control class and the command bar class by calling the **InitCommonControlsEx** function, and passing in the **INITCOMMONCONTROLSEX** structure.

3. Create the image list to use for the band images.

4. Create the commands bands control by calling the **CommandBands_Create** function, and then passing the image list handle in the *himl* parameter.

5. Initialize an array of **REBARBANDINFO** structures, one for each band in the command bands control.

6. Add the bands by calling the **CommandBands_AddBands** function, passing the array of **REBARBANDINFO** structures in the *prbbi* parameter.

7. Add controls to the command bars in the bands by calling the appropriate command bar functions for the controls you want to add.

8. Call the **CommandBands_AddAdornments** function to add the **Close** and **Help** buttons. When you do this, the **Close** button is added by default.

The following code example demonstrates how to register a command band and command bar.

```
INITCOMMONCONTROLSEX icex;
icex.dwSize = sizeof(icex);
icex.dwICC = ICC_BAR_CLASSES | ICC_COOL_CLASSES;
InitCommonControlsEx(&icex);

HWND hwndCmdBands, hwnd;
REBARBANDINFO arbbi[2];

HIMAGELIST himl = ImageList_Create(16, 16, ILC_COLOR, 2, 0);
hwndCmdBands = CommandBands_Create(g_hinst, hwndParent, BANDS_ID,
   RBS_VARHEIGHT | RBS_BANDBORDERS, himl);

arbbi[0].cbSize = sizeof(REBARBANDINFO);
arbbi[0].fMask = RBBIM_ID | RBBIM_STYLE| RBBIM_SIZE |   RBBIM_IMAGE;
arbbi[0].fStyle = RBBS_NOGRIPPER ;
arbbi[0].wID = ID_MENUBAND;
arbbi[0].cx = 100;
arbbi[0].iImage = 0;

arbbi[1].cbSize = sizeof(REBARBANDINFO);
arbbi[1].fMask = RBBIM_ID |  RBBIM_IMAGE | RBBIM_SIZE;
arbbi[1].wID = ID_BUTTONBAND;
arbbi[1].cx = 125;
arbbi[1].iImage = 1;

CommandBands_AddBands(hwndCmdBands, g_hinst, 2, arbbi);

hwnd = CommandBands_GetCommandBar(hwndCmdBands, 0);
CommandBar_InsertMenubar(hwnd, g_hinst, IDM_MAINMENU, 0);

hwnd = CommandBands_GetCommandBar(hwndCmdBands, 1);
CommandBar_AddBitmap(hwnd, HINST_COMMCTRL, IDB_STD_SMALL_COLOR, 0, 0,
0);
CommandBar_AddButtons(hwnd, sizeof(tbButtons)/sizeof(TBBUTTON),
tbButtons);

CommandBands_AddAdornments(hwndCmdBands, g_hinst, CMDBAR_HELP, NULL);
```

Command bands controls support the custom draw service, which makes it easy to customize the appearance of a command bands control. For information on the custom draw service, see Chapter 10, "Overview of Controls."

Using Command Bands

Windows CE supports the following functions for creating and manipulating command bands controls.

Use the **CommandBands_AddAdornments** function to add a band with the **Close** (**X**) button, the **Help** (**?**) button, and the **OK** button. This band will always have a **Close** button. The **OK** button and the **Help** button are optional.

Use the **CommandBands_AddBands** function to add one or more bands to the control. By default, each band has a command bar as its child window.

Use the **CommandBands_Create** function to create a command bands control.

You can retrieve a command bar from a band in a command bands control by using the **CommandBands_GetCommandBar** function. Pass it the zero-based index of the band that contains the command bar you want to retrieve.

Unlike scroll bars and status bars, the command bar is part of the client area of your application. To determine the useable portion of the application window, use the **CommandBands_Height** function to retrieve the command bar's height in pixels and subtract the height of the command bar from the size of the client rectangle, which you obtain by calling **GetClientRect**.

Use the **CommandBands_IsVisible** function to determine whether a command bands control is visible.

Use the **CommandBands_GetRestoreInformation** function to retrieve information about the bands in a command band control, before you close the application window, so you can save the information in the registry. The next time the application is opened, you can use this information to restore the command bands control to its previous state.

Although you should always have a command bar or a command bands control in a Windows CE-based application that has a graphical user interface, you can provide users with the option to hide the command bands control, as long as it can be retrieved. Use the **CommandBands_Show** function show or hide the command bands control.

A command band is a rebar control and a toolbar control and can be manipulated using the rebar and toolbar messages.

Tab Controls

A tab control is analogous to a set of dividers in a notebook or labels in a file cabinet. In a property sheet, a user selects a tab to move from one property sheet page to another.

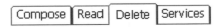

Windows CE tab control

You send messages to a tab control to add tabs and otherwise affect the control's appearance and behavior. Each message has a corresponding macro, which you can use instead of sending the message explicitly. Though you cannot disable an individual tab in a tab control, you can disable a tab control in a property sheet by disabling the corresponding page.

Each tab in a tab control consists of a label and application-defined data. This information is specified by a **TCITEM** structure. You can add tabs to a tab control, get the number of tabs, retrieve and set the contents of a tab, and delete tabs. Tabs are identified by their zero-based index.

Tab Control Styles

Tab control styles supported by Windows CE are described in the following table.

Style	Description
TCS_BOTTOM	Displays the tabs at the bottom of the control. If the TCS_VERTICAL style is also specified, this style is interpreted as TCS_RIGHT.
TCS_BUTTONS	Displays all tabs as buttons with no border drawn around the display area.
TCS_FIXEDWIDTH	Specifies that all tabs are the same width. You can not combine this style with the TCS_RIGHTJUSTIFY style.
TCS_FLATBUTTONS	Changes the appearance of a selected tab to indented while other tabs appear to be on the same plane as the background. This style only applies to tab controls that have the TCS_BUTTONS style.
TCS_FLIP	Flips all tabs from top to bottom or left to right, and visa versa.
TCS_FOCUSNEVER	Creates a tab control that never receives the input focus.
TCS_FOCUSONBUTTONDOWN	Specifies that a tab which, when selected, receives the input focus.

Style	Description
TCS_FORCEICONLEFT	Aligns an icon with the left edge of a fixed-width tab. This style can only be used with the TCS_FIXEDWIDTH style.
TCS_FORCELABELLEFT	Aligns a label with the left edge of a fixed-width tab; that is, it displays the label immediately to the right of the icon instead of centering it. This style can only be used with the TCS_FIXEDWIDTH style, and it implies the TCS_FORCEICONLEFT style.
TCS_MULTILINE	Displays multiple rows of tabs, if necessary, so that all tabs are visible at once.
TCS_MULTISELECT	Specifies that multiple tabs can be selected by holding down CTRL when selecting a tab. This style only applies to tabs that have the TCS_BUTTONS style.
TCS_OWNERDRAWFIXED	Specifies that the parent window is responsible for drawing tabs.
TCS_RAGGEDRIGHT	Leaves a ragged right edge by not stretching a row of tabs to fill the entire width of the control. This style is the default.
TCS_RIGHT	Displays multiple tabs vertically on the right side of controls that use the TCS_VERTICAL style. If the TCS_VERTICAL style is not specified, this style is interpreted as TCS_BOTTOM.
TCS_RIGHTJUSTIFY	Increases the width of each tab, if necessary, so that each row of tabs fills the entire width of the tab control. This style is valid only when used with the TCS_MULTILINE style.
TCS_SCROLLOPPOSITE	Specifies that unused tabs move to the opposite side of the control when a new tab is selected.
TCS_SINGLELINE	Displays only one row of tabs. The user can scroll to see more tabs, if necessary. This style is the default.
TCS_VERTICAL	Displays multiple tabs vertically on the left side of the control. This style is valid only when used with the TCS_MULTILINE style. To make tabs appear on the right side of the control, combine this style with the TCS_RIGHT style.

Because Windows CE does not support ToolTips for any controls other than command bar buttons, it does not support the TCS_TOOLTIPS style.

Extended Tab Control Styles

Windows CE supports two extended tab control styles. The first style uses the TCM_SETEXTENDEDSTYLE message or its corresponding macro, **TabCtrl_SetExtendedStyle**, to set the extended style. It uses the TCM_GETEXTENDEDSTYLE message or its corresponding macro, **TabCtrl_GetExtendedStyle**, to retrieve the extended style.

Note Because an extended tab control style is not the same as an extended window style, you cannot pass an extended tab control style to **CreateWindowEx** when you create a tab control.

The second extended tab control style, TCS_EX_FLATSEPARATORS, draws separators between tab items in tab controls that have the TCS_BUTTONS or TCS_FLATBUTTONS style. When you create a tab control with the TCS_FLATBUTTONS style, this extended style is set by default.

Using Tab Controls

You create a tab control by specifying WC_TABCONTROL in the *lpClassName* parameter to the **CreateWindowEx** function. Windows CE registers this class when it loads the common control DLL. You can use the **InitCommonControls** function to ensure that this DLL is loaded. To register the tab control class using the **InitCommonControlsEx** function, specify the ICC_TAB_CLASSES flag as the **dwICC** member of the **INITCOMMONCONTROLSEX** structure you pass in the *lpInitCtrls* parameter.

To add tabs to a tab control, use the TCM_INSERTITEM message, which specifies the position of the tab and the address of its **TCITEM** structure. You can retrieve and set the contents of an existing tab by using the TCM_GETITEM and TCM_SETITEM messages. For each tab, you can specify an icon, a label, or both. You can also specify application-defined data to associate with the tab.

Other messages that you can use with a tab control are described in the following table.

Message	Description
TCM_GETITEMCOUNT	Retrieves the current number of tabs.
TCM_DELETEITEM	Deletes a tab.
TC_DELETEALLITEMS	Deletes all tabs in a tab control.

You can associate application-defined data with each tab. For example, you might save information about each page with its corresponding tab. By default, a tab control allocates four extra bytes per tab for application-defined data. You can change the number of extra bytes per tab by using the TCM_SETITEMEXTRA message. You can only use this message when the tab control is empty.

The **lParam** member of the **TCITEM** structure specifies application-defined data. If you use more than four bytes of application-defined data, you need to define your own structure and use it instead of **TCITEM**. You can retrieve and set application-defined data the same way you retrieve and set other information about a tab: Use the TCM_GETITEM and TCM_SETITEM messages.

Note Windows CE does not support vertical text. If you create vertical tabs, and want to use vertical text, you have to create a text bitmap and rotate it. Then, you can add the bitmap to an image list and attach it to the tab by specifying its image list index in the **iImage** member of the **TCITEM** or **TCITEMHEADER** structure.

Tab Control Display Area

The tab control display area is the area of the control in which an application displays the current page. An application creates a child window or dialog box to display the current page, and then it sets the window size and position to fit the display area. You can use the TCM_ADJUSTRECT message to calculate a tab control's display area based on the dimensions of a specified rectangle, or to calculate the dimensions of rectangle given the coordinates of a display area.

Tab Control Messages

When the user selects a tab, a tab control sends notification messages to its parent window in the form of WM_NOTIFY messages. The tab control sends the TCN_SELCHANGING notification message before the selection changes, and it sends the TCN_SELCHANGE notification message after the selection changes.

You can process TCN_SELCHANGING to save the state of the outgoing page. You can return TRUE to prevent the selection from changing. For example, you might not want to switch away from a child dialog box in which a control has an invalid setting.

To display the incoming page in the display area, you must process TCN_SELCHANGE. Though processing might entail changing the information displayed in a child window, it will more likely entail destroying or hiding the outgoing child window or dialog box and creating or showing the incoming child window or dialog box.

You can retrieve and set the current table selection by using the TCM_GETCURSEL and TCM_SETCURSEL messages.

Tab Control Image Lists

Each tab can have an icon associated with it. An index specifies the icon into the image list for the tab control. When you create a tab control, it has no image list associated with it. You can use the **ImageList_Create** function to create an image list. You can assign it to a tab control by using the TCM_SETIMAGELIST message.

You can add an image to a tab control's image list just as you would add one to any other image list. To ensure that each tab remains associated with its assigned image, remove images by using the TCM_REMOVEIMAGE message instead of the **ImageList_Remove** function.

Because destroying a tab control does not destroy an image list that is associated with it, you must destroy the image list separately. Retaining the image list may be useful if you want to assign the same image list to multiple tab controls.

To retrieve the handle of the image list currently associated with a tab control, you can use the TCM_GETIMAGELIST message.

Tab Size and Position

Each tab in a tab control has a size and a position. You can set the size of tabs, retrieve the bounding rectangle of a tab, or determine which tab is located at a specified position.

For fixed-width and owner-drawn tab controls, you can set the exact width and height of tabs by using the TCM_SETITEMSIZE message. In other tab controls, you calculate each tab's size based on the icon and label for the tab. The tab control includes space for a border and an additional margin. You can set the thickness of the margin by using the TCM_SETPADDING message.

You use messages and styles to learn about tabs. You can determine the current bounding rectangle for a tab by using the TCM_GETITEMRECT message. You can determine which tab, if any, is at a specified location by using the TCM_HITTEST message. And, in a tab control with the TCS_MULTILINE style, you can determine the current number of rows of tabs by using the TCM_GETROWCOUNT message.

Tab Control Structures

In Windows CE, the **TCITEM** structure replaces the **TC_ITEM** structure that is used by Windows-based desktop platforms. **TCITEM** has two members that are not available in its desktop computer counterpart. The **dwState** member, which contains the item states, replaces the **lpReserved1** member, and the **dwStateMask** member replaces the **lpReserved2** member. The **dwStateMask** member is a bit member that specifies which bits of the value in the **dwState** member are valid. The **mask** member supports a value unique to Windows CE, TCIF_STATE, which indicates whether the **dwState** member is valid. Windows CE structures that have been renamed to conform to windows standard naming conventions are described in the following table. These structures are otherwise the same as the corresponding structures in Windows-based desktop platforms.

Windows CE	Windows-based desktop platforms
TCITEMHEADER	TC_ITEMHEADER
NMTCKEYDOWN	TC_KEYDOWN

Tab Control Item States

Tab control item states supported by Windows CE are described in the following table.

Item state	Description
TCIS_BUTTONPRESSED	The tab control item is selected.
TCIS_HIGHLIGHTED	The tab control item is highlighted and the tab and text are drawn using the current highlight color.

Toolbars

A toolbar is a control that contains buttons. The buttons in a toolbar usually correspond to items on the application's menu, providing a quick way for the user to access these commands. When a user taps a toolbar button with the stylus, the toolbar sends the command message associated with the button to the toolbar's parent window. The Windows CE alternative to the toolbar is the command bar. A command bar combines a menu bar and a toolbar in a single control, which conserves limited screen space.

Windows CE toolbar

You create a toolbar by using the **CreateToolbarEx** function. Windows CE registers this class when it loads the common control DLL. You can use the **InitCommonControls** function to ensure that this DLL is loaded. To register the toolbar class using the **InitCommonControlsEx** function, specify the ICC_BAR_CLASSES flag as the **dwICC** member of the **INITCOMMONCONTROLSEX** structure you pass in the *lpInitCtrls* parameter. You can also use the **CreateWindowEx** function to register the toolbar class by specifying the **TOOLBARCLASSNAME** window class. However, this method creates a toolbar that initially contains no buttons. You can then add buttons to the toolbar by using the TB_ADDBUTTONS or TB_INSERTBUTTON message.

A toolbar must be created as a child window with the WS_CHILD style. If you use **CreateWindowEx** to create a toolbar, you must specify the WS_CHILD window style. **CreateToolbarEx** includes the WS_CHILD style by default. You must specify the initial parent window when creating the toolbar, but you can change the parent window after creation by using the TB_SETPARENT message.

Windows CE does not support user customization of toolbars or drag-and-drop operations for toolbars.

Toolbar Styles

Toolbar styles that are the same in both Windows CE and Windows-based desktop platforms are described in the following table.

Style	Description
TBSTYLE_CUSTOMERASE	Creates a toolbar that generates NM_CUSTOMDRAW notification messages when it processes WM_ERASEBKGND messages.
TBSTYLE_FLAT	Creates a flat toolbar, in which both the toolbar and the buttons are transparent. Button text appears under button bitmaps.
TBSTYLE_LIST	Places button text to the right of button bitmaps. This style can only be used with the TBSTYLE_FLAT style.
TBSTYLE_TRANSPARENT	Creates a transparent toolbar, in which the toolbar is transparent but the buttons are not. Button text appears under button bitmaps.
TBSTYLE_WRAPABLE	Creates a toolbar that can have multiple rows of buttons. Toolbar buttons can wrap to the next line when the toolbar becomes too narrow to include all buttons on the same line. Wrapping occurs on separation and non-group boundaries.

In Windows CE, the TBSTYLE_LIST style creates a toolbar with variable width buttons. If you want to use the TBSTYLE_LIST style with fixed width buttons, you can override the default behavior by sending a TB_SETBUTTONSIZE or TB_SETBUTTONWIDTH message.

Windows CE does not support the TBSTYLE_ALTDRAG style or the TBSTYLE_REGISTERDROP style for toolbars because it does not support drag-and-drop operations.

Note Because Windows CE does not support an actual ToolTip control, you cannot pass it a handle to a ToolTip control. Instead, the TB_SETTOOLTIPS message in Windows CE takes a *wParam*, which is the number of ToolTip strings to associate with the toolbar, and an *lParam*, which is the array of ToolTip strings to associate with the toolbar buttons.

Toolbar Size and Position

The window procedure for a toolbar automatically sets the size and position of the toolbar window. The height is based on the height of the buttons in the toolbar. The width is the same as the width of the parent window's client area. The CCS_TOP and CCS_BOTTOM common control styles determine whether the toolbar is positioned along the top or bottom of the client area. By default, a toolbar has the CCS_TOP style.

The toolbar window procedure automatically adjusts the size of the toolbar whenever it receives a WM_SIZE or TB_AUTOSIZE message. An application should send either of these messages whenever the size of the parent window changes or after sending a message that requires the size of the toolbar to be adjusted, for example, after sending the TB_SETBUTTONSIZE message.

Toolbar Buttons

Toolbar buttons are bit images, not child windows as other buttons are. When a user clicks a toolbar button, the toolbar sends its parent window a WM_COMMAND message with the button's command identifier.

If you want to assign a shortcut key to a toolbar button, you can use the button's ToolTip to let the user know what the shortcut is.

Each button in a toolbar can include a bitmap image. A toolbar maintains an internal list that contains all of the bitmaps that have been assigned to each of its toolbar buttons. When you call the **CreateToolbarEx** function, you specify a monochrome or color bitmap that contains the initial images. The toolbar then adds the information to the internal list of images. You can add additional images later by using the TB_ADDBITMAP message.

Each image has a zero-based index. The first image added to the internal list has an index of zero, the second image has an index of one, and so on. TB_ADDBITMAP adds images to the end of the list and returns the index of the first new image that it added. You use an image's index to associate the image with a button.

Windows CE assumes that all of a toolbar's bitmaps are the same size. You specify the size when you create the toolbar by using **CreateToolbarEx**. If you use the **CreateWindowEx** function to create a toolbar, the size of its bitmaps is set to the default dimensions of 16 x 15 pixels. You can use the TB_SETBITMAPSIZE message to change the dimensions of the bitmaps, but you must do so before adding any images to the internal list of images.

Each button can display a string in addition to, or instead of, an image. A toolbar maintains an internal list that contains all of the strings available to toolbar buttons. You add strings to the internal list by using the TB_ADDSTRING message, specifying the address of the buffer containing the strings to add. Each string must be null-terminated, and the last string must be terminated with two null characters.

Each string has a zero-based index. The first string added to the internal list of strings has an index of zero, the second string has an index of one, and so on. TB_ADDSTRING adds strings to the end of the list and returns the index of the first new string. You use a string's index to associate the string with a button.

Toolbar Button Styles

Toolbar styles that are the same in both Windows CE and Windows-based desktop platforms are described in the following table.

Style	Description
TBSTYLE_BUTTON	Creates a toolbar button that looks like a standard Windows push button.
TBSTYLE_CHECK	Creates a button that toggles between the pressed and not pressed states each time the user clicks it. The button has a different background color when it is in the pressed state.
TBSTYLE_CHECKGROUP	Creates a check button that stays pressed until another button in the group is pressed.
TBSTYLE_GROUP	Creates a button that stays pressed until another button in the group is pressed.
TBSTYLE_AUTOSIZE	Calculates a button's width based on the text of the button, not on the size of the image.

Style	Description
TBSTYLE_DROPDOWN	Creates a drop-down list button.
TBSTYLE_SEP	Creates a separator, which provides a small gap between button groups. A button that has this style does not receive user input.

Toolbar Button States

Each button in a toolbar has a current state that indicates whether the button is hidden or visible, enabled or disabled, and pressed or not pressed. You set a button's initial state when adding the button to the toolbar, and the toolbar updates the button state in response to a user's actions, for example, when the user taps it with the stylus. You can use the TB_GETSTATE and TB_SETSTATE messages to retrieve and set the state of a button.

Toolbar button states that are the same in both Windows CE and Windows-based desktop platforms are described in the following table.

State	Description
TBSTATE_CHECKED	The button has the TBSTYLE_CHECKED style and is being pressed.
TBSTATE_ENABLED	The button accepts user input. A button without this state does not accept user input and is dimmed.
TBSTATE_HIDDEN	The button is not visible and cannot receive user input.
TBSTATE_HIGHLIGHTED	The button is highlighted.
TBSTATE_INDETERMINATE	The button is dimmed.
TBSTATE_PRESSED	The button is being pressed.
TBSTATE_WRAP	The button has a line break following it. The button must also have the TBSTATE_ENABLED state.

The toolbar button state TBSTATE_ELLIPSES is unique to Windows CE. When a button has this style, if its text does not fit the size of the button, the text is cut off and ellipses are displayed.

Toolbar Features

Windows CE supports messages that allow you to customize the look and behavior of toolbars and toolbar buttons.

You can create transparent toolbars by specifying the TBSTYLE_FLAT or TBSTYLE_TRANSPARENT styles. If you give a toolbar the TBSTYLE_FLAT style, the toolbar displays its buttons, but the toolbar itself is transparent. If you give a toolbar the TBSTYLE_TRANSPARENT style, the client area shows through the buttons as well as through the underlying toolbar.

You can use image lists to customize the way a toolbar displays buttons in various states. You can set and retrieve image lists for toolbar buttons by using the TB_GETIMAGELIST and TB_SETIMAGELIST messages for buttons in their default unpressed state, and the TB_GETDISABLEDIMAGELIST and TB_SETDISABLEDIMAGELIST messages for buttons in their disabled state. Use the TB_LOADIMAGES message to load images into a toolbar's image list.

Windows CE supports a toolbar button style called a drop-down button. When a user taps a button that has the TBSTYLE_DROPDOWN style, the toolbar sends a TBN_DROPDOWN notification to its parent window. The parent window usually responds by displaying a pop-up menu or list box under the drop-down button.

Note In Windows CE, the **TBNOTIFY** structure has been renamed **NMTOOLBAR** to conform to standard naming conventions, but the two structures are identical.

Because toolbars in Windows CE support the custom draw service, you have flexibility to customize a toolbar's appearance. If a toolbar provides this service, it sends the new NM_CUSTOMDRAW notification at specific times during drawing operations. The *lParam* of the NM_CUSTOMDRAW notification is a pointer to an **NMCUSTOMDRAW** structure, which contains the information necessary to draw the customized toolbar. For information on the custom draw service, see Chapter 10, "Overview of Controls."

CHAPTER 1 2

File and Scale Controls

Two types of controls are described in this chapter: controls that display and manage files and data, and controls that change scaled values. The file controls allow a user to readily display and manipulate files or other data. The scale controls allow a user to increase or decrease a scaled value. For example, the user can use a trackbar or an up-down control to adjust the volume in an application that includes sound.

The following file and scale controls are described in this chapter.

- Header controls
- Image lists
- List views
- Tree views
- Trackbars
- Up-Down controls

Header Controls

A *header control* is a horizontal window that is usually positioned above columns of data. It is divided into partitions that correspond to the columns, and each partition contains the title for the column below it. The user can drag the dividers between the partitions to set the width of each column. A header can also perform an action, such as sorting the rows of data according to the values in a column the user selects.

Windows CE header control

To create a header control, specify WC_HEADER in the *lpClassName* parameter to the **CreateWindowEx** function. This class is registered when the common control dynamic-link library (DLL) is loaded. Use the **InitCommonControls** function to ensure that this DLL is loaded.

To register the header control class using the **InitCommonControlsEx** function, specify the ICC_ LISTVIEW_CLASSES flag as the **dwICC** member of the **INITCOMMONCONTROLSEX** structure you pass in the *lpInitCtrls* parameter.

Header Control Styles

Header control styles supported by Windows CE are described in the following table.

Style	Description
HDS_BUTTONS	Causes each header item to look and behave like a button. This style is useful if an application carries out a task when the user clicks an item in the header control.
HDS_DRAGDROP	Allows drag-and-drop reordering of header items.
HDS_FULLDRAG	Causes the header control to display column contents even while a user resizes a column.
HDS_HIDDEN	Creates a header control that you can hide by setting its height to zero. This style is useful when you use the control as an information container instead of a visual control.
HDS_HORZ	Creates a horizontal header control.

Header Control Size and Position

Typically, you must set the size and position of a header control to fit within the boundaries of a particular rectangle, such as the client area of a window. By using the HDM_LAYOUT message, you can retrieve the appropriate size and position values from the header control.

When sending the HDM_LAYOUT message, you specify the address of an **HDLAYOUT** structure that contains the coordinates of the rectangle that the header control is to occupy and that provides a pointer to a **WINDOWPOS** structure. The control fills **WINDOWPOS** with size and position values appropriate for positioning the control along the top of the specified rectangle. The height value is the sum of the heights of the control's horizontal borders and the average height of characters in the font currently selected into the control's device context.

Header Control Items

A header control typically has several header items that define the columns of the control. To add an item to a header control, send the HDM_INSERTITEM message to the control. The message includes the address of an **HDITEM** structure. This structure defines the properties of the header item.

The **fmt** member of an item's **HDITEM** structure can include either the HDF_STRING or HDF_BITMAP flag to indicate whether the control displays the item's string or bitmap. If you want to display both a string and a bitmap, create an owner-drawn item by setting the **fmt** member to include the HDF_OWNERDRAW flag. You can combine a string and an image from an image list by combining the HDF_IMAGE and HDF_STRING flags.

The **HDITEM** structure also specifies formatting flags that tell the control whether to center, left-align, or right-align the string or bitmap in the item's rectangle.

HDM_INSERTITEM returns the index of the newly added item. You can use the index in other messages to set properties or retrieve information about the item. To delete an item, use the HDM_DELETEITEM message, which specifies the index of the item to delete.

The HDM_SETITEM message sets the properties of an existing header item and the HDM_GETITEM message retrieves the current properties of an item. To retrieve a count of the items in a header control, use the HDM_GETITEMCOUNT message.

You can define individual items of a header control to be owner-drawn items. Using this technique gives you more control than you would otherwise have over the appearance of a header item.

Use the HDM_INSERTITEM message to insert a new owner-drawn item into a header control or the HDM_SETITEM message to change an existing item to an owner-drawn item. Both messages include the address of an **HDITEM** structure, which should have the **fmt** member set to the HDF_OWNERDRAW value.

Header Control Messages

A header control sends notification messages to its parent window when the user clicks or double-clicks an item, when the user drags an item divider, and when the attributes of an item change. The parent window receives the notifications in the form of WM_NOTIFY messages.

Windows CE supplies macros to send header control messages as well as to support the use of image lists, drag-and-drop functionality, and custom ordering of header control items.

Advanced Header Control Features

Windows CE enables you to use image lists in header controls, as well as text and bitmaps. An *image list* is a collection of images that are all the same size, such as bitmaps or icons. For more information, see "Image Lists" later in this chapter.

You can use the HDM_SETIMAGELIST message to associate an image list with a header control. Use the HDM_GETIMAGELIST message to retrieve the handle of the image list that is associated with a header control. To display an image with a header control item, specify HDI_IMAGE as the **mask** member, HDF_IMAGE as the **fmt** member, and the zero-based index of an image in the list as the **iImage** member of the **HDITEM** structure you use to add the item to the header control.

Header controls support callback requests for text and images in header control items. To create a callback item, set the **pszText** member to LPSTR_TEXTCALLBACK, or the **iImage** member to I_IMAGECALLBACK, in the **HDITEM** structure you fill in when you add the item to the header control. This causes the header control to send the HDN_GETDISPINFO notification message when the item is about to be drawn. The *lParam* of the WM_NOTIFY message is a pointer to an **NMHDDISPINFO** structure. When the header control sends the notification, it sets the **NMHDDISPINFO** structure's members to specify the type of information it needs in order to draw the item. Return the requested information to the header control by filling in the appropriate members of the structure. If you set the **mask** member to HDI_DI_SETITEM, the header control stores the information and does not request it again. Otherwise, the header control sends the NMHDDISPINFO notification each time the item is redrawn.

Header controls also support drag-and-drop functionality. To create a header control that supports drag-and-drop operations, specify the HDS_DRAGDROP style when you create the header control. You can also customize a header control's drag-and-drop behavior by handling the HDN_BEGINDRAG and HDN_ENDDRAG notification messages and by sending HDM_CREATEDRAGIMAGE and HDM_SETHOTDIVIDER messages.

You can support custom ordering of items in a header control by setting the **iOrder** member in the **HDITEM** structure when you add an item to a header control and by using the HDM_GETORDERARRAY, HDM_SETORDERARRAY, and HDM_ORDERTOINDEX messages.

Header controls support the custom draw service, which gives you flexibility to customize a header control's appearance. If a header control provides this service, it sends the NM_CUSTOMDRAW notification at specific times during drawing operations. The *lParam* of the NM_CUSTOMDRAW notification is a pointer to an **NMCUSTOMDRAW** structure, which contains the information necessary to draw the customized header control. For information on the custom draw service, see Chapter 10, "Overview of Controls."

Image Lists

An image list is a collection of images that are all the same size. You can create the images in a single wide bitmap or as individual bitmaps that you add to the list one at a time. Image lists manage images, but they do not display the images directly. They can be used independently or in conjunction with list view and tree view controls.

There are two types of image lists, nonmasked and masked. A nonmasked image list consists of a color bitmap that contains one or more images. A masked image list consists of two bitmaps of equal size. The first is a color bitmap that contains the images, and the second is a monochrome bitmap that contains a series of masks—one for each image in the first bitmap.

Windows CE draws a nonmasked image by simply copying it into the target device context and drawing it over the existing background color of the device context. Windows CE draws a masked image by combining its bits with the bits of the mask, typically producing transparent areas in the bitmap where the background color of the target device context shows through.

Note Most Windows CE-based platforms do not support cursors except for the wait cursor, which resembles a spinning hourglass. Therefore, image lists cannot contain cursors.

Using Image Lists

To create an image list, call the **ImageList_Create** function. For a nonmasked image list, this function creates a single bitmap large enough to hold a specified number of images of the specified dimensions. Then, it creates a screen-compatible device context and selects the bitmap into it. For a masked image list, the function creates two bitmaps and two screen-compatible device contexts. **ImageList_Create** selects the image bitmap into one device context and the mask bitmap into the other.

In **ImageList_Create**, you specify the initial number of images that will be in an image list, as well as the number of images by which the list can grow. If you attempt to add more images than you initially specified, the image list automatically grows to accommodate the images.

If **ImageList_Create** succeeds, it returns a handle to the HIMAGELIST type. Use this handle in other image list functions to access the image list and manage the images. You can add and remove images, copy images from one image list to another, and merge images from two different image lists. When you no longer need an image list, destroy it by specifying its handle in a call to the **ImageList_Destroy** function.

Use the **ImageList_Duplicate**, **ImageList_SetImageCount**, and **ImageList_RemoveAll** functions to respectively copy, resize, or remove all images from an image list.

The **IMAGELISTDRAWPARAMS** structure, which is used with the **ImageList_DrawIndirect** function, contains information about how to draw an image from an image list, such as what part of the image to draw, the foreground and background colors, the style, and a raster operation (ROP) code specifying how to combine the image's colors with the background colors.

Using Images in Image Lists

You can add icons or other bit images to an image list. To add bit images, specify the handles to two bitmaps in a call to the **ImageList_Add** function. The first bitmap contains one or more images to add to the image bitmap, and the second bitmap contains the masks to add to the mask bitmap. Windows CE ignores the second bitmap handle for nonmasked images; you can set it to NULL.

The **ImageList_AddMasked** function adds bit images to a masked image list. This function is similar to **ImageList_Add**, in which you do not specify a mask bitmap. Instead, you specify a color that the system combines with the image bitmap to automatically generate the masks. Windows CE changes each pixel of the specified color in the image bitmap to black and sets the corresponding bit in the mask to one. As a result, any pixel in the image that matches the specified color is transparent when the image is drawn.

The **ImageList_AddIcon** function adds an icon to an image list. If the image list is masked, **ImageList_AddIcon** adds the mask provided with the icon to the mask bitmap. If the image list is nonmasked, the mask for the icon is not used when drawing the image.

To create an icon based on an image and mask in an image list, use the **ImageList_GetIcon** function. The function returns the handle to the icon. **ImageList_Add**, **ImageList_AddMasked**, and **ImageList_AddIcon** assign an index to each image as it is added to an image list. When more than one image is added at a time, the functions return the index of the first image. The **ImageList_Remove** function removes an image from an image list.

The **ImageList_Replace** and **ImageList_ReplaceIcon** functions replace an image in an image list with a new image. **ImageList_Replace** replaces an image with a bit image and mask, and **ImageList_ReplaceIcon** replaces an image with an icon. Use the **ImageList_Copy** function to move or copy images within an image list.

The **ImageList_Merge** function merges two images, storing the new image in a new image list. The new image is created by drawing the second image transparently over the first. The mask for the new image is the result of performing a logical **OR** operation on the bits of the masks for the two original images.

The **ImageList_GetImageInfo** function fills an **IMAGEINFO** structure with information about a single image, including the handles of the image and mask bitmaps, the number of color planes and bits per pixel, and the bounding rectangle of the image within the image bitmap. Use this information to directly manipulate the bitmaps for the image. The **ImageList_GetImageCount** function retrieves the number of images in an image list.

Use the **ImageList_DrawIndirect** function to specify custom drawing properties for an image in an image list. This function takes a pointer to an **IMAGELISTDRAWPARAMS** structure as a parameter. The **IMAGELISTDRAWPARAMS** structure contains information about how to draw the image.

Using Overlays in Image Lists

Every image list includes a list of indexes to use as overlays. An overlay is an image that is drawn transparently over another image. Any image currently in the image list can be used as an overlay. You can specify up to four overlays for each image list.

Add the index of an image to the list of overlays by using the **ImageList_SetOverlayImage** function, specifying the handle to the image list, the index of the existing image, and the desired overlay index. The overlay indexes are one-based rather than zero-based because an overlay index of zero means that no overlay will be used.

Specify an overlay when drawing an image with the **ImageList_Draw** or **ImageList_DrawEx** function. The overlay is specified by performing a logical **OR** operation between the desired drawing flags and the result of the **INDEXTOOVERLAYMASK** macro. The **INDEXTOOVERLAYMASK** macro formats the overlay index for inclusion with the flags for these functions.

List Views

A *list view* is a common control that displays a collection of items, such as files or folders. Each item has an icon and a label. A user can choose whether to have the items displayed as large icons, small icons, a list, or a detailed list. You can design list views so that a user can drag an item to a new location within the list view or sort the collection by tapping a column header.

Image list in list view

Create a list view by specifying WC_LISTVIEW in the *lpClassName* parameter to the **CreateWindowEx** function. This class is registered when the common control DLL is loaded. Use the **InitCommonControls** function to ensure that this DLL is loaded.

To register the list view class using the **InitCommonControlsEx** function, specify the ICC_ LISTVIEW_CLASSES flag as the **dwICC** member of the **INITCOMMONCONTROLSEX** structure you pass in the *lpInitCtrls* parameter.

You can speed up the creation of large list views by disabling the painting of the list view before adding the items. You do this by sending a WM_SETREDRAW message with the redraw flag in *wParam* set to FALSE. When you are finished adding items, re-enable painting by sending a WM_SETREDRAW message with the redraw flag *wParam* set to TRUE. Before inserting items, send the LVM_SETITEMCOUNT message with the *cItems* parameter set to the number of items in question. When you do this, the list view will allocate the memory it needs all at once, instead of having to reallocate more memory incrementally as the internal data structures grow.

You can change the view type after a list view control is created. To retrieve and change the window style, use the **GetWindowLong** and **SetWindowLong** functions. To determine the window styles that correspond to the current view, use the LVS_TYPEMASK value.

Note Windows CE does not support hot tracking, hover selection, background images, or list view ToolTips.

List View Styles

List view styles supported by Windows CE are described in the following table.

Style	Description
LVS_ALIGNLEFT	Specifies that items are left-aligned in icon view and small icon view.
LVS_ALIGNTOP	Specifies that items are aligned with the top of the list view control in icon view and small icon view.
LVS_AUTOARRANGE	Specifies that icons automatically remain arranged in icon view and small icon view.
LVS_BUTTON	Specifies that item icons look like buttons in icon view.
LVS_EDITLABELS	Allows item text to be edited in place. The parent window must process the LVN_ENDLABELEDIT notification message.
LVS_ICON	Specifies icon view.
LVS_LIST	Specifies list view.
LVS_NOCOLUMNHEADER	Specifies that no column header is displayed in report view, which is the default view.
LVS_NOLABELWRAP	Displays item text on a single line in icon view. By default, item text may wrap in icon view.

Style	Description
LVS_NOSCROLL	Disables scrolling, so all items must be displayed within the client area.
LVS_NOSORTHEADER	Specifies that column headers do not work like buttons. This style is useful if clicking a column header in report view does not carry out any action, such as sorting.
LVS_OWNERDATA	Creates a virtual list view control.
LVS_OWNERDRAWFIXED	Enables the owner window to paint items in report view. The list view control sends a WM_DRAWITEM message to paint each item; it does not send separate messages for each subitem. The **itemData** member of the **DRAWITEMSTRUCT** structure contains the item data for the specified list view item.
LVS_REPORT	Specifies report view.
LVS_SHAREIMAGELISTS	Specifies that the control does not destroy the image lists assigned to it when it is destroyed. This style enables the same image lists to be used with multiple list view controls.
LVS_SHOWSELALWAYS	Always shows the selection highlighted, even if the control is not activated.
LVS_SINGLESEL	Allows only one item to be selected at a time. By default, multiple items can be selected.
LVS_SMALLICON	Specifies small icon view.
LVS_SORTASCENDING	Sorts items based on item text in ascending order.
LVS_SORTDESCENDING	Sorts items based on item text in descending order.

You can control the way items are arranged in icon view or small icon view by specifying either the LVS_ALIGNTOP windows style, which is the default, or the LVS_ALIGNLEFT window style. You can change the alignment after a list view control is created. To isolate the window styles that specify the alignment of items, use the LVS_ALIGNMASK value.

Extended List View Styles

Extended list view styles supported by Windows CE are described in the following table.

Extended style	Description
LVS_EX_CHECKBOXES	Enables items in a list view control to be displayed as check boxes. This style uses item state images to produce the check box effect.
LVS_EX_FULLROWSELECT	Specifies that when an item is selected, the item and all its subitems are highlighted. This style is available only in conjunction with the LVS_REPORT style.
LVS_EX_GRIDLINES	Displays gridlines around items and subitems. This style is available only in conjunction with the LVS_REPORT style.
LVS_EX_HEADERDRAGDROP	Enables drag-and-drop reordering of columns in a list view control. This style is only available to list view controls that use the LVS_REPORT style.
LVS_EX_SUBITEMIMAGES	Allows images to be displayed for subitems. This style is available only in conjunction with the LVS_REPORT style.

Use the LVM_SETEXTENDEDLISTVIEWSTYLE message or its corresponding macro, **ListView_SetExtendedListViewStyle**, to set these extended styles, and use the LVM_GETEXTENDEDLISTVIEWSTYLE message or its corresponding macro, **ListView_GetExtendedListViewStyle**, to retrieve these extended styles.

Note   These extended styles are not the same as extended window styles; you cannot pass them to **CreateWindowEx** when you create a list view control.

List View Structures

Windows CE structures that have been renamed to conform to Windows standard naming conventions are described in the following table. These structures are otherwise the same as the corresponding structures in Windows-based desktop platforms.

Windows CE	Previous Win32 name
NMLISTVIEW	NM_LISTVIEW
NMLVKEYDOWN	LV_KEYDOWN

List View Item States

Every list view item has a current state that determines its appearance and functionality. Retrieve and set this state by sending the LVM_GETITEM, LVM_SETITEM, and LVM_SETITEMSTATE messages or by using the **ListView_GetItem** and **ListView_SetItem** macros. You set or retrieve the item state in the **state** member of the **LV_ITEM** structure that you pass in the *pItem* parameter, *lParam*, to these messages and macros. List view item states supported by Windows CE are described in the following table.

State	Description
LVIS_CUT	The item is marked for a cut-and-paste operation.
LVIS_DROPHILITED	The item is highlighted as a target for a drag-and-drop operation.
LVIS_FOCUSED	The item has the focus, so it is surrounded by a standard focus rectangle. Although more than one item can be selected, only one item can have the focus.
LVIS_LINK	The item is a link.
LVIS_PUSHED	The button-like item appears pushed. This value has no effect, unless the LVS_BUTTON window style is used.
LVIS_SELECTED	The item is selected. The appearance of a selected item depends on whether it has the focus and on the system colors used for selection.

Use the LVIS_OVERLAYMASK mask to isolate the state bits that contain the one-based index of the overlay image. You can use the LVIS_STATEIMAGEMASK mask to isolate the state bits that contain the one-based index of the state image.

List View Image Lists

By default, a list view control does not display item images. To display item images, you must create image lists and associate them with the control. A list view control can have three image lists:

- One that contains full-sized icons displayed when the control is in icon view.
- One that contains small icons displayed when the control is in small icon view, list view, or report view.

- One that contains state images, which are displayed to the left of the full-sized icon or small icon.

You can use state images, such as checked or cleared check boxes, to indicate application-defined item states. State images are displayed in icon view, small icon view, list view, or report view.

To assign an image list to a list view control, use the LVM_SETIMAGELIST message to specify whether the image list contains full-sized icons, small icons, or state images. To retrieve the handle to an image list currently assigned to a list view control, use the LVM_GETIMAGELIST message. You can use the **GetSystemMetrics** function to determine appropriate dimensions for the full-sized icons and small icons. Use the **ImageList_Create** function to create an image list, and use other image list functions to add bitmaps to the image list.

Create only the image list that the control will use. For example, if the list view control will never be in icon view, do not create and assign a large image list because the large images will never be used. If you create large and small icon image lists, each image list must contain the same images in the same order. This is because a single value is used to identify a list view item's icon in both image lists. You can associate an icon index with an item when you call the **ListView_InsertItem** or **ListView_SetItem** macro.

The full-sized icon and small icon image lists can also contain overlay images, which are designed to be drawn transparently over the item icons.

▶ **To use overlay images in a list view control**

1. Call the **ImageList_SetOverlayImage** function to assign an overlay image index to an image in the full-sized icon and small icon image lists.

   An overlay image is identified by a one-based index.

2. Call the **ListView_InsertItem** or **ListView_SetItem** macro to associate an overlay image index with an item.

3. Use the **INDEXTOOVERLAYMASK** macro to specify an overlay image index in the **state** member of the item's **LVITEM** structure.

   You must also set the **LVIS_OVERLAYMASK** bits in the **stateMask** member.

To associate a state image with an item, use the **INDEXTOSTATEIMAGEMASK** macro to specify a state image index in the **state** member of the **LVITEM** structure.

By default, when a list view control is destroyed, it destroys the image lists assigned to it. However, if a list view control has the LVS_SHAREIMAGELISTS window style, you are responsible for destroying the image lists when they are no longer in use. You should specify this style if you assign the same image lists to multiple list view controls; otherwise, more than one control might try to destroy the same image list.

Items and Subitems

Each item in a list view control has an icon, a label, a current state, and an application-defined value. By using list view messages, you can add, modify, and delete items as well as retrieve information about items. You can also find items with specific attributes.

Each item can also have one or more subitems. A subitem is a string that, in report view, is displayed in a column to the right of an item's icon and label. To specify the text of a subitem, use the LVM_SETITEMTEXT or LVM_SETITEM message. All items in a list view control have the same number of subitems. The number of subitems is determined by the number of columns in the list view control.

The **LVITEM** structure defines a list view item or subitem. To add an item to a list view control, use the LVM_INSERTITEM message. Before adding multiple items, you can send the control an LVM_SETITEMCOUNT message to specify the number of items the control will ultimately contain. This message enables the list view control to reallocate its internal data structures only once rather than every time you add an item. Determine the number of items in a list view control by using the LVM_GETITEMCOUNT message.

Use the LVM_SETITEM message to change the attributes of a list view item. The LVM_SETITEMTEXT message only changes the text of an item or subitem.

To retrieve information about a list view item, use the LVM_GETITEM message specifying the address of the **LVITEM** structure to fill in. To retrieve only an item or subitem's text, use the LVM_GETITEMTEXT message. To delete a list view item, use the LVM_DELETEITEM message. Delete all items in a list view control by using the LVM_DELETEALLITEMS message.

Callback Items and the Callback Mask

For each of its items, a list view control typically stores the label text, the image list index of the item's icons, and a set of bit flags for the item's state. A callback item in a list view control is an item for which the application stores the text, icon index, or both. You can define callback items or change the control's callback mask to indicate that the application—rather than the control—stores some or all of this information. You may want to use callbacks if your application already stores some of this information. You can define callback items when you send the LVM_INSERTITEM message to add an item to the list view control.

The callback mask of a list view control is a set of bit flags that specify the item states for which the application, rather than the control, stores the current data. The callback mask applies to all of the control's items, unlike the callback item designation, which applies to a specific item. The callback mask is zero by default, meaning that the list view control stores all item-state information. After creating a list view control and initializing its items, you can send the LVM_SETCALLBACKMASK message to change the callback mask. To get the current callback mask, send the LVM_GETCALLBACKMASK message.

When a list view control must display or sort a list view item for which the application stores callback information, the control sends the LVN_GETDISPINFO notification message to the control's parent window. This message specifies an **NMLVDISPINFO** structure that indicates the type of information required. The parent window must process LVN_GETDISPINFO to provide the requested data.

If the list view control detects a change in an item's callback information, the control sends an LVN_SETDISPINFO notification message to notify you of the change. Changes that the list view control detect are alterations to the text, the icon, or the state information being tracked by the application.

If you change a callback item's attributes or state bits, you can use the LVM_UPDATE message to force the control to repaint the item. This message also causes the control to arrange its items if it has the LVS_AUTOARRANGE style. You can use the LVM_REDRAWITEMS message to redraw a range of items by invalidating the corresponding portions of the list view control's client area.

Columns

Columns control the way items and their subitems are displayed in report view. Each column has a title and width and is associated with a specific subitem. The attributes of a column are defined by an **LVCOLUMN** structure.

To add a column to a list view control, use the LVM_INSERTCOLUMN message. To delete a column, use the LVM_DELETECOLUMN message. You can retrieve and change the properties of an existing column by using the LVM_GETCOLUMN and LVM_SETCOLUMN messages. To retrieve or change a column's width, use the LVM_GETCOLUMNWIDTH and LVM_SETCOLUMNWIDTH messages.

Unless the LVS_NOCOLUMNHEADER window style is specified, column headers appear in report view. The user can click a column header, which causes the live view control to send an LVN_COLUMNCLICK notification message to the parent window. Typically, the parent window sorts the list view control by the specified column when the user clicks the column header.

List view controls can set the order in which columns are displayed. To implement this feature, specify the LVCF_ORDER value and assign the proper value to the **iOrder** member in the **LVCOLUMN** structure.

Arranging, Sorting, and Finding List Views

You can use list view messages to arrange and sort items and to find items based on their attributes or positions. Although arranging items repositions them to align on a grid, the indexes of the items do not change. Sorting changes the sequence of items and their corresponding indexes, and then repositions them in the order specified. You can arrange items only in icon and small icon views, but you can sort items in any view.

To arrange items, use the LVM_ARRANGE message. You can ensure that items are arranged at all times by specifying the LVS_AUTOARRANGE window style.

To sort items, use the LVM_SORTITEMS message. When you sort using this message, you specify an application-defined callback function that the list view control calls to compare the relative order of any two items. By specifying the appropriate item data and supplying an appropriate comparison function, you can sort items by their labels, by any subitems, or by any other properties. Note that sorting items does not reorder the corresponding subitems. Thus, if any subitems are not callback items, you must regenerate the subitems after sorting.

Ensure that a list view control is always sorted by specifying the LVS_SORTASCENDING or LVS_SORTDESCENDING window style. Controls with these styles use the label text of the items to sort them in ascending or descending order. You cannot supply a comparison function when using these window styles.

You can find a list view item with specific properties by using the LVM_FINDITEM message. Use the LVM_GETNEXTITEM message to find a list view item that is in a specified state and bears a specified geometrical relationship to a specified item.

List View Item Position

Every list view item has a position and size, which you can retrieve and set using messages. You can also determine which item, if any, is at a specified position. The position of list view items is specified in view coordinates, which are client coordinates offset by the scroll position.

To retrieve and set an item's position, use the LVM_GETITEMPOSITION and LVM_SETITEMPOSITION messages, respectively. LVM_GETITEMPOSITION works for all views, but LVM_SETITEMPOSITION works only for icon and small icon views.

You can determine which item, if any, is at a particular location by using the LVM_HITTEST message. To get the bounding rectangle for a list item, or for only its icon or label, use the LVM_GETITEMRECT message.

Scroll Position

Unless the LVS_NOSCROLL window style is specified, you can use messages to perform a variety of scrolling operations. You can scroll a list view control to show items that do not fit in the client area of the control, determine a list view control's scroll position, scroll a list view control by a specified amount, or scroll a list view control so that a specified list item is visible.

In icon view or small icon view, the current scroll position is defined by the view origin. The view origin is the set of coordinates, relative to the visible area of the list view control, that correspond to the view coordinates (0, 0). To get the current view origin, use the LVM_GETORIGIN message. This message should be used only in icon or small icon view; it returns an error in list or report view.

In list or report view, the current scroll position is defined by the top index. The top index is the index of the first visible item in the list view control. To get the current top index, use the LVM_GETTOPINDEX message. This message returns a valid result only in list view or report view; it returns zero in icon or small icon view.

Use the LVM_GETVIEWRECT message to get the bounding rectangle of all items in a list view control relative to the visible area of the control.

The LVM_GETCOUNTPERPAGE message returns the number of items that fit in one page of the list view control. This message returns a valid result only in list and report views; in icon and small icon views, it returns the total number of items.

To scroll a list view control by a specific amount, use the LVM_SCROLL message. Using the LVM_ENSUREVISIBLE message, you can scroll the list view control, if necessary, to ensure that a specified item is visible.

Editing Labels

A list view control that has the LVS_EDITLABELS window style enables a user to edit item labels in place. The user begins editing by clicking the label of an item that has the focus. An application can begin editing automatically by using the LVM_EDITLABEL message. The list view control notifies the parent window when editing begins and when it is canceled or completed. When editing is completed, the parent window is responsible for updating the item's label, if appropriate.

When label editing begins, a list view control sends its parent window an LVN_BEGINLABELEDIT notification message. You can process this message to allow selective editing of specific labels; returning a nonzero value prevents label editing.

When label editing is canceled or completed, a list view control sends its parent window an LVN_ENDLABELEDIT notification message. The parent window is responsible for updating the item's label if it keeps the new label.

During label editing, you can get the handle to the edit control used for label editing by using the LVM_GETEDITCONTROL message. To limit the amount of text a user can type, you can send the edit control an EM_LIMITTEXT message. You can even subclass the edit control to intercept and discard invalid characters.

Advanced List View Features

In Windows CE, you can set the order of the columns that display in report view by setting the **iOrder** member in the **LVCOLUMN** structure when you add a column to a list view control. You can also set the column order by using the LVM_GETCOLUMNORDERARRAY and LVM_SETCOLUMNORDERARRAY messages.

To display an image from an image list next to the title of a column in report view, specify LVCF_IMAGE in the **mask** member and LVCFMT_IMAGE in the **fmt** member. When you add a column to a list view control, specify the zero-based index of an image in the list in the **iImage** member of **LVCOLUMN**.

List view controls in Windows CE support a custom draw service, which gives you flexibility to customize a list view's appearance. If a list view provides this service, it sends the NM_CUSTOMDRAW notification at specific times during drawing operations. For information on the custom draw service, see Chapter 10, "Overview of Controls."

Windows CE supports a list view style, LVS_OWNERDATA, for creating a virtual list view. The only data that a virtual list view manages is input focus and item selection information. All other data is managed by the owner of the list view. This enables a list view to handle very large data sets, especially in cases where the data is stored in a database that has its own data access methods.

Trackbars

A *trackbar*, also known as a slider control, is a common control that consists of a bar with tick marks on it and a slider, also known as a thumb. When a user drags the slider or clicks on either side of it, the slider moves in the appropriate direction, tick by tick.

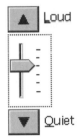

Window CE trackbar

Create a trackbar by specifying TRACKBAR_CLASS in the *lpClassName* parameter to the **CreateWindowEx** function. This class is registered when the common control DLL is loaded. You can use the **InitCommonControls** function to ensure that this DLL is loaded.

To register the trackbar class using the **InitCommonControlsEx** function, specify the ICC_BAR_CLASSES flag as the **dwICC** member of the **INITCOMMONCONTROLSEX** structure you pass in the *lpInitCtrls* parameter.

A trackbar can have either one or two buddy windows. A buddy window is a companion control.

Trackbars in Windows CE support the custom draw service, which gives you flexibility to customize a trackbar's appearance. For information on the custom draw service, see Chapter 10, "Overview of Controls."

Trackbar Messages

You can send messages to the trackbar to retrieve information about the window and to change its characteristics.

To retrieve the position of the slider, which is the value that the user has chosen, use the TBM_GETPOS message. To set the position of the slider, use the TBM_SETPOS message.

The range of a trackbar is the set of contiguous values that the trackbar can represent. Use the TBM_SETRANGE message to set the range of a trackbar when it is first created. You can dynamically alter the range by using the TBM_SETRANGEMAX and TBM_SETRANGEMIN messages. An application that allows the range to be changed dynamically usually retrieves the final range settings when the user has finished working with the trackbar. To retrieve these settings, use the TBM_GETRANGEMAX and TBM_GETRANGEMIN messages.

A trackbar automatically displays tick marks at each end, unless you specify the TBS_NOTICKS style. Use the TBS_AUTOTICKS style to automatically display additional tick marks at regular intervals along the trackbar. By default, a TBS_AUTOTICKS trackbar displays a tick mark at each increment of the trackbar's range. To specify a different interval for the automatic tick marks, send the TBM_SETTICFREQ message to the trackbar.

To set the position of a single tick mark, send the TBM_SETTIC message. A trackbar maintains an array of DWORD values that stores the position of each tick mark. The array does not include the first and last tick marks that the trackbar creates automatically. You can specify an index in this array when you send the TBM_GETTIC message to get the position of the corresponding tick mark. Alternatively, you can send the TBM_GETPTICS message to get a pointer to the array. To retrieve the physical position of a tick mark, send the TBM_GETTICPOS message. The TBM_CLEARTICS message removes all but the first and last of a trackbar's tick marks.

A trackbar's line size determines how far the slider moves in response to keyboard input from the arrow keys, such as the RIGHT ARROW or DOWN ARROW key. To retrieve or set the line size, send the TBM_GETLINESIZE and TBM_SETLINESIZE messages, respectively.

A trackbar's page size determines how far the slider moves in response to keyboard input, such as the PAGE UP or PAGE DOWN key, or mouse input, such as clicks in the trackbar channel. To retrieve or set the page size, send the TBM_GETPAGESIZE and TBM_SETPAGESIZE messages.

An application can send messages to retrieve the dimensions of a trackbar. The TBM_GETTHUMBRECT message retrieves the bounding rectangle for the slider. The TBM_GETTHUMBLENGTH message retrieves the length of the slider. The TBM_GETCHANNELRECT message retrieves the bounding rectangle for the trackbar's channel, which is the area over which the slider moves. If a trackbar has the TBS_FIXEDLENGTH style, you can send the TBM_SETTHUMBLENGTH message to change the length of the slider.

A trackbar with the TBS_ENABLESELRANGE style can indicate a selection range by highlighting a range of the trackbar's channel and displaying triangular tick marks at the start and end of the selection. When a trackbar has this style, you can send messages to set and retrieve the selection range. Typically, an application handles the trackbar notification messages and sets the trackbar's selection range according to the user's input. The TBM_SETSEL message sets the starting and ending positions of a selection. To set just the starting position or just the ending position of a selection, use the TBM_SETSELSTART or TBM_SETSELEND message. To retrieve the starting and ending positions of a selection range, send the TBM_GETSELSTART and TBM_GETSELEND messages. To clear a selection range, send the TBM_CLEARSEL message.

Tree Views

A *tree view control* is a hierarchical display of labeled items. The top item in the hierarchy is called the root. An item that has other items below it in the hierarchy is referred to as those items' parent, and the items below it are its children. Child items, when displayed, are indented below their parent item. The hierarchy can be expanded or collapsed at any level to display or hide any parent item's children.

You create a tree view by specifying WC_ TREEVIEW in the *lpClassName* parameter to the **CreateWindowEx** function. This class is registered when the common control dynamic-link library (DLL) is loaded. You can use the **InitCommonControls** function to ensure that this DLL is loaded.

To register the tree view class using the **InitCommonControlsEx** function, specify the ICC_ TREEVIEW_CLASSES flag as the **dwICC** member of the **INITCOMMONCONTROLSEX** structure you pass in the *lpInitCtrls* parameter.

Windows CE does not support hot tracking, hover selection, or ToolTips for tree views.

Tree views in Windows CE support the custom draw service, which gives you greater flexibility to customize a tree view's appearance.

Tree View Styles

Tree view styles govern aspects of a tree view control's appearance. You set the initial styles when you create the tree view control. You can retrieve and change the styles after creating the tree view control by using the **GetWindowLong** and **SetWindowLong** functions.

Tree view styles supported by Windows CE are described in the following table.

Style	Description
TVS_CHECKBOXES	Enables items in a tree view control to be displayed as check boxes. This style uses item state images to produce the check box effect.
TVS_DISABLEDRAGDROP	Prevents the tree view control from sending TVN_BEGINDRAG notification messages.
TVS_EDITLABELS	Allows the user to edit the labels of tree view items.
TVS_HASBUTTONS	Displays plus (+) and minus (-) buttons next to parent items. The user clicks the buttons to expand or collapse a parent item's list of child items. To include buttons with items at the root of the tree view, you must also specify the TVS_LINESATROOT style.
TVS_HASLINES	Uses lines to show the hierarchy of items.
TVS_LINESATROOT	Uses lines to link items at the root of the tree view control. This value is ignored if TVS_HASLINES is not also specified.
TVS_SHOWSELALWAYS	Uses the system highlight colors to draw the selected item.
TVS_SINGLESEL	Specifies that when a new tree view item is selected, the selected item will automatically expand and the previously selected item will collapse.

Parent and Child Items

Any item in a tree view control can have a list of subitems—called child items—associated with it. An item that has one or more child items is called a parent item. A child item is displayed below its parent item and is indented to indicate that it is subordinate to the parent. An item that has no parent appears at the top of the hierarchy and is called a root item.

To add an item to a tree view control, send the TVM_INSERTITEM message to the control. The message returns a handle to the HTREEITEM type, which uniquely identifies the item. When adding an item, specify the handle to the new item's parent item. If you specify NULL or the TVI_ROOT value instead of a parent item handle in the **TVINSERTSTRUCT** structure, the item is added as a root item.

At any time, the state of a parent item's list of child items can be either expanded, partially expanded, or collapsed. When the state is expanded, the child items of the expanded section are displayed below the parent item. When it is collapsed, the child items are not displayed. The list automatically toggles between the expanded and collapsed states when the user double-taps the parent item or, if the parent has the TVS_HASBUTTONS style, when the user clicks the button associated with the parent item. You can expand or collapse the child items by using the TVM_EXPAND message.

A tree view control sends the parent window a TVN_ITEMEXPANDING notification message when a parent item's list of child items is about to be expanded or collapsed. The notification gives an application the opportunity to prevent the change or to set any attributes of the parent item that depend on the state of the list of child items. After changing the state of the list, the tree view control sends the parent window a TVN_ITEMEXPANDED notification message.

When a list of child items is expanded, it is indented relative to the parent item. Set the amount of indentation by using the TVM_SETINDENT message or retrieve the current amount by using the TVM_GETINDENT message.

A tree view control uses mcmory allocated from the heap of the process that creates the tree view control. The maximum number of items in a tree view is based on the amount of memory available in the heap.

Item Labels

You typically specify the text of an item's label when you add the item to the tree view control. The TVM_INSERTITEM message includes a **TVITEM** structure that defines the item's properties, including a string containing the text of the label.

A tree view control allocates memory for storing each item; the text of the item labels takes up a significant portion of this memory. If you maintain a copy of the strings in the tree view control, you can decrease the memory requirements of the control by specifying the LPSTR_TEXTCALLBACK value in the **pszText** member of **TVITEM** instead of passing actual strings to the tree view. Using LPSTR_TEXTCALLBACK causes the tree view control to retrieve the text of an item's label from the parent window whenever the item needs to be redrawn.

Tree View Item States

Every tree view item has a current state that determines its appearance and functionality. You can retrieve and set this state by sending the TVM_GETITEM and TVM_SETITEM messages, or by using the **TreeView_GetItem** and **TreeView_SetItem** macros. You set or retrieve the item state by using the **state** member of the **TV_ITEM** structure that you pass in the *pItem* parameter *(lParam)* to these messages and macros.

Windows CE supports the TVIS_EXPANDPARTIAL item state. This state indicates that a tree view item is partially expanded. This could happen if an error occurs during data retrieval and some of the child items cannot be retrieved from the data source. The tree view displays the items that were successfully retrieved, but continues to display the plus symbol next to the parent item as well. This indicates to the user that more information is available. When the user clicks the plus symbol again, the application repeats the query.

Item states supported by Windows CE are described in the following table.

State	Description
TVIS_BOLD	Windows CE uses a bold font to draw the item.
TVIS_CUT	Windows CE selects the item for cutting and pasting.
TVIS_DROPHILITED	Windows CE selects the item for dropping and dragging.
TVIS_EXPANDED	Windows CE expands the items list of child items so that the child items are visible. This state applies only to parent items.
TVIS_EXPANDEDONCE	Windows CE expands the the item's list of child items at least once. Windows CE does not send the TVN_ITEMEXPANDING and TVN_ITEMEXPANDED notifications for parent items that have specified this value. This value applies only to parent items.
TVIS_EXPANDPARTIAL	Windows CE partially expands the items. This could happen if an error occurs during data retrieval and some of the child items cannot be retrieved from the data source.
TVIS_FOCUSED	Windows CE gives the item the focus and surrounds it with a standard focus rectangle. Although more than one item can be selected, only one item can have the focus.

Style	Description
TVIS_OVERLAYMASK	Windows CE includes the item's overlay image when it draws the image. The index of the overlay image must be specified in the **state** member of the **TV_ITEM** structure by using the **INDEXTOOVERLAYMASK** macro. The overlay image must be added to the tree view's image list by using the **ImageList_SetOverlayImage** function. This value should not be combined with any other value.
TVIS_SELECTED	Windows CE selects the item. The appearance of a selected item depends on whether it has the focus and on whether the system colors are used for selection.
TVIS_STATEIMAGEMASK	Windows CE includes the item's state image when it draws the item. The index of the state image must be specified in the **state** member of the **TV_ITEM** structure by using the **INDEXTOSTATEIMAGEMASK** macro. This value should not be combined with any other value.

Editing Tree View Labels

The user can directly edit the labels of items in a tree view control that has the TVS_EDITLABELS style. The user begins editing by clicking the label of the item that has the focus. An application begins editing by using the TVM_EDITLABEL message. The tree view control notifies the parent window when editing begins and when it is canceled or completed. When the user or application completes editing, the parent window is responsible for updating the item's label, if appropriate.

When the user begins editing the label, a tree view control sends its parent window a TVN_BEGINLABELEDIT notification message. By processing this notification, an application can allow editing of some labels and prevent editing of others. Returning zero allows editing, and returning nonzero prevents it.

When the user cancels or completes editing the label, a tree view control sends its parent window a TVN_ENDLABELEDIT notification message. The **pszText** member of TVITEM is zero if editing is canceled.

Tree View Item Position

To add an item to a tree view control, send the TVM_INSERTITEM message to the control. The message includes a **TVINSERTSTRUCT** structure that specifies the handle to the parent item and the handle to the item after which the new item is to be inserted. The second handle must identify either a child item of the specified parent or one of these values: TVI_FIRST, TVI_LAST, or TVI_SORT.

When you specify TVI_FIRST or TVI_LAST, the tree view control places the new item at the beginning or end of the specified parent item's list of child items. When you specify TVI_SORT, the tree view control inserts the new item into the list of child items in alphabetical order based on the text of the item labels.

Put a parent item's list of child items in alphabetical order by using the TVM_SORTCHILDREN message. The TVM_SORTCHILDRENCB message allows you to sort child items based on criteria that you define. When you use this message, you specify an application-defined callback function that the tree view control can call whenever the relative order of two child items needs to be determined.

Item Selection

A tree view control notifies the parent window when the selection changes from one item to another by sending the TVN_SELCHANGING and TVN_SELCHANGED notification messages. The notifications also include information about the item that gains the selection and the item that loses the selection. You can use this information to set item attributes that depend on the selection state of the item. Returning TRUE in response to TVN_SELCHANGING prevents the selection from changing, and returning FALSE allows the selection to change. Change the selection by sending the TVM_SELECTITEM message.

Item Information

Tree view controls support a number of messages that retrieve information about items in the control.

The TVM_GETITEM message can retrieve an item's handle and attributes. An item's attributes include its current state, the indexes in the control's image list of the item's selected and nonselected bit images, a flag that indicates whether the item has child items, the address of the item's label string, and the item's application-defined 32-bit value.

The TVM_GETNEXTITEM message retrieves the tree view item that bears the specified relationship to the current item. The message can retrieve an item's parent, the next or previous visible item, the first child item, and so on.

The TVM_GETITEMRECT message retrieves the bounding rectangle for a tree view item. The TVM_GETCOUNT and TVM_GETVISIBLECOUNT messages retrieve a count of the items in a tree view control and a count of the items that can be fully visible in the tree view control's window, respectively. You can ensure that a particular item is visible by using the TVM_ENSUREVISIBLE message.

Tree View Image Lists

Each item in a tree view control can have four bit images associated with it:

- An image, such as an open folder, displayed when the item is selected.
- An image, such as a closed folder, displayed when the item is not selected.
- An overlay image that is drawn transparently over the selected or nonselected image.
- A state image, which is an additional image displayed to the left of the selected or nonselected image. You can use state images, such as checked and cleared check boxes, to indicate application-defined item states.

By default, a tree view control does not display item images. To display item images, you must create image lists and associate them with the control.

A tree view control can have two image lists: a normal image list and a state image list. A normal image list stores the selected, nonselected, and overlay images. A state image list stores state images. Use the **ImageList_Create** function to create an image list, and use other image list functions to add bitmaps to the image list. Then, to associate the image list with the tree view control, use the TVM_SETIMAGELIST message. The TVM_GETIMAGELIST message retrieves a handle to one of a tree view control's image lists.

In addition to the selected and nonselected images, a tree view control's normal image list can contain up to four overlay images. Overlay images are designed to be drawn transparently over the selected and nonselected images. To assign an overlay mask index to an image in the normal image list, call the **ImageList_SetOverlayImage** function.

By default, all items display the first image in the normal image list for both the selected and nonselected states. Also, by default, items do not display overlay images or state images. You can change these default behaviors for an item by sending the TVM_INSERTITEM or TVM_SETITEM messages. These messages use the **TVITEM** structure to specify image list indexes for an item.

To associate an overlay image with an item, use the **INDEXTOOVERLAYMASK** macro to specify an overlay mask index in the **state** member of the item's **TVITEM** structure. You must also set the TVIS_OVERLAYMASK bits in the **stateMask** member. Overlay mask indexes are one-based; an index of zero indicates that the application not specify an overlay image.

To associate a state image with an item, use the **INDEXTOSTATEIMAGEMASK** macro to specify a state image index in the state member of the item's **TVITEM** structure. The index identifies an image in the control's state image list.

Note You can speed up the creation of large tree views by disabling the painting of the tree view before adding the items. You do this by sending a WM_SETREDRAW message with the redraw flag set to FALSE. When you are finished adding items, re-enable painting by sending a WM_SETREDRAW message with the redraw flag set to TRUE.

Drag-and-Drop Operations

A tree view control notifies the parent window when the user starts to drag an item with a mouse. The parent window receives a TVN_BEGINDRAG notification message when the user begins dragging an item with the left mouse button and a TVN_BEGINRDRAG notification message when the user begins dragging with the right button. You can prevent a tree view control from sending these notifications by giving the tree view control the TVS_DISABLEDRAGDROP style.

You obtain an image to display during a drag operation by using the TVM_CREATEDRAGIMAGE message. The tree view control creates a dragging bitmap based on the label of the item being dragged. Then, the tree view control creates an image list, adds the bitmap to it, and returns the handle to the image list.

You must provide the code that actually drags the item. This typically involves using the dragging capabilities of the image list functions and including code for processing the WM_MOUSEMOVE and WM_LBUTTONUP messages sent to the parent window after the drag operation has begun.

To use an item in a tree view control as the target of a drag-and-drop operation, use the **SendMessage** function to send a TVM_HITTEST message to determine when the stylus is on a target item. To do this, specify the address of a **TVHITTESTINFO** structure that contains the current coordinates of the stylus. When the **SendMessage** function returns, the structure contains a flag indicating the location of the stylus relative to the tree view control. If the stylus is over an item in the tree view control, the structure contains the handle to the item as well.

You indicate that an item is the target of a drag-and-drop operation by using the TVM_SETITEM message to set the state to TVIS_DROPHILITED. An item that has this state is drawn in the style used to indicate a target for a drag-and-drop operation.

Up-Down Controls

An *up-down control*, also known as a spin button control, is a pair of arrow buttons that a user can tap with the stylus to increment or decrement a value. An up-down control is most often used with a companion control, called a buddy window, in which the current value is displayed. In Windows CE-based applications, up-down controls can only be "buddies" with edit controls.

Up-Down control and buddy window

You create an up-down control by using the **CreateUpDownControl** function. This class is registered when the common control DLL is loaded. You can use the **InitCommonControls** function to ensure that this DLL is loaded.

To register the up-down control class using the **InitCommonControlsEx** function, specify the ICC_UPDOWN_CLASS flag as the **dwICC** member of the **INITCOMMONCONTROLSEX** structure you pass in the *lpInitCtrls* parameter.

Windows CE does not support hot tracking.

Up-Down Control Styles

Control styles for up-down controls supported by Windows CE are described in the following table.

Style	Description
UDS_ALIGNLEFT	Positions the up-down control next to the left edge of the buddy window. The buddy window is moved to the right and its width is decreased to accommodate the width of the up-down control.
UDS_ALIGNRIGHT	Positions the up-down control next to the right edge of the buddy window. The width of the buddy window is decreased to accommodate the width of the up-down control.
UDS_ARROWKEYS	Causes the up-down control to process the UP ARROW and DOWN ARROW keys on the keyboard.
UDS_AUTOBUDDY	Automatically elects the previous window in the Z order as the up-down control's buddy window. In Windows CE, the window must be an edit control.
UDS_HORZ	Causes the up-down control's arrows to point left and right instead of up and down.
UDS_NOTHOUSANDS	Refrains from inserting a thousands separator between every three decimal digits.
UDS_SETBUDDYINT	Causes the up-down control to set the text of the buddy window, using the WM_SETTEXT message, when the position changes. The text consists of the position formatted as a decimal or hexadecimal string.
UDS_WRAP	Causes the position to wrap if it is incremented or decremented beyond the end or beginning of the range.

Position and Acceleration

After you have created an up-down control, you can change it in several ways. You can change its current position, minimum position, and maximum position by sending messages. You can change the radix base, that is, either base 10 or base 16, used to display the current position in the buddy window. And, you can change the rate at which the current position changes when the up or down arrow is clicked.

To retrieve the current position of an up-down control, use the UDM_GETPOS message. For an up-down control with a buddy window, the current position is the number in the buddy window's caption. The up-down control retrieves the current caption and updates its current position if the caption has changed because the user edited the text of an edit control.

The buddy window's caption can be either a decimal or hexadecimal string, depending on the radix base of the up-down control. Set the radix base by using the UDM_SETBASE message and retrieve the radix base by using the UDM_GETBASE message.

The UDM_SETPOS message sets the current position of a buddy window. Note that unlike a scroll bar, an up-down control automatically changes its current position when the up and down arrows are clicked. Therefore, an application does not need to set the current position when processing the WM_VSCROLL or WM_HSCROLL message.

You can change the minimum and maximum positions of an up-down control by using the UDM_SETRANGE message. The maximum position may be less than the minimum, in which case clicking the up arrow button decreases the current position. Put another way, up moves toward the maximum position. To retrieve the minimum and maximum positions for an up-down control, use the UDM_GETRANGE message.

You can control the rate at which the position changes when the user holds down an arrow button by setting the up-down control's acceleration. The acceleration is defined by an array of **UDACCEL** structures. Each structure specifies a time interval and the number of units by which to increment or decrement at the end of that interval. To set the acceleration, use the UDM_SETACCEL message. To retrieve acceleration information, use the UDM_GETACCEL message.

C H A P T E R   1 3

Informational Controls

Windows CE contains a set of common controls that provide information about tools, processes, or time. These informational controls are described in this chapter:

- Date and time picker controls
- Month calendar controls
- Status bars
- ToolTips
- Progress bars

Date and Time Picker Controls

The *date and time picker* (DTP) is a control that displays information about dates and times, and provides users with an easy way to modify this information. Each field in the control displays a time element, such as month, day, hour, or minute. A user selects a field by tapping it with the stylus and then types a new value from the keyboard.

| Wednesday, December 03, 1997 | ▼ |

Windows CE date and time picker

The way date and time information is displayed is determined by a format string. A DTP control can display time information in any of three preset formats, or you can create custom format strings to specify a different order in which to display the fields. For more information on the three preset formats, see "Preset DTP Display Formats" later in this chapter. You can also add customized date and time information to a DTP control by using callback fields.

To create a date and time picker control, specify DATETIMEPICK_CLASS in the *lpClassName* parameter to the **CreateWindowEx** function. This class is registered when the common control dynamic-link library (DLL) is loaded. You can use the **InitCommonControls** function to ensure that this DLL is loaded.

To register the date and time picker class using the **InitCommonControlsEx** function, specify the ICC_DATE_CLASSES flag as the **dwICC** member of the **INITCOMMONCONTROLSEX** structure you pass in the *lpInitCtrls* parameter.

Date and Time Picker Styles

Date and time picker styles supported by Windows CE are described in the following table.

Style	Description
DTS_APPCANPARSE	Allows the owner to parse user input. When a DTP control has this style, a user can make changes within the client area of the control by pressing the F2 key. The control sends a DTN_USERSTRING notification message when the user is finished editing.
DTS_LONGDATEFORMAT	Displays the date in long format. The default format string for this style is defined by LOCALE_SLONGDATEFORMAT, which produces output like "Friday, April 19, 1996."
DTS_SHOWNONE	Enables the control to accept "no date" as a valid selection state. This state can be set with the DTM_SETSYSTEMTIME message or verified with the DTM_GETSYSTEMTIME message.
DTS_SHORTDATEFORMAT	Displays the date in short format. The default format string for this style is defined by LOCALE_SSHORTDATE, which produces output like "4/19/96."
DTS_TIMEFORMAT	Displays the time. The default format string for this style is defined by LOCALE_STIMEFORMAT, which produces output like "5:31:42 PM." An up-down control is placed to the right of the DTP control to modify time values.
DTS_UPDOWN	Places an up-down control to the right of a DTP control to modify time values. This style can be used instead of the drop-down month calendar, which is the default style.

Date and Time Picker User Interface

Each field in the DTP control displays a portion of the time information that the control stores internally. The user can select a field to set the keyboard focus, and then provide keyboard input to change the time information represented by that field. The DTP control automatically updates internal time information based on the user's input. Input types recognized by the control as valid are described in the following table.

Input type	Description
Arrow keys	The control accepts arrow keys to navigate the fields in the control and change values. The user can press the LEFT ARROW key or RIGHT ARROW key to move in that direction through the control. If the user attempts to move past the last field in a specified direction, the keyboard focus moves to the field on the opposite side of the control. The UP ARROW and DOWN ARROW keys change values in the current field incrementally.
END and HOME Keys	The control accepts the VK_END and VK_HOME virtual keys to change the value within the current field to its upper and lower limits, respectively.
Numbers	The control accepts numeric input in two-character segments. If the value typed by the user is invalid, such as setting the month to 14, the control rejects it and resets the display to the previous value.

Format Strings

As stated earlier, a DTP control relies on a format string to determine how it will display fields of information. By default, a DTP control can display time information in the format DTS_LONGDATEFORMAT.

Custom format strings provide flexibility for your application. In a custom format string, you can specify the order in which the control will display fields of information or indicate specific callback fields. The format characters of the format string define the DTP control's display and field layout.

Preset DTP Display Formats

By default, a DTP control can display time information fields in three preset formats or according to a custom format string. Window styles used by the preset formats, which are format strings, are described in the following table.

Style	Description
DTS_LONGDATEFORMAT	The control displays the date in long format. The default format string for this style is defined by LOCALE_SLONGDATEFORMAT, which produces output like "Friday, April 19, 1996."
DTS_SHORTDATEFORMAT	The control displays the date in short format, which is the default style setting. The default format string for this style is defined by LOCALE_SSHORTDATE, which produces output like "4/19/96."
DTS_TIMEFORMAT	The control displays the time. The default format string for this style is defined by LOCALE_STIMEFORMAT, which produces output like "5:31:42 PM." An up-down control is placed to the right of the DTP control to modify time values.

Custom Format Strings

You can customize the display of a DTP control using custom format strings. DTP controls support specified format characters that you can combine to create a format string. To assign the format string to the DTP control, use the DTM_SETFORMAT message.

You can add body text to the format string. For example, if you want the control to display the current date with the format "Today is: 04:22:31 Tuesday Mar 23, 1996", use the following format string: Today is: 'hh':'m':'s ddddMMMdd', 'yyy. Body text must be enclosed in single quotation marks.

Note that segments of nonformat characters in the preceding example are delimited by single quotation marks. Failure to surround body text in this way will result in unpredictable display by the DTP control.

Format Characters

Format characters supported by DTP controls are described in the following table.

String fragment	Description
"d"	The one-digit or two-digit day.
"dd"	The two-digit day. Single-digit day values are preceded by a zero.
"ddd"	The three-character weekday abbreviation.
"dddd"	The full weekday name.
"gg"	The period and era string contained in the CAL_SERASTRING value associated with the specified locale. Windows CE ignores this element if the date to be formatted does not have an associated era or period string.
"h"	The one-digit or two-digit hour in 12-hour format.
"hh"	The two-digit hour in 12-hour format. Single-digit values are preceded by a zero.
"H"	The one-digit or two-digit hour in 24-hour format.
"HH"	The two-digit hour in 24-hour format. Single-digit values are preceded by a zero.
"m"	The one-digit or two-digit minute.
"mm"	The two-digit minute. Single-digit values are preceded by a zero.
"M"	The one-digit or two-digit month number.
"MM"	The two-digit month number. Single-digit values are preceded by a zero.
"MMM"	The three-character month abbreviation.
"MMMM"	The full month name.
"t"	The one-letter AM and PM abbreviation (that is, "AM" is displayed as "A").
"tt"	The two-letter AM and PM abbreviation (that is, "AM" is displayed as "AM").
"X"	The callback field. The control uses the other valid format characters and queries the application to fill in the "X" portion of the string. The application must be prepared to handle the DTN_WMKEYDOWN, DTN_FORMAT, and DTN_FORMATQUERY notification messages. Multiple "X" characters can be used in a series to signify unique callback fields.
"y"	The one-digit year. For example, 1996 would be displayed as "6."
"yy"	The last two digits of the year. For example, 1996 would be displayed as "96."
"yyy"	The full year. For example, 1996 would be displayed as "1996."

Callback Fields

In addition to the standard format characters that define DTP fields, you can customize your output by specifying certain parts of a format string as callback fields. To declare a callback field, include one or more ASCII Code 88 "X" characters anywhere in the body of the format string. Like other DTP control fields, callback fields are displayed in left-to-right order, based on their location in the format string.

You can create unique callback fields by repeating the "X" character. Thus, the following format string contains two callback fields: XXddddMMMdd', 'yyyXXX. Remember, because callback fields are treated as valid fields, your application must be prepared to handle DTN_WMKEYDOWN notification messages.

When the DTP control parses the format string and encounters a callback field, it sends DTN_FORMAT and DTN_FORMATQUERY notification messages. The owner of the control must respond to these notifications to ensure that the custom information is properly displayed.

Month Calendar Controls

A *month calendar control* is a child window that displays a monthly calendar. The calendar can display one or more months at a time.

Month calendar control

When a user taps the name of a month with the stylus, a pop-up menu appears that lists all the months of the year. A user can select a month by tapping its name on the menu. A user who is using the DTP control can use ALT+DOWN ARROW to activate the month calendar control. The user can scroll the displayed months forward or backward either by tapping the left arrow or right arrow at the top of the control or by pressing the PAGE UP or PAGE DOWN keys on the keyboard. When a user taps the year displayed at the top of the calendar next to the month, an up-down control appears. The user can use this control to change the year. The user can also use CTRL+PAGE UP or CTRL+PAGE DOWN to scroll from one year to another. A user can press keys on the keyboard to navigate; the arrow keys scroll between days, the HOME key moves to the beginning of a month, and the END key moves to the end of a month. Unless the calendar has the MCS_NOTODAY style, the user can return to the current day by tapping the **Today** label at the bottom of the month calendar control.

You create a month calendar control by specifying MONTHCAL_CLASS in the *lpClassName* parameter to the **CreateWindowEx** function. This class is registered when the common control DLL is loaded. You can use the **InitCommonControls** function to ensure that this DLL is loaded.

To register the month calendar control class using the **InitCommonControlsEx** function, specify the ICC_DATE_CLASSES flag as the **dwICC** member of the **INITCOMMONCONTROLSEX** structure you pass in the *lpInitCtrls* parameter.

Month Calendar Styles

Month calendar styles supported by Windows CE are described in the following table.

Style	Description
MCS_DAYSTATE	Specifies that the month calendar will send MCN_GETDAYSTATE notifications to request information about which days should be displayed in bold.
MCS_MULTISELECT	Allows the user to select a range of dates. By default, the maximum range is one week. You can change the maximum selectable range using the MCM_SETMAXSELCOUNT message.
MCS_NOTODAY	Creates a month calendar that does not display a Today selection.
MCS_NOTODAYCIRCLE	Creates a month calendar that does not circle the current date.
MCS_WEEKNUMBERS	Displays the week number, from 1 through 52, to the left of each week in the calendar.

Day States

A month calendar control that uses the MCS_DAYSTATE style supports day states. The control uses day state information to determine how it draws specific days within the control. Day state information is expressed as a 32-bit data type, MONTHDAYSTATE. Each bit in a MONTHDAYSTATE bit field, from 1 through 31, represents the state of a day in a month. If a bit is on, the corresponding day will be displayed in bold; otherwise it will be displayed with no emphasis.

An application can explicitly set day state information by sending the MCM_SETDAYSTATE message or by using the corresponding macro, **MonthCal_SetDayState**. Additionally, month calendar controls that use the MCS_DAYSTATE style send MCN_GETDAYSTATE notification messages to request day state information.

Times

Because the month calendar control is created, it will insert the current time into its "today" date and time. When a time is later set programmatically, the control will either copy the time fields as they are or validate them first, and then, if invalid, store the current default times. Messages that set a date and the manner in which those messages treat time fields are described in the following table.

Message	Description
MCM_SETCURSEL	The control copies the time fields as they are, without validation or modification.
MCM_SETRANGE	The control validates the time fields of the structures passed in. If they are valid, the time fields are copied without modification. If they are invalid, the control copies the time fields from the "today" date and time.
MCM_SETSELRANGE	The control validates the time fields of the structures passed in. If they are valid, the time fields are copied without modification. If they are invalid, the control retains the time fields from the current selection ranges.
MCM_SETTODAY	The control copies the time fields as they are, without validation or modification.

When a date is retrieved from the month calendar control, the time fields will be copied from the stored times without modification. Handling of the time fields by the control is provided as a convenience to you. The control does not examine or modify the time fields as a result of any operation other than those previously listed.

Status Bars

A *status bar*, also known as a status window, is a horizontal window positioned at the bottom of a parent window. It displays status information defined by the application.

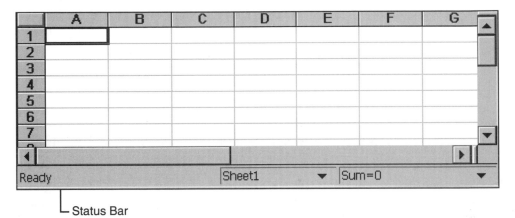

Status Bar

Status bar

You create a status bar by calling the **CreateStatusWindow** function. This class is registered when the common control DLL is loaded. You can use the **InitCommonControls** function to ensure that this DLL is loaded. To register the status bar class using the **InitCommonControlsEx** function, specify the ICC_ BAR_CLASSES flag as the **dwICC** member of the **INITCOMMONCONTROLSEX** structure you pass in the *lpInitCtrls* parameter.

Size and Height

The window procedure for the status bar control automatically sets the initial size and position of the window. The width is the same as that of the parent window's client area. The height is based on the width of the window's borders and on the metrics of the font that is currently selected into the status bar's device context.

The window procedure automatically adjusts the size of the status bar whenever it receives a WM_SIZE message. Typically, when the size of the parent window changes, the parent sends a WM_SIZE message to the status bar.

An application can set the minimum height of a status bar's drawing area by sending the window an SB_SETMINHEIGHT message that specifies the minimum height in pixels. The drawing area does not include the window's borders.

You retrieve the widths of the borders of a status bar by sending the window an SB_GETBORDERS message. The message includes the address of a three-element array that receives the widths.

Multiple-Part Status Bars

A status bar can have many different parts, each displaying a different line of text. You divide a status bar into parts by sending the window an SB_SETPARTS message, which specifies the number of parts to create and the address of an integer array. The array contains one element for each part, and each element specifies the client coordinate of the right edge of a part.

A status bar can have a maximum of 255 parts, although applications typically use far fewer than that. You retrieve a count of the parts in a status bar, as well as the coordinate of the right edge of each part, by sending the window an SB_GETPARTS message.

A simple mode status bar is useful for displaying Help text for menu items while the user is scrolling through the menu. You put a status bar in simple mode by sending it an SB_SIMPLE message. A simple mode status bar displays only one part. When the text of the window is set, the window is invalidated, but it is not redrawn until the next WM_PAINT message. Waiting for the message reduces screen flicker by minimizing the number of times the window is redrawn.

The string that a status bar displays while in simple mode is maintained separately from the strings that it displays while it is not in simple mode. This means you can put the window in simple mode, set its text, and switch out of simple mode without the original text being changed.

Windows CE supports a status bar notification, SBN_SIMPLEMODECHANGE, that a status bar sends when the simple mode changes as a result of receiving an SB_SIMPLE message.

Status Bar Text

You set the text of any part of a status bar by sending the SB_SETTEXT message, specifying the zero-based index of a part, an address of the string to draw in the part, and the technique for drawing the string. The drawing technique determines whether the text has a border and, if it does, the style of the border. It also determines whether the parent window is responsible for drawing the text.

By default, text is left-aligned within the specified part of a status bar. You can embed tab characters, for example, \ t, in the text to center it or right-align it. Text to the right of a single tab character is centered, and text to the right of a second tab character is right-aligned.

To retrieve text from a status bar, use the SB_GETTEXTLENGTH and SB_GETTEXT messages.

If your application uses a status bar that has only one part, you can perform text operations by using the WM_SETTEXT, WM_GETTEXT, and WM_GETTEXTLENGTH messages. These messages deal only with the part that has an index of zero, allowing you to treat the status bar much like a static text control.

To display a line of status information without creating a status bar, use the **DrawStatusText** function. The function uses the same techniques to draw the status information as it uses to draw the window procedure for the status bar, but it does not automatically set the size and position of the status information. When calling the **DrawStatusText** function, you must specify the size and position of the status information as well as the device context of the window in which to draw it.

ToolTips

A *ToolTip* is a tiny, rectangular pop-up window that displays a brief description of a command bar button's purpose when the user holds the stylus on the button for more than 0.5 second. If the user lifts the stylus from the screen while it is still positioned over the button, the button is activated. If the user moves the stylus away from the button before raising the stylus from the screen, the button is not activated.

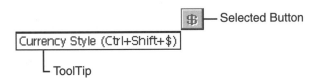

ToolTip

Windows CE supports ToolTips only for command bar and toolbar buttons. it does not support ToolTips for the menus or combo boxes in a command bar. To add ToolTips to a command bar, use the **CommandBar_AddTooltips** function.

The **CommandBar_AddtoolTips** function does not make a copy of the array of ToolTip strings you pass to it. It directly uses the memory address you pass to it in the *lpToolTips* parameter. Do not release the memory allocated for this array until the program exits.

ToolTips usually display only the name of a button's command, but they can also display the shortcut key for the command. For more information about shortcut keys, see Chapter 16, "Dialog Boxes, Menus, and Other Resources."

Progress Bars

A *progress bar* is a common control that indicates the progress of a lengthy operation by displaying a colored bar inside a horizontal rectangle. The length of the bar in relation to the length of the rectangle corresponds to the percentage of the operation that is complete.

Progress bar

You create a progress bar by specifying PROGRESS_CLASS in the *lpClassName* parameter to the **CreateWindowEx** function. This class is registered when the common control DLL is loaded. You can use the **InitCommonControls** function to ensure that this DLL is loaded.

To register the progress bar class using the **InitCommonControlsEx** function, specify the ICC_PROGRESS_CLASS flag as the **dwICC** member of the **INITCOMMONCONTROLSEX** structure you pass in the *lpInitCtrls* parameter.

Progress Bar Styles

Progress bar styles supported by Windows CE are described in the following table.

Style	Description
PBS_SMOOTH	Displays progress status in a smooth scrolling bar instead of the default segmented bar.
PBS_VERTICAL	Displays progress status vertically, from bottom to top.

Range and Current Position

A progress bar's range represents the entire duration of the operation, and the current position represents the progress that the application has made toward completing the operation. The window procedure uses the range and the current position to determine the percentage of the progress bar to fill with the highlight color as well as to determine what text, if any, to display within the progress bar.

If you do not set the range values, the system sets the minimum value to zero and the maximum value to 100. You can adjust the range to convenient integers by using the PBM_SETRANGE message.

A progress bar provides several messages that you can use to set the current position. The PBM_SETPOS message sets the position to a specified value. The PBM_DELTAPOS message advances the position by adding a specified value to the current position. The PBM_SETSTEP message allows you to specify a step increment for a progress bar. Subsequently, whenever you send the PBM_STEPIT message to the progress bar, the current position advances by the specified increment. By default, the step increment is set to 10.

Note The range values in a progress bar are considered signed integers. Any number greater than 0x7FFFFFFF is interpreted as a negative number.

C H A P T E R   1 4

Buttons

Windows CE provides dialog boxes and controls to support communication between an application and the user. A button is a Windows control that a user can turn on or off to provide input to an application. Buttons can be used alone or in groups and can appear with or without application-defined text, known as a label. Buttons belong to the BUTTON window class.

The user turns a button on or off by selecting it with the stylus or keyboard. Selecting a button changes its visual appearance and state, for example, from checked to unchecked. A button can send messages to its parent window, and a parent window can send messages to a button.

Although you can use buttons in overlapped, pop-up, and child windows, they are designed for use in dialog boxes where Windows CE standardizes their behavior. If you use buttons outside dialog boxes, you increase the risk that your application may behave in a nonstandard fashion. You can create customized buttons by using window subclassing procedures.

Windows CE provides four kinds of buttons: push buttons, check boxes, radio buttons, and group boxes. Each type has one or more styles that affect the button's appearance, behavior, or both.

The following button types are described in this chapter:

- Check boxes
- Group boxes
- Push buttons
- Radio buttons

Button States

A button's state can be characterized by its focus state, push state, and check state. The focus state applies to a check box, radio button, or push button. A button receives the keyboard focus when the user selects it and loses the focus when the user selects another control. Only one control can have the keyboard focus at a time.

The push state applies to a push button, check box, radio button, or three-state check box, but does not apply to other buttons. The push state of a button can be either pushed or not pushed. When a push button is pushed, the button is drawn as a sunken button. When it is not pushed, it is drawn as a raised button. When a check box, radio button, or three-state check box is pushed, the background of the button appears dimmed. When it is not pushed, the background of the button does not appear dimmed.

The check state applies to a check box, radio button, or three-state check box, but does not apply to other buttons. The state can be checked, unchecked, or indeterminate; the latter state applies only to three-state check boxes. A check box is checked when it contains a check mark, and is unchecked when it does not. A radio button is checked when it contains a black dot and it is unchecked when it does not. A three-state check box is checked when it contains a check mark, unchecked when it does not, and indeterminate when it contains a box that appears dimmed. Windows CE changes the check state of an automatic button, but the application must change the check state of a button that is not automatic.

Changes to a Button State

When the user selects a button, either the operating system or the application must change one or more of the button's state elements. Windows CE automatically changes the focus state for all button types, the push state for push buttons, and the check state for all automatic buttons. The application must make all other state changes, taking into account the button's type, style, and current state. For example, an application must change the check state for a check box or a radio button. When an application changes the check state for a radio button, it may also need to change the check state of other radio buttons in the same group to ensure the mutually exclusive nature of radio buttons.

An application can determine a button's state by sending it a BM_GETCHECK or BM_GETSTATE message; the application can set a button's state by sending it a BM_SETCHECK or BM_SETSTATE message.

Selecting a Button

Windows CE provides three ways for a user to select a button: by touching it with a stylus, by tabbing to it and then pressing the ENTER key, or by tabbing to the selected button in the group and using the arrow keys to move within that group. This last method is only available if the button is part of a group defined by the WS_GROUP style. In addition to these predefined methods, you can create a keyboard accelerator to a button. A *keyboard accelerator*, also known as a shortcut key, is a keystroke or combination of keystrokes that generates a WM_COMMAND message. For more information about keyboard accelerators, see Chapter 16, "Dialog Boxes, Menus, and Other Resources."

Selecting a button generally causes the following events:

1. Windows gives the button the keyboard focus.
2. The button sends its parent window a message to notify it of the selection.
3. The parent window or Windows CE sends the button a message to change its state.
4. The parent window or Windows CE repaints the button to reflect its new state.

Notification Messages from Buttons

When the user selects a button, its state changes, and the button sends notification messages to its parent window about the changed state. For example, a push button control sends the BN_CLICKED notification message whenever the user chooses the button. In all cases, the low-order word of the *wParam* parameter contains the control identifier, the high-order word of *wParam* contains the notification code, and the *lParam* contains the control window handle.

Both the message and the parent window's response to it depend on the type, style, and current state of the button. Button notification messages that an application should monitor and process are described in the following table.

Message	Description
BN_CLICKED	The user clicked a button.
BN_DISABLE	A button is disabled.
BN_PUSHED	The user pushed a button.
BN_KILLFOCUS	The button lost the keyboard focus.
BN_PAINT	The button should be painted.
BN_SETFOCUS	The button gained the keyboard focus.
BN_UNPUSHED	The button is no longer pushed.

A button sends the BN_DISABLE, BN_PUSHED, BN_KILLFOCUS, BN_PAINT, BN_SETFOCUS, and BN_UNPUSHED notification messages only if it has the BS_NOTIFY style. It sends the BN_CLICKED notification message regardless of the BS_NOTIFY style.

For automatic buttons, the operating system performs pushing, unpushing, and painting. In this case, the application typically processes only the BN_CLICKED notification message. For buttons that are not automatic, the application usually responds to the notification message by sending a message to change the state of the button.

When the user selects an owner-drawn button, the button sends its parent window a WM_DRAWITEM message containing the identifier of the control to be drawn and information about its dimensions and state.

Messages to Buttons

A parent window can send messages to a button in an overlapped or child window by using the **SendMessage** function. It can send messages to a button in a dialog box by using the **SendDlgItemMessage** and **CheckRadioButton** functions.

An application can use the BM_GETCHECK message to retrieve the check state of a check box or radio button. An application can also use the BM_GETSTATE message to retrieve the button's current states, that is, the check state, push state, and focus state.

The BM_SETCHECK message sets the check state of a check box or radio button and the BM_SETSTATE message sets the push state of a button. You can change the style of a button by using the BM_SETSTYLE message, which changes the button styles within a type. For example, it changes a check box to an automatic check box. This message is not designed for changing between types, for example, changing a check box to a radio button. An application should not change a button from one type to another.

You can use the DM_GETDEFID message to retrieve the identifier of the default push button control in a dialog box. You can use the DM_SETDEFID message to set the default push button for a dialog box. When you use the **SetFocus** function on a dialog box control, you should use the WM_NEXTDLGCTL message, rather than the DM_SETDEFID message, to change the default button style.

Button Color Messages

Windows provides default color values for buttons. The system sends a WM_CTLCOLORBTN message to a button's parent window before the button is drawn. This message contains a handle of the button's device context and a handle of the child window. The parent window can use these handles to change the button's text and background colors. Default button-color values are described in the following table.

Value	Element colored
COLOR_BTNFACE	Button faces.
COLOR_BTNHIGHLIGHT	Highlight area—the top and left edges—of a button.
COLOR_BTNSHADOW	Shadow area—the bottom and right edges—of a button.
COLOR_BTNTEXT	Regular text in buttons.
COLOR_GRAYTEXT	In buttons, disabled text appears dimmed. This color is set to zero if the current display driver does not support a solid gray color.
COLOR_WINDOW	Window backgrounds.
COLOR_WINDOWFRAME	Window frames.
COLOR_WINDOWTEXT	Text in windows.

An application can retrieve the default values for these colors by calling the **GetSysColor** function, or it can set the values by calling the **SetSysColors** function.

Button Default Message Processing

The window procedure for the predefined button control window class processes defaults for all messages that the button control procedure does not process. When the button control procedure returns FALSE for any message, the predefined window procedure checks the messages and performs the default actions described in the following table.

Message	Default action
BM_CLICK	Sends the button a WM_LBUTTONDOWN and a WM_LBUTTONUP message, and sends the parent window a BN_CLICKED notification message.
BM_GETCHECK	Returns the check state of the button.
BM_GETSTATE	Returns the current check state, push state, and focus state of the button.

Message	Default action
BM_SETCHECK	Sets the check state for all styles of radio buttons and check boxes. If the *wParam* parameter is greater than zero for radio buttons, the button is given the WS_TABSTOP style.
BM_SETSTATE	Sets the push state of the button. For owner-drawn buttons, a WM_DRAWITEM message is sent to the parent window if the state of the button has changed.
BM_SETSTYLE	Sets the button style. If the low-order word of the *lParam* parameter is TRUE, the button is redrawn.
WM_CHAR	Changes the check state of a check box when the user presses the space bar.
WM_ENABLE	Paints the button.
WM_ERASEBKGND	Erases the background for owner-drawn buttons. The backgrounds of other buttons are erased as part of the WM_PAINT and WM_ENABLE processing.
WM_GETFONT	Returns a handle of the current font.
WM_KEYDOWN	Pushes the button, if the user presses the SPACEBAR.
WM_KEYUP	Releases the mouse capture for all cases except the TAB key.
WM_KILLFOCUS	Removes the focus rectangle from a button. For push buttons and default push buttons, the focus rectangle is invalidated. If the button has the mouse capture, the capture is released, the button is not clicked, and any push state is removed.
WM_LBUTTONDBLCLK	Sends a BN_DBLCLK notification message to the parent window for radio buttons and owner-drawn buttons. For other buttons, a double-click is processed as a WM_LBUTTONDOWN message.
WM_LBUTTONDOWN	Highlights the button if the position of the mouse cursor is within the button's client rectangle.
WM_LBUTTONUP	Releases the mouse capture if the button has the mouse capture.
WM_PAINT	Draws the button according to its style and current state.
WM_SETFOCUS	Draws a focus rectangle on the button getting the focus. For radio buttons and automatic radio buttons, the parent window is sent a BN_CLICKED notification message.
WM_SETFONT	Sets a new font and, optionally, updates the window.

Message	Default action
WM_SETTEXT	Sets the text of the button. In the case of a group box, the message paints over the preexisting text before repainting the group box with the new text.
WM_SYSKEYUP	Releases the mouse capture for all cases except the TAB key.

Check Boxes

A check box is a small square box with a label next to it. A user can turn a check box on or off by tapping it with the stylus or pressing the space bar when the check box has the keyboard focus. The box is empty in its default off state and has a check mark in it when it is turned on.

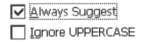

Check box

Applications display check boxes in a group box to permit the user to choose from a set of related but independent options. For example, an application might present a group of check boxes from which the user can select error conditions that produce warning beeps.

When the user selects a check box of any style, the check box receives the keyboard focus from Windows CE, which sends the check box's parent window a WM_COMMAND message containing the BN_CLICKED notification code. The parent window does not acknowledge this message if it comes from an automatic check box or automatic three-state check box, because Windows CE automatically sets the check state for those styles. But the parent window must acknowledge the message if it comes from an application-defined check box or three-state check box because the parent window, not Windows CE, is responsible for setting the check state for those styles. Regardless of the check box style, Windows CE automatically repaints the check box once its state is changed.

Check Box Styles

Check box styles supported by Windows CE are described in the following table.

Style	Description
BS_3STATE	Creates a check box in which the box can be unavailable as well as checked or unchecked. Use the unavailable state to show that the state of the check box is not determined.
BS_AUTO3STATE	Creates a three-state check box in which the state cycles through checked, unavailable, and unchecked each time the user selects the check box.
BS_AUTOCHECKBOX	Creates a check box in which the check state automatically toggles between checked and unchecked each time the user selects the check box.
BS_CHECKBOX	Creates a small, empty check box with a label displayed to the right of it. To display the text to the left of the check box, combine this flag with the BS_RIGHTBUTTON style.
BS_LEFT	Left-aligns the text in the button rectangle that is on the right side of the check box.
BS_RIGHT	Right-aligns text in the button rectangle that is on the right side of the check box.
BS_RIGHTBUTTON	Positions a check box's square on the right side of the button rectangle.
WS_TABSTOP	Turns the control into a tab stop, which allows the user to select the control by tabbing through the controls in a dialog box.

Group Boxes

A group box is a rectangular area within a dialog box in which you can group together controls that are semantically related. The controls are grouped by drawing a rectangular border around them. Any text associated with the group box is displayed in its upper-left corner. The sole purpose of a group box is to organize controls related by a common purpose, which is usually indicated by the label. The group box has only one style, defined by the constant BS_GROUPBOX. Because a group box cannot be selected, it has no check state, focus state, or push state. An application cannot send messages to a group box.

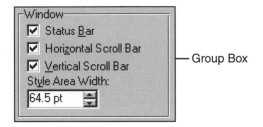

Group Box

Group box

Because group boxes are opaque in Windows CE, you must always add them to your dialog box template after you have added everything else. Anything you add to the template after you add the group box will be hidden underneath it. By adding group boxes last, you ensure that the group boxes are at the bottom of the Z order and will not hide your other controls.

You create a group box by specifying the BS_GROUPBOX style in the **CreateWindow** or **CreateWindowEx** function.

Push Buttons

A push button, also known as a command button, is a small, rectangular control that a user can turn on or off by tapping it with the stylus. A push button has a raised appearance in its default, or off, state and a depressed appearance when it is turned on. Windows CE supports owner-drawn push buttons, which are discussed later in this chapter.

Push button

When the user clicks a push button, it receives the keyboard focus from Windows CE, which sends the button's parent window a WM_COMMAND message containing the BN_CLICKED notification code. In response, the dialog box closes and carries out the operation indicated by the button.

Push Button Styles

Button styles supported by Windows CE are described in the following table.

Style	Description
BS_BOTTOM	Places the text at the bottom of the button rectangle.
BS_CENTER	Centers the text horizontally in the button rectangle.
BS_DEFPUSHBUTTON	Creates a push button with a heavy black border. If the button is in a dialog box, the user can select the button by pressing the ENTER key, even when the button does not have the input focus. This style is useful for enabling the user to quickly select the most likely option, or default.
BS_LEFT	Left-aligns the text in the button rectangle.
BS_NOTIFY	Enables a button to send BN_DBLCLK, BN_KILLFOCUS, and BN_SETFOCUS notification messages to its parent window. Note that the button sends the BN_CLICKED notification message regardless of whether it has this style.
BS_OWNERDRAW	Creates an owner-drawn button. The owner window receives a WM_MEASUREITEM message when the button is created and a WM_DRAWITEM message when a visual aspect of the button has changed.
BS_PUSHBUTTON	Creates a push button that posts a WM_COMMAND message to the owner window when the user clicks the button.
BS_RIGHT	Right-aligns text in the button rectangle.
BS_TOP	Places text at the top of the button rectangle.
BS_VCENTER	Vertically centers text in the button rectangle.
WS_TABSTOP	Turns the control into a tab stop, which allows the user to select the control by tabbing through the controls in a dialog box.

Owner-Drawn Push Buttons

When you use the BS_OWNERDRAW style for a button, you assume all responsibility for drawing the button. You cannot use any other button styles with the BS_OWNERDRAW style. When you use an owner-drawn button, you have to trap the WM_DRAWITEM message in the window procedure for the button's parent window, and you must insert the code that erases the background, if necessary, and draws the button.

The WM_DRAWITEM message is not generated by the window manager; it is part of the interface between a button and its owner. When you use a built-in button class, the button's window procedure automatically sends the WM_DRAWITEM message to the button's parent window when the button receives a WM_PAINT message. If you create a new class of button—a button that is not a built-in button—and you want it to support the WM_DRAWITEM message, you must send the WM_DRAWITEM message to the button's parent window whenever the button needs to be redrawn.

Note Windows CE does not support the BS_BITMAP, BS_FLAT, BS_ICON, BS_PUSHBOX, BS_TEXT, or BS_USERBUTTON styles. Use the BS_OWNERDRAW style to create the effects you would otherwise achieve by using the BS_BITMAP, BS_ICON, or BS_USERBUTTON button styles.

Radio Buttons

A radio button, also known as an option button, is a small, round button with a label next to it. The label may be text, an icon, or a bitmap. A user can select a radio button by tapping it with the stylus. Radio buttons are usually grouped together in a group box, representing a set of related, but mutually exclusive options. When a user selects a radio button, all other radio buttons in the same group are automatically cleared.

◉ None
○ Bulleted
○ Numbered

Radio button

When the user selects an automatic radio button, Windows CE automatically sets the check state of all other radio buttons within the same group to unchecked. For standard radio buttons, use the WS_GROUP style to achieve the same effect.

Radio Button Styles

Windows CE supports most of the radio button styles that Windows-based desktop platforms support, but it does not support the BS_LEFTTEXT style, which places the radio button to the right of the assoicated text. You can achieve the same effect by using the BS_RIGHTBUTTON style.

Radio button styles are described in the following table. They are the same in Windows CE as they are in Windows-based desktop platforms.

Style	Description
BS_AUTORADIOBUTTON	Creates a radio button that, when selected by a user, clears all other buttons in the same group.
BS_RADIOBUTTON	Creates a small circle with a label displayed to the right of it. To display the text to the left of the circle, combine this flag with the BS_RIGHTBUTTON style.
BS_LEFT	Left-aligns the text in the button rectangle on the right side of the check box.
BS_RIGHT	Right-aligns the text in the button rectangle on the right side of the check box.
BS_RIGHTBUTTON	Positions a check box's square on the right side of the button rectangle.
WS_TABSTOP	Turns the control into a tab stop, which allows the user to select the control by tabbing through the controls in a dialog box.

C H A P T E R   1 5

Window Controls

Windows controls send WM_COMMAND messages. This distinguishes them from common controls, which send WM_NOTIFY messages. In this chapter you will learn about all of the windows controls except for those that belong to the button class. For more information on windows controls and common controls, see Chapter 10, "Overview of Controls." For information about buttons, see Chapter 14, "Buttons."

The following windows controls are described in this chapter:

- Edit controls
- Combo boxes
- List boxes
- Scroll bars
- Static controls

Edit Controls

An *edit control*, which is also called a text box, is a rectangular window in which a user can type and edit text from the keyboard.

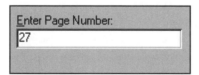

Edit control

Generally, you provide a label for an edit control by placing a static control with the appropriate text above or next to the edit control. However, if you do not have enough space to do this, you can include the label as the default text inside the edit control, enclosed between angle brackets, for example, <edit control label>.

An edit control is selected and receives the input focus when a user touches it with a stylus or presses the TAB key. After it is selected, the edit control displays its text, if any, and a flashing caret that indicates the insertion point. The user can then type text, move the insertion point, or select text to be moved or deleted by using the stylus or keys on the keyboard. An edit control can send notification messages to its parent window in the form of WM_COMMAND messages. A parent window can send messages to an edit control in a dialog box by calling the **SendDlgItemMessage** function.

Windows provides both single-line edit controls (SLEs), and multiline edit controls (MLEs). Edit controls belong to the EDIT window class.

Because Windows CE does not support rich edit controls, you cannot use edit control masks.

Edit Control Styles

Windows provides several edit control styles. An individual edit control can have several styles at the same time. If you use stand-alone tools to develop dialog boxes, you may not need to specify edit control styles explicitly. However, if you create an edit control for your application using the **CreateWindow** or **CreateWindowEx** function, you must specify these edit control styles.

Every edit control specifies a combination of style values that define the appearance and features of the edit control. The style values can establish the appearance of a single-line or multiline edit control, align the text in the control, and determine if and how text appears in the edit control. The number and type of styles the application uses depend on the type and purpose of the edit control.

Edit control styles supported by Windows CE are described in the following table.

Style	Description
ES_AUTOHSCROLL	Automatically scrolls text to the right by 10 characters when the user types a character at the end of the line. When the user presses the ENTER key, the control scrolls all text back to position zero.
ES_AUTOVSCROLL	Scrolls text up one page when the user presses the ENTER key on the last line.
ES_CENTER	Centers text in a multiline edit control.
ES_COMBOBOX	Indicates that the edit control is part of a combo box.
ES_LEFT	Left-aligns text.
ES_LOWERCASE	Converts all characters to lowercase as they are typed into the edit control.

Style	Description
ES_MULTILINE	Designates a multiline edit control. The default is a single-line edit control.
	When the multiline edit control is in a dialog box, the default response to pressing the ENTER key is to activate the default button. To use the ENTER key as a carriage return, use the ES_WANTRETURN style.
	When the multiline edit control is not in a dialog box and the ES_AUTOVSCROLL style is specified, the edit control shows as many lines as possible and scrolls vertically when he user presses the ENTER key. If you do not specify ES_AUTOVSCROLL, the edit control shows as many lines as possible and beeps if the user presses the ENTER key when no more lines can be displayed.
	If you specify the ES_AUTOHSCROLL style, the multiline edit control automatically scrolls horizontally when the caret goes past the right edge of the control. To start a new line, the user must press the ENTER key. If you do not specify ES_AUTOHSCROLL, the control automatically wraps words to the beginning of the next line when necessary. A new line is also started if the user presses the ENTER key. The window size determines the position of the word wrap. If the window size changes, the word wrapping position changes and the text is redisplayed.
	Multiline edit controls can have scroll bars. An edit control with scroll bars processes its own scroll bar messages. Note that edit controls without scroll bars scroll as described in the previous paragraphs and process any scroll messages sent by the parent window.
ES_NOHIDESEL	Negates the default behavior for an edit control. The default behavior hides the selection when the control loses the input focus and inverts the selection when the control receives the input focus. If you specify ES_NOHIDESEL, the selected text is inverted, even if the control does not have the focus.
ES_NUMBER	Allows only digits to be typed into the edit control.
ES_OEMCONVERT	Converts text typed in the edit control from the Windows character set to the OEM character set, and then converts it back to the Windows set. This style is most useful for edit controls that contain file names.
ES_PASSWORD	Displays an asterisk (*) for each character typed into the edit control. You can use the EM_SETPASSWORDCHAR message to change the character that is displayed.
ES_READONLY	Prevents the user from typing or editing text in the edit control.
ES_RIGHT	Right-aligns text in a multiline edit control.

Style	Description
ES_UPPERCASE	Converts all characters to uppercase as they are typed into the edit control.
ES_WANTRETURN	Specifies that a carriage return be inserted when the user presses the ENTER key while typing text into a multiline edit control in a dialog box. If you do not specify this style, pressing the ENTER key has the same effect as pressing the dialog box's default push button. This style has no effect on a single-line edit control.
WS_TABSTOP	Turns the control into a tab stop, which allows the user to select the control by tabbing through the controls in a dialog box.

Text Buffer

When Windows CE creates an edit control, it automatically creates a text buffer, sets its initial size, and increases the size as necessary. Windows CE stores edit control text in a buffer and copies it to the control. The size can be up to a predefined limit of approximately 30,000 characters for single-line edit controls. Because this limit can change, it is called a soft limit. You can set a hard limit to the buffer size by sending an EM_SETLIMITTEXT message to the edit control. If the buffer exceeds either limit, Windows sends the application an EN_ERRSPACE message. You can retrieve the current text limit by sending an EM_GETLIMITTEXT message.

You free the buffer by calling the **LocalFree** function, or you can obtain a new buffer, and buffer handle, by calling the **LocalAlloc** function.

You can initialize or reinitialize an edit control's text buffer by calling the **SetDlgItemText** function. It can retrieve the content of a text buffer by calling the **GetDlgItemText** function.

For each edit control, Windows CE maintains a read-only flag that indicates whether the control's text is read/write, which is the default, or read-only. An application can set the read/write or read-only flag for the text by sending the control an EM_SETREADONLY message. To determine whether an edit control is read-only, an application can call the **GetWindowLong** function using the GWL_STYLE constant. The EM_SETREADONLY message applies to both single-line and multiline edit controls.

You can change the font that an edit control uses by sending the WM_SETFONT message. Changing the font does not change the size of the edit control; applications that send the WM_SETFONT message may have to retrieve the font metrics for the text and recalculate the size of the edit control.

Changing the Formatting Rectangle

The visibility of an edit control's text is governed by the dimensions of its window rectangle and its formatting rectangle. The window rectangle is the client area of the window containing the edit control. The formatting rectangle is a construct maintained by Windows CE for formatting the text displayed in the window rectangle. When an edit control is first displayed, the two rectangles are identical on the screen. An application can make the formatting rectangle larger or smaller than the window rectangle. Making the formatting rectangle larger limits the visibility of the edit control's text, whereas making it smaller creates extra white space around the text.

You can set the coordinates of an edit control's formatting rectangle by sending it an EM_SETRECT message. The EM_SETRECT message automatically redraws the edit control's text. To establish the coordinates of the formatting rectangle without redrawing the control's text, send the control an EM_SETRECTNP message. To retrieve the coordinates of the formatting rectangle, send the control an EM_GETRECT message. These messages apply to multiline edit controls only.

Working with Text

After selecting an edit control, the user can select text in the control by using the mouse or keys on the keyboard. You can retrieve the starting and ending character positions of the current selection in an edit control by sending the control an EM_GETSEL message.

You can also select text in an edit control by sending the control an EM_SETSEL message with the starting and ending character indexes for the selection. For example, you can use EM_SETSEL with EM_REPLACESEL to delete text from an edit control. These three messages apply to both single-line and multiline edit controls.

Replacing Text

You can replace selected text in an edit control by sending the control an EM_REPLACESEL message with a pointer to the replacement text. If there is no current selection, EM_REPLACESEL inserts the replacement text at the insertion point. You might receive an EN_ERRSPACE notification message if the replacement text exceeds the available memory. This message applies to both single-line and multiline edit controls. You can use EM_REPLACESEL to replace part of an edit control's text or the **SetDlgItemText** function to replace all of it.

Cut, Copy, Paste, and Clear Operations

Windows CE provides four messages for moving text between an edit control and the clipboard. The WM_COPY message copies the current selection, if any, from an edit control to the clipboard without deleting it from the edit control. The WM_CUT message deletes the current selection, if any, in the edit control and copies the deleted text to the clipboard. The WM_CLEAR message deletes the current selection, if any, from an edit control, but does not copy it to the clipboard unless the user pressed the SHIFT key. The WM_PASTE message copies text from the clipboard into an edit control at the insertion point. These four messages apply to both single-line and multiline edit controls.

Modifying Text

The user can select, delete, or move text in an edit control. Windows CE maintains an internal flag for each edit control indicating whether the content of the control has been modified. Windows CE clears this flag when it creates the control and sets the flag whenever the text in the control is modified. You can retrieve the modification flag by sending the control an EM_GETMODIFY message and set or clear the modification flag by sending the control an EM_SETMODIFY message. These messages apply to both single-line and multiline edit controls.

Limiting User-Entered Text

The default limit to the amount of text a user can type in an edit is 30,000 characters. An application can change the amount of text the user can type by sending the control an EM_SETLIMITTEXT message. This message sets a hard limit to the number of bytes the user can type into an edit control, but affects neither text that is already in the control when the message is sent nor text copied to the control by the **SetDlgItemText** function or the WM_SETTEXT message. For example, suppose that the application uses the **SetDlgItemText** function to place 500 characters in an edit control, and the user also typed 500 characters, for a total of 1,000 characters. If the application then sends an EM_SETLIMITTEXT message limiting user-entered text to 300 characters, the 1,000 characters already in the edit control remain there, and the user cannot add any more text. On the other hand, if the application sends an EM_SETLIMITTEXT message limiting user-entered text to 1,300 characters, the 1,000 characters remain, but the user can add 300 more characters.

When the user reaches the character limit of an edit control, Windows CE sends the application a WM_COMMAND message containing an EN_MAXTEXT notification message. This notification message does not mean that memory has been exhausted, but that the limit for user-entered text has been reached; the user cannot type any more text. To change this limit, an application must send the control a new EM_SETLIMITTEXT message with a higher limit.

Wordwrap Functions

An application may direct a multiline edit control to add or remove a soft linebreak character—two carriage returns and a linefeed—automatically at the end of wrapped text lines. An application can turn this feature on or off by sending the edit control an EM_FMTLINES message. This message applies only to multiline edit controls and does not affect a line that ends with a hard linebreak —one carriage return and a linefeed typed by the user.

Retrieving Points and Characters

You can determine which character is closest to the specified point in an edit control by sending the EM_CHARFROMPOS message. The message returns the character index and line index of the character nearest the point. Similarly, you can determine the client coordinates of the specified character in an edit control by sending the EM_POSFROMCHAR message. You specify the index of a character and the message returns the x- and y-coordinates of the upper-left corner of the character.

Undoing Text Operations

Every edit control maintains an undo flag that indicates whether an application can reverse, or undo, the most recent operation on the edit control; for example, to undo a text deletion. The edit control sets the undo flag to indicate that the operation can be undone and resets it to indicate that the operation cannot be undone. You can determine the setting of the undo flag by sending the control an EM_CANUNDO message.

You can undo the most recent operation by sending the control an EM_UNDO message. An operation can be undone provided no other edit control operation occurs first. For example, the user can delete text; replace the text or undo the deletion; and then delete the text again or undo the replacement. The EM_UNDO message applies to both single-line and multiline edit controls and always works for single-line edit controls.

Scrolling Text in an Edit Control

To implement scrolling in an edit control, you can use the automatic scrolling styles, or you can explicitly add scroll bars to the edit control. To add a horizontal scroll bar, use the style WS_HSCROLL; to add a vertical scroll bar, use the style WS_VSCROLL. An edit control with scroll bars processes its own scroll bar messages.

Windows CE provides three messages that you can send to an edit control with scroll bars. The EM_LINESCROLL message can scroll a multiline edit control both vertically and horizontally. The *lParam* parameter specifies the number of lines to scroll vertically starting from the current line and the *wParam* parameter specifies the number of characters to scroll horizontally, starting from the current character. The edit control does not acknowledge messages to scroll horizontally if it has the ES_CENTER or ES_RIGHT style. This message applies to multiline edit controls only.

The EM_SCROLL message scrolls a multiline edit control vertically, which is the same effect as sending a WM_VSCROLL message. The *wParam* parameter specifies the scrolling action. The EM_SCROLL message applies to multiline edit controls only.

Tab Stops and Margins

To set tab stops in a multiline edit control use the EM_SETTABSTOPS message. The default for a tab stop is eight characters. When you add text to the edit control, tab characters in the text automatically generate space up to the next tab stop. The EM_SETTABSTOPS message does not automatically cause Windows CE to redraw the text. To do that, you can call the **InvalidateRect** function. The EM_SETTABSTOPS message applies to multiline edit controls only.

You can set the width of the left and right margins for an edit control by using the EM_SETMARGINS message. After sending this message, Windows CE redraws the edit control to reflect the new margin settings. You can retrieve the width of the left or right margin by sending the EM_GETMARGINS message. By default, the edit control margins are set to be just wide enough to accommodate the largest character horizontal overhang, known as a negative ABC width, for the font currently in use in the edit control.

Password Characters

You can use a password character in an edit control to conceal user input. When a password character is set, it is displayed in place of each character the user types. When a password character is removed, the control displays the characters the user types. If you create an edit control using the style ES_PASSWORD, the default password character is an asterisk (*). An application can use the EM_SETPASSWORDCHAR message to remove or define a different password character and the EM_GETPASSWORDCHAR message to retrieve the current password character. These messages apply to single-line edit controls only.

Combo Boxes

A *combo box* is a control that combines a list box with an edit control. Selecting an item in the list box displays the selected text in the edit control. If the combo box style allows keyboard input, typing characters into the edit control highlights the first list box item that matches the characters typed. A combo box can appear either in a dialog box or on the command bar.

Combo box

To create a command bar combo box and insert it into a command bar, use the **CommandBar_InsertComboBox** function.

Note If you provide **Style**, **Font**, and **Font Size** combo boxes, you must position them in the order they are listed in this note.

Combo Box Styles

Because of limited screen space, Windows CE-based devices use either the CBS_DROPDOWN or CBS_DROPDOWNLIST style rather than the CBS_SIMPLE style that is popular on Windows-based desktop platforms. In the CBS_SIMPLE style, the list box is always visible and the current selection is displayed in the edit control. In the the CBS_DROPDOWN or CBS_DROPDOWNLIST styles, the list box is not displayed until the user selects an icon next to the edit control, which conserves space on the screen. The difference between the two styles is that the CBS_DROPDOWNLIST style has a static text field that always displays the current selection instead of having an edit control.

Window CE does not support owner-drawn combo boxes.

Note If you specify the CBS_EX_CONSTSTRINGDATA style when the application inserts a string into the list part of a combo box, the combo box stores the pointer passed to it by the application rather than copying the string. This saves RAM resources when you have a large table of strings in ROM that you want to insert into a combo box.

All combo boxes in Windows CE have the LBS_HASSTRINGS style by default.

Combo box styles supported by Windows CE are described in the following table.

Style	Description
CBS_AUTOHSCROLL	Automatically scrolls the text in an edit control to the right when the user types a character at the end of the line. If this style is not set, only text that fits within the rectangular boundary is allowed.
CBS_DISABLENOSCROLL	Shows a disabled vertical scroll bar in the list box when the box does not contain enough items to scroll. Without this style, the scroll bar is hidden when the list box does not contain enough items.
CBS_DROPDOWN	Displays only the edit control by default. The user can display the list box by selecting an icon next to the edit control.
CBS_DROPDOWNLIST	Displays a static text field that displays the current selection in the list box.
CBS_LOWERCASE	Converts any uppercase characters typed into the edit control of a combo box to lowercase.
CBS_NOINTEGRALHEIGHT	Specifies that the combo box will be exactly the size specified by the application when it created the combo box. Usually, Windows sizes a combo box so that it does not display partial items.
CBS_OEMCONVERT	Converts text typed in the combo box edit control from the Windows character set to the OEM character set and then back to the Windows set. This style is most useful for combo boxes that contain file names. It applies only to combo boxes created with the CBS_DROPDOWN style.
CBS_SORT	Automatically sorts strings typed into the list box.
CBS_UPPERCASE	Converts any lowercase characters typed into the edit control of a combo box to uppercase.
WS_TABSTOP	Turns control into a tab stop, which allows the user to select the control by tabbing through the controls in a dialog box.

Windows CE does not support the CBS_OWNERDRAWFIXED or CBS_OWNERDRAWVARIABLE styles for combo boxes.

Edit Control Selection Fields

The edit control selection field is the portion of a combo box that displays the currently selected list item. In drop-down combo boxes, which are combo boxes that have the CBS_DROPDOWN style, the selection field is an edit control and can be used to type text that is not in the list.

You can retrieve or set the contents of the edit control selection field and can determine or set the edit selection. You can also limit the amount of text a user can type in the selection field. When the contents of the selection field change, Windows CE sends notification messages to the parent window or dialog box procedure.

To retrieve the content of the edit control selection field, send a WM_GETTEXT message to the combo box. To set the contents of the selection field of a drop-down combo box, send the WM_SETTEXT message to the combo box.

List Boxes

A *list box* is a window that displays a list of character strings. The user selects a string from the list by tapping it with the stylus. When a string is selected, it is highlighted. You can use a vertical or horizontal scroll bar with a list box to scroll lists that are too long for the control window. The list box automatically hides or shows the scroll bar, as needed.

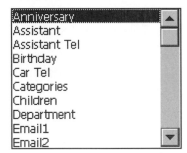

List box

A dialog box procedure is responsible for initializing and monitoring its child windows, including any list boxes. The dialog box procedure communicates with the list box by sending messages to it and by processing the notification messages sent by the list box.

Windows CE does not support owner-drawn list boxes.

List Box Styles

There are two types of list boxes: single-selection, which is the default, and multiple-selection. In a single-selection list box, the user can select only one item at a time. In a multiple-selection list box, the user can select more than one item at a time. To create a multiple-selection list box, specify the LBS_MULTIPLESEL or the LBS_EXTENDEDSEL style.

Note Windows CE supports the LBS_EX_CONSTSTRINGDATA style, which saves RAM resources when you have a large table of strings in ROM that you want to insert into a list box.

All list boxes in Windows CE have the LBS_HASSTRINGS style by default.

List box styles supported by Windows CE are described in the following table.

Style	Description
LBS_DISABLENOSCROLL	Shows a disabled vertical scroll bar for the list box when the box does not contain enough items to scroll. If you do not specify this style, the scroll bar is hidden when the list box does not contain enough items.
LBS_EXTENDEDSEL	Allows the user to select multiple items by using the SHIFT key and the mouse or special key combinations.
LBS_MULTICOLUMN	Specifies a multicolumn list box that the user scrolls horizontally. You set the width of the columns by using the LB_SETCOLUMNWIDTH message.
LBS_MULTIPLESEL	Turns string selection on or off each time a user clicks or double-clicks a string in the list box. A user can select any number of strings simultaneously.
LBS_NOINTEGRALHEIGHT	Specifies that the list box will be exactly the size specified by the application when it created the list box. Usually, Windows sizes a list box so that it does not display partial items.
LBS_NOREDRAW	Specifies that the list box's appearance is not automatically updated when changes are made. You can change this style by sending a WM_SETREDRAW message.
LBS_NOSEL	Specifies that the user can view list box strings but cannot select them.
LBS_NOTIFY	Notifies the parent window whenever the user clicks or double-clicks a string in the list box.

Style	Description
LBS_SORT	Sorts strings in the list box alphabetically.
LBS_STANDARD	Sorts strings in the list box alphabetically. The parent window receives an input message whenever the user clicks or double-clicks a string. The list box has borders on all sides.
LBS_USETABSTOPS	Enables a list box to recognize and expand tab characters when drawing its strings. The default tab positions are 32 dialog box units. A dialog box unit is equal to one-fourth of the current dialog box base-width unit. Windows CE calculates these units based on the height and width of the current system font.
LBS_WANTKEYBOARDINPUT	Specifies that the owner of the list box receives WM_VKEYTOITEM messages whenever the user presses a key and the list box has the input focus. This enables an application to perform special processing on the keyboard input.
WS_TABSTOP	Turns control into a tab stop, which allows the user to select the control by tabbing through the controls in a dialog box.

Windows CE supports the LBS_NODATA style for compatibility with applications written for earlier versions of Windows.

Scroll Bars

A *scroll bar* is a rectangle that contains a scroll box and has direction arrows at both ends. The user can tap the arrows, click on the gray area between the arrows, or drag the scroll box to scroll the scroll bar's parent window.

Scroll bar

Scroll bars should be included in any window for which the content of the client area extends beyond the window's borders. A scroll bar's orientation determines the direction in which scrolling occurs when the user operates the scroll bar. A horizontal scroll bar enables the user to scroll the content of a window to the left or right. A vertical scroll bar enables the user to scroll the content up or down.

You can use as many scroll bar controls as needed in a single window. When you create a scroll bar control, you must specify the scroll bar's size and position. However, if a scroll bar control's window can be resized, your application must adjust the scroll bar's size whenever the size of the window changes.

Scroll Bar Styles

A scroll bar control can have a number of styles to control the orientation and position of the scroll bar. You specify the styles that you want when you call the **CreateWindowEx** function to create a scroll bar control. Some of the styles create a scroll bar control that uses a default width or height. However, you must always specify the x- and y-coordinates and the other dimensions of the scroll bar.

Scroll bar styles supported by Windows CE are described in the following table.

Style	Description
SBS_BOTTOMALIGN	Aligns the bottom edge of the scroll bar with the bottom edge of the rectangle defined by the **CreateWindowEx** parameters x, y, *nWidth*, and *nHeight*. The scroll bar has the default height for system scroll bars. Use this style with the SBS_HORZ style.
SBS_HORZ	Designates a horizontal scroll bar. If the SBS_TOPALIGN style is not specified, the scroll bar has the height, width, and position specified by the parameters of **CreateWindow**.
SBS_LEFTALIGN	Aligns the left edge of the scroll bar with the left edge of the rectangle defined by the parameters of **CreateWindow**. The scroll bar has the default width for system scroll bars. Use this style with the SBS_VERT style.
SBS_RIGHTALIGN	Aligns the right edge of the scroll bar with the right edge of the rectangle defined by the parameters of **CreateWindowEx**. The scroll bar has the default width for system scroll bars. Use this style with the SBS_VERT style.
SBS_SIZEBOX	Designates a size box. If you do not specify the SBS_SIZEBOXTOPLEFTALIGN style, the size box has the height, width, and position specified by the parameters of **CreateWindowEx**.

Style	Description
SBS_SIZEBOXBOTTOMRIGHTALIGN	Aligns the lower-right corner of the size box with the lower-right corner of the rectangle specified by the parameters of **CreateWindowEx**. The size box has the default size for system size boxes. Use this style with the SBS_SIZEBOX style.
SBS_SIZEBOXTOPLEFTALIGN	Aligns the upper-left corner of the size box with the upper-left corner of the rectangle specified by the parameters of **CreateWindowEx**. The size box has the default size for system size boxes. Use this style with the SBS_SIZEBOX style.
SBS_TOPALIGN	Aligns the top edge of the scroll bar with the top edge of the rectangle defined by the parameters of **CreateWindow**. The scroll bar has the default height for system scroll bars. Use this style with the SBS_HORZ style.
SBS_VERT	Designates a vertical scroll bar. If you do not specify the SBS_LEFTALIGN style, the scroll bar has the height, width, and position specified by the parameters of **CreateWindow**.

Parts of a Scroll Bar

A scroll bar consists of a gray area with an arrow button at each end and a scroll box, which is sometimes called a thumb, between the arrow buttons. A scroll bar represents the overall length or width of a data object in a window's client area; the scroll box represents the portion of the object that is visible in the client area. The position of the scroll box changes whenever the user scrolls a data object to display a different portion of it. Windows CE also adjusts the size of a scroll bar's scroll box so that it indicates what portion of the entire data object is currently visible in the window. If most of the object is visible, the scroll box occupies most of the scroll bar's shaft. Similarly, if only a small portion of the object is visible, the scroll box occupies a small part of the shaft.

The user scrolls the content of a window by clicking one of the arrow buttons, by clicking in the gray area, or by dragging the scroll box. When the user clicks an arrow button, the application scrolls the content by one unit, which is typically a single line or column. When the user clicks one of the gray areas, the application scrolls the content by one window. The amount of scrolling that occurs when the user drags the scroll box depends on the distance the user drags the scroll box and on the scrolling range of the scroll bar.

Scroll Box Position and Scrolling Range

The position of the scroll box is represented as an integer; it is relative to the left or upper end of the scroll bar, depending on whether the scroll bar is horizontal or vertical. The position must be within the minimum and maximum values of the scrolling range. For example, in a scroll bar with a range of zero through 100, position 50 is in the middle, with the remaining positions distributed equally along the scroll bar. The initial range depends on the scroll bar. Standard scroll bars have an initial range of zero through 100. Scroll bar controls have an empty range—both minimum and maximum values are zero—unless you supply an explicit range when you create the control. You can alter the range at any time after its initial creation. You can use the **SetScrollInfo** function to set the range values, and the **GetScrollInfo** function to retrieve the current range values.

You can set a page size for a scroll bar. The page size represents the number of data units that can fit in the client area of the owner window given its current size. For example, if the client area can hold eight lines of text, an application would set the page size to eight. Windows CE uses the page size, along with the scrolling range and length of the scroll bar's gray area, to set the size of the scroll box. Whenever a window containing a scroll bar is resized, an application should call the **SetScrollInfo** function to set the page size. An application can retrieve the current page size by calling the **GetScrollInfo** function.

Scroll Bar Requests

The user makes scrolling requests by clicking various parts of a scroll bar. Windows CE sends the request to the specified window in the form of a WM_HSCROLL or WM_VSCROLL message for horizontal and vertical scroll bars, respectively. Each message includes a notification code that corresponds to the user's action to the handle of the scroll bar, for scroll bar controls only, and, in some cases, to the position of the scroll box.

Usually an application scrolls the content of a window in the direction opposite that indicated by the scroll bar. For example, when the user clicks the gray area below the scroll box, an application scrolls the object in the window upward to reveal a portion of the object that is below the visible portion. An application can also scroll a rectangular region using the **ScrollDC** function.

When you process the WM_CREATE message you can set scrolling units. It is convenient to base the scrolling units on the dimensions of the font associated with the window's display context (DC). To retrieve the font dimensions for a specific DC, use the **GetTextMetrics** function. When you process the WM_SIZE message, you can adjust the scrolling range and scrolling position to reflect the dimensions of the client area as well as the number of lines of text that will be displayed.

The scroll bar sends WM_HSCROLL and WM_VSCROLL messages to the window procedure whenever the user clicks the scroll bar or drags the scroll box. The low-order words of WM_VSCROLL and WM_HSCROLL each contain a notification message that indicates the direction and magnitude of the scrolling action.

When you process the WM_HSCROLL and WM_VSCROLL messages, you should examine the scroll bar notification message and calculate the scrolling increment. After you apply the increment to the current scrolling position, you can scroll the window to the new position by using the **ScrollWindowEx** function. You can use the **SetScrollInfo** function to adjust the position of the scroll box.

After you scroll a window, it makes part of the window's client area invalid. To ensure that the invalid region is updated, you use the **UpdateWindow** function to generate a WM_PAINT message.

Static Controls

A *static control* is a control used to display text, to draw frames or lines separating other controls, or to display icons. A static control does not accept user input, but it can notify its parent window of stylus taps if the static control is created with **SS_NOTIFY** style.

Static control

Although you can use static controls in overlapped, pop-up, and child windows, they are designed for use in dialog boxes where Windows CE standardizes their behavior. If you use static controls outside of dialog boxes, you increase the risk that the application might behave in a nonstandard fashion.

Windows CE does not support owner-drawn static controls.

Static Control Styles

Static control styles supported by Windows CE are described in the following table.

Style	Description
SS_BITMAP	Specifies that a bitmap will be displayed in the static control. The text is the name of a bitmap defined elsewhere in the resource file, not a file name. The style ignores the *nWidth* and *nHeight* parameters; the control automatically sizes itself to accommodate the bitmap.
SS_CENTER	Specifies a simple rectangle and centers the error value text in the rectangle. Windows CE formats the text before display. The control automatically wraps words that extend past the end of a line to the beginning of the next centered line.
SS_CENTERIMAGE	Specifies that the midpoint of a static control with the SS_BITMAP style will remain fixed when you resize the control. The four sides are adjusted to accommodate a new bitmap. If the bitmap is smaller than the control's client area, the rest of the client area is filled with the color of the pixel in the upper-left corner of the bitmap.
SS_ICON	Specifies that an icon will be displayed in the static control. The text is the name of an icon defined elsewhere in the resource file, not a file name. The style ignores the *nWidth* and *nHeight* parameters; the icon automatically sizes itself.
SS_LEFT	Specifies a rectangle and left-aligns the text in the rectangle. Windows CE formats the text before display. The control automatically wraps words that extend past the end of a line to the beginning of the next left-aligned line.
SS_LEFTNOWORDWRAP	Specifies a rectangle and left-aligns the text in the rectangle. Tabs are expanded but words are not wrapped. Text that extends past the end of a line is clipped.
SS_NOPREFIX	Prevents interpretation of any ampersand (&) characters in the control's text as accelerator prefix characters.
	An application can combine SS_NOPREFIX with other styles by using the bitwise OR (|) operator. This can be useful when file names or other strings that may contain an ampersand (&) must be displayed within a static control in a dialog box.
SS_NOTIFY	Sends the parent window the STN_CLICKED notification when the user clicks the control.

Style	Description
SS_RIGHT	Specifies a rectangle and right-aligns the specified text in the rectangle. Windows CE formats the text before display. The control automatically wraps words that extend past the end of a line to the beginning of the next right-aligned line.

In Windows CE, you can use only the SS_CENTERIMAGE style in conjunction with the SS_BITMAP style. Even if you specify SS_ICON, you cannot set the image by calling:

```
SendMessage( hStatic, STM_SETIMAGE, IMAGE_ICON, (LPARAM) hIcon );
```

You have to use:

```
SendMessage( hStatic, STM_SETIMAGE, IMAGE_BITMAP, (LPARAM) hBitmap );
```

If you specify SS_CENTERIMAGE, and do not specify either SS_ICON or SS_BITMAP, the static control will behave as though you had specified the SS_BITMAP style.

Windows CE does not support the SS_SIMPLE static control styles but you can emulate this style by using the SS_LEFT or SS_LEFTNOWORDWRAP style. Windows CE also does not support the SS_BLACKFRAME, SS_BLACKRECT, SS_GRAYFRAME, SS_GRAYRECT, SS_OWNERDRAW, SS_WHITEFRAME, SS_WHITERECT styles but you can use the WM_PAINT message to achieve the same results.

C H A P T E R   1 6

Dialog Boxes, Menus, and Other Resources

A resource is binary data, such as a bitmap, an image, or a string, that you can add an application's executable file. Windows CE resources include cursors, icons, menus, dialog boxes, bitmaps, string-table entries, message-table entries, keyboard-accelerator tables, and user-defined data. The Windows CE-based platform you are targeting will determine which Windows resources are available for use.

Before using a resource, you must load it into memory. The **FindResource** function finds a resource in a module and returns a handle to the binary resource data. The **LoadResource** function uses the resource handle returned by **FindResource** to load the resource into memory. After you load a resource by using **LoadResource**, Windows CE automatically unloads and reloads the resource as memory conditions and application execution require. Thus, you need not explicitly unload a resource you no longer need.

You can use **FindResource** and **LoadResource** to find and load any type of resource, but you should use these functions only if you must access the binary resource data for subsequent function calls. To use a resource immediately, you should use one of the resource-specific functions described in the following table to find and load resources in one call.

Function	Action
FormatMessage	Loads and formats a message-table entry
LoadAccelerators	Loads an accelerator table
LoadBitmap	Loads a bitmap resource
LoadCursor	Loads a cursor resource
LoadIcon	Loads an icon resource
LoadImage	Loads an icon, cursor, or bitmap
LoadMenu	Loads a menu resource
LoadString	Loads a string-table entry

Before terminating, an application should release the memory occupied by accelerator tables, bitmaps, cursors, icons, and menus by using one of the functions described in the following table.

Resource	Release function
Accelerator table	**DestroyAcceleratorTable**
Bitmap	**DeleteObject**
Cursor	**DestroyCursor**
Icon	**DestroyIcon**
Menu	**DestroyMenu**

Dialog Boxes

A dialog box is a temporary window that contains controls. You can use it to display status information and to get input from the user. Most applications use dialog boxes to prompt for additional information. Many applications also use dialog boxes to display information or options while the user works in another window. For example, word processing applications often use a dialog box with a text-search command. While the application searches for text, the dialog box remains on the screen. The user can return to the dialog box and continue searching for the word or search for a new word. Applications that use dialog boxes in this way create a dialog box when the user chooses a command. The application continues to display the dialog box for as long as the application runs or until the user closes the dialog box.

Windows CE supports two types of dialog boxes to accommodate different application uses—modal and modeless. A *modal dialog box* requires the user to supply information or dismiss the dialog box before allowing the application to continue. Applications use modal dialog boxes in conjunction with commands that require additional information before they can proceed. A *modeless dialog box* allows the user to supply information and return to a previous task without closing the dialog box. Modal dialog boxes are simpler to manage than their modeless counterparts because they are created, perform their task, and are destroyed by calling a single function.

To create either a modal or modeless dialog box, you must supply a dialog box template to describe the dialog box style and content. You must also supply a dialog box procedure to carry out tasks. The *dialog box template* is a binary description of the dialog box and the controls it contains. You can create this template as a resource that you can load from your executable file. The *dialog box procedure* is an application-defined callback function that the system calls when it has input for the dialog box or tasks for the dialog box to carry out. Although a dialog box procedure is similar to a window procedure, it does not have the same responsibilities.

You typically create a dialog box by using either the **DialogBox** or **CreateDialog** function. **DialogBox** creates a modal dialog box; **CreateDialog** creates a modeless dialog box. These two functions load a dialog box template from your executable file and create a pop-up window that matches the template's specifications. There are other functions that create a dialog box by using templates in memory; they pass additional information to the dialog box procedure as the dialog box is created.

Dialog boxes usually belong to a predefined, exclusive window class. The system uses this window class and its corresponding window procedure for both modal and modeless dialog boxes. When the function is called, it creates the window for the dialog box, as well as the windows for the controls in the dialog box, and then sends selected messages to the dialog box procedure. While the dialog box is visible, the predefined window procedure manages all messages, processing some messages and passing others to the dialog box procedure so that the procedure can carry out tasks. You do not have direct access to the predefined window class or window procedure, but you can use the dialog box template and dialog box procedure to modify the style and behavior of a dialog box. Dialog box types are described in the following table.

Dialog box type	Description
Application-defined dialog box	Helps a user perform tasks specific to an application.
Common dialog box	Provides a familiar way for users to perform tasks that are common to many applications.
Message box	Notifies a user of an event or situation and offers limited responses.
Property sheet, a collection of tabbed dialog boxes	Provides a convenient way to view and modify object properties. These are discussed in Chapter 11, "Foundation Controls."

Application-Defined Dialog Boxes

An application-defined dialog box is a child window that you design to suit the needs of your application. You can use any kind of control in a dialog box and lay it out in any format you like.

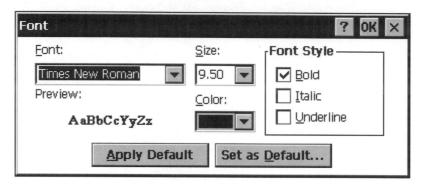

Application-defined dialog box

In Windows CE, all dialog boxes are control parents. They are also recursive. This means that if a dialog box has a child dialog box when a user tabs through the parent dialog box, the dialog box manager tabs into the child dialog box as well. If a dialog box is outside the visible area of the screen, Windows CE does not automatically reposition it.

If a user presses ALT+H while the dialog box has the input focus, the system posts a WM_HELP message to the dialog box procedure. Respond to this message by displaying context-sensitive Help for the dialog box.

Note Sometimes it is necessary for a dialog box to appear on top of all other windows. For example, under low memory conditions, the **System Out of Memory Dialog Box** will send a WM_CLOSE message to an application. If the application is not in the foreground, any dialog box it displays will be hidden behind the current foreground window, unless you create the dialog box with the DS__SETFOREGROUND style. Because putting the dialog box in the foreground will not bring the application's main window forward, put in the dialog box any information that the user may need to decide what action to take.

In Windows CE, dialog boxes have the WS_POPUP style by default. If you want to use the WS_CHILD style instead, specify it in the **style** member of the **DLGTEMPLATE** structure you pass in the *lpTemplate* parameter to any of these functions. You can also specify the DS_SETFOREGROUND or DS_CENTER styles.

Dialog box styles supported by Windows CE are described in the following table.

Dialog box style	Description
DS_ABSALIGN	Indicates that the coordinates of the dialog box are screen coordinates. If this style is not specified, Windows CE assumes they are client coordinates.
DS_CENTER	Centers the dialog box vertically and horizontally in the working area.
DS_MODALFRAME	Creates a dialog box with a modal dialog-box frame that you can combine with a title bar and **System** menu by specifying the WS_CAPTION and WS_SYSMENU styles.
DS_SETFONT	Indicates that the header of the dialog box template contains additional data specifying the font to use for text in the client area and the controls of the dialog box. The font data begins on the WORD boundary that follows the title array. It specifies a 16-bit point size value and a Unicode font name string. If possible, the system creates a font according to the specified values. The system then passes the handle of the font to the dialog box and to each control by sending them the WM_SETFONT message.
DS_SETFOREGROUND	Brings the dialog box to the foreground.

Common Dialog Boxes

A common dialog box is a system-defined dialog box that standardizes how users perform complex operations that are common to most applications. Windows CE supports the **Color**, **Open**, **Save As** and **Print** common dialog boxes. The following screen shot illustrates a **Print** dialog box.

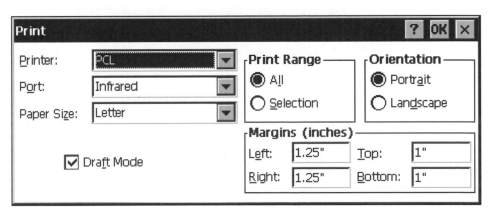

Print common dialog box

Each of the common dialog boxes has a unique purpose. The **Color** dialog box provides a user with a way to select a color from a set of custom colors or from a set of basic colors that are determined by the display driver. The **Open** dialog box provides users with a way to select a file to open. The **Save As** dialog box provides users with a way to save a file under a name other than the name with which it was opened. The **Print** dialog box provides users with a way to select print options. Users must print the entire document or the currently selected portion and can print only one copy at a time. The settings in the **Print** dialog box are always initialized to the current default printer. If the user has never used the **Print** dialog box before, the first printer registered in the registry is the default. After that, the last printer the user selected is the default.

Note You can set the widths and minimum widths of the left, top, right, and bottom margins of the printed page by including values for the **rcMargin** and **rcMinMargin** members of the **PRINTDLG** structure.

Common dialog boxes are centered vertically and horizontally on the screen and are not movable. They always have the **Help** button displayed.

Message Boxes

A message box is a special kind of modal dialog box that an application uses to display messages and prompt for simple input. A message box typically contains a text message and one or more predefined buttons. You do not need to provide a dialog box template or dialog box procedure for a message box. Windows creates the template based on the text and buttons you specify and supplies its own dialog box procedure.

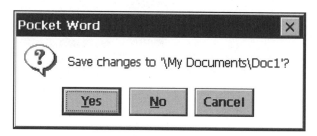

Message box

Use the **MessageBox** function to create a message box, specifying the text and the number and types of buttons to display. Because Windows CE controls the creation and management of the message box, you do not provide a dialog box template and dialog box procedure. Windows CE creates its own template based on the text and buttons specified for the message box and supplies its own dialog box procedure.

Note As with dialog boxes, sometimes it is necessary for a message box to appear on top of all other windows. In particular, under low-memory conditions, the **System Out of Memory Dialog Box** sends a WM_CLOSE message to an application. If the application is not in the foreground, any message box it puts up is hidden behind the current foreground window, unless you create the message box with the MB_SETFOREGROUND style. Because putting the message box in the foreground will not bring the application's main window forward, put any information in the message box that the user may need to decide what action to take.

The **MessageBeep** function, generally used with message boxes, plays a waveform sound. The waveform sound for each sound type is identified by an entry in the sounds section of the registry.

Message box styles that are supported by Windows CE are described in the following table.

Message Box Style

Button	Description
MB_ABORTRETRYIGNORE	The message box contains three buttons: **Abort**, **Retry**, and **Ignore**.
MB_OK	The message box contains one button: **OK**.
MB_OKCANCEL	The message box contains two buttons: **OK** and **Cancel**.
MB_RETRYCANCEL	The message box contains two buttons: **Retry** and **Cancel**.
MB_YESNO	The message box contains two buttons: **Yes** and **No**.
MB_YESNOCANCEL	The message box contains three buttons: **Yes**, **No**, and **Cancel**.
MB_DEFBUTTON1	The first button is the default button. Note that the first button is always the default unless you specify MB_DEFBUTTON2.
MB_DEFBUTTON2	The second button is the default button.
MB_DEFBUTTON3	The third button is the default button.
Icon	**Description**
MB_ICONASTERISK MB_ICONINFORMATION	An icon consisting of a lowercase letter i in a circle appears in the message box.
MB_ICONEXCLAMATION MB_ICONWARNING	An exclamation-point icon appears in the message box.

Message Box Style

Icon	Description
MB_ICONERROR MB_ICONHAND MB_ICONSTOP	A stop-sign icon appears in the message box.
MB_ICONQUESTION	A question-mark icon appears in the message box.

Window style	Description
MB_APPLMODAL	The user must respond to the message box before continuing work in the window identified by the *hWnd* parameter. However, the user can move to the windows of other applications and work in those windows.
	Depending on the hierarchy of windows in the application, the user may be able to move to other windows within the application. All child windows of the message box's parent window are automatically disabled, but pop-up windows are not.
	MB_APPLMODAL is the default value. Windows CE does not support either MB_SYSTEMMODAL or MB_TASKMODAL.
MB_SETFOREGROUND	The message box becomes the foreground window.
MB_TOPMOST	The message box is created with the WS_EX_TOPMOST window style.

Menus

A *menu* is a list of *menu items*. Choosing a menu item opens a submenu or causes the application to carry out a command. Each menu must have an owner window. Windows CE sends messages to a menu's owner window when the user selects the menu or chooses an item from the menu.

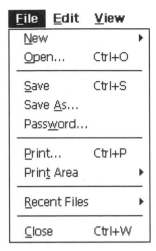

Menu

All menus in Windows CE are implemented as top-level, pop-up windows. A pop-up menu is a floating menu that displays commands specific to the object selected by the user or to the object's immediate context.

Windows CE sends a WM_COMMAND message to the window that owns the menu when the user chooses a command item. Each menu item that opens a submenu is associated with a handle to that corresponding submenu. When the user points to such an item, Windows CE opens the submenu. No command message is sent to the owner window; however, Windows CE sends it a WM_INITMENUPOPUP message before displaying the submenu. You can get the handle to the submenu associated with an item by using the **GetSubMenu** or **GetMenuItemInfo** function.

Command Bar Menus

The command bar combines the functionality of the menu bar and toolbar in one control. The menu names on a command bar represent the main categories of commands that an application provides. Selecting a menu name from the command bar opens a menu whose menu items correspond to the commands in a specified category. For example, a command bar might contain a **File** menu name that, when selected by the user, activates a menu with menu items such as **New**, **Open**, and **Save**. For more information about command bars, see Chapter 11, "Foundation Controls."

Menu Items

Windows CE generates a unique handle for each menu. A *menu handle* is a value of the **HMENU** type. You must specify a menu handle in many of the Windows CE menu functions. To retrieve the handle to the submenu associated with a menu item, use the **GetSubMenu** or **GetMenuItemInfo** function.

In addition to having a unique handle, each menu item in a command bar or menu has a unique position value. The leftmost item in a command bar, or the top item in a menu, has position zero. The position value is incremented for subsequent menu items. Windows CE assigns a position value to all items in a menu, including separators. When calling a menu function that modifies or retrieves information about a specific menu item, specify the item using either its handle or its position.

A menu item can be checked or unchecked. Windows CE displays a bitmap next to checked menu items to indicate their checked state; it does not display a bitmap next to unchecked items. Only menu items in a menu can be checked; items in a command bar cannot be checked.

Applications check or uncheck a menu item to indicate whether an option is in effect. For example, suppose an application has a toolbar that the user can show or hide by using a **Toolbar** command on a menu. When the toolbar is hidden, the **Toolbar** menu item is unchecked. When the user chooses the command, the application checks the menu item and shows the toolbar. A check mark attribute controls whether a menu item is checked. Set a menu item's check mark attribute by using the **CheckMenuItem** function.

Sometimes, a group of menu items corresponds to a set of mutually exclusive options. In this case, indicate the selected option by using a checked radio menu item—analogous to a radio button control. Checked radio items are displayed with a bullet bitmap instead of a check mark bitmap. To check a menu item and make it a radio item, use the **CheckMenuRadioItem** function.

When a menu item is not available to the user, the item should be dimmed. Dimmed menu items cannot be chosen. An application dims an unavailable menu item to provide a visual cue to the user that a command is not available. You can use a dimmed item when an action is not appropriate. For example, you can dim the **Print** command in the **File** menu when the system does not have a printer installed.

A menu item can be enabled or dimmed by using the **EnableMenuItem** function. To determine whether a menu item is enabled or dimmed, use the **GetMenuItemInfo** function.

Owner-Drawn Menu Items

You can completely control the appearance of a menu item by using an owner-drawn item. Owner-drawn items require an application to take total responsibility for drawing selected, checked, and unchecked states. For example, if an application provides a font menu, it can draw each menu item by using the corresponding font; the item for Roman will be drawn in Roman, the item for Italic will be drawn in Italic, and so on.

Windows CE handles owner-drawn menu items differently than Windows-based desktop platforms do. In some respects, it treats an owner-drawn item as it would any other menu item. On other Windows-based platforms, the device context (DC) is initialized to its default state. Under Windows CE, however, the DC is initialized to the dimmed or highlighted status of the current item. Also, unlike other Windows-based platforms, Windows CE automatically highlights an owner-drawn menu item when it has the keyboard focus.

Menu Item Separators and Line Breaks

Windows provides a special type of menu item, called a separator, that appears as a horizontal line. You can use a separator to divide a menu into groups of related items. A separator cannot be used in a command bar, and the user cannot select a separator.

When a menu contains more items than will fit in one column, the menu is truncated unless you force the line to break. You can cause a column break to occur at a specific item in a menu by assigning the MFT_MENUBREAK type flag to the item or using the MENUBREAK option in the MENUITEM statement. Windows places that item and all subsequent items in a new column. The MFT_MENUBARBREAK type flag has the same effect, except that a vertical line appears between the new column and the old. If you use the **AppendMenu** or **InsertMenu** function to assign line breaks, you should assign the type flags MFT_MENUBREAK or MFT_MENUBARBREAK.

Scrolling Menus

Some Windows CE-based platforms include scrolling menus. On these platforms, if a menu does not fit on the screen, Windows CE automatically adds scrolling arrows so users can scroll the menu up and down.

When the user cannot scroll any further in one direction or the other, the associated arrow is dimmed. Pressing the up or down arrow scrolls the menu one item at a time. No menu item is highlighted while the user is scrolling. Changing the selection by using a keyboard arrow or keyboard mnemonic causes the newly selected item to scroll into view if it is not already displayed. If a menu has too many columns to fit the width of the display area, Windows CE ignores all column breaks and makes the menu a single-column scrolling menu.

If an individual menu item is too large to be drawn without being clipped by the up or down arrow, the item is not drawn at all. This may leave a large blank space next to an arrow.

Creating, Displaying, and Destroying Menus

Most applications create menus using menu-template resources. A *menu template* defines a menu, including the items in the menu bar and all submenus. For information about creating a menu-template resource, see the documentation included with your development tools.

After you create a menu-template resource and add it to your application's executable (.exe) file, use the **LoadMenu** function to load the resource into memory. Implementing menus as resources makes an application easier to localize for use in multiple countries because only the resource-definition file needs to be localized for each language, not the application's source code.

To create an empty menu bar, use the **CreateMenu** function; to create an empty menu, use the **CreatePopupMenu** function. To add items to a menu, use the **AppendMenu** and **InsertMenu** functions.

To display a shortcut menu, use the **TrackPopupMenuEx** function. Shortcut menus, also called floating pop-up menus or context menus, are typically displayed when the WM_CONTEXTMENU message is processed. The older **TrackPopupMenu** function is still supported, but new applications should use the **TrackPopupMenuEx** function.

If a menu is assigned to a window and that window is destroyed, Windows CE automatically destroys the menu, freeing the menu's handle and the memory occupied by the menu. Windows CE does not automatically destroy a menu that is not assigned to a window. An application must destroy the unassigned menu by calling the **DestroyMenu** function.

For general guidelines on menu design, see Chapter 6, "Designing a User Interface for Windows CE."

Carets

A *caret* is a flashing line or block in the client area of a window that indicates the place at which the user will insert text or graphics. To display a solid caret, Windows CE inverts every pixel in the window rectangle. Windows CE does not support bitmap carets. The following screen shot illustrates a caret as it appears in text.

Microsoft Windows CE

⌐ Caret

Caret

▶ **To create and display a caret**

1. Call the **CreateCaret** function.

   Windows CE formats a caret by inverting the pixel color within the rectangle specified by the caret's position, width, and height.

2. Call the **SetCaretPos** function to set the caret's position.

3. Call the **ShowCaret** function to make the caret visible. When the caret appears, it automatically begins flashing.

The system sends the WM_SETFOCUS message to the window receiving the keyboard focus; therefore, an application should create and display the caret while processing this message.

The elapsed time, in milliseconds, required to invert the caret is called the *blink time*. The caret will blink as long as the thread that owns the message queue has a message pump processing the messages. The user can set the blink time of the caret using Control Panel, and applications should respect the settings that the user has chosen. An application can determine the caret's blink time by using the **GetCaretBlinkTime** function. If you are writing an application that allows the user to adjust the blink time, such as a Control Panel applet, use the **SetCaretBlinkTime** function to set the rate of the blink time to a specified number of milliseconds.

The *flash time* is the elapsed time, in milliseconds, required to display, invert, and restore the caret's display. The flash time of a caret is twice as much as the blink time.

You can determine the position of the caret using the **GetCaretPos** function. An application can move a caret in a window by using the **SetCaretPos** function. A window can move a caret only if it already owns the caret. **SetCaretPos** can move the caret whether it is visible or not.

You can temporarily remove a caret by hiding it, or you can permanently remove the caret by destroying it. To hide the caret, use the **HideCaret** function. This is useful when your application must redraw the screen while processing a message, but must keep the caret out of the way. When the application finishes drawing, it can display the caret again by using the **ShowCaret** function. Hiding the caret does not destroy its shape or invalidate the insertion point. Hiding the caret is cumulative; that is, if the application calls **HideCaret** five times, it must also call **ShowCaret** five times before the caret will reappear.

To remove the caret from the screen and destroy its shape, use the **DestroyCaret** function. **DestroyCaret** destroys the caret only if the window involved in the current task owns the caret.

Cursors

A cursor is a small bit image that reflects the position of the mouse, or other pointing device, as it tracks across the screen. Windows CE platforms implement cursors in different ways.

On many Windows CE-based platforms, users interact with applications by tapping the stylus on the screen. Because there is no mouse, there is no need for a cursor to indicate the current mouse position. However, even if your target platform does not support a pointing device, every application should display the wait cursor, which is a spinning hourglass, whenever it executes a command that renders the current window or the system unresponsive to user input.

Target platforms that support mouse cursors support cursors the same way that Windows-based desktop platforms do, except that they do not support color cursors.

Some Windows CE-based platforms only support the wait cursor and the **SetCursor** and **LoadCursor** functions. On these platforms, you can use the following code example to load the wait cursor.

```
SetCursor(LoadCursor(NULL, IDC_WAIT));
```

Icons

An *icon* is a picture that is used to identify an application, file, or other object. It consists of a bit image combined with a mask. An application's icon always appears on the taskbar while the application is running, and it can be used to recover the application's main window when another window has the foreground. The icon also can be used to identify the application in the Windows CE Explorer.

Icon

Every application should register both 16 x 16-pixel and 32 x 32-pixel icons for its main executable file and the types of files it stores in the file system.

Icons are associated with window classes rather than with individual windows. Use the WM_GETICON message to retrieve the handle of the icon associated with a window class and the WM_SETICON message to associate an icon with a window class.

Windows CE does not support any of the standard predefined icons (IDI_*) that Windows-based desktop platforms support.

For information on icon design, see Chapter 6, "Designing a User Interface for Windows CE."

Bitmaps, Images, and Strings

Initialize a bitmap with the **LoadBitmap** function. The bitmap you create with this function will be read-only. This is because Windows CE does not copy the bitmap into RAM, as Windows-based desktop platforms do.

In Windows CE, the bitmap only exists in a resource, which is part of the program's executable file. When you select the bitmap into a DC, you cannot modify the DC—for example, by drawing text into it—because that would require the ability to write to the bitmap.

Use the **LoadImage** function to load an image. Windows CE does not support stretching and shrinking of images or any loading options other than LR_DEFAULTCOLOR.

Use the **LoadString** function to load a string. Windows CE only supports Unicode strings.

Keyboard Accelerators

A *keyboard accelerator*, also known as a shortcut key, is a keystroke, or combination of keystrokes, that generates a WM_COMMAND message. Keyboard accelerators are often used as shortcuts for commonly used menu commands, but you can also use them to generate commands that have no equivalent menu items. Include keyboard accelerators for any common or frequent actions, and provide support for the common shortcut keys wherever they apply.

You can use an ASCII character code or a virtual-key code to define the accelerator. An ASCII character code makes the accelerator case-sensitive. The ASCII "C" character can define the accelerator as ALT+c rather than ALT+C. Because accelerators do not need to be case-sensitive, most applications use virtual-key codes for accelerators rather than ASCII character codes.

If an application defines an accelerator that is also defined in the system accelerator table, the application-defined accelerator overrides the system accelerator, but only within the context of the application. Avoid this practice, however, because it prevents the system accelerator from performing its standard role in the Windows user interface. For general guidelines on assigning shortcut keys, see Chapter 6, "Designing a User Interface for Windows CE."

Accelerator Tables

An *accelerator table* consists of an array of **ACCEL** structures, each defining an individual accelerator. Each **ACCEL** structure includes the following information:

- The accelerator's keystroke combination
- The accelerator's identifier
- Various flags

Call the **TranslateAccelerator** function in the message loop associated with the thread's message queue to process accelerator keystrokes for a specified thread. This function monitors keyboard input to the message queue, checking for key combinations that match an entry in the accelerator table. When **TranslateAccelerator** finds a match, it translates the keyboard input, that is, the WM_KEYUP and WM_KEYDOWN messages, into a WM_COMMAND or WM_SYSCOMMAND message. It then sends the message to the window procedure of the specified window.

The WM_COMMAND message includes the identifier of the accelerator that caused **TranslateAccelerator** to generate the message. The window procedure examines the identifier to determine the source of the message and then processes the message accordingly.

Note Unlike Windows-based desktop platforms, Windows CE does not maintain a system-wide accelerator table that applies to all applications.

Windows CE maintains accelerator tables for each application. An application can define any number of accelerator tables for use with its own windows. A unique 32-bit handle, **HACCEL**, identifies each table. However, only one accelerator table can be active at a time for a specified thread. The handle of the accelerator table passed to the **TranslateAccelerator** function determines which accelerator table is active for a thread. The active accelerator table can be changed at any time by passing a different accelerator-table handle to **TranslateAccelerator**.

▶ **To create an accelerator table**

1. Use a resource compiler to create an accelerator table resource and to add it your executable file.

2. Call the **LoadAccelerators** function at run time to load the accelerator table and to retrieve the handle of the accelerator table.

3. Pass a handle to the accelerator table to the **TranslateAccelerator** function to activate the accelerator table.

You can create an accelerator table for an application at run time by passing an array of **ACCEL** structures to the **CreateAcceleratorTable** function. This method supports user-defined accelerators in the application. Like the **LoadAccelerators** function, **CreateAcceleratorTable** returns an accelerator-table handle that can be passed to **TranslateAccelerator** to activate the accelerator table.

Accelerator tables loaded by **LoadAccelerators** are automatically destroyed by Windows CE. **CreateAcceleratorTable** creates a table that must be destroyed before an application closes. Use the **DestroyAcceleratorTable** function to destroy an accelerator table.

Creating an Accelerator Table Resource

Create an accelerator-table resource by using the **ACCELERATORS** statement in your resource-definition file. You must assign a name or a resource identifier to the accelerator table, preferably unlike that of any other resource. Windows CE uses this identifier to load the resource at run time.

Each accelerator you define requires a separate entry in the accelerator table. In each entry, you define the keystroke that generates the accelerator and the accelerator's identifier. The keystroke is either an ASCII character code or virtual-key code. You must also specify whether the keystroke must be used in some combination with the ALT, SHIFT, or CTRL keys.

An ASCII keystroke is specified either by enclosing the ASCII character in double quotation marks or by using the integer value of the character in combination with the ASCII flag. The following code examples show how to define ASCII accelerators.

```
"A",   ID_ACCEL1        ; SHIFT+A
65,    ID_ACCEL2, ASCII  ; SHIFT+A
```

A keystroke that generates a virtual-key code is specified differently depending on whether the keystroke is an alphanumeric key or a non-alphanumeric key. For an alphanumeric key, the key's letter or number, enclosed in double quotation marks, is combined with the VIRTKEY flag. For a non-alphanumeric key, the Windows virtual-key code for the specific key is combined with the VIRTKEY flag. The following code examples show how to define virtual-key code accelerators.

```
"a",       ID_ACCEL3, VIRTKEY    ; A (caps-lock on) or a
VK_INSERT, ID_ACCEL4, VIRTKEY    ; INSERT key
```

If you want the user to press the ALT, SHIFT, or CTRL keys in some combination with the accelerator keystroke, specify the ALT, SHIFT, and CONTROL flags in the accelerator's definition. The following code examples show possible combinations.

```
"B",   ID_ACCEL5, ALT                       ; ALT_SHIFT+B
"I",   ID_ACCEL6, CONTROL, VIRTKEY          ; CTRL+I
VK_F5, ID_ACCEL7, CONTROL, ALT, VIRTKEY     ; CTRL+ALT+F5
```

P A R T   4

Connection Services

CHAPTER 17

Invoking Functions from a Desktop Computer

Windows CE supports a remote application programming interface (RAPI) that gives an application running on a desktop computer the ability to invoke function calls on a Windows CE-based platform. The desktop computer is the RAPI client and the Windows CE-based platform is the RAPI server. The communication uses Windows Sockets (Winsock) and can take place over a serial link, a modem connection, or a network connection.

The function calls behave much like the equivalent Windows CE functions. For the most part, RAPI functions have the same syntax, parameters, and return values as the corresponding Windows CE versions. Any differences are noted in the reference documentation for the RAPI functions.

Note String and character parameters must be in Unicode format. Use the appropriate conversion routines, if necessary.

Initializing and Terminating Remote Application Programming Interface

Before making RAPI calls, you must call the **CeRapiInit** or **CeRapiInitEx** function. These functions perform routine initialization and set up the communications link between the desktop computer and the platform.

The CeRapiInit call is a synchronous operation. It does not return control to the application until a connection is made or an error occurs. In contrast, the **CeRapiInitEx** call is an asynchronous operation and it returns immediately. **CeRapiInitEx** continues the initialization until a connection is made, an error occurs, or there is a call to **CeRapiUninit**. Although **CeRapiInitEx** avoids blocking any threads, it is a more complicated method of initialization.

▶ **To initialize RAPI using CeRapiInitEx**

1. Call **CeRapiInitEx**.

2. If an error is returned, exit.

3. If successful, call **WaitForSingleObject** or **WaitForMultipleObjects** to wait on the event handle passed back in the **heRapiInit** member of **RAPIINIT**.

4. When **heRapiInit** is signaled, check for a successful connection or an error value.

5. Check the **hrRapiInit** member of the **RAPIINIT** structure for the final return value.

When you are finished with RAPI, call **CeRapiUninit** to terminate the connection and perform any necessary cleanup. Because creating and terminating connections are fairly expensive operations, establish and terminate the link only once per session, not on a per-call basis.

The following code example shows how to use the **CeRapiInitEx** function. Following the **CeRapiInitEx** call, the **MsgWaitForMultipleObjects** function is used to wait on one of two events. The first event is when the event handle is passed back through the **heRapiInit** member of the **RAPIINIT** structure. The second event is when a user terminates a connection.

```
HRESULT InitRapi(HEVENT hExit)
{
   RAPIINIT ri = { sizeof(RAPIINIT) };
   HRESULT hr = CeRapiInitEx(&ri);
   if ( FAILED( hr ) )
   {
      return(hr);
   }

   HANDLE ahWait[] = { hExit                  , ri.heRapiInit };
   enum              { WAIT_EXIT=WAIT_OBJECT_0, WAIT_INIT     };

   DWORD dwObj = WaitAndDispatch(ARRAYSIZE(ahWait), ahWait);

   if (WAIT_INIT == dwObj)              //Event signaled by RAPI
   {
      if (FAILED(ri.hrRapiInit))        //Connection failed
      {
         CeRapiUninit();
      }

      return(ri.hrRapiInit);
   }
```

```
                                  //Event signaled by user or timeout occurred
        CeRapiUninit();

        if (WAIT_EXIT == dwObj)
        {
            return(HRESULT_FROM_WIN32(ERROR_CANCELLED));
        }

        return(E_FAIL);
}

enum
{
    WAD_ALLINPUT    = 0x0000,
    WAD_SENDMESSAGE = 0x0001,
} ;

DWORD WaitAndDispatch(DWORD nCount, HANDLE *phWait, DWORD dwTimeout,
UINT uFlags)
{
    DWORD dwObj;
    DWORD dwStart = GetTickCount();
    DWORD dwTimeLeft = dwTimeout;

    for ( ; ; )
    {
        dwObj = MsgWaitForMultipleObjects(nCount, phWait, FALSE,
            dwTimeLeft, (uFlags&WAD_SENDMESSAGE) ? QS_SENDMESSAGE :
QS_ALLINPUT);
        if (dwObj == (DWORD)-1)
        {
            dwObj = WaitForMultipleObjects(nCount, phWait, FALSE, 100);
            if (dwObj == (DWORD)-1)
            {
                break;
            }
        }
        else if (dwObj == WAIT_TIMEOUT)
        {
            break;
        }

        if ((UINT)(dwObj-WAIT_OBJECT_0) < nCount)
        {
            break;
        }

        MSG msg;
        if (uFlags & WAD_SENDMESSAGE)
        {
```

```
                    PeekMessage(&msg, NULL, 0, 0, PM_NOREMOVE);
        }
        else
        {
           while (PeekMessage(&msg, NULL, 0, 0, PM_REMOVE))
           {
               DispatchMessage(&msg);
           }
        }

        if (INFINITE != dwTimeout)
        {
           dwTimeLeft = dwTimeout - (GetTickCount() - dwStart);
           if ((int)dwTimeLeft < 0)
           {
               break;
           }
        }
     }

     return(dwObj);
}
```

Executing Functions and Applications

Among all RAPI functions, there are two functions that execute functions and applications residing on the Windows CE-based platform:

- **CeCreateProcess**

  This function creates a new process that runs a specified executable file residing on the Windows CE-based platform.

- **CeRapiInvoke**

  This function remotely executes a function residing on the Windows CE-based platform and provides for both input parameters and output data. It operates in either of two modes: block, known as synchronous, or stream, known as asynchronous.

  In *block mode*, the caller passes both input parameters and output data in a single buffer. Because this is a synchronous call, all input data must be present in memory at the time of the call and all output data must be present before the function finishes.

In *stream mode*, an **IStream** type interface is used to exchange arbitrarily-sized data in any order and direction. The caller can pass input data in a single buffer, but from that point on all data should be exchanged through the stream. Because the data can be read, written, and stored in chunks, stream code is significantly faster than block mode. The interface used is based on **Istream**, but has two additional methods to allow you to do timeouts.

Note **LocalAlloc** allocates the memory passed for both the *pInput* and *ppOutput* parameters of **CeRapiInvoke**. The called function frees the input memory allocation, and the calling application frees the output memory allocation.

Retrieving Information

▶ **To retrieve path information**

- Call the **CeGetTempPath** function to get the path to the directory that is designated for temporary files.

    –Or–

- Call the **CeGetSpecialFolderPath** function to get the path to a specific shell folder, which depends on the input parameter. The possibilities include the recycle bin, **Start** menu directory, document template directory, network directory, and folders for fonts or installed printers.

▶ **To retrieve other information**

- Call the **CeFindAllDatabases** function to get information about all databases of a specified type.

    –Or–

- Call the **CeFindAllFiles** function to get information about all files and directories in a specified directory of the Windows CE object store.

In both cases, the information is returned in an array of **CE_FIND_DATA** structures.

You must free the memory allocated by the **CeFindAllDatabases**, **CeFindAllFiles**, or **CeReadRecordProps** function by calling the **CeRapiFreeBuffer** function.

Handling RAPI Errors

In addition to errors associated with their non-RAPI counterparts, RAPI functions can fail because of RAPI-related errors. Network errors, for example, will need to be communicated back to the calling application.

RAPI functions that fail due to a RAPI-related error will return the error value defined for their Win32-based counterpart. To distinguish between RAPI and non-RAPI errors, use either the **CeRapiGetError** function or the **CeGetLastError** function. To determine if a function failed because of RAPI errors, call **CeRapiGetError**. To determine if a function failed because of non-RAPI errors, call **CeGetLastError**, which works the same as the **GetLastError** function does on Windows-based platforms.

Sample RAPI Program

The following code example shows the basics of initializing the RAPI client, making calls, and handling errors.

```
#include <stdio.h>
#include <rapi.h>
#include <string.h>

void PrintDirectory( LPWSTR Path, UINT Indent )
{
   if ( !Path )
      return;

   DWORD           foundCount;
   LPCE_FIND_DATA findDataArray;

   WCHAR searchPath[MAX_PATH];
   wcscpy( searchPath, Path );
   wcscat( searchPath, L"*" );

   if ( !CeFindAllFiles( searchPath,
                         FAF_ATTRIBUTES | FAF_NAME,
                         &foundCount,
                         &findDataArray ) )
   {
      printf( "*** CeFindAllFiles failed. ***\n" );
```

```
        if ( CeGetLastError() != ERROR_SUCCESS )
           printf( "failure occurred on the HPC function\n" );

        return;
     }

     if ( !foundCount )
     {
        for ( UINT indCount = 0 ; indCount < Indent ; indCount++ )
           printf( "   " );
        printf( "No files found.\n" );
        return;
     }

     for ( UINT i = 0 ; i < foundCount ; i++ )
     {
        for ( UINT indCount = 0 ; indCount < Indent ; indCount++ )
           printf( "   " );
        wprintf( findDataArray[i].cFileName );
        printf( "\n" );

        if ( findDataArray[i].dwFileAttributes &
FILE_ATTRIBUTE_DIRECTORY )
        {
           WCHAR newPath[MAX_PATH];

           wcscpy( newPath, Path );
           wcscat( newPath, findDataArray[i].cFileName );
           wcscat( newPath, L"\\" );
           PrintDirectory( newPath, Indent + 1 );
        }
     }

     CeRapiFreeBuffer( findDataArray )
}

void main()
{
   HRESULT hr = CeRapiInit();
   if ( FAILED(hr) )
   {
      printf( "*** CeRapiInit() failed. ***\n" );
      return;
   }

   PrintDirectory( L"\\", 0 );

   CeRapiUninit();
}
```

CHAPTER 18

Receiving Connection Notification

There are two methods to register the desktop application:

- Registry-based notification using command lines that are registered in the system registry.
- COM interface-based notification using two Component Object Model (COM) interfaces, one implemented by the connection manager and the other by the application, to perform the registration.

Registry-Based Notification

In registry-based notification, an application places a command line in the desktop system registry in one of two keys. When the event specified by the key occurs, the command line is executed. Registry-based notification is appropriate for applications that do not need some control of the connection manager nor the ability to register and unregister for connection notifications.

The keys used in registry-based notification are **HKEY_LOCAL_MACHINE \SOFTWARE\Microsoft\Windows CE Services\AutoStartOnConnect** and **AutoStartOnDisconnect**. When a Windows CE-based device is connected to a desktop computer, the command line under **AutoStartOnConnect** is executed. Likewise, when the device is disconnected, the command line under **AutoStartOnDisconnect** is executed.

▶ **To register an application for automatic execution**

1. Construct a named value that uniquely identifies the application. It should include a company and product name—for example, **MicrosoftHPCExplorerAutoConnect**. Enter the named value under the appropriate key, either **AutoStartOnConnect** or **AutoStartOnDisconnect**.

2. Define the named value as the application that is to be executed. Include command line arguments.

The following registry editor (.reg) file shows how to register a command line for both **AutoStartOnConnect** and **AutoStartOnDisconnect**. In this example, when the Windows CE-based device is connected, Notepad.exe is started with a command line argument of **c:\config.sys**. When the device is disconnected, Notepad.exe is started with a command line argument of **c:\autoexec.bat**.

```
REGEDIT4
[HKEY_LOCAL_MACHINE\SOFTWARE\Microsoft\Windows CE
Services\AutoStartOnConnect]
"MicrosoftAutoConnectSample"="notepad c:\\config.sys"
[HKEY_LOCAL_MACHINE\SOFTWARE\Microsoft\Windows CE
Services\AutoStartOnDisconnect]
"MicrosoftAutoDisconnectSample"="notepad c:\\autoexec.bat"
```

COM Interface-Based Notification

The second method you can use to register a desktop application is COM interface-based notification. In this method, two COM interfaces, **IDccMan** and **IDccManSink**, are used to register an application in the desktop registry. The Windows CE Services connection manager implements the **IDccMan** interface, while the application implements the **IDccManSink** interface. Although the COM interface-based notification method is more complex than registry-based notification, by using it you get some control of the connection manager and the ability to register and unregister for connection notifications.

The Windows CE Services connection manager, which resides on the desktop, displays an icon next to the clock in the taskbar when the Windows CE-based device is connected or is waiting to be connected to the desktop computer. This icon—two terminals with a connecting cable—indicates the connection status. By right-clicking the icon you can start Windows CE Explorer.

Notification and Unregistration Procedures

The notification process follows the same basic steps for connection and disconnection of the Windows CE-based device. The following procedure assumes that the **IDccMan** and **IDccManSink** interfaces have been implemented.

1. Initialize the COM library and register the application for the appropriate event.

2. Connect or disconnect the Windows CE-based device.

3. Perform the application processing.

The Connection Notification Client sample program shows several connection notification scenarios, including a new remote connect, a disconnect, and a reconnect. To see the actual sequence of interface method calls for any of these scenarios, build and run the program. Then, view the **Notification Messages** list box output in the **Connection Notification Test** dialog box. For a description of this sample, see "Windows CE Sample Applications" in the online Help.

▶ **To receive notification when the Windows CE-based device connects to a desktop computer**

1. Initialize the COM library and register with the Windows CE Services connection manager.

   a. Call the COM function **CoInitialize** to initialize the Component Object library.

   b. Call the COM function **CoCreateInstance** with the **DccMan** class identifier (CLSID_DccMan) and **IDccMan** interface identifier (IID_IDccMan) and receive a pointer to the **IDccMan** interface. For more information on CLSID_DccMan and IID_IDccMan, see "Registering the IDccMan Class Identifier" later in this chapter.

   c. Call the **IDccMan::Advise** method, which provides the connection manager with a pointer to the **IDccManSink** interface that you implemented. It also registers the application with the connection manager.

   d. The Windows CE Services connection manager calls the **IDccManSink::OnLogInactive** method, notifying the application that there is no connection between the desktop computer and the mobile device.

2. Establish the connection between the desktop and the mobile device.

   a. The Windows CE Services connection manager calls the **IDccManSink::OnLogListen** method. Then, it waits for the remote connection services for both the desktop computer and the Windows CE-based device to respond. Until they are both running, the connection manager will not proceed.

   b. For Windows 95-based systems only, the connection manager calls the **IDccManSink::OnLogAnswered** method when the connection manager has detected the communications interface.

   c. The Windows CE Services connection manager calls the **IDccManSink::OnLogActive** method when the connection is established between the Windows CE-based device and Windows CE Services connection manager.

   d. The Windows CE Services connection manager calls the **IDccManSink::OnLogIpAddr** method, providing the IP address that it obtained for the communications socket.

> **Note** Only when the **IDccManSink::OnLogIpAddr** notification occurs is the connection completely established.

3. Perform the desired processing in the application, which can include processing on the desktop, remote processing on the Windows CE-based device using remote application programming interface (RAPI), or calling the **IDccMan** methods. However, the application should wait to initialize RAPI, using **CeRapiInit**, until the **IDccManSink::OnLogActive** notification is received. This ensures that a connection is established between the desktop computer and the device.

▶ **To receive notification when the Windows CE-based device disconnects from the desktop**

1. Initialize the COM library and register the application, as described in the previous section.

2. Disconnect the device from the desktop computer. Windows CE Services notifies the application when the desktop computer and device are disconnected by calling the **IDccManSink::OnLogDisconnection** method.

3. Perform the desired processing in the application. Because there is no connection to the device, this processing can only take place on the desktop computer.

Notification when Reestablishing a Remote Connection

If a connection was established, but then was disconnected by the desktop computer or the Windows CE-based device, the **IDccMan::OnLogActive** notification occurs when the connection is reestablished.

When an application calls the **IDccMan::ShowCommSetting** function and the **OK** button is clicked in the **Communications Properties** dialog box, the following notification sequence occurs:

1. **IDccManSink::OnLogListen**
2. **IDccManSink::OnLogDisconnection**
3. **IDccManSink::OnLogInactive**
4. **IDccManSink::OnLogListen**

If instead the **Cancel** button is clicked in the dialog box, no notification is sent and a Listen state is maintained.

The Connection Notification Client source code uses the **IDccMan** interface and implements the **IDccManSink** interface.

Unregistering an Application

One of the advantages to using the COM interface-based notification process is that it allows an application to unregister itself from being notified. This might be helpful when an application needs to run only once.

▶ **To unregister an application from being notified**

1. Call **IDccMan::Unadvise**, which releases the memory associated with the **IDccManSink** interface.

2. Call **IDccMan::Release**, which releases the **IDccMan** object.

3. Call **CoUninitialize** to perform any OLE cleanup. Note that a call to **CoUninitialize** is required for each successful call to **CoInitialize**.

Registering the IDccMan Class Identifier

As mentioned earlier, both the **DccMan** class identifier, CLSID_DccMan, and the **IDccMan** interface identifier, IID_IDccMan, are passed in the call to **CoCreateInstance**. Because the Windows CE Services setup application registers CLSID_DccMan, your application only needs to register IID_IDccMan.

The following sample registry file shows the **IDccMan** class identifier being initialized in the registry.

```
REGEDIT4
[HKEY_CLASSES_ROOT\CLSID\499c0c20-A766-11cf-8011-00A0c90A8F78]
@="Connection Manager"

[HKEY_CLASSES_ROOT\CLSID\499c0c20-A766-11cf-8011-    /
  00A0c90A8F78\InprocServer32]
@="C:\\Windows\\System\\Rapi.dll"
   "ThreadingModel"="Apartment"

[HKEY_LOCAL_MACHINE\SOFTWARE\Classes\CLSID\499c0c20-A766-11cf-8011-    /
  00A0c90A8F78]
@="Connection Manager"

[HKEY_LOCAL_MACHINE\SOFTWARE\Classes\CLSID\499c0c20-A766-11cf-8011-    /
  00A0c90A8F78\InprocServer32]
@="C:\\Windows\\System\\Rapi.dll"
   "ThreadingModel" = "Apartment"
```

CHAPTER 19

Transferring Files

A file filter is a dynamic-link library (DLL) that controls the transfer of data between the desktop computer and the Windows CE-based device. File filters are used by the Windows CE Services application on the desktop computer to automatically convert files as they are transferred.

File formats used by the Windows CE operating system and Windows CE-based applications are generally different from those of the corresponding Windows-based applications. For example, Pocket Word does not support OLE compound files. Windows CE Services automatically adjusts file formats as files are transferred between the desktop computer and the Windows CE-based device.

Some of the common filters provided with Windows CE Services include:

- Pocket Word (.pwd) to Microsoft® Word (.doc)
- Microsoft Word (.doc) to Pocket Word (.pwd)
- Pocket Excel (.pxl) to Microsoft® Excel 5.0 (.xls)
- Microsoft Excel (.xls) to Pocket Excel (.pxl)
- Windows bitmap (.bmp) to Windows CE 4-color bitmap (.2bp)

You can extend the file-filtering capability of Windows CE Services by defining your own application-specific filters. This section describes file filters and the interfaces used to create them.

Implementing a file filter is similar for importing and exporting files. The only differences are in the registry settings and in how the body of the file filter—the converter function—changes data. The examples in this section demonstrate the procedure for importing files, but typically you would write a converter function that handles both importing and exporting, using dual registry settings that indicate both the import and export functionality.

> **Note** The words "importing" and "exporting" in this chapter are from the perspective of the Windows CE-based device. Thus, importing a file with a file filter transfers a file from the desktop computer to the device, whereas exporting a file with a file filter transfers a file from the device to the desktop.

Registering File Types and File Filters

Windows CE Services uses the registry entries to determine which conversions are available for a given file type and how to invoke the filter that supports the conversion. For this reason, you must register each file type and file filter properly using the following procedure.

▶ **To register file types and their filters**

1. Register the file extension type.
2. Generate a class identifier (CLSID) for the file filter.
3. Register the file filter.

The following sections describe each step in detail.

> **Note** CEUTIL, a utility DLL, has functions that are especially helpful when dealing with the desktop registry entries for Windows CE Services. For information about CEUTIL, see Chapter 21, "Installing and Managing Applications."

Registering a File Extension Type

Windows CE Explorer, like Windows Explorer, allows you to customize a type name, as displayed in the details view of Explorer, and an icon for any file extension, for example, .pwd. File filters must be registered under HKEY_CLASSES_ROOT.

The following is the structure of HKEY_CLASSES_ROOT:

```
HKEY_CLASSES_ROOT\.<file extension>
    \(Default) = <Class Name>
HKEY_CLASSES_ROOT\<Class Name>
    \(Default) = <Name to be displayed in the "Type" column of Explorer>
    \DefaultIcon = <filename or index of the icon for this type>
```

Generating a Class Identifier for a File Filter

Every file filter must be given a unique CLSID, which identifies class objects to OLE. CLSIDs are universally unique identifiers (UUIDs), also called globally unique identifiers (GUIDs). The file filter's CLSID must be included in your application and it must be registered with the operating system when your application is installed.

If the file filter supports both importing and exporting, a unique CLSID must be associated with each file filter that is to be registered for the respective import and export registry setting.

The GUID Generator tool lets you generate a GUID that you can use to identify your file filter. A GUID Generator application, named Guidgen.exe, is provided with Microsoft Visual C++. The GUID Generator calls the **CoCreateGuid** function to generate a new GUID. It also lets you copy the GUID to the clipboard for insertion into your application's source code using one of the following formats:

- IMPLEMENT_OLECREATE macro format

  Defined in an IMPLEMENT_OLECREATE macro, which allows instances of a *CCmdTarget*-derived class to be created by Automation clients. For example:

  ```
  // {CA761230-ED42-11CE-BACD-00AA0057B223}
  IMPLEMENT_OLECREATE(<<class>>, <<external_name>>,
  0xca761230, 0xed42, 0x11ce, 0xba, 0xcd, 0x0, 0xaa,
  0x0, 0x57, 0xb2, 0x23);
  ```

- DEFINE_GUID macro format

  Defined in an IMPLEMENT_OLECREATE macro, which is included with Microsoft Visual C++ in the file Afxdisip.h. It allows instances of a *CCmdTarget*-derived class to be created by Automation clients. For example:

  ```
  // {CA761230-ED42-11CE-BACD-00AA0057B223}
  DEFINE_GUID(<<name>>,
  0xca761230, 0xed42, 0x11ce, 0xba, 0xcd, 0x0, 0xaa, 0x0, 0x57, 0xb2,
  0x23);
  ```

- Statically allocated structure format

  Declared as a statically allocated structure. For example:

  ```
  // {CA761232-ED42-11CE-BACD-00AA0057B223}
  static const GUID <<name>> = { 0xca761232, 0xed42, 0x11ce,
  { 0xba, 0xcd, 0x0, 0xaa, 0x0, 0x57, 0xb2, 0x23 } };
  ```

- Registry entry format

  Specified in a form suitable for registry entries or registry editor scripts. For example:

  ```
  {CA761233-ED42-11CE-BACD-00AA0057B223}
  ```

Registering a File Filter

A file filter is registered by placing its CLSID in two locations. The first place is under the file type's extension key in the **InstalledFilters** subkey. This registration associates the file filter with the file type it converts. The other place to register a file filter is under the **HKEY_CLASSES_ROOT\CLSID** key. This registration provides information on the file filter's capabilities and its DLL.

Optionally, a file filter can be registered under the file type's extension key as the **DefaultImport** or **DefaultExport** named value. As the names imply, these values define the default file filters for the file type.

Each key under **HKEY_LOCAL_MACHINE\SOFTWARE\Microsoft\Windows CE Services\Filters** is the name of a file extension. This is called the file type's *extension key*. Under each extension key is the **InstalledFilters** subkey, which contains the CLSID of each file filter that can convert this file type. The CLSID must identify an OLE Component Object Model (COM) object that is used for the conversion. The filters that are registered under the **InstalledFilters** subkey will be listed in the Windows CE Services user interface as filter options. Whichever file filter is also listed under the extension key as the **DefaultImport** or **DefaultExport** value will be shown as the default.

Note Any filter defined as the **DefaultImport** or **DefaultExport** named value must be an **InstalledFilters** value also.

The following is the structure of the **Filters** key and the **InstalledFilters** subkey.

```
HKEY_LOCAL_MACHINE\SOFTWARE\Microsoft\Windows CE Services\Filters

    \.<file extension>
       [DefaultImport = <Default import filter CLSID>]
       [DefaultExport = <Default export filter CLSID>]
       \InstalledFilters
          [<clsid1>]

          . . .
          [more CLSID's for this extension]
       . . .
    [more extensions]
```

The HKEY_CLASSES_ROOT\CLSID key gives basic information concerning file filters. Each file filter that has been identified in the **HKEY_LOCAL_MACHINE\SOFTWARE\Microsoft\Windows CE Services\Filters** key must be registered in this key. The following is the key's structure and its subkeys.

```
HKEY_CLASSES_ROOT\CLSID

\<clsid>
   \(Default) = <Description in "Edit Conversion Settings" listbox>
   \DefaultIcon = <filename,index for the icon for this type>
   \InProcServer32 = <filename of the DLL that handles his type>
      ThreadingModel = Apartment
   \PegasusFilter
      [Import]
      [HasOptions]
      Description = <String to display in the conversion dialog>
      NewExtension = <extension of converted file>
\. . . [more clsids for filters]
```

The *clsid* key is a named value that is the CLSID of the registered file filter. This key contains the following subkeys:

- **DefaultIcon**

  Defines the icon name string or icon resource identifier for the icon associated with the file filter DLL.

- **InProcServer32**

  Identifies the file filter DLL using the default value, and defines the Apartment model capabilities of the file filter in the **ThreadingModel** named value.

- **PegasusFilter**

  Provides information on the specific capabilities of the file filer. Possible named values for this key are described in the following table.

Named Value	Description
Import	If this named value exists, the conversion type is for importing files from the desktop computer to the Windows CE-based device. Otherwise, the conversion type is for exporting files from the desktop computer to the Windows CE-based device.
HasOptions	If this named value exists, the file filter supports the **ICeFileFilter::FilterOptions** method.

Named Value	Description
Description	The data for this named value is a string that describes the conversion. Windows CE Services displays this text on the property sheets displayed by selecting the **Device→Desktop** or **Desktop→Device** tab control selections from the **File Conversion Properties** dialog box and then clicking the **Edit** button to display the **Edit Conversion Settings** dialog box. For example, if the **Import** named value exists, then, on the **Desktop→Device** property sheet, the data value defined by the **Description** named value will be displayed under the file conversions details "Convert to HPC files of the type."
NewExtension	Defines the extension of the file that will be created on the destination device.

Sample File Filter Registry Entry

The following is a sample registry editor (.reg) file used to register the Bitmap Image file filter converter. It is to be used when a bitmap file is imported from a desktop computer to a Windows CE-based device. The sample file can be used to convert a bitmap file with a .bmp format to a bitmap file with the .2bp format used by Windows CE. The last three entries register the .2bp file extension to be displayed with a specific icon and name.

Note The 2bp.dll file converter is registered and installed when Windows CE Services is installed on the desktop computer.

```
REGEDIT4

[HKEY_LOCAL_MACHINE\SOFTWARE\Microsoft\Windows CE Services\Filters\.bmp]
"DefaultImport"="{DA01ED80-97E8-11cf-8011-00A0C90A8F78}"

[HKEY_LOCAL_MACHINE\SOFTWARE\Microsoft\Windows CE
Services\Filters\.bmp\InstalledFilters]
"{DA01ED80-97E8-11cf-8011-00A0C90A8F78}"=""

[HKEY_CLASSES_ROOT\CLSID\{DA01ED80-97E8-11cf-8011-00A0C90A8F78}]
@="Bitmap Image"

[HKEY_CLASSES_ROOT\CLSID\{DA01ED80-97E8-11cf-8011-
00A0C90A8F78}\DefaultIcon]
@="c:\Program Files\Windows CE Services\2bp.dll,-1000"
```

```
[HKEY_CLASSES_ROOT\CLSID\{DA01ED80-97E8-11cf-8011-
00A0C90A8F78}\InProcServer32]
@="2bp.dll"
"ThreadingModel"="Apartment"

[HKEY_CLASSES_ROOT\CLSID\{DA01ED80-97E8-11cf-8011-
00A0C90A8F78}\PegasusFilter]
"Import"=""
"Description"="Bitmap Image."
"NewExtension"="2bp"

[HKEY_CLASSES_ROOT\.2bp]
@="2bpfile"

[HKEY_CLASSES_ROOT\2bpfile]
@="Bitmap Image"

[HKEY_CLASSES_ROOT\2bpfile\DefaultIcon]
@="c:\Program Files\Windows CE Services\minshell.dll,-2025"
```

Implementing and Using a File Filter

The Windows CE SDK includes a sample file filter named Copyfilt that imports
a binary file (.bin) from a desktop computer to a binary file (.pbn) on a Windows
CE-based device. The Copyfilt sample file filter demonstrates basic operations for
implementing a file filter, which are described in the following procedure.

▶ **To implement a file filter**

1. Register the file filter DLL.

   See "Registering a File Filter" earlier in this chapter.

2. Implement the **ICeFileFilter** interface and methods.

   For a list of file filter interfaces, see the appendix "Lists of Functions
   and Interfaces."

3. Windows CE Services calls the **QueryInterface** method for the file filter's
   ICeFileFilterOptions interface. If this interface is available, it then calls the
   ICeFileFilterOptions::SetFilterOptions method with a correctly initialized
   CFF_CONVERTOPTIONS structure. The **bNoModalUI**
   member specifies whether the converter is allowed to bring up modal UI
   while performing the conversion.

   For a file filter that includes selectable conversion options, the
   ICeFileFilter::FilterOptions method should be implemented. This allows
   a user to select among the conversion options supported by the file filter.

▶ **To use a file filter**

1. The user uses the drag-and-drop method to transfer a file between Windows CE Explorer on the desktop and on the device.

2. Windows CE Services prompts the user for a conversion type, using the **File Conversion Properties** dialog box.

3. Windows CE Services calls the file filter's **ICeFileFilter::NextConvertFile** method to perform the custom file conversion. Information about the file conversion and about the source and destination files is passed by pointers to the **CFF_CONVERTINFO**, **CFF_DESTINATIONFILE**, and **CFF_SOURCEFILE** structures.

   Within the **ICeFileFilter::NextConvertFile** method:

   a. Call **ICeFileFilterSite::OpenSourceFile** to open the source file.

   b. Call **ICeFileFilterSite::OpenDestinationFile** to open the destination file.

   c. Read data from the stream file that was opened using the **OpenSourceFile** method.

   d. Convert the data. This can include ISV-developed code and RAPI calls.

   e. Check on the status of the **NextConvertFile** *pbCancel* parameter occasionally to ensure that the user has not aborted the conversion process. If the conversion has been aborted, perform all cleanup operations and exit.

   f. Write the converted data to the stream file that was opened using the **OpenDestinationFile** method.

   g. Report the progress of the file conversion by occasionally calling the **ICeFileFilterSite::ReportProgress** method. Windows CE Services uses this information to update a status bar showing the percentage completion of the conversion. You should limit your use of this method because it can add substantially to the conversion time.

   h. Report data that is intentionally discarded during conversion by calling the **ICeFileFilterSite::ReportLoss** method. Windows CE Services displays a message with this information when the file conversion is complete. Depending on the error format passed in the call, Windows CE Services may call the file filter's **ICeFileFilter::FormatMessage** method, in order to properly format the message.

   i. Close the source file, using the **ICeFileFilterSite::CloseSourceFile** method, and then close the destination file, using the **ICeFileFilterSite::CloseDestinationFile** method.

Using Remote API Calls in a File Filter

It is possible to use remote application programming interface (RAPI) calls in a file filter. This allows use of any RAPI functions that are appropriate to your application, such as registry or file functions.

Do not initialize RAPI in the file filter DLL by using **CeRapiInit**. Rather, the **NextConvertFile** method should have already performed the RAPI initialization and established a connection between the desktop computer and the Windows CE-based device. If a RAPI call fails because there is no connection established, the file converter should perform some type of default action rather than just failing. For example, this could involve querying the user to select from various options.

To determine if a call failed due to a failure in the RAPI, use **CeRapiGetError**. To diagnose non-RAPI related errors, use **CeGetLastError**.

For more information on RAPI, see Chapter 17, "Invoking Functions from a Desktop Computer."

Filter-Defined Error Values

There are two ways that file filter errors are returned. First, the **NextConvertFile** method uses the **HRESULT_FROM_WIN32** macro to return an HRESULT error value if the method fails.

But, there is a way to have an error value that is customized to your data type. The **NextConvertFile** function can return a filter-defined error value in the variable pointed to by the *perr* parameter. To use this method, the error value must be defined by using the **CF_DECLARE_ERROR** macro defined in the Replerr.h header file. Also, the filter DLL must include a message table that contains the error value and a corresponding message string. When Windows CE Services gets the filter-defined error value, it then uses the Win32 **FormatMessage** function to create the error string, using **ICeFileFilter::FormatMessage** to check the filter object first for the relevant string (). For more information about message tables, see the Microsoft Platform SDK.

Implementing a Dummy File Filter

A dummy file filter gives the appearance that files are being converted without actually implementing a file filter or performing a filter conversion. Instead, the file is passed without any conversion whatsoever.

Implementing such a dummy filter may be desirable for a file that has a unique file type or one that has not been registered already in the desktop registry. It might also be useful for a file that does not need any conversion when it is transferred between Windows Explorer on the desktop computer and Explorer for the device.

Usually, if a file with an unregistered file type is copied to the device, the device will display the warning **No Converter Selected**. This warns the user that the file will be transferred without conversion. In this situation, implementing a dummy filter would avoid alarming the user with the file conversion warning.

Note The **No Converter Selected** warning will be displayed only if the mobile device's **File Conversions Properties** is set to enable file conversion. If the **Enable File Conversion** check box is unchecked, then the **No Converter Selected** warning will not be displayed.

▶ **To register a dummy file filter**

1. Modify **HKLM\Software\Microsoft\Windows CE Services\Filters**, the desktop computer registry key, by adding a subkey. This subkey should name the file extension for the type of files that should be converted using the NULL file conversion. For example, if you are converting files with extension .abc, then you must add a subkey **.abc**.

2. Under the **.abc** subkey, create a string value named **DefaultImport** that is set to Binary Copy. This string value identifies the conversion for files with .abc extensions that are imported from the desktop computer to the Windows CE-based device.

3. Under the **.abc** subkey, create a string value named **DefaultExport** that is set to Binary Copy. This identifies the conversion for files with .abc extensions that are exported from the device to the desktop computer.

The following registry editor (.reg) file registers the example .abc dummy file filter.

```
REGEDIT4
[HKEY_LOCAL_MACHINE\SOFTWARE\Microsoft\Windows CE Services\Filters\.abc]
"DefaultImport"="Binary Copy"
"DefaultExport"="Binary Copy"
```

In this example, when a file with an .abc extension is copied between the desktop computer and the Windows CE-based device, it will seem as though a conversion process is taking place because you do not receive the warning **No Converter Selected** from Windows CE Services. However, no filter actually is being used, because an **InstalledFilters** subkey has not been added under the **.abc** key.

C H A P T E R   2 0

Synchronizing Data

A computer user with a Windows CE-based device and a desktop computer may need to ensure that data is the same, or *synchronized*, on both. For example, when a user updates information in a personal information manager (PIM) application, that information needs to be synchronized with Schedule+ data on the desktop computer.

Windows CE Services provides interfaces that simplify the synchronization process. Because it takes care of many common services, such as connectivity, conflict resolution, and detection of changes and deletions, you need to develop only the code for your specific data.

You use the synchronization interfaces of Windows CE Services to develop a client and a server. The ActiveSync™ Service Provider, known as the client, has two parts, one that resides on the Windows CE-based device and another that resides on the desktop computer. The ActiveSync Service Manager, known as the server, is the synchronization engine built into Windows CE Services on the desktop computer. Together, the server and the client make up ActiveSync. Once ActiveSync is installed and the required registry entries have been made, user-defined data is automatically synchronized between the device and the desktop computer.

For a sample application that implements ActiveSync for a stock portfolio, see the Stockpor program in the SDK.

When discussing synchronization, the *store* is a database that holds the data to be synchronized. An *object* is a logical unit of data in the store, for example, an appointment. An *object type* is a name for a particular group of objects, for example, appointment. A *folder* is a logical container for an object type, for example, all appointments in Schedule+.

Design Considerations

To develop ActiveSync for your application, you first analyze the data to be synchronized. Define the object, the object type, the folder, the object identifier, and the database to hold the objects. Decide on the way to compare objects and the method for indicating that an object has changed. As you do this, keep the following requirements in mind:

- The object definition depends entirely on your application. It could be an appointment, an address, or some other item. The object type and the folder depend upon the object.

- The object identifier must satisfy several criteria. It cannot change once it is created; it cannot be reused for any other object; and it must be ordered. This allows object identifiers to be compared. Globally unique identifiers (GUIDs), for example, would satisfy these criteria.

- The database must accommodate the objects to be synchronized, but it can be a flat file, a Windows CE database, or some other custom format.

- Time stamps and version numbers are common ways to indicate that an object has changed.

Once these requirements are met, you can design and implement ActiveSync.

ActiveSync Service Provider

As mentioned earlier, the ActiveSync Service Provider, or client, that you implement has two parts: one for the desktop computer and one for the Windows CE-based device. The ActiveSync Service Manager, or server, communicates with the clients on the desktop computer and the device during synchronization. Each client must be registered on its respective device.

Desktop Client

The desktop client is an OLE in-process (Inproc) server dynamic-link library (DLL) that must:

- Have access to the store while synchronization is taking place.
- Be able to create, read, write, and delete any object in the store.
- Determine if an object has changed since the last time it was synchronized.
- Enumerate all objects that need to be synchronized.

- Be able to read an object and convert it into a series of bytes, a process called serialization.

- Take such a series of bytes and convert them back to an object, a process called deserialization.

▶ **To implement the desktop client**

1. Create one GUID for the store, using the Visual C++ GUID generator tool, Guidgen.exe.

2. Define **HREPLITEM** and **HREPLFLD**. These handles can be simply pointers to data structures.

3. Define **HREPLOBJ**, which is a generic handle that can be either **HREPLITEM** or **HREPLFLD**.

4. Implement all methods in **IReplStore**.

   These methods implement the following functionality:

   - Initialize the store.

   - Provide a folder handle for the specified object type and return a pointer to the **IReplObjHandler** interface.

   - Provide for management of the object types.

   - Provide a way for Windows CE Services to display related information in the main window.

   - Enumerate objects for a specified object type.

5. Implement all methods in **IReplObjHandler**.

Windows CE Client

The Windows CE client can be a single DLL that exports the following functions:

- **InitObjType**, which initializes the data for an object type and, at termination, frees allocated resources.

- **GetObjTypeInfo**, which gets information for an object type.

- **ObjectNotify**, which allows the server to prompt the Windows CE client whether it is interested in the current change or deletion to the device's store. Also, it sends the object identifier to the desktop client.

- **ReportStatus**, which is an optional function that allows the server to get the status on the Windows CE-based platform synchronization objects.

Besides implementing the previous functions, you must also implement the methods in **IReplObjHandler**. However, these methods can be stubbed, rather than fully implemented.

Registering the ActiveSync Service Provider

For Windows CE Services to use ActiveSync, valid registry entries must exist in the registry on both the desktop computer and on the Windows CE-based device.

Note The CEUTIL utility DLL functions are especially helpful when dealing with desktop registry entries for Windows CE. For more information, see Chapter 21, "Installing and Managing Applications."

Registry Settings for a Desktop Computer

On the desktop computer, you must register the object type to be synchronized and you must also register ActiveSync as an in-process server. For object-type registration, you must enter values under **HKEY_LOCAL_MACHINES \Software\Microsoft\Windows CE Services\Services\Synchronization\Objects**. The keys under **Objects** are the object types to be synchronized. For each object type, you must define five values: *Default, Display Name, Plural Name, Store,* and *Disabled.*

The *Default* value can be anything; it is usually a description of the object type. The *Display Name* and *Plural Name* are names for the object, for example, "Appointment" and "Appointments." The *Store* value is the OLE programmatic identifier, ProgID, of the store that implements the **IReplStore** and **IReplObjHandler** interfaces. The *Disabled* value indicates whether the service is shown as disabled or enabled in Windows CE Services. A non-zero value indicates the service is disabled.

Using Schedule+ synchronization as an example, the desktop component is Scdstore.dll. This DLL synchronizes data for five different object types: Appointment, Contact, File, Inbox, and Task. A 32-bit OLE in-process server implements **IReplStore** and various **IReplObjHandler** interfaces, one for each object type. The following screen shot illustrates the desktop registry location for synchronization objects.

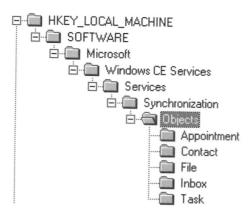

📝 (Default)	"OutLook Appointment Object"
📝 Display Name	"Appointment"
📝 Plural Name	"Appointments"
📝 Store	"MS.WinCE.OutLook"
🔢 Disabled	0x00000000 (0)

Desktop registry structure

You must register ActiveSync for OLE to recognize it as a valid in-process server. To do this, you must register the ProgID, the Class ID, and the GUID under **HKEY_CLASSES_ROOT**. Register the ProgID under **HKEY_CLASSES_ROOT\<ProgID>\Clsid**, where the *Default* value of the **Clsid** key is the GUID for the store; in this case, it is {a417bc10-7be1-11ce-ad82-00aa006ec559}.

To specify the location of the OLE in-process server, use the following keys: **HKEY_CLASSES_ROOT\Clsid\<Class ID>\InProcServer32** and **HKEY_CLASSES_ROOT\Clsid\<Class ID>\ProgID**. The *Default* value of the **InprocServer32** key is the full path of the 32-bit DLL that implements the **IReplStore** interface. In the Schedule+ example, this is the path to Scdstore.dll. The *Default* value of **ProgID** key is the ProgID of the store. In this example, it is **MS.WinCE.Outlook**. For more information on registration, see the OLE documentation in the Microsoft Platform SDK.

For another example of the required desktop registry keys, see the Stockpor program in the SDK.

Registry Settings for Windows CE-Based Platforms

On the Windows CE-based platform, the registry settings are similar to those for the desktop computer. You must register the object types and the corresponding DLL under **HKEY_LOCAL_MACHINE\Windows CE Services \Synchronization\Objects**. Under the **Objects** key, there is a list of keys, one key for each object type. The only value needed is for *Store*, which specifies the name of the DLL that exports the necessary functions.

Using the Schedule+ example, the Windows CE-based platform component is a DLL named Pegobj.dll, which exports the four functions mentioned previously.

You can set these registry entries when you install your application with the device connected. The following screen shot illustrates the Windows CE-based device registry location for synchronization objects.

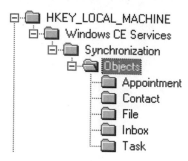

Device registry structure

For an example of the required registry keys on the Windows CE-based platform, see the Stockpor program in the SDK.

CHAPTER 21

Installing and Managing Applications

Windows CE uses a cabinet file to install an application on a Windows CE-based device. A cabinet (.cab) file is composed of multiple files that have been compressed into one. Compressing all files into one has three main benefits: it ensures that all the files for your application are present, it prevents a partial installation, and it allows installation from several sources, such as a desktop computer or Web site.

You use CAB Wizard to generate a .cab file for your application. The Windows CE Application Manager uses that .cab file to install the application. The Application Manager also removes an application from the Windows CE-based device. This chapter describes the methods and tools involved in these processes, and it includes a checklist for troubleshooting application installations.

This chapter also describes how to manage applications by registering desktop file filters, synchronizing services, adding custom menu items, and accessing partnership settings.

General Procedure for Application Installation

Because the .cab files are self-contained setup packages, they are source-independent. For example, they can be installed from a companion desktop computer or transferred from another device using an infrared (IR) link.

▶ **To create the multiple device-specific .cab files for a single application**

1. Create a single Win32 setup .inf file with Windows CE-specific modifications.

2. Optionally, create a Setup.dll file to provide custom control of the installation process.

3. Start CAB Wizard with the Setup .inf file and the device-specific application files.

▶ **To install an application on the Windows CE-based device from a desktop computer**

1. Create a single Application Manager initialization (.ini) file to provide information about the application for Application Manager.

2. Create a desktop setup program using any available third-party desktop setup program. This program will:

   ▪ Copy the multiple device-specific .cab files to the desktop computer.

   ▪ Launch the Application Manager, with the Application Manager .ini file as a parameter.

For more information, see ".inf File" and "Setup.dll File" later in this chapter.

CAB Wizard

The CAB Wizard creates a Windows CE-specific .cab file using the Win32 Setup information (.inf) file, an optional Setup.dll file created by an independent software vendor (ISV), and the application files.

The command-line syntax for CAB Wizard is:

cabwiz.exe *"inf-file"* [/dest *dest-directory*] [/err *error-file*] [/cpu *cpu-type* [*cpu-type*]]

Note The /cpu parameter, followed by multiple CPU values, must be the last qualifier in the command line.

The Windows CE SDK files that must be installed in the same directory on the desktop computer are: Cabwiz.exe, Makecab.exe, and Cabwiz.ddf. Cabwiz.exe must be called with its full path in order to run correctly.

---

inf-file
    Absolute full path for the setup .inf file.

dest-directory
    Absolute destination directory for the.cab files. If no directory is specified, the .cab files are created in the directory of *inf-file*.

error-file
    File name for a log file that contains all warnings and errors encountered during the compilation of the .cab files. If no file name is specified, errors are displayed in message boxes. If a file name is used, CAB Wizard runs without the user interface (UI); this is useful for automated builds.

cpu-type
> Creates a .cab file for each processor tag that you specify. A processor tag is a label used in the Win32 setup .inf file to differentiate between different processor types.

The following command line example creates .cab files for the SH3 and MIPS chips, assuming that the Win32 setup .inf file contains the SH3 and MIPS tags:

```
cabwiz.exe  "c:\myfile.inf"  /err myfile.err  /cpu  sh3  mips
```

.inf File

CAB Wizard can create multiple .cab files with a single setup .inf file and multiple application binaries. This is useful for creating multiple .cab files, each one for a specific processor type. To indicate information for a specific processor, append an extension describing the processor, known as a processor tag, to these section names: CEDevice, DefaultInstall, SourceDisksNames, and SourceDisksFiles. For example:

```
[DefaultInstall]        ;shared by all platforms, processed first
[DefaultInstall.sh3]    ;specific to the SH3 chip
[DefaultInstall.mips]   ;specific to the MIPS chip
```

Information in sections without an extension is valid, unless it is specifically overridden by information in a section with an extension. The exception to this is the *UnsupportedPlatforms* key in the CEDevice section, described later.

Version

```
[Version]
Signature = "signature-name"
Provider = "INF-creator"
CESignature = "$Windows CE$"
```

signature-name
> Must be "$Windows NT$" or "$Windows 95$."

INF-creator
> The company name of the application. For example:

```
Provider = "Microsoft"
```

CEStrings

This is a section specific to Windows CE that specifies string substitutions for the application name and the default install directory.

```
[CEStrings]
    AppName = app-name
InstallDir = default-install-dir
```

app-name
> Name of the application. Other instances of %AppName% in the .inf file will be replaced with this string value.

default-install-dir
> Default installation directory on the device. Other instances of %InstallDir% in the .inf file will be replaced with this string value.

For example, to have AppName mean "Game Pack," and to have InstallDir mean %CE1%\%AppName%, use this code:

```
[CEStrings]
AppName="Game Pack"
InstallDir=%CE1%\%AppName%
```

Strings

```
[Strings]
string-key = value
[string-key = value]
```

CEDevice

```
[CEDevice]
[ProcessorType    =[processor-type]]
[UnsupportedPlatforms = platform-family-name[,platform-family-name]]
[VersionMin      = [major-version.minor-version]]
[VersionMax      = [major-version.minor-version]]
[BuildMin        = [build-number]]
[BuildMax        = [build-number]]
```

All keys are optional. If a key is non-existent, no checking is performed. If a key exists but there is no data, then no checking is performed. The exception is **UnsupportedPlatforms**; if this key exists but there is no data, the previous value is not overridden.

processor-type

> Value returned by SYSTEMINFO.dwProcessorType. For example, the value for the SH3 CPU is 10003 and the MIPS CPU is 4000.

platform-family-name

> List of platform family names known to be unsupported. If the name specified in [CEDevice.xxx] is different from that in [CEDevice], both platform family name values are unsupported for processor "xxx." That is, the list of specific unsupported platform family names is appended to the previous list of unsupported platform family names. Application Manager will not display the application for an unsupported platform. Also, the user will be warned during setup if the .cab file is copied to an unsupported device. For example:

```
[CEDevice]
UnsupportedPlatforms = pltfrm1      ; pltfrm1 is unsupported
[CEDevice.SH3]
UnsupportedPlatforms =              ; pltfrm1 is still unsupported
```

minor-version or *major-version*

> Numeric value returned by OSVERSIONINFO.dwVersionMinor and OSVERSIONINFO.dwVersionMajor. The .cab file is valid for the currently connected device, if the version of the currently connected device is less than or equal to VersionMax and also greater than or equal to VersionMin.

build-number

> Numeric value returned by OSVERSIONINFO.dwBuildNumber. The .cab file is valid for the currently connected device, if the version of the currently connected device is less than or equal to BuildMax and also greater than or equal to BuildMin.

The following code example shows three CEDevice sections, one that gives basic information for any \cpu and two that are specific to the SH3 and the MIPS processor chips.

```
[CEDevice]                          ; a "template" for all platforms
UnsupportedPlatforms = pltfrm1      ; does not support pltfrm1
; the following specifies version 1.0 devices only
VersionMin = 1.0
VersionMax = 1.0


[CEDevice.SH3]                      ; inherits all [CEDevice] settings
; this will create a CAB file specific for "SH3" devices
ProcessorType = 10003              ; the SH3 CAB file is only valid for the
SH3 processors
UnsupportedPlatforms =             ; pltfrm1 is still unsupported
; the following overrides the version settings so that no version
checking is performed
VersionMin =
VersionMax =
```

```
[CEDevice.MIPS]                      ; inherits all [CEDevice] settings
; this will create a CAB file specific for "MIPS" devices
ProcessorType = 4000                 ; the "MIPS" CAB file is only valid for
the MIPS processor
UnsupportedPlatforms =pltfrm2        ; pltfrm1 and pltfrm2 are unsupported
for the "MIPS" CAB file
```

Note To create the two CPU-specific .cab files for the setup .inf file in the previous example, CAB Wizard must be run with the parameter */cpu sh3 mips*.

DefaultInstall

```
[DefaultInstall]
Copyfiles=copyfile-list-section[,copyfile-list-section]
AddReg=add-registry-section[,add-registry-section]
[CEShortcuts=shortcut-list-section[,shortcut-list-section]]   ; new key
[CESetupDLL=setup-DLL]                                        ; new key
[CESelfRegister=self-reg-DLL-filename[,self-reg-DLL-filename] ; new key
```

shortcut-list-section
> String that identifies one more section that defines shortcuts to a file; see the CEShortcuts description later in this section.

setup-DLL
> Optimal string that specifies a Setup.dll. It is written by the ISV and contains customized functions for operations during installation and removal of the application. The file must be specified in the [SourceDisksFiles] section. For more information, see the associated description later in this section.

self-reg-DLL-filename
> String that identifies files that self-register, exporting the COM functions **DllRegisterServer** and **DllUnregisterServer**. You must specify the files in the SourceDiskFiles section.
>
> If installation on the device fails to call the file's exported **DllRegisterServer** function, then the file's exported **DllUnregisterServer** function will not be called during uninstallation.

SourceDisksNames

```
[SourceDisksNames]
disk-ordinal= ,disk-label,,path
[disk-ordinal= ,disk-label,,path]
```

SourceDisksFiles

```
[SourceDisksFiles]
filename=disk_number[,subdir]
[filename=disk_number[,subdir]]
```

DestinationDirs

```
[DestinationDirs]
file-list-section = 0,subdir
[file-list-section = 0,subdir]
[DefaultDestDir=0,subdir]
```

Note Windows CE does not support directory identifiers (DirID).

Subdir

String that identifies the destination directory. String substitutions supported by Windows CE are described in the following table. These can only be used for the beginning of the path.

String	Replacement value
%CE1%	\Program Files
%CE2%	\Windows
%CE3%	\Windows\Desktop
%CE4%	\Windows\Startup
%CE5%	\My Documents
%CE6%	\Program Files\Accessories
%CE7%	\Program Files\Communication
%CE8%	\Program Files\Games
%CE9%	\Program Files\Pocket Outlook
%CE10%	\Program Files\Office
%CE11%	\Windows\Programs
%CE12%	\Windows\Programs\Accessories
%CE13%	\Windows\Programs\Communications
%CE14%	\Windows\Programs\Games
%CE15%	\Windows\Fonts
%CE16%	\Windows\Recent
%CE17%	\Windows\Favorites

For example:

```
[DestinationDirs]
Files.Common   = 0,%CE1%\My Subdir    ;\Program Files\My Subdir
Files.Shared   = 0,%CE2%              ;\Windows
```

CopyFiles

```
[copyfile-list-section]
destination-file-name,[source-file-name],[,flags]
[destination-file-name,[source-file-name],[,flags]]
```

Source-file-name is optional if it is the same as *destination-file-name*.

Flags

Numeric value that specifies an action to be done while copying files. Values supported by Windows CE are described in the following table.

Flag	Value	Description
COPYFLG_WARN_IF_SKIP	0x00000001	Warn user if attempt is made to skip a file after an error has occurred.
COPYFLG_NOSKIP	0x00000002	Do not allow user to skip copying a file.
COPYFLG_NO_OVERWRITE	0x00000010	Do not overwrite an existing file in the destination directory.
COPYFLG_REPLACEONLY	0x00000400	Copy source file to the destination directory only if the file is already in the destination directory.
CE_COPYFLG_NO_DATE_DIALOG	0x20000000	Do not copy if target is newer.
CE_COPYFLG_NODATECHECK	0x40000000	Ignore date while overwriting the target file.
CE_COPYFLG_SHARED	0x80000000	Reference when a shared DLL is counted.

AddReg

```
[add-registry-section]
registry-root-string , subkey,[value-name], flags, value[,value]
[registry-root-string, subkey,[value-name], flags, value[,value]]
```

registry-root-strings
> String that specifies the registry root location. Values supported by Windows CE are described in the following table.

Root string	Description
HKCR	Same as HKEY_CLASSES_ROOT.
HKCU	Same as HKEY_CURRENT_USER.
HKLM	Same as HKEY_LOCAL_MACHINE.

value-name
> Registry value name. If empty, the registry value name "(default)" is used.

flags
> Numeric value that specifies information about the registry key. Values supported by Window CE are described in the following table.

Flag	Value	Description
FLG_ADDREG_NOCLOBBER	0x00000002	If the registry key exists, do not overwrite it. This flag can be used in combination with any of the flags later in this table.
FLG_ADDREG_TYPE_SZ	0x00000000	Registry data type REG_SZ.
FLG_ADDREG_TYPE_MULTI_SZ	0x00010000	Registry data type REG_MULTI_SZ. The value field that follows can be a list of strings separated by commas.
FLG_ADDREG_TYPE_BINARY	0x00000001	Registry data type REG_BINARY. The value field that follows must be a list of numeric values separated by commas, one byte per field, and must not use the 0x hex prefix.
FLG_ADDREG_TYPE_DWORD	0x00010001	Data type REG_DWORD. Only the noncompatible format in the Win32 Setup .inf documentation is supported.

The following code example shows how the AddReg section is used.

```
[RegSection]
; the following uses (FLG_ADDREG_TYPE_MULTI_SZ | FLG_ADDREG_NOCLOBBER)
to create a multi-string with the "noclobber" flag
   HKLM,Software\Microsoft\Games,Title,0x00010002, "Game","Pack"
; the following uses FLG_ADDREG_TPE_BINARY to create an 8-byte binary
registry value
   HKLM,Software\Microsoft\Games,Data,0x00000001,2,F,B,3,0,A,6,D
; the following uses (FLG_ADDREG_TYPE_DWORD | FLG_ADDREG_NOCLOBBER) to
create a dword with the "no clobber" flag
   HKLM,Software\Microsoft\Games,HighScore,0x00010003,456
```

CEShortcuts

This is a Windows CE-specific section.

[shortcut-list-section]

```
shortcut-file-name,shortcut-type-flag,target-file/path[,standard-
destination-path]
[shortcut-file-name,shortcut-type-flag,target-file/path[,standard-
destination-path]]
```

shortcut-file-name
>   String that identifies the shortcut name. It does not require the .lnk extension.

shortcut-type-flag
>   Numeric value. Zero or empty represents a shortcut to a file; any non-zero numeric value represents a shortcut to a folder.

target-file/path
>   String value that specifies the destination location. For a file, use the target file name, for example, MyApp.exe, that must be defined in a file copy list. For a path, use a *file-list-section* name defined in [*DestinationDirs*], for example, *DefaultDestDir*, or the %InstallDir% string.

standard-destination-path
>   Optional string value. A standard %CEx% path or %InstallDir%. If no value is specified, the *shortcut-list-section* name of the current section or the "*DefaultDestDir*" from the [*DestinationDirs*] section is used.

The following code example shows how the CEShortcuts section is used.

```
[DestinationDirs]
file_list  = 0%CE2%
Links = 0%CE3%
DefaultDestDir = 0%InstallDir%
[file_list]
"my final app.exe",app.exe,,0
[Links]
; shortcut name is "file 1"
; this is a shortcut to a file; the target is "my final app.exe"
; shortcut is created in the folder used in "[DestinationDirs] Links"
section, which is currently %CE3%
"file 1",0,"my final app.exe"

;shortcut name is "file2"
;this is a shortcut to a file; the target is "my final app.exe"
;shortcut is created in the %InstallDir% folder
"file 2",0,"my final app.exe",%InstallDir%

;shortcut name is "path 1"
;this is a shortcut to a folder
;the shortcut target is the folder used in "[DestinationDirs]
DefaultDestDir" section, which is currently %InstallDir%
;shortcut is created in the folder used in "[DestinationDirs] Links"
section which is currently %CE3%
"path 1",1,DefaultDestDir

;shortcut name is "path 2"
;this is a shortcut to a folder
;the target is the folder used in "[DestinationDirs] Links" section
which is currently %CE3%
;shortcut is created in the %InstallDir% folder
"path 2",1,Links,%InstallDir%
```

Sample .inf File

```
[Version]                 ; required section
Signature = "$Windows NT$"
Provider = "Microsoft"
CESignature = "$Windows CE$"

[CEDevice.SH3]
ProcessorType = 10003      ; SH3 processor

[CEDevice.MIPS]
ProcessorType = 4000       ; MIPS processor
```

```
[DefaultInstall]                ; required section
AddReg = RegSettings.All
CEShortcuts = Shortcuts.All

[DefaultInstall.SH3]
CopyFiles = Files.Common, Files.SH3

[DefaultInstall.MIPS]
CopyFiles = Files.Common, Files.MIPS

[SourceDisksNames]              ; required section
1 = ,"Common files",,C:\app\common    ;using an absolute path

[SourceDisksNames.SH3]
2 = ,"SH3 files",,sh3          ;using a relative path

[SourceDisksNames.MIPS]
2 = ,"MIPS files",,mips        ;using a relative path

[SourceDisksFiles]              ; required section
begin.wav = 1
end.wav = 1
sample.hlp = 1

[SourceDisksFiles.SH3]
sample.exe = 2                  ; uses the SourceDisksNames.SH3 id of 2

[SourceDisksFiles.MIPS]
sample.exe = 2                  ; uses the SourceDisksNames.MIPS id of 2

[DestinationDirs]               ; required section
Shortcuts.All = 0,%CE3%         ; \Windows\Desktop
Files.Common = 0,%CE2%          ; \Windows
Files.SH3 = 0,%InstallDir%
Files.MIPS = 0,%InstallDir%
DefaultDestDir = 0,%InstallDir%

[CEStrings]                     ; required section
AppName = My Test App
InstallDir = %CE1%\%AppName%

[Strings]                       ; optional section
reg_path = Software\Microsoft\My Test App

[Shortcuts.All]
Sample App,0,sample.exe                 ; uses path in DestinationDirs
Sample App,0,sample.exe,%InstallDir% ; path is explicitly specified
```

```
[Files.Common]
begin.wav,,,0
end.wav,,,0
Sample Help File.hlp,sample.hlp,,0   ; rename destination file

[Files.SH3]
sample.exe,,,0

[Files.MIPS]
sample.exe,,,0

[RegSettings.All]
HKLM,%reg_path%,,0x00000000,alpha      ; <default> = "alpha"
HKLM,%reg_path%,test,0x00010001,3      ; test = 3
HKLM,%reg_path%\new,another,0x00010001,6 ; new\another = 6
```

Setup.dll File

The device-specific Setup.dll file is an optional file, written by the ISV, that enables you to perform custom operations during installation and removal of your application. The file exports the following functions:

- **Install_Init** is called before installation begins. You can use this function to check the application version in a reinstall scenario and to determine if a dependent application is present.

- **Install_Exit** is called after installation completes. You can use this function to handle errors that occurred during installation of the application.

- **Uninstall_Init** is called before uninstallation begins. You can use this function to close the application, if it is running.

- **Uninstall_Exit** is called after uninstallation completes. You can use this function to save database data into a file and delete the database, telling the user where the user data files are stored and how to reinstall the application.

Note Once the Setup.dll file is incorporated into the .cab file, it is renamed. You cannot make any assumptions on file name or location of this DLL on the device. Thus, you must specify the full path and file name when you write these functions. Also, you must include the SDK public header file, Ce_setup.h.

Application Manager

The Application Manager program, CeAppMgr.exe, resides on a user's desktop computer. It is responsible for adding and removing applications on the Windows CE-based device, as well as deleting the application files from the desktop computer.

▶ **To register an application with Application Manager**

1. Copy the application .cab file to the desktop computer.
2. Copy the Application Manager .ini file for the application to the desktop computer.
3. Run Application Manager with the .ini file as a parameter.

This process can be done using a third-party desktop computer installation program. With this approach, Application Manager automatically installs the application on the Windows CE-based device. If the Windows CE device is not connected, Application Manager notes that the application has not been installed. When the device is subsequently connected, Application Manager automatically completes the installation.

The command line syntax for the Application Manager, CeAppMgr.exe is:

```
CEAppMgr.exe [/report]  "CEAppMgr-INI-file"  ["CEAppMgr-INI-file"]
```

CEAppMgr-INI-file
  Full file name and path of the CEAppMgr .ini file for a single application. If the application has multiple components, you can run Application Manager once with the multiple .ini files, one for each component.

report
  Optional parameter that provides information concerning the installation process in the event of problems. This parameter should not be included in the final setup program.

You can extract the full file name and path of Application Manager from the default registry value of the registry key: **HKLM\Software\Microsoft\Windows\CurrentVersion\App Paths\CEAppMgr.exe**. Because the returned value is the full file name and path of CEAppMgr.exe, you can remove the CEAppMgr.exe file name to get the desktop installation directory of Windows CE Services. You can use the desktop installation directory to copying files to the desktop computer. The location for your files will be the installation directory with your application's subdirectory appended.

Because the installation procedure registers the application's .cab files with Application Manager, the application can be reinstalled on the device at a later time or installed on another device.

.ini File Format for Application Manager

The .ini file contains information that registers an application with Application Manager. The .ini file has the following format:

```
[CEAppManager]
Version      = version-number
Component    = component-name

[component-name]
Description  = descriptive-name
[Uninstall   = uninstall-name]
[InstallDir  = install-directory]
[IconFile    = icon-filename]
[IconIndex   = icon-index]
[DeviceFile  = device-filename]
CabFiles     = cabfile-name [, cabfile-name]
```

version-number
> Numeric version of Application Manager, which is 1.0.

component-name
> String that identifies the name of the section for the application.

descriptive-name (string)
> String that will appear in the description field of Application Manager when the user chooses the application.

uninstall-name
> String that identifies the application's Windows uninstall registry key name. This name must match the application's registered Windows uninstall key name, found in the registry **HKLM\Software\Microsoft\Windows \CurrentVersion\Uninstall**. Providing this key name enables Application Manager to automatically uninstall the application on the desktop and on the device when the user clicks the **Remove** button in the Application Manager user interface.

install-directory
> String that identifies the desktop install directory containing the location of the .cab files. If this key is non-existent, which is recommended, then the path of the .inf file is used for the install directory.

icon-filename
> String that identifies the relative path from *install-directory* to the desktop icon file. This string is used to display the *device-filename* when the file name is viewed in Windows CE Services.

icon-index
> Numeric index into *icon-filename*. The value is used to display the *device-filename* when viewed in Windows CE Services. If this key is non-existent, then the first icon in *icon-filename* is used.

device-filename
> File name on the device that will display the icon specified by *icon-filename* and *icon-index* when the *device-filename* is viewed in Windows CE Services.

cabfile-name
> File name of the .cab files available, relative to *install-directory*.

Sample Application Manager .ini File

```
[CEAppManager]
Version    = 1.0
Component  = Games

[Games]
Description = Game Pack for your Windows CE-based device
Uninstall   = Game Pack

;do not specify the "InstallDir" key so that CEAppMgr will use the
directory of this INI file as the install directory

IconFile    = gamepack.ico
IconIndex   = 0
DeviceFile  = gamepack.exe

;we have multiple CAB files specific to a CPU type
;these files are relative to the install directory
CabFiles= SH3\gamepack.cab, MIPS\gamepack.cab
```

Troubleshooting Application Installation

To identify and avoid problems that may occur when you install an application on Windows CE, follow these guidelines:

CAB Wizard

- Use %% for a % character when using this character in an .inf file string, as specified in the Win32 SDK documentation. This will not work under the [Strings] section.

- Do not use .inf files created for Windows CE for installing to Windows-based desktop platforms.

- Do not use .cab files created for Windows CE for installing to Windows-based desktop platforms.

- Ensure that the files "Makecab.exe" and "Cabwiz.ddf," included in the Windows CE SDK, are in the same directory as "Cabwiz.exe."

- Call Cabwiz.exe with the full path.

- Do not create a .cab file using the Makecab.exe file included in the Windows CE SDK. You must use Cabwiz.exe, which uses Makecab.exe to generate the .cab files for Windows CE.

- Do not make .cab files with the read-only file attribute set.

Application Manager (CeAppMgr)

- Use the full path for the location of the CeAppMgr .ini file when you call Ceappmgr.exe to register an application.

- Use the /report parameter in debug versions to verify that CeAppMgr is using the correct information for the .cab files.

- Verify in the CeAppMgr .ini file that the string list in the CabFiles key contains no unnecessary spaces.

- Verify in the CeAppMgr .ini file that the string list in the CabFiles key matches the actual .cab files name and relative path.

- Verify in the CeAppMgr .ini file that the string value in the Component key exists elsewhere in the .ini file.

- Verify that the desktop computer's setup program is calling the correct CeAppMgr .ini file, using the full path.

- There are various third-party desktop setup programs that will not correctly update the actual file sizes when overwriting existing files. Because the Application Manager will verify the actual file size with the embedded file size of the .cab file, be sure that the installed .cab file sizes are correct. To ensure this happens for future upgrade scenarios, delete the known existing .cab files when you reinstall an application.

Adding Custom Menus to Windows CE Explorer

Windows CE Services allows additional menu items to be added to the **Tools** menu in the Explorer window in two different ways. The method described in this section uses code to directly place values in the proper registry locations. You can also use the CEUTIL utility DLL to create custom menus and perform other tasks.

In order to add a custom menu, create a subkey and add several values under **HKEY_LOCAL_MACHINE\SOFTWARE\Microsoft\Windows CE Services\ CustomMenus** as follows:

```
[HKEY_LOCAL_MACHINE\SOFTWARE\Microsoft\WINDOWS CE Services\CustomMenus]
[HKEY_LOCAL_MACHINE\SOFTWARE\Microsoft\WINDOWS
CE Services\CustomMenus\subkey]
"DisplayName"="displayName"
"Command"="myApp.exe"
"StatusHelp"="StatusHelpText"
"Version"=version_number
```

subkey
String that identifies the subkey to be created under the **Tools** menu.

DisplayName
String that identifies the display name of the menu item. An ampersand (&) specifies a hot key.

myApp.exe
String that identifies the command that will be executed by WinExec when a user chooses the menu item.

StatusHelpText
String that identifies the status and Help text that appears in the status bar when a user browses the menu item.

version_number
Application version. This value should be 0x00020000.

The following sample registry file adds a calculator menu item.

```
REGEDIT4
[HKEY_LOCAL_MACHINE\SOFTWARE\Microsoft\WINDOWS CE Services\CustomMenus]
[HKEY_LOCAL_MACHINE\SOFTWARE\Microsoft\WINDOWS
CE Services\CustomMenus\MyApp]
"DisplayName"="&My Calculator"
"Command"="calc.exe"
"StatusHelp"="Brings up the calculator"
"Version"=dword:00020000
```

CEUTIL: Helper DLL for Windows CE Services

Use CEUTIL, a utility DLL, to handle the desktop registry entries for Windows CE Services. CEUTIL encapsulates the registry top-level locations, to ensure forward-compatibility for applications. It also provides helper functions for browsing device partnerships and querying the currently connected, or selected, device settings. In general, this DLL is a replacement for, and compatible with, the Win32 registry application programming interface (API) used when referring to any subkeys under the Windows CE Services root.

Use CEUTIL to do the following tasks:

- Register desktop file filters.
- Register desktop synchronization services.
- Access device-partnership settings used for both file filters and synchronization services.
- Add custom menu items.

For a list of the CEUTIL functions, see the appendix "Lists of Functions and Interfaces."

Desktop Registry Structure

The following list describes the desktop registry structure used by Windows CE Services and the corresponding identifiers used in CEUTIL to refer to particular keys in the structure:

- **HKEY_LOCAL_MACHINE\Software\Microsoft\Windows CE Services**, hereafter referred to as **MACHINE_ROOT**, stores general information.
- **HKEY_CURRENT_USER\Software\Microsoft\Windows CE Services**, hereafter referred to as **LOCAL_ROOT**, stores partnership information.

The first time a device is connected to a desktop computer and a partnership is created, the various synchronization and filter settings are copied from the **MACHINE_ROOT** to the partnership subkey under **LOCAL_ROOT**.

Examples of CEUTIL Functions

The following code example shows how to enumerate device partnerships and get file sync folder path.

```
HCESVC    hsvc            = NULL;
HCESVC    hsvcSync        = NULL;
HCESVC    hsvcProfile     = NULL;
DWORD     cProfilesEnum   = 0;
DWORD     nProfileID      = 0;

while (SUCCEEDED (CeSvcEnumProfiles(&hsvc, cProfilesEnum, &nProfileID)))
{
   if (nProfileID != (DWORD)-1)
   {
      if (SUCCEEDED(CeSvcOpenEx(hsvcProfile,
TEXT("Services\\Synchronization"), FALSE, &hsvcSync)))
        {
           TCHAR szPath[MAX_PATH];
           if (SUCCEEDED(CeSvcGetString(hsvcSync, TEXT("Briefcase
Path"), szPath, sizeof(szPath)/sizeof(TCHAR))))
           {
               //complete tasks
           }
           CeSvcClose(hsvcSync);
        }
        CeSvcClose(hsvcProfile);
   }
   cProfilesEnum++;
}
```

The following code example shows how to add a custom menu.

```
HCESVC  hsvcMyMenu = NULL;

if (SUCCEEDED(CeSvcOpen(CESVC_CUSTOM_MENUS, TEXT("MyApp"), TRUE,
&hsvcMyMenu)))
{
   CeSVCSetString(hsvcMyMenu, TEXT("DisplayName"), TEXT("&My
Calculator"));
   CeSVCSetString(hsvcMyMenu, TEXT("Command"), TEXT("calc.exe"));
   CeSVCSetString(hsvcMyMenu, TEXT("StatusHelp"), TEXT("Displays
calculator"));
   CeSVCSetString(hsvcMyMenu, TEXT("Version"), 0x00020000);
   CeSvcClose(hsvcMyMenu);
}
```

Web Services

C H A P T E R   2 2

Mobile Channels

Windows CE users can access the World Wide Web using a Windows CE-based device, such as a Palm PC, with the underlying technology Mobile Channels. This Windows CE technology adopts and extends Microsoft Internet Explorer 4.0 (IE4) standards for offline Web browsing on a Windows CE-based device.

IE4 defines a channel standard for delivering information for offline Web browsing on a desktop computer. An IE4 channel is a self-describing Web site that contains all the information necessary for efficient download of Web content to a desktop computer. The Channel Definition Format (CDF) is a standard that contains meta information about a Web site and encapsulates the instructions to IE4 on how to download the site for offline browsing. IE4 defines three basic types of channels that all use the standard CDF technology or extensions to it: Active Channels, Desktop Components, and Software Distribution Channels.

The Mobile Channels technology introduces a fourth type of channel with its own extensions designed to offer offline browsing experiences to Windows CE users. A mobile channel is a Web site that conforms to the Mobile Channels CDF extensions.

Mobile Channels technology provides the following benefits for you:

- A convenient mechanism for ad-hoc transfer of Web information to a Windows CE-based device.

- The notion of a channel subscription as implemented in IE4, whereby the transfer of Web information is performed on a recurring basis.

- An efficient mechanism to transfer and store the information, given the limited bandwidth of Windows CE-based device connections to the desktop computer and on-device storage capacities.

The Mobile Channels technology embodies the following aspects:

- Creation

  Following Mobile Channels design guidelines, you create a mobile channel by developing a Web site. The site must be suitable for a Windows CE-based device in terms of format and quantity of information. A mobile channel uses standard HTML scripting techniques to render data-driven pages. It has three fundamental components: the CDF to define the channel, a set of script files to render the channel, and a set of data files to be rendered.

- Publishing

  A content provider publishes a mobile channel on the Web or a corporate intranet by providing HTML links to the CDF. These links can appear on any HTML Web page, such as an existing standard Web site or desktop Active Channel. A mobile channel makes an excellent mobile complement to a traditional Web site. In addition, a mobile channel may be featured within the Mobile Channel Guide, which is similar in concept to the Active Channel Guide for IE4. For more information about publishing your mobile channel in the Mobile Channel Guide, see the http://www.microsoft.com/windowsce /palmpc/channels/ Web site.

- Subscription

  A channel subscription is a recurring update of information. It does not mean that the user makes payment for receiving the content. A user can subscribe to a mobile channel in a manner consistent with IE4 in the following ways:

  - By accessing a link to a mobile channel CDF.
  - By accessing the Mobile Channel Guide on the Web.
  - By clicking on any channel link.

  A user can access a Mobile Channels CDF file within the context of a standard Web site or channel. Once the subscription is established, the Mobile Channels content is downloaded by IE4 to the desktop computer.

  A channel provider can let a user choose to update a subscription, that is, to download new content on a one-time or recurring basis. Mobile Channels downloads information on a regular basis, keeping the channel up-to-date at all times.

- Synchronization

  Once a mobile channel has been downloaded by IE4 into a desktop computer's Internet channel cache, a user can synchronize the content of the site with a Windows CE-based device using Windows CE Services. In general, a mobile channel is synchronized each time the Windows CE-based device is attached to the desktop computer.

- Viewing

  A user can view a mobile channel on a Windows CE-based device using an offline Web browser, such as Channel Browser on the Palm PC. A user can also view a mobile channel directly on a desktop computer using the IE4 browser or Active Desktop. An IE4 user can download and view Mobile Channels content without having a Windows CE-based device, provided that he or she has the appropriate desktop computer software.

- Logging

  Because a mobile channel is intended to be viewed offline, there is no direct way for the system to track what links or pages a user is viewing. However, because you might need such traffic information to determine the usage pattern for a site, Mobile Channels provides a way to log and report this information to a Web site. Similar to IE4's offline logging mechanism, any page in a mobile channel can be marked for logging. As a user browses the channel, visited items are kept in a list. When the mobile device is next synchronized, this information is optionally transferred to the IE4 desktop computer. From there, it is uploaded to a Web site in the manner established for the IE4 offline logging feature.

- Mobile Desktop Components

  A Mobile Desktop Component is a one-page channel designed to fit in a very small space. A mobile-channel provider may elect to have a Mobile Desktop Component appear in the Mobile Channels Active Desktop, or simply in Active Desktop on a Windows CE-based device, such as a Palm PC.

Creating Mobile Channels

The foundation of Mobile Channels rests upon two key technologies: CDF and Active Server Pages (ASP) scripting. Mobile Channels has developed a streamlined and optimized subset of functionality that allows devices to work with limited storage space over the narrow bandwidth of Windows CE connectivity. For information on client-side scripting in a mobile channel, see the appendix "Mobile Channels Scripting Environment" in the online Help.

There are two ways to construct a mobile channel. In the first approach, a group of standard HTML pages are connected by hyperlinks. This approach is sufficient for small page sets that do not have repetitive data. The CDF file serves primarily as an inventory of files to be brought over to the device. This non-scripted, page-group approach may be desirable when the page set consists of few pages with highly dissimilar content, and when the content is static and does not need to be incrementally updated.

In the second approach, more complex page sets are organized with the help of a scripting language to build pages "on the fly." This is more desirable when the page set consists of:

- Highly repetitive data.
- Small data portions that need to be updated dynamically without changing the overall structure of the page.
- Template pages that can load and display similar data dynamically.

The design rules are simple and familiar for the first method of constructing a mobile channel. The documentation for IE4 channels describes how to create channels of this type. Scripted channels operate on principles similar to any dynamic Web site, and because scripted channels provide the most flexibility, this chapter discusses them in detail. Be aware that all Windows CE-based devices have a limited HTML control that does not support frames or dynamic HTML.

Scripted Mobile Channels

A scripted mobile channel has three components: scripts, data, and a CDF file. The scripts define templates to specify the appearance and layout of the channel, subchannels, and item views. The data is typically dynamic and is formatted in a manner specific to the content. Scripts are written in a subset of Visual Basic Script (VBS). The scripting environment is similar to the scripting environment of the Active Server Pages in Internet Information Server (IIS).

Data is packaged in small and simple text files for use with devices that have limited bandwidth and storage capacity. This data is readily accessible through the script. Mobile Channels stores scripts, data files, and all content on the Windows CE-based device in a special-purpose cache similar to the IE4 cache. URL references are made to the Mobile Channels Transport Protocol. This transport then invokes the script interpreter to run scripts to access data and CDF files. Both scripts and data are fetched from the cache. The interpreter outputs pure HTML back to the transport and eventually to the Channel Browser application.

At display time, scripts are executed on the Windows CE-based device to construct HTML pages. These pages render data in a browser using structural information contained in the CDF file. For example, a script might determine what subchannel of a CDF file is being displayed and fetch the title and logo for that subchannel from the CDF file, incorporating them into the page layout. Items or additional subchannels within the subchannel may be fetched from the CDF file to present an index to the subchannel. Item titles can be fetched directly from the items.

Although this blending of scripts, data items, and CDF files is more complex than a standard channel or Web pages, it is beneficial when properly applied. By separating the content into a template and data, Mobile Channels is able to deliver content in small segments of data instead of full HTML pages. This incremental approach makes it economical to update time-critical information. It also makes it possible to create default, or generic, scripts that can render channels, subchannels, and data, if a script is missing.

▶ **To create a scripted mobile channel**

1. Describe the channel content using Channel Definition Format (CDF) and its Mobile Channels extensions.

2. Separate the content into Mobile Channels script files and Mobile Channels files.

3. Write script files to comply with the scripting protocol for the Windows CE-based device.

4. Package incremental data, such as news articles or stock quotes, in one or more text files.

Mobile Channels Extension to CDF

CDF is a standard for creating Active Channels in IE4. It is based on the Extensible Markup Language (XML). For the complete specifications, see the Microsoft Internet SDK Web site http://www.microsoft.com/msdn/sdk /inetsdk/help/. As mentioned earlier, Mobile Channels adds a channel to the existing IE4 channels. It calls for additional tags to extend CDF for optimizing the mobile-channel performance on a Windows CE-based device. Mobile Channels uses these additional tags to navigate through CDF files and to reduce the storage space required on the device.

Top-level Channel URL

You use the path to the CDF in two attributes of the top-level **CHANNEL** element. The **HREF** attribute references the CDF path using the Mobile Channels Transport Protocol (MCTP). The **SELF** attribute references the CDF path using the standard HTTP prefix. Unlike the IE4 implementation, the **SELF** attribute is a required attribute of the top-level **CHANNEL** element.

The **HREF** attribute uses the MCTP prefix to indicate the CDF file as a mobile channel. This causes special processing when referenced under IE4 where the mobile channel is registered for synchronization to the Windows CE-based device. Unlike the **HREF** under IE4, in a mobile channel, the URL does not directly indicate the page to render. Rather, it references the top-level channel as specified by the CDF file. The appropriate **CHANSCRIPT** tag determines what script is used to render the top-level of the channel. For a detailed description of **CHANSCRIPT**, see "CDF Tags for Mobile Channels" later in this chapter. The **BASE** attribute has the same functionality for Mobile Channels as it does for Active Channels in IE4. The following code example illustrates that the attribute's URL is an HTTP URL.

```
<CHANNEL HREF="mctp://www.microsoft.com/test.cdf" ID="test"
 BASE = "http://www.microsoft.com/test/
 SELF = "http://www.microsoft.com/test.cdf" />
    <ITEM HREF="microsoft.com/START.MCS" ID="Start"/>
    <CHANSCRIPT VALUE="Start"/>
    . . .
</CHANNEL>
```

In this code example, the **CHANSCRIPT** tag is used to specify the starting page or script by referencing the **ID** tag of the script that is defined in the **ITEM** tag. The START.MCS file is a Mobile Channels script that defines how to display the top-most page of the channel.

In the mobile channel CDF file, the HREF for the **CHANNEL** tag is the only one that has an MCTP-style URL. All other HREF values are of the HTTP-style.

Extensions to Standard Tags and Attributes

Mobile Channels recognizes several attributes and attribute values that may appear in standard CDF tags. These tags are described in the following table.

Attribute	Description
ID	A short string identifier for the **CHANNEL**, **ITEM**, and **LOGO** elements.
DEFAULTPREF	A Boolean operator indicating the suggested preference setting for a **CHANNEL** element. It can be On or Off.
USAGE	New usage values for Mobile Channels are **MobileChannel** and **MobileDesktopComponent**.
CHANNEL	**CHANNEL** element may take a **USAGE** tag specifying either of the two new **USAGE** values previously defined. It is required for the top-level **CHANNEL** element of a Mobile Desktop Component.

Each tag or attribute is discussed in detail in the following list:

- **ID**

  An **ID** tag is a text string used as an attribute to identify the specified element. An **ID** tag must be provided for all **CHANNEL**, **ITEM**, and **LOGO** elements in a mobile channel.

  ```
  ID = "ChanId"
  ID = "ItemId"
  ID = "LogoId"
  ```

  An **ID** tag is used for short and quick references of a mobile channel element both within a CDF and within scripts. Within the CDF, the **ID** tag is used as a value for both **CHANSCRIPT** and **ITEMSCRIPT** tags to refer to the associated **ITEM** tag that represents the script file.

  Within a script, the **ID** tag is used, along with the MCTP syntax, to form unique URLs in the Mobile Channels namespace. The **ID** tag is used in the MCTP transport to uniquely reference a channel or item. MCTP references are of the form "*mctp://CDFid/ChanID*" for a channel or "*mctp://CDFid/ItemID*" for an item.

  Keep the string length of an **ID tag** to the minimum necessary to uniquely define it within the CDF over time. Keeping the **ID** string length to the minimum is important to conserve network bandwidth and storage space.

  In a CDF file, the **ID** tag of the top-level channel is used as a handle to the channel. The maximum length of the **ID** string is 64 characters, but a handle of between 6 and 10 characters is recommended for the top-level **ID** to be unique. The following are three CDF examples that define IDs.

  ```
  <CHANNEL ID = "Sports" >
  <ITEM HREF = "www.microsoft.com/test/sports/article001.mcd"
          ID = "Art1" >
  <LOGO HREF =  "www.microsoft.com/test/sports/sportslogo.gif"
       STYLE = "IMAGE"
          ID = "L_Sports" >
  ```

The **ID** tag is required for each parent element and can be of a single occurrence. There are no applicable child elements for this tag.

- **USAGE**

For the **USAGE** tag, Mobile Channels defines the following two new values:

- **MobileChannel**

  The statement

  ```
  <USAGE VALUE = "MobileChannel"/>
  ```

  specifies the channel as a mobile channel, or an item as a special Mobile Channels data item. The top-level channel should be given a **USAGE** value of "**MobileChannel**." When the **USAGE** value is set to "**MobileChannel**," Mobile Channels items will be seen on Channel Explorer on the device but not on the channel bar on IE4. This feature makes it possible to properly display the items as the special Mobile Channels Data (MCD) files on the device and to ignore them in IE4. For example,

  ```
  <ITEM HREF="http://www.microsoft.com/test1.mcd" ID="T1">
      <USAGE VALUE="MobileChannel"/>
  </ITEM>
  <ITEM HREF="http://www.microsoft.com/test2.mcs" ID="T2">
      <USAGE VALUE="None"/>
  </ITEM>
  ```

  Item T1 is a Mobile Channels data item and will be seen in the Channel Explorer feature on the device, but not by IE4 on the desktop computer. Item T2 is a Mobile Channels script and will not be seen by either IE4 or the Channel Explorer on the device. The **USAGE** tag has no applicable child element.

  Note that the statement

  ```
  <USAGE VALUE=""/>
  ```

  is equivalent to

  ```
  <USAGE VALUE="None"/>
  ```

The former is recommended because it helps to save storage space on the device.

- **MobileDesktopComponent**

  The statement

  ```
  <USAGE VALUE = "MobileDesktopComponent"/>
  ```

  specifies the channel as a Mobile Channels desktop component. This is used strictly on a Windows CE-based device to make the channel available as a component for the Windows CE Active Desktop. For example:

  ```
  <CHANNEL HREF="http://www.mydomain.com/myChannel.cdf">
      <USAGE VALUE="MobileDesktopComponent"/>
  </CHANNEL>
  ```

  The channel, as specified by "myChannel.cdf" can be registered as a component for the Windows CE Active Desktop.

  There can be only one occurrence of this usage value in a given desktop component CDF file. And there are no applicable child elements.

- **DEFAULTPREF**

  The **DEFAULTPREF** tag can be used as follows:

  ```
  <CHANNEL ID = "ChanId">
      <DEFAULTPREF VALUE="ON"|"OFF"/>
  </CHANNEL>
  ```

  The tag marks a subchannel with specific default preferences. You can use this attribute to control what subchannels a user receives content for by default. By default, when a new channel is synchronized to a Windows CE-based device, items within subchannels marked with the attribute **DEFAULTPREF** = "OFF" are not transferred.

  This mechanism allows you to create a channel that offers more content than can reasonably be accommodated by the limited storage resources available on a Windows CE-based device, and yet does no, by default, overwhelm the device with all of this content. The **DEFAULTPREF** setting is applied only when the channel is first synchronized to the device. After this, the user can change his or her preferences to include more or less content than the **DEFAULTPREF** settings allow.

  The **DEFAULTPREF** tag can have values of either "ON" or "OFF." If **DEFAULTPREF** attribute is not specified, the Windows CE-based device treats the subchannel as if it were marked with **DEFAULTPREF** = "ON."

For Example:

```
<CHANNEL ID="SubChan1">
    <DEFAULTPREF VALUE="OFF"/>
    . . .
</CHANNEL>
```

The **DefaultPref** tag can appear only once in a **CHANNEL** element.

CDF Tags for Mobile Channels

Additional tags recognized by Mobile Channels are described in the following table.

Tag	Description
CHANSCRIPT	Identifies the **ID** of the script file to render the channel and subchannels.
ITEMSCRIPT	Identifies the **ID** of the script file to render the item data file.
ITEMFORMAT	Defines the file structure for data files.

The following list describes each tag in detail:

- **CHANSCRIPT**

  The **CHANSCRIPT** tag is used as follows:

  ```
  <CHANSCRIPT VALUE="ChannelID"/>
  ```

  The **CHANSCRIPT** tag specifies a Mobile Channels script (MCS) to be used to render the display of a channel. The **CHANSCRIPT** tag value applies to all child channels of the current channel or subchannel. This tag supersedes the **CHANSCRIPT** value previously defined by a parent **CHANNEL** element, if any exist. The **VALUE** attribute specifies the **ID** of the **ITEM** element corresponding to the script to be run to render this level of the channel. For example,

  ```
  <CHANSCRIPT VALUE="ChanScript1"/>
  ```

  where the channel script identified by "*ChanScript1*" has been defined elsewhere in the CDF file, say, as follows:

  ```
  <ITEM HREF="http://www.microsoft.com/channel.mcs" ID="ChanScript1">
      <USAGE VALUE="None"/>
  </ITEM>
  ```

The top-level **CHANNEL** element can have at least one **CHANSCRIPT** tag as the child element. Each subchannel can have at most one such tag.

- **ITEMSCRIPT**

The **ITEMSCRIPT** tag is used as follows:

```
<ITEMSCRIPT VALUE = "ItemID"/>
```

The **ITEMSCRIPT** tag specifies a script to be used to render the display of MCD items. The **ITEMSCRIPT** tag value applies to all child items of the current channel or subchannel. This tag supersedes the **ITEMSCRIPT** value previously defined by a parent **CHANNEL** element, if any exist. The **VALUE** attribute specifies the **ID** of the **ITEM** element corresponding to the script to run to render this level of the channel. For example,

```
<ITEMSCRIPT VALUE = "A_Script" />
```

The item script file here refers to the following **ITEM** element defined elsewhere in the CDF file:

```
<ITEM HREF="http://www.microsoft.com/items.mcs" ID="A_Script">
    <USAGE VALUE="None"/>
</ITEM>
```

You can set the **VALUE** attribute to "None" or "" for the **USAGE** tag to prevent the script file from appearing in the Channel Explorer.

The topmost **CHANNEL** element can have at least one **ITEMSCRIPT** tag. At all other channel levels there can be at most one such tag.

- **ITEMFORMAT**

The **ITEMFORMAT** tag is used as follows:

```
<ITEMFORMAT VALUE="header_block ; repeat_block"/>
```

The tag specifies the format of a class of MCD items by identifying the associated file structure. MCD items are simple text files that can have a unique header and a repeating block structure for record-oriented data. Special helper functions are provided in the scripting environment to access the MCD content using information contained in the **ITEMFORMAT** tag. Both *header_block* and *repeat_block* are optional, but at least one of them must exist. If *repeat_block* exists, it must be preceded by the semi-colon (;). The header block typically contains the description about the items. And the repeatable data block contains description about items. The *header_block* and *repeat_block* are of the form

```
v1[=t1], v2[=t2], … , vn[=tn]
```

Here *vi* is the field name of the block value and *ti* is the optional type of the block value. If *ti* is omitted, the default value "HTML" is assumed. Valid types are listed in the following table.

Type	Description
HTML	HTML text including markup.
TEXT	Same as HTML.
IMG	ID of image item in CDF files.
HREF	URL to a page, for example, data file and channel script.

A data block is merely a group of values. There is one value per line. Any meaningful data file should have at least one data block. For example, three data blocks might be used to show a portfolio of three stocks. In the following example, the Market mobile channel displays stock values listed in the Stocks.mcd file. The header gives the title and displays the date of the shown stocks. The data to be listed includes the name, the low price, high price, and closing prices of each stock.

```
<ITEM HREF="http://www.market.com/Stocks.mcs" ID="Stock_S">
    <USAGE VALUE="None">
</ITEM>
. . .
<CHANNEL ID= "Stock_C">
    <TITLE>Market</TITLE>
    <ITEM HREF="http://www.market.com/Stocks.mcd" ID="Stock_D">
        <USAGE VALUE="MobileChannel"/>
        <ITEMSCRIPT VALUE="Stock_S"/>
        <ITEMFORMAT VALUE ="Title,Date,Picture=IMG;
                            Name,Low,High,Close"/>
    </ITEM>
</CHANNEL>
```

Here the header block has three values, *Title, Date,* and *Picture,* and the data block has four: *Name, Low, High,* and *Close.*

IMG indicates the field that represents an image, such as a JPEG or GIF file. The field value is the identifier of the item defining the URL of the image. The built-in item script creates an IMG value to display this item.

The data block may be repeated to build a table of stock prices. If the Stocks.mcd file contains a single data block, the script displays a single stock per page. If it has multiple data blocks, the script could display a table of stocks.

The repeat block can be omitted, as shown in the following example, which is represents a news article with a title, an image, and the body of text:

```
<ITEMFORMAT VALUE="TITLE, PICTURE=IMG, BODY"/>
```

The header block can also be omitted, as shown in the following example that represents a page with stock listings. The semi-colon (;) is used to indicate the value list. It is the repeat block and not a header block.

```
<ITEMFORMAT VALUE ="; Name, Low, High, Close"/>
```

CDF Omissions

Not all the standard IE4 tags are supported in Mobile Channels. In particular, Mobile Channels does not support any Software Update Channel tags. In addition, the Mobile Channels parser ignores the **LOGIN** tag. However, while the **EARLIESTTIME**, **INTERVALTIME**, and **LASTTIME** tags are ignored on the device, they are supported on the desktop computer and used by IE4 to download the channel from the Web.

Mobile Channels Data Files

Data files are used to deliver incremental data for a channel. These are simple text files that contain data with one data item per line in the file. Within the CDF file, a structure for the data file may be declared using an **ITEMFORMAT** tag as discussed earlier.

Each data file must have a .mcd extension. The CDF file must include an **ITEM** tag to define the MCD file. Within the **ITEM** tag, the **ID** attribute is used as a shorthand reference for the MCD file from within a script without having to reference its complete URL.

Unlike the conventional script-drives-data approach, where script files are run and call for data to display, Mobile Channels does the opposite for displaying incremental data. Because new information can come in at any time within a new MCD file, it is more efficient to activate the script to display data when it arrives. This data-triggers-script approach has an added benefit: it permits the inheritance of scripts.

The file format for data files is flexible. It is simply a text file that contains the data, such as references to images, with each item on a separate line. Mobile Channels exposes methods within the scripting environment for reading this content from the file.

The **ITEMFORMAT** tag is used to specify the type of data present in the file. Generally, files have the following format:

```
[Header Block]
[Data Block 1]
[Data Block 2]
...
[Data Block n]
```

Each block may consist of zero or more fields, as specified in the **ITEMFORMAT**. This allows a single data file to be used as a simple database that can have rows of data. In the following code example file, data items are organized in the structure, as specified by the following **ITEMFORMAT** tag:

```
<ITEMFORMAT VALUE="TITLE,DATE,PICTURE=IMG;NAME,LOW,HIGH,CLOSE"/>
```

The different blocks are commented for the purpose of illustration. Comments should not be present in any MCD file. The first block is the header block, which contains general information such as a title, date, and image. The remaining repeating data blocks follow the header block.

```
Stock Info              'header block
April 24, 1997
ClintonPic
MSFT                    'data block 1
110.25
112.50
111.00
DEC                     'data block 2
21
23
22
IBM                     'data block 3
132.50
132.75
132.75
```

Mobile Channels Script Files

Mobile Channels employs two types of scripts: channel scripts and item scripts. In the CDF, a **CHANNELSCRIPT** tag identifies a script for a channel and an **ITEMSCRIPT** tag identifies a script for an item. All Mobile Channels script files end with an .mcs extension.

Scripts are invoked in a data-driven manner. When it is time to display a particular data file, the reference is made to the data file and the appropriate item script is located to display it. Likewise, when it is time to show channel content, such as a listing of subchannels or data items, the reference to the channel is made and the appropriate channel script is located to display it. For more detail on how scripts are associated with the data or channels, see "Item Script Selection" and "Channel Script Selection" later in this chapter.

The following code example illustrates a CDF file that is referenced later.

```
<!-- Declare item scripts -->
<ITEM HREF="Http://www.microsoft.com/test/script1.mcs" ID="IS1">
    <USAGE VALUE="None"/>
</ITEM>
<ITEM HREF="Http://www.microsoft.com/test/script2.mcs" ID="IS2">
    <USAGE VALUE="None"/>
</ITEM>


<!-- Declare channel scripts -->
<ITEM HREF="Http://www.microsoft.com/test/script3.mcs" ID="CS1">
    <USAGE VALUE="None"/>
</ITEM>
<ITEM HREF="Http://www.microsoft.com/test/script4.mcs" ID="CS2">
    <USAGE VALUE="None"/>
</ITEM>

<CHANNEL HREF - "Http://www.microsoft.com/test/test.cdf" ID="test">
    <TITLE>Test Channel</TITLE>
    <!—IS1 is the general item script to use within the channel -->
    <ITEMSCRIPT VALUE="IS1"/>

    <!—CS1 is the general channel script to use within the channel -->
    <CHANSCRIPT VALUE = "CS1"/>
     . . .
    <CHANNEL ID = "C1">
        <TITLE>Test Subchannel 2</TITLE>

        <!—This channel is rendered by the general channel script CS1 -->
         . . .
        <ITEM HREF="http://www.microsoft.com/test/item-a.mcd" ID="ITA">
            <!—This item is rendered by the item-specific IS2 script-->
            <ITEMSCRIPT VALUE="IS2"/>
            <USAGE VALUE="MobileChannel"/>
        </ITEM>
        ......
    </CHANNEL>
    <CHANNEL ID = "C2">
            <TITLE>Test Subchannel 2</TITLE>

        <!—This channel is rendered by the channel-specific script CS2-->
        <CHANSCRIPT VALUE = "CS2" />
        <ITEM HREF="http://www.microsoft.com/test/item-b.mcd" ID="ITB">
            <!—This item is rendered by the general IS1 item script-->

            <USAGE VALUE="MOBILECHANNEL"/>
        </ITEM>
    </CHANNEL>
</CHANNEL>
```

Item Script Selection

When it is necessary to render a particular data file in the browser, the appropriate script must be selected. Item scripts are responsible for rendering MCD data files and are invoked as a result of referencing the URL of the data file. The appropriate script is selected based upon the proximity of an **ITEMSCRIPT** tag to the particular MCD data file.

An item URL, as appears in scripts, is in the following form:

```
mctp://CDFid/ItemId
```

Here "mctp://" specifies the use of the Mobile Channels Transport Protocol to resolve the URL and to invoke the scripting engine. *CDFid* is the **ID** tag of the top-level **CHANNEL** element and is used to scope the channel identifier to the correct CDF file. *ItemId* is the **ID** tag of the **ITEM** element for the MCD data file to be rendered.

The MCD data file appears in an **ITEM** element within the channel hierarchy. The location of the **ITEM** element relative to an **ITEMSCRIPT** element determines which script will be used to render the data. The script file is identified by matching the **ID** value in the **ITEMSCRIPT** element with the **ID** value of an **ITEM** element, which is the item for the script file, within the CDF.

ITEMSCRIPT elements can be children of either **CHANNEL** elements or **ITEM** elements. An **ITEMSCRIPT** determines the script to be used for all items of the current channel and its subchannels. An item script, as identified by **ITEMSCRIPT**, for a **CHANNEL** or **ITEM** element supercedes any previously defined **ITEMSCRIPT** value.

Thus, an inheritance model is used. When it is necessary to render a particular MCD item, the nearest **ITEMSCRIPT** element in the hierarchy is used to determine what script should render the data. In the event that the appropriate script is not available on the device, a built-in script is used to render the data. The default item script simply enumerates through all the fields specified in the **ITEMFORMAT** tag and for each one displays the appropriate data from the specified MCD file. If the MCD file contains a repeating block, all the block values are enumerated on the page in a list until the end of the MCD file.

By convention, item scripts are specified at the top-level of a channel, usually at the top of the file. Each item script is assigned a unique **ID**. The script can then be referenced using an **ITEMSCRIPT** element from any location in the CDF hierarchy. In a script, data links are anchored using a regular HREF link to the MCTP transport, rather than the usual HTTP protocol.

Given the previous CDF example specified, the following statement in a script file shows the data in the *item-a.mcd* file:

```
<A HREF="MCTP://TEST/ITA"> Click Here to See Item A</A>
```

Referencing by MCTP is based on the channel identifier "TEST" and the data file identifier "ITA," not the item script file. The appropriate **ITEMSCRIPT** tag is sought in the hierarchy to show the data. This conforms to the inheritance model. The *script1.mcs* script renders the *item-b.mcd file* whereas *script2.mcs* renders the *item-a.mcd* data file.

Note In order for an image to be rendered on IE4 desktop computer, you should reference images using standard HTTP references, rather than MCTP. If allowing the channel to be viewed on IE4 is not important, then the MCTP type URLs may be used. They will render correctly on the Windows CE-based device.

Channel Script Selection

In addition to rendering data from data files, it is usually necessary to render the current location within the CDF so that the user can navigate to the desired data. When it is necessary to render a CDF navigation page in the browser, the appropriate script must be selected. Channel scripts are responsible for rendering the CDF navigation pages supplied by a content provider. As with an item script, referencing the URL of the subchannel results in the invocation of a channel script. The appropriate script is selected based upon the proximity of a **CHANSCRIPT** tag to the particular **CHANNEL** element in the URL.

A channel URL, as appears in scripts, is of the following form:

```
mctp://CDFid/ChanId
```

Here, "mctp://" specifies the use of the Mobile Channels Transport Protocol to resolve the URL and to invoke the scripting engine. *CDFid* is the **ID** tag of the top-level **CHANNEL** element. It is used to scope *ChanId* to the correct CDF file. *ChanId* is the **ID** tag of the **CHANNEL** element for the subchannel within the CDF to be rendered. As a user navigates through the channel, he or she is effectively moving up and down through the CDF channel hierarchy accessing data files. At each level in the channel hierarchy, it is possible to associate a script to display the channel content, which is usually a list of subchannels or available items.

The **CHANSCRIPT** element identifies the script to be used to display the current channel location in a way similar to how the **ITEMSCRIPT** element identifies the script to display data. The location of a **CHANNEL** element relative to a **CHANSCRIPT** element determines which script will be used to render the subchannel. The script file is identified by matching the **ID** value in the **CHANSCRIPT** element with the **ID** value of an **ITEM** element—that is, the **ITEM** for the script file—within the CDF.

CHANSCRIPT elements are children of **CHANNEL** elements. A **CHANSCRIPT** element determines the script to be used for the current channel and its subchannels. A **CHANSCRIPT** tag specified for a **CHANNEL** element supercedes any previously defined **CHANSCRIPT** value.

Thus, an inheritance model is used. When it is necessary to render a particular subchannel, the nearest **CHANSCRIPT** element upward in the hierarchy is used to determine what script should render the data. In the event that the appropriate script is not available on the device, a built-in script is used to render the channel as best it can.

In the previous CDF example, the following statement in a script file shows the Test Subchannel 2:

```
<A HREF="MCTP://TEST/C2">Click Here to See Subchannel 2</A>
```

Referencing by MCTP is based on the channel identifier "TEST" and the subchannel identifier "C2," not the channel script file. The appropriate **CHANSCRIPT** tag is located in the hierarchy, in conformance to the inheritance model, to show the channel. The *script4.mcs* script renders the "C2" subchannel whereas *script3.mcs* renders the "C1" subchannel.

Scripting

A script specifies the layout and behavior of HTML pages. Script segments are enclosed between the *<%* and *%>* or *<%=* and *%>* delimiter pairs. The second pair of delimiters entails special use and meaning in the script file. In each script segment, there must be at least one valid executable, or non-comment, statement. There must also be at least one scripting segment in the MCS file. Any empty script segment generates a syntax error. Scripting segments can be freely intermixed with standard HTML text, provided that the script-generated HTML output has the valid syntax within the context of the standard HTML display code. In the following sections are code examples of channel script and item script files.

Example Channel Script

```
<html>
<%
    Set MC    = Server.CreateObject("MobileChannels.Utilities")
    URL       = Request.ServerVariables("URL")
    DataID    = Request.QueryString("DATAID")
    Pieces    = Split(URL,"/")
    ChanID    = Pieces(2)
```

```
' Get logo and title of channel
    TopElem = MC.Locate(ChanID)
    ChanTitle = ""
    LogoHref = 0
    If TopElem Then
        ChanTitle = MC.Title(TopElem)
        LogoElem = TopElem
        LogoElem = MC.Navigate(LogoElem,"INMATCH","LOGO")
        Do While LogoElem
            LogoStyleElem = MC.Navigate(LogoElem,"INMATCH","STYLE")
            If LogoStyleElem Then
                If StrComp(MC.Value(LogoStyleElem),"IMAGE",1) = 0 Then
                    LogoHref = MC.Href(LogoElem)
                    If LogoHref Then
                        If MC.HrefExists(LogoHref) Then
                            Exit Do
                        Else
                            LogoHref = 0
                        End If
                    End If
                End If
            End If
            LogoElem = MC.Navigate(LogoElem,"NEXT")
                If LogoElem Then
                    LogoElem = MC.Navigate(LogoElem,"MATCH","LOGO")
                End If
        Loop
    End If

    NeedTitle = 1
    Response.Write("<head><title>" & ChanTitle & "</title></head>")
    If LogoHref Then
        Response.Write("<body><a href=mctp://" & ChanID & ">
            <img src=" & LogoHref & "></a><br> <br>")
    ElseIf ChanTitle And Len(ChanTitle) Then
        Response.Write("<body><a href=mctp://" & ChanID & ">
            <h3>" & ChanTitle & "</h3></a>")
        NeedTitle = 0
    Else
        Response.Write("<body>")
    End If

' Decide whether you need a title for this chan/subchan
    If DataID And (DataID <> ChanID) Then
        NeedTitle = 1
    Else
        DataID = ChanID
    End If
```

```
        SubTitle = 0
        SubElem = MC.Locate(DataID)
        If SubElem Then
            SubTitle = MC.Title(SubElem)
            If SubTitle And NeedTitle Then
                Response.Write("<b>" & SubTitle & "</b><br> <br>")
            End If

' Display contents of chan/subchan
        Response.Write("<table border=0 cellpadding=-2 cellspacing=-2>")
        ChildElem = MC.Navigate(SubElem,"In")
        Do While ChildElem
            ShowIt = 1
            IsChan = 0
            If MC.Tag(ChildElem) = "CHANNEL" Then
                IsChan = 1
                If Not MC.IsSubscribed(ChildElem) Then
                    ShowIt = 0
                End If
            ElseIf MC.Tag(ChildElem) = "ITEM" Then
                VisParElem = MC.Navigate(ChildElem,"InMatch","USAGE")
                    If VisParElem Then
                        Usage = MC.Value(VisParElem)
                            If Usage Then
                                If StrComp(Usage,"None",1) = 0 Then
                                    ShowIt  = 0
                                End If
                            End If
                    End If
' Be sure item exists
                If ShowIt Then
                    ChildHref = MC.Href(ChildElem)
                    If ChildHref Then
                        If Not MC.HrefExists(ChildHref) Then
                            ShowIt = 0
                        End If
                    Else
                        ShowIt = 0
                    End If
                End If
            Else
                ShowIt = 0
            End If
```

```
            If ShowIt Then
' Be sure you can get the ID
                IDVal = 0
                IDElem = MC.Navigate(ChildElem,"InMatch","ID")
                    If IDElem Then
                        IDVal         = MC.Value(IDElem)
                    End If
                    If Not IDVal Then
                        ShowIt = 0
                    End If
            End If
' Get title
        If ShowIt Then
            ItemTitle = MC.Title(ChildElem)
            If Not ItemTitle Or (Len(ItemTitle) = 0) Then
                ShowIt = 0
            Else
                If Len(ItemTitle) > 26 Then
                    ItemTitle = Mid(ItemTitle,0,25) & "..."
                End If
            End If
        End If
' You know what it is and are going to try to show it
        If ShowIt Then
            If IsChan Then
                Response.Write("<tr><td>*")
            Else
                Response.Write("<tr><td>")
            End If
            Response.Write("<td> <a href=mctp://" & ChanID & "/"
                & IDVal & ">" & ItemTitle & "</a>")
        End If
        ChildElem         = MC.Navigate(ChildElem,"Next")
        Loop
        Response.Write("</table>")
    Else
        Response.Write("Data ID not found.")
    End If
%>

<br> <br><hr>
<b>Note:</b> This page was automatically generated because the correct
scripts could not be found.  If this problem persists after
synchronization,
please contact the content provider.
</body>
</html>
```

Example Item Script

```
<html>

<%
    Set MC    = Server.CreateObject("MobileChannels.Utilities")
    URL       = Request.ServerVariables("URL")
    DataID    = Request.QueryString("DATAID")
    Pieces    = Split(URL,"/")
    ChanID    = Pieces(2)


' Get logo and title of channel
    TopElem = MC.Locate(ChanID)
    ChanTitle = ""
    LogoHref = 0
    If TopElem Then
        ChanTitle = MC.Title(TopElem)
        LogoElem = TopElem
        LogoElem = MC.Navigate(LogoElem,"INMATCH","LOGO")
    Do While LogoElem
        LogoStyleElem = MC.Navigate(LogoElem,"INMATCH","STYLE")
            If LogoStyleElem Then
                If StrComp(MC.Value(LogoStyleElem),"IMAGE",1) = 0 Then
                    LogoHref = MC.Href(LogoElem)
                        If LogoHref Then
                            If MC.HrefExists(LogoHref) Then
                                Exit Do
                            Else
                                LogoHref = 0
                            End If
                        End If
                End If
            End If
        LogoElem = MC.Navigate(LogoElem,"NEXT")
        If LogoElem Then
            LogoElem = MC.Navigate(LogoElem,"MATCH","LOGO")
        End If
    Loop
    End If

    Response.Write("<head><title>" & ChanTitle & "</title></head>")
    If LogoHref Then
        Response.Write("<body><a href=mctp://" & ChanID & ">
            <img src=" & LogoHref & "></a><br> <br>")
    ElseIf ChanTitle And Len(ChanTitle) Then
        Response.Write("<body><a href=mctp://" & ChanID & ">
            <h3>" & ChanTitle & "</h3></a>")
    Else
        Response.Write("<body>")
    End If
```

```
' Dump article out best we can
    ArtElem = 0
    If DataID Then
        ArtElem = MC.Locate(DataID)
    End If
    If ArtElem Then
    For Blk=0 To 100
        Data = MC.Data(ArtElem,Blk)
        If Not Data.Count Then
            Exit For
        End If
    For Field=0 To Data.Count - 1
        Tag = Data(Field).Tag
        Val = Data(Field).Value
        Type = Data(Field).Type
        If Val And Len(Val) Then
            If (StrComp(Type,"Html",1) = 0) Or (StrComp(Type,"Text",1)
                = 0) Then
' Output text in standard html
                If Tag And Len(Tag) Then
                    Response.Write("<b>" & Tag & ": </b>")
                End If
                Response.Write(Val & "<br>")
            ElseIf StrComp(Type,"Img",1) = 0 Then
' Try to create an image
                ImgElem = MC.Locate(Val)
                If ImgElem Then
                    ImgHref = MC.Href(ImgElem)
                    If ImgHref Then
                        Response.Write("<img src=" & ImgHref
                            & "><br>")
                    End If
                End If
            ElseIf StrComp(Type,"Href",1) = 0 Then
' Write an href
            Response.Write("<a href=" & Val & ">" & Tag & "</a><br>")
            End If
        End If
    Next
    Next
    End If
%>


<br> <br><hr>
<b>Note:</b> This page was automatically generated because the correct
scripts could not be found.  If this problem persists after
synchronization,
please contact the content provider.
</body>
</html>
```

Mobile Channels User Interface Elements

Mobile Channels user interface elements include the Channel Browser and Active Desktop, as well as controls panels for changing settings for channel synchronization. The following discussion focuses on how these are used and point out features that you should be aware of in order for the elements to work properly.

Channel Synchronization

As a synchronizing agent, Microsoft Windows CE Services copies mobile channel contents into the channel cache of the Windows CE-based device. Channel synchronization is a two-way operation. From the desktop computer to the device, the synchronization agent copies channel content, such as CDF, scripts, data, and images. From the device to the desktop computer, the agent posts the usage logging data to the logging host site.

When the agent synchronizes mobile channels, it consults with a list of subscribed channels that a user can select from the Channel Synchronization Options panel. The list covers the subscribed channels with associated CDF files on both the desktop computer and the device. The CDF files must have the top-level channels defined with the following **USAGE** tag:

```
<USAGE VALUE="MobileChannel"/>
```

Channel Browser

A user launches Channel Browser to select and to view a mobile channel. The browser follows the special Mobile Channels transport protocol to render the content. To conserve storage space and bandwidth, channel content is expressed both in terms of a template, which is a script file, and data to be filled into that template. When data arrives and must be displayed, Channel Browser runs the appropriate script to process the data and display it in HTML format.

Channel Browser's main window holds a command bar, a channel bar, and an HTML control. The command bar features a menu and a toolbar. The channel bar displays icons of subscribed channels. The icon files can be of the GIF, or JPEG format. You specify the icons in CDF files using the **LOGO** tag with **STYLE** setting to "ICON."

```
<LOGO STYLE="Icon"
      ID="icon1"
      HREF ="http://www.msnbc.com/mobileChannels/icon1.gif"/>
```

The HTML control displays the content for the current channel. You are responsible for supplying the content, specifying page layout, and providing the navigation scheme from within the channel. Except for a smaller screen size, Channel Browser is modeled after the IE4 browser on a desktop computer. This similarity provides a consistent Web experience for Windows CE users.

Channel Browser includes Home Channel, a virtual channel at the top of the channel hierarchy, which you can see in Channel Explorer. Home Channel contains links to the main pages of all subscribed channels. A built-in home channel script displays the subscribed channels. Users can access this channel using the **Home Channel** command from either the **Go** menu or the appropriate button on the toolbar.

From the **Go** menu of Channel Browser, a user can choose "**Explore Channel...**" to bring up the **Channel Explorer** dialog box. This pop-up window provides a hierarchical view of the mobile channels. It offers users a shortcut to channel navigation without having to trace through all the intermediate pages. Each channel and item may have an icon associated with it. Top-level channels are listed in order, as specified in **Preferences**. Within a channel, the subchannels and items are listed according to the hierarchy specified in the CDF file. The icon displayed at each level is derived from the **LOGO** tag in CDF, as explained earlier. If you fail to supply a logo, the default channel or item icon is used. The **<TITLE>** flag specifies the name of each channel. For example,

```
<CHANNEL>
    <TITLE>Mobile Channel Tips</TITLE>
    ...
</CHANNEL>
```

By choosing the **Properties** command on the **File** menu of Channel Browser, a user can examine item properties from the Item Properties panel for any item page displayed in the browser. The information, including the title of the item and the date of creation and last modification, is extracted from the CDF file defining the item.

Active Desktop

Windows CE Active Desktop shares many features with Channel Browser and uses the underlying Mobile Channels infrastructures. Its main window uses HTML controls to display the system information and selected shortcuts to applications. Each control represents a desktop component. On a Windows CE-based device, such as the Palm PC, Active Desktop components typically include the Windows CE Logo, Owner Information, Appointments, Tasks, Messages, and custom desktop components. Tapping the Appointment component launches the Calendar application. Similarly, the Tasks and Messages items provide shortcuts to the Tasks and Inbox applications, respectively.

Each desktop component is driven by a Mobile Channels script. You can supply the script file for defining desktop components. The following MCS file for the Owner component, as supplied by the Palm PC operating system, gives you a working example.

```
<%
    Set MC = Server.CreateObject("MobileChannels.Utilities")
    URL    = Request.ServerVariables("URL")
    Q      = Chr(34)
%>

<HTML>
<HEAD>
<META HTTP-EQUIV="Content-Type" content="text/html; charset=iso-8859-1">
<META HTTP-EQUIV="LAUNCHAPP" content="ctlpnl.exe?passwrdg,1,0">

<%
    Refresh = ";URL=MCTP://owner"
    Notify  = Q & "PRIVUPDATE=756" & Refresh & Q
    Response.Write("<META HTTP-EQUIV=NOTIFY content=" & Notify & ">")
%>

<TITLE>Owner</TITLE>
</HEAD>
<BODY>
<%
    Response.Write("<FONT SIZE=5>")
        Response.Write(MC.LibraryCall("owner.dll", "GetOwnerInfo"))
    Response.Write("</FONT>")
%>
</BODY>
```

You create a desktop component in a CDF file in which the desktop component is defined as a child element of a channel. To do this, you must use the following tag in the CDF file containing the desktop component:

```
<USAGE VALUE="MobileDesktopComponent"/>
```

Any such script is appropriately registered as a desktop component. The script files are then fed into the MCTP transport to process the data into the HTML format for display in the viewer. All the usual HTML tags are allowed.

P A R T   6

Interfaces to Bundled Applications

C H A P T E R   2 3

Contacts Database

Contacts, a Windows CE personal information manager (PIM) application, is organized as a series of records, called address cards. Each address card contains a number of fields, called properties. Among the many predefined properties are name, address, telephone number, birthday, and anniversary. Contacts is bundled with Windows CE and includes a graphical user interface.

Contacts can be used as is, if the default application settings meet the needs of the user. However, you can take advantage of the open application programming interface and design new Contacts database applications. For example, you can design an application to track a doctor's patient-contact information, including dates of previous and future office visits. You can retrieve, store, and query the records and properties in your Contacts database.

Because Contacts is built on the Windows CE object store, you need to be familiar with the object store to completely understand the database. For more information about the object store, see Chapter 4, "Accessing Persistent Storage."

A Contacts database includes the following basic elements.

- Address card

  An address card stores information about one individual. The information is parsed into a set of predetermined properties. Each address card is represented by an **AddressCard** structure. The number of address cards in a Contacts database depends on the amount of available memory on the hardware device. To determine the number of records in the database, call the **GetNumberOfAddressCards** function.

- Object identifier and position index

  A typical operation performed against an address card requires identification of the record and specification of its location in the database. To accomplish this, Windows CE assigns each address card a unique object identifier and a position index value. If you know the object identifier for an address card, you can get its position index by calling the **GetAddressCardIndex** function. Conversely, by calling **GetAddressCardOid** and passing in the position index as a variable, you can get the object identifier.

- Property and property tag

  A property has an associated identifier called a property tag that is unique within the context of a single address card. To manipulate a property, you set the property tag with a call to the **SetMask** function. For example, you set the HHPR_HOME_TELEPHONE_NUMBER property tag to enable the home telephone number property of an address card. When accessing a property, you use the **GetPropertyDataStruct** function to specify whether the information should be retrieved by the position index, property name, or property tag. The information is then passed into a **PropertyDataStruct** structure.

- Sort order

  Sort order specifies how the records are indexed. For example, records can be sorted according to the names or telephone numbers of the individuals. You can use up to four properties as the position indexes for sorting. However, you can sort only one property at a time. You specify an array of sort order options when you create a new database using **CreateAddressBook** and you specify a sort order out of the options list when you open an existing database using **OpenAddressBook**. You can change and retrieve the sort-order properties using the **SetColumnProperties** or **GetColumnProperties** function. In addition, you can change or retrieve the current sort order in an opened database using the **SetSortOrder** or **GetSortOrder** function.

Programming with the Contacts Database

Designing your database application involves calling the Contacts API to manipulate the database elements. In general, your application will include the following processes:

- Opening your database
- Adding and removing address cards
- Opening address cards
- Searching for a named property

- Modifying address cards
- Closing the opened address cards
- Closing your database

You can use wrapper functions to map a user-defined setting to a system-defined one. For an application that tracks patient visits to a doctor, you can use the *stBirthDate* and *stAnniversary* properties to hold the time and dates of previous and future office visits. The following code example shows how to write a **SetOfficeVisitDates** function to set these two properties.

```
void SetOfficeVisitDates(SYSTEMTIME stVisit, BOOL fPrev, ADDRESSCARD *
myAC)
{
    if(fPrev)
        myAC.stBirthdate=stVisit;        // previous office visit
    else
        myAC.stAnniversary=stVisit;      // future office visit
}
```

Similarly, the following code example shows how to write a **GetOfficeVisitDates** to return the appropriate date for the office visit.

```
SYSTEMTIME GetofficeVisitDate(BOOL fPrev, ADDRESSCARD myAC)
{
    if(fPrev)
        return myAC.stBirthdate;         // previous office visit
      else
        return myAC.stAnniversary;       //  future office visit
}
```

Opening the Contacts Database

Before you can work with any address cards, you must first open your database and specify a sort order and a handle to a window. The window receives notification messages from the object store. Before you can open the database, you must create it by calling the **CreateAddressBook** function.

▶ **To open the Contacts database**

1. Call the **OpenAddressBook** function.
2. Define a sort order to be used and specify a window to receive the notification message.

   If the Boolean function returns TRUE, you can proceed to work with the opened database. The function returns FALSE if you attempt to open a non-existing database. If another Contacts database application has altered the sort order in an existing database, the function returns FALSE as well.

3. Call **GetLastError** to get error information. If the error value is ERROR_FILE_NOT_FOUND, the database does not exist.

4. Call the **CreateAddressBook** function to create the database before re-opening it.

   –Or–

   If the error value is ERROR_INVALID_PARAMETER, the database does exist, but the sort order has been altered. Call **OpenAddressBook** again, but without specifying a sort order.

The **CreateAddressBook** function can take as input a NULL array for the sort order properties. In this case, the function uses the surname, company name, office telephone number, and home telephone number properties as the default sort order parameters.

Multiple applications can open the Contacts database simultaneously. To coordinate data access and preserve data integrity, the operating system sends object-store notification messages to attached applications whenever the database is modified. The notification messages have the DB_CEOID_ prefix and are defined in the Windbase.h header file. After receiving a notification message, an application calls the **RecountCards** function to recalculate the number of records in the database.

The following code example illustrates how to open the Contacts database. When **OpenAddressBook** fails because the database does not exist, **CreateAddressBook** is invoked to create the database before **OpenAddressBook** is called again. The **GetPropertyDataStruct** function examines address card properties to ensure that the database has not been corrupted. The sample function returns TRUE if the database was successfully opened or FALSE if it was not.

```
BOOL OpenUpTheAddressBook(HWND hwndParent, HHPRTAG hhSortProp)
{
    DWORD dwError;                      // Error code
    HHPRTAG propList[MAX_COLUMNS];      // Sort-order property tags
    int nColumns;                       // Number of sortable columns
    int index;                          // Loop index

    if (!OpenAddressBook(hwndParent, hhSortProp)) {
        dwError = GetLastError();
        if (dwError == ERROR_FILE_NOT_FOUND)
        {

            if (!CreateAddressBook(NULL, 0))
                {
                goto InitError;
                }
```

```
                    if (!OpenAddressBook(hwndParent, hhSortProp))
                        {
                        goto InitError;
                        }

            } else if (dwError == ERROR_INVALID_PARAMETER)
            {
                    if (!OpenAddressBook(hwndParent, 0))
                        {
                        goto InitError;
                        }

                    nColumns = MAX_COLUMNS;
                    if (!GetColumnProperties(&propList, &nColumns))
                        {
                        goto InitError;
                        }

                    for (index = 0; index < nColumns; index++)
                        {
                        if (GetPropertyDataStruct(GPDS_PROPERTY,
                                propList[index], NULL) == GPDS_ERR)
                            {
                            MessageBox(hwndParent, IDS_CORRUPT_DATABASE,
                                MB_ICONEXCLAMATION | MB_OK);
                            goto InitError;
                            }
                        }

                    hhSortProp = propList[0];
                    if (!OpenAddressBook(hwndParent, hhSortProp))
                        {
                        goto InitError;
                        }
            } else
                    {
                    goto InitError;
                    }
    }
    return TRUE;

InitError:
    return FALSE;
}
```

Adding and Removing Address Cards

Follow these procedures for adding and deleting records from your Contacts database.

▶ **To add an address card to the Contacts database**

1. Initialize an **AddressCard** structure to hold whatever properties the new card is to have.

2. For each property you will include in the new card, call the **SetMask** function on the initialized **AddressCard** with a (HHPR _*) property tag. Only properties that are enabled by **SetMask** can be saved to the object store.

3. Call the **AddAddressCard** function to insert the new address card into the database.

If the operation is successful, **AddAddressCard** returns the object identifier in the *myAC_oid* parameter and the position index in the *myAC_posIndex* parameter. The position index is determined by the current sort order. The following code example illustrates how to add an address to the Contacts database.

```
ADDRESSCARD myAC;
PEGOID myAC_oid;
int myAC_posIndex;

memset(myAC,0,sizeof(myAC));    // to be sure everything starts from 0
myAC.stBirthday.wYear=1969;
myAC.stBirthday.wMonth=1;
myAc.stBirthday.wDay=19;
myAC.pszGivenName="Mimmo";
SetMask(&myAC, HHPR_BIRTHDAY);
SetMask(&myAC, HHPR_GIEVN_NAME);
if(!AddAddressCard(&myAC, &myAC_oid, &myAC_posIndex))
{
                        // error handling
}
```

▶ **To remove an address card from the Contacts database**

▪ Call the **DeleteAddressCard** function on the object identifier of the card.

Retrieving and Modifying Address Cards

Before you can modify an address card, you must first retrieve its current properties. There are two ways to retrieve the properties.

▶ **To retrieve an address card**

- Call **GetAddressCardProperties** to open the address card and retrieve a selected set of properties. This is the preferred method because this function allocates less memory.

  –Or–

- Call **OpenAddressCard** to allocate memory for an address card and retrieve all of the card's properties.

▶ **To modify an address card**

1. Change members of the **AddressCard** structure retrieved by **OpenAddressCard** or **GetAddressCardProperties**.

2. Set the property tag for each modified property with a call to the **SetMask** function to make the modification persistent.

3. Call the **ModifyAddressCard** function on the modified **AddressCard** structure to complete the process.

To save system resources, you should free the memory allocated by **OpenAddressCard** or **GetAddressCardProperties** after the modification is finished by calling the **FreeAddressCard** function. For every call to **OpenAddressCard** or **GetAddressCardProperties**, there should be a corresponding call to **FreeAddressCard**.

C H A P T E R   2 4

Inbox

The Windows CE Inbox application provides users with access to electronic mail by means of Simple Mail Transport Protocol (SMTP) and Post Office Protocol 3 (POP3). Inbox works with any Transmission Control Protocol/Internet Protocol (TCP/IP) network, including the Internet.

Inbox is a Windows CE-based companion to a Microsoft Exchange client running on the user's desktop computer. It is an integral part of the personal information management (PIM) software that comes bundled with some Windows CE-based devices, such as an H/PC.

Inbox has an open application programming interface. The mail interface enables any application to send and receive mail messages mediated through Inbox. When a specified type of message is received, Inbox can automatically launch an application and pass it the message. You can take advantage of this open application programming interface (API) to write additional mail transport and storage applications.

Note Windows CE does not support the Microsoft Messaging API (MAPI) standard. Messaging applications must use the mail interface described in this chapter.

Writing a mail application involves:

- Maintaining a local message heap to work with a message.
- Working with the **MailMsg** and **MailAtt** structures to manipulate a message and its attachment.
- Working with the message store to store, retrieve, and query messages.

Before we discuss how to work with mail messages, you should be familiar with some of the basic mail message elements, including message heap, message store, messages, and message attachments.

Message Heap

Opening a message usually creates a private heap for dynamic storage of data from the message store. A handle to this private heap is registered as the **hHeap** member of a **MailMsg** structure, discussed later in this chapter. To optimize memory use, you should free the private heap when you are done with the message by calling the **MailFree** function. To prevent fragmentation of the global heap, use local heaps to work with mail messages. To conserve the memory resource, open messages one at a time.

Message Store

The message store is a database in the object store used to store messages. It is partitioned into folders arranged in a flat hierarchy. Windows CE defines five types of folders:

- **Inbox**

  A built-in folder for storing all incoming messages.

- **Outbox**

  A built-in folder for queuing messages to be sent the next time a connection is made.

- **Sent Items**

  A built-in folder for storing a copy of sent messages.

- **Deleted Items**

  A built-in pseudofolder that displays messages marked for deletion.

- **User-Defined**

  Additional folders (up to 21) that a user can create. Folder names are limited to 31 characters.

You may not rename or delete any of the built-in folders. Deleted messages remain in their original folders, but are marked with a flag. They are visible only in the **Deleted Items** pseudofolder. When a user recovers a deleted message, the flag is unmarked and the message become visible again in the original folder.

Mail Messages

Windows CE uses the **MailMsg** structure to encapsulate information about a mail message. The data structure contains the following elements:

- The message's object identifier
- The message's header and body
- The time the message is received
- Additional status information about the message and the operation to be performed against it

You must create and initialize a **MailMsg** structure in order to use it to read and write messages to and from the message store. If you declare a **MailMsg** structure on the stack, to be sure that the structure is cleanly initialized, you should call:

```
memset(&MailMsg, 0, sizeof(MailMsg));
```

The unique object identifier is registered as the **oid** member of the **MailMsg** structure. You use this identifier for direct access to messages in the message store. There are a number of flags you can use to perform specific operations on the message. These flags are assigned to the **dwFlags** member of the **MailMsg** structure. The mail and transport functions assign flags to denote the status of the message. You can assign flags to specify how to handle a message. For example, you can selectively retrieve messages of certain types, and you can flag a new message to be sent after the user issues the **Send** command.

Mail flags are divided into four categories:

- Folder flags

  Determine which folder to locate or store the message in, or which folder the message will be moved or copied into. The flags have the MAIL_FOLDER_ prefix.

- Status flags

  Determine the type of message being searched for before a call is made to retrieve a message. After the function call they contain the status of the message. The flags have the MAIL_STATUS_ prefix.

- Message store flags

  Determine how much of the message is read into memory when the message is retrieved. The flags have the MAIL_ prefix.

- Message attachment flags

  Determine the status of message attachments and the mode of operation to be performed on them. The flags have the ATT_ prefix.

When you assign MAIL_FOLDER_SENT to **dwFlag**, the system will move the message to the **Sent Items** folder. Messages that are flagged with MAIL_STATUS_DELETE are displayed in the **Deleted Items** folder and are invisible from the original folder. MAIL_STATUS_ATTACHMENTS indicates that the message has attachments. If you want to fetch the full body of a message from the message store, set **dwFlags** to MAIL_FULL. All the mail flags are defined in the Msgstore.h header file.

Message Header

The message header *pwcHeaders* usually contains information, such as the name and address of the sender and receiver of the message. It consists of one or more entries, each of which contains two fields: *Name* and *Value*. Both fields are Unicode strings that can be read with **MailGetField** and modified with **MailSetField**. Entries a message header might contain are described in the following table.

Name Field	Value Field
To	john@street.com
From	frank@hill.com
cc	bob@river.com
Subject	The way it was, is and will be

When creating a message header string, you should terminate the *Name* and *Value* strings with a NULL character. For the last *Value* field, you must terminate it with two NULL characters to indicate the end of the header.

For the most part, the strings assigned to the *Name* fields have no special meaning to the system, unless the string is "*Type.*" In this case, the system checks the corresponding value field to see if it matches the name of a dynamic-link library (DLL) registered with the system. The body of the message is passed to the DLL for processing.

Message Attachments

Windows CE uses a **MailAtt** structure to hold information about an attachment to a mail message. The members identify the attachment and specify the name and status of the attached file. An attachment is the attached file plus a header. The file name is registered in the **szOriginalName** member of the **MailAtt** structure and the header is the **MailAtt** structure itself.

An attachment can be classified as local or non-local. A local attachment consists of the header and a locally-stored copy of the original file. A non-local attachment has only the header with the name of the attached file. The actual file is not stored on the Windows CE-based device. The file name is simply a placeholder for the attachment. Non-local attachments are possible only when they are attached to a service-linked message.

Multiple attachments to a message are arranged in the **MailAttArray** structure. Because a file can be attached to a message more than once, it is possible that conflicts arise in the name space of the local files of the attachment. When this happens, Windows CE automatically resolves the name conflicts.

Working with Mail Messages

You can follow the general procedure for working with messages.

▶ **To work with mail messages**

1. Open the message store with **MailOpen**.
2. Perform tasks such as retrieving messages, inserting messages, sending messages, copying and moving messages, and updating Message Store.
3. If you use **MailFirst**, **MailGet**, or **MailNext** in step 2, free the heap with **MailFree**.
4. Close the message store with **MailClose**.

Retrieving Mail Messages

Before using a message and its related information, you must retrieve it from the message store. If you know the object identifier of the message, you can call **MailGet** to retrieve the message directly from the message store. Otherwise, you need to use **MailFirst** to get the first message. You can then step through the message store with repeated calls to **MailNext**.

Using Message Flags

Message flags provide you with many options to manipulate mail messages. In fact, you do not write code to perform the low-level operations. You simply set appropriate flags and the system takes care of the rest. For example, if you want to retrieve a message from the **Inbox** folder only, you set the **dwFlags** member of the **MailMsg** structure to MAIL_FOLDER_INBOX before you call **MailFirst**.

You can use other message flags to enhance the performance of your application. You use MAIL_GET_BODY and MAIL_GET_FLAGS to determine how much of the message is to be read into memory. If you set MAIL_GET_BODY, the entire message is read into memory. Otherwise, everything except the message body is read into memory. In either case, the system allocates memory from the local heap. A handle to the heap is passed back through the **hHeap** member of the **MailMsg** structure.

To get minimal information about the messages, without allocating memory, you set **dwFlags** to MAIL_GET_FLAGS. MAIL_GET_FLAGS instructs the system to read only the **dwFlags** member of the **MailMsg** structure. For example, you can build an array of pointers to unopened messages stored in the Inbox folder.

▶ **To build an array of pointers to unopened messages stored in the Inbox folder**

1. Call **MailFirst** to get the flags and object identifier of the first unopened message in the Inbox.

2. Store the identifier number and any other desired information.

3. Reset the flags to specify the same folder and type of message.

4. Call **MailNext** with the MAIL_GET_FLAGS flag set to retrieve the flags and object identifier of the next message.

5. Save the information.

6. Repeat steps 3, 4, and 5 until you have handled all of the messages in the Inbox.

To retrieve a particular message body, you can pass the object identifier to **MailGet**.

Inserting Mail Messages

▶ **Follow this procedure to insert a new message into a message store folder**

1. Create the message body and header string.

2. Create a **MailMsg** structure.

3. Point the **szBody** member of the structure to the message body.

4. Use **MailSetField** to put the header string into the **pwcHeaders** member.

5. Set the message flags to point to the folder.

6. Set any other relevant flags, for example, MAIL_STATUS_COMPOSED.

7. Fill in the **dwMsgLen**, **ftDate**, and **szSvcNam** members, if relevant.

8. Use **MailPut** to put the message in the desired folder.

The procedure just described works well for simple mail messages without attachments or for a non-Interpersonal Message (non-IPM), which is any message that is processed by an application, rather than read directly by a user. If you need to add non-IPM properties or attachments to the newly created message, be aware that a transport may be registered to receive database notifications and may attempt to manipulate the message as soon as it is written. For example, a transport may move or delete a message in the Outbox folder before the call to **MailPutAttachment**. To avoid unexpected deletion, create outgoing messages in the **Inbox** folder only after the message is completely written to the message store and is ready to be sent. Use **MailUpdate** to move the message to the **Outbox** folder. Set the Boolean variable to FALSE.

Sending Mail Messages

Sending a message is a simple task, requiring a few lines of code. When a user finishes composing a message and activates the **Send** command, the application sets flags and the system performs all the necessary actions required to send the message to its destination or destinations. To send a mail message, the application sets the MAIL_STATUS_COMPOSED flag, and sets the MAIL_FOLDER_OUTBOX flag to direct the message to the **Outbox** folder. The next time a user connects to the service specified on the message, the message is sent.

Updating the Message Store

If your application changes any of the members of **MailMsg**, for example, setting the MAIL_STATUS_READ flag, the message store is not affected until the message is reinserted. You must call the **MailUpdate** function to make the modifications permanent in the message store.

Moving and Copying Mail Messages

An application can move and copy mail messages in the message store. To move an existing message, change the folder flag and pass the resulting **MailMsg** structure to **MailUpdate**. To copy a message, change the folder flag and pass the structure to **MailPut**.

A user can move and copy service-linked mail messages. When Inbox downloads messages from a service provider, it checks the copy and move status flags of all messages in the **Inbox** folder that belong to the service provider, which is specified by the **szSvcID** and **szSvNam** members of the **MailMsg** structure. If MAIL_STATUS_MOVE is set, the message is moved to the specified folder. If MAIL_STATUS_COPY is set, the message is copied to the specified folder, with the original message remaining in the **Inbox** folder.

Attaching Files to Mail Messages

You can use the **MailPutAttachment**, **MailGetAttachment**, **MailDeleteAttachment**, **MailRequestAttachment**, and **MailLocalAttachmentLen** functions to work with mail attachments. With these functions you can create, open, or delete an attachment. You can also request to download one or query for its length.

You work with attachments the way you would work with a message: You register an intended operation in the *dwFlags* parameter of the **MailAtt** structure. For example, you set the parameter to ATT_DISP_RETRIEVE when you want the attachment downloaded to the local device.

The Mail Interface API uses the **szLocalName** member of **MailAtt** to determine whether the attachment is local or non-local. For a non-local attachment, you must set **szLocalName** to NULL before passing it to **MailPutAttachment** for example. For a non-local attachment, you must specify the length, *ulSize*, of the original file. For local attachments, the size is determined by examining the file.

Handling Mail Errors

When an error occurs, call the **MailError** function to obtain the error information. You can also call **MailErrorMsg** to obtain a more descriptive error condition.

CHAPTER 25

Mail Transport Service

Transport services, available as dynamic-link libraries (DLLs), allow a mail client to interact with a server to transmit or receive messages. The Windows CE mail transport service, Smtp.dll, is a message broker between Inbox, the Windows CE mail client, and an Internet mail server that is compliant with the Simple Mail Transfer Protocol (SMTP) and Post Office Protocol 3 (POP3) protocols. The operations of the mail transport service are transparent to the user.

Transport services are not limited to electronic mail. You can write a custom transport for paging, fax, file systems and other services. Similarly, you can write a custom client application. In any case, a transport is responsible for implementing a set of transport application programming interfaces (APIs) and making it available for a client to call. If you write a transport that uses Inbox as a client, you must declare and implement all the transport service interface functions and structures that Inbox expects. For lists of these functions and structures, see the appendix "Lists of Functions and Interfaces."

Note You can use the mail message API to deliver messages to the mail client without server interaction, for example, for a built-in, one-way pager card. However, this chapter describes interactive transports only.

As part of initialization, the mail transport service retrieves from the registry information about the name of an SMTP or POP3 server, port, user name, password, return address, and so on. The transport service uses a private **SERVICE** structure to represent the server it communicates with and the **MailMsg** structure to transport mail messages between the client and the server.

A mail transport service works closely with a client application. For example, Inbox calls functions exported by Smtp.dll to perform standard mail operations, such as connecting and sending mail to an Internet mail server, and receiving and deleting mail from that server. A transport service must implement a minimum number of functions that the client application needs to call. Additionally, it may choose to implement a few optional functions. Before the client can communicate with a transport library, the transport must register itself in the registry and the client must add the transport to its list of interactive services.

Registering a Transport Service

A transport service library must register itself in the registry under the **HKLM\PMail\ServicLibs** key so that a client application can locate and load the DLL. Register Smtp.dll as the **SMTP** subkey.

All interactive transport services must register with the client application so that a user can choose one for connecting to the server. An interactive transport is the transport that appears in the service list visible to users. On the other hand, passive services are those that deliver mail without requiring the user's interaction. In Inbox, interactive services are added to the **Service** menu once they are registered as a named key under **HKLM\PMail\ServiceInfo**. If the user removes an interactive service, Inbox deletes the associated registry entry. Passive services are registered as a named key under **HKLM\PMail\PassiveServiceInfo**. The client uses the passive service registration information to allow the user to select the transport for outgoing messages. Unlike interactive services, passive services have no subkeys.

The user can add registered interactive services to the **Service** menu of the Inbox application by tapping the **Compose** menu followed by the **Options** dialog box, and then the **Add** dialog box. The following sections provide sample registry entries and demonstrate how to install a transport service and add it to the Inbox client application.

Registering a Transport Service Library

Following is a sample registry, with Inbox running as the mail client, that makes use of a sample transport service.

▶ **To register a transport service library**

1. Under the **ServiceLibs** key, create a transport subkey that uniquely identifies the name of the transport service.

   In this example, the transport subkey is named **SAMPLE** to refer to the sample transport service DLL, Sample.dll.

2. Under the **SAMPLE** subkey, register a **SvcName** named value to identify the name of the service. In this example, the string value is "Sample Transport Service."

3. Under the **SAMPLE** subkey, register a **SvcLib** named value that defines the name of the transport service DLL.

   Inbox will load this DLL when it makes a connection to the specified service by calling the service's **TransportConnect** function.

Adding a Transport Service for Inbox

Using Inbox, a user has added the "Sample Transport Service" to the list of **Installed Services**. The service has been mapped to the **MyMail** key.

▶ **To add a transport service for Inbox**

1. From Inbox, tap **Compose**, tap **Options**, tap the **Services** tab control, and tap the **Add** button to bring up installed services. Highlight the **Sample** transport service called "Sample Transport Service."

2. Tap the **OK** button, and then type **MyMail** as a unique name for the selected service.

   The **SvcKey** value is the **HKLM\PMail\ServiceLibs\SAMPLE** subkey. Inbox uses this key to identify the name of the DLL to be loaded into memory when the desired service is connected. In this example, the DLL is Sample.dll.

3. Finish making choices in the dialog box to define the service's properties appropriately and tap **OK** to close the dialog box.

   Inbox adds the **MyMail** subkey under **HKLM\PMail\ServiceInfo** that includes information and properties for the service. Note that these properties can be modified by the service's **TransportProps** routine, once the new service is connected.

4. The **SvcKey** value is the **HKLM\PMail\ServiceLibs\SAMPLE** subkey. Inbox uses this key to identify the name of the DLL to be loaded into memory when the desired service is connected. In this example, the DLL is Sample.dll.

Note The **PMail** key refers to the Inbox application.

The previous procedure could result in the following registry entries.

```
'HKEY_LOCAL_MACHINE'
  [PMail]
      [ServiceInfo]
        [MyMail]
            REG_DWORD: CopyMaxLines = 0x32
            REG_DWORD: CopyAllLines = 0x0
            REG_DWORD: GrabRead = 0x1
            REG_DWORD: TypeOfGrab = 0x0
            REG_DWORD: SvcAutoDisco = 0x0
            REG_DWORD: NewMailNotify = 0x1
            REG_DWORD: RefreshTime = 0x5
            REG_DWORD: DoRefresh = 0x1
            REG_SZ: SvcAddrBook = Internet
            REG_SZ: SvcProfile = Direct
            REG_DWORD: SvcRemember = 0x1
            REG_SZ: SvcRtn =
            REG_SZ: SvcSMTPHost =
            REG_SZ: SvcPass =
            REG_SZ: SvcUser = thisuser
            REG_SZ: SvcPOP3Host = pop3svr-msg
            REG_SZ: SvcKey = SAMPLE
      [ServiceLibs]
        [SMTP]
            REG_SZ: SvcName = Internet Mail
            REG_SZ: SvcLib = smtp.dll
        [SAMPLE]
            REG_SZ: SvcName = Sample Transport Service
            REG_SZ: SvcLib = sample.dll
```

Registry Entries Used by Inbox and the Transport Service

Registry values under the **MyMail** subkey that are specific to, and set by, the transport, but that are also used by Inbox, are described in the following table. These registry values are usually set by the **Service Definition** dialog box that gets called when a mail service is being added, for example, **MyMail**. Once the **MyMail** service is connected, these and other values under the **MyMail** registry subkey may be modified or added by the service's **TransportProps** routine.

Note The "Type" entry in the table defines the registry value type.

Registry value	Type	Description
CopyMaxLines	REG_DWORD	Indicates the maximum number of messsage body lines to copy from the server.
		This value is relevant only if the **CopyAllLines** value is set to zero.
CopyAllLines	REG_DWORD	Indicates that the entire message body should be copied from the server, if the value is non-zero.
		If this value is zero, **CopyMaxLines** lines of the message body are copied.
GrabRead	REG_DWORD	Indicates whether a remote message should be saved locally when it is read from the server.
		If the **TypeOfGrab** value is one, and the messages are not remote, **GrabRead** will be ignored. If this value is not zero, the remote message is saved locally.
		If this value is zero, the remote message is not stored locally when read. If your service allows this option, messages with attachments and non-Interpersonal Messages (non-IPMs) will not work properly in this scenario.
TypeOfGrab	REG_DWORD	Indicates whether the entire message or only the message header should be copied from the server.
		If this value is zero, only the message headers are copied. If this value is one, all messages, headers, and bodies are copied. However, the amount of the body to be copied is limited to **CopyMaxLines**.
SvcAutoDisco	REG_DWORD	Indicates whether Inbox should force an automatic disconnect after the service sends or receives messages.
		If this value is zero, the user must manually disconnect the service. If this value is one, Inbox automatcally disconnects the service after connecting and performing the implied send-and-receive operations.
NewMailNotify	REG_DWORD	Indicates what type of notification Inbox should perform when a new message arrives.
		If this value is zero, Inbox beeps. If this value is one, Inbox beeps and also displays a message box.

Registry value	Type	Description
RefreshTime	REG_DWORD	Indicates the number of minutes between refreshes. This is relevant only if the **DoRefresh** value is one.
DoRefresh	REG_DWORD	Indicates whether messages should periodically be refreshed; the refresh interval is defined by the **RefreshTime** registry value.
		If this value is zero, Inbox does not do a periodic refresh. If this value is one, Inbox refreshes every **RefreshTime** minutes.
SvcAddrBook	REG_SZ	Indicates which address book (data base contacts) field to use for queries. This is a Unicode string.
		For example, you could set **SvcAddrBook** to the value "Internet," or the value "2-Way Paging." Each of these strings is a long name, called a *property name* of a database property. You can obtain this property name by specifying a property with a call to **GetPropertyDataStruct** function. **GetPropertyDataStruct** also returns a database position index of the specified property. The property name returned can then be used with **GetMatchingEntry**.
		The transport service can set **SvcAddrBook** to the long name of any property identifier that it will search.
SvcRemember	REG_DWORD	Indicates whether the password should be remembered.
		If this value is zero, Inbox displays a dialog box and prompts the user for a password each time the service connects. If this value is one, the system remembers the password, and Inbox does not display the dialog box.

Registry value	Type	Description
SvcRtn	REG_SZ	A Unicode string that defines the default return address to use. On a "Reply," Inbox will place this string in the "From:" field of the message header.
		The service driver could check or modify this entry to provide an appropriate or desired return address.
SvcPass	REG_SZ	A Unicode string that stores the password provided at the time of logon.
SvcKey	REG_SZ	An encrypted Unicode string that identifies the registry key that corresponds to the currently connected service; this key is under the **ServiceLibs** subkey.
		This indicates to Inbox the DLL that is to be loaded when the **SvcName** service is connected by the user within the Inbox application.
		See "Registering a Transport Service" earlier in this chapter.

Implementing a Sample Transport Service

The SDK includes a sample transport service. For a description of this sample, see Windows CE Sample Applications in the online Help. This Svcsampl sample transport service performs message service routines, such as creating, writing to, and reading from files that are located in the **Inbox** folder. This is performed, for demonstration purposes, using file system functions, such as **CreateFile**, **ReadFile**, and **WriteFile**. For transport functions that perform such tasks as sending, receiving, and deleting messages, a handle to a **MailMsg** structure is passed. The **MailMsg** structure contains the message header and body, and information about the message.

The sample transport service provided with the SDK sample code allocates a local heap in **TransportInit** for a transport-defined **SERVICE** structure. This structure supports handling the messages and provides a number of service functions that you can use for message handling. For example, the sample service locates messages in a mail directory specified by the **szMailDir** member of the **SERVICE** structure. These messages are stored as individual text files; file names are numbers with a .txt suffix, assigned in sequence.

Every mail message that arrives on a server is given a persistent *unique ID*. The system guarantees that this ID is different for every mail message and that it never changes. However, because these IDs are long—up to 70 characters—and are not convenient to use inside the transport service, Windows CE provides an alternative. For each session, the service generates a non-persistent *session ID* to reference a long unique ID. Each time a connection is made to the server—that is, each time a POP3 session is created—the server looks at all of the currently stored messages and assigns a session ID to each message. The messages are numbered from one through the total number of messages. This makes it easier to reference a particular message without having to use its long unique ID. The drawback is that you have no guarantee that message number five on this session with a session ID of five will still be message number five the next time the service is connected. Because of this, the session ID can not be trusted from one connection of a service to the next connection of that service.

Managing Memory for Mail Allocations

Inbox uses **HeapCreate** and **HeapAlloc** to allocate a private heap for each mail message; however, Inbox opens only one mail message at a time, in order to conserve memory. When Inbox is finished working with a message, it frees the allocated memory by calling **HeapDestroy**. If a service or application needs to create a memory heap, following this method can help to minimize memory fragmentation.

When working with a mail message, if Inbox has already allocated a heap for a message, then the service can reallocate memory on the existing heap. For example, if the handle **hHeap** in the **MailMsg** structure is not NULL, that is, if the handle exists, the service can allocate additional memory to this existing heap. In this way, Inbox takes care of freeing memory when it calls the **MailFree** function.

When following the method just described, the **TransportRecv** routine should create a private heap using **HeapCreate** for each mail message. A good initial size is 2 Kb. **TransportRecv** should store this heap handle in the **hHeap** member of the **MailMsg** structure. All dynamic storage in the **MailMsg** structure will use this private heap. Heap allocated storage should include the **szSvcId**, **szSvcNam**, **pwcHeaders**, and **szBody** members of the **MailMsg** structure.

The **TransportFreeMsg** routine should check for a NULL heap handle, delete the heap, and set the **hHeap** member of the **MailMsg** structure to NULL.

Handheld PC

CHAPTER 26

Programming for an H/PC

The Handheld PC (H/PC) is a category of mobile computing devices based on the Windows CE operating system. More than a personal digital assistant, the H/PC is a full-featured computer that extends the Microsoft Windows family to compact platforms. An H/PC is housed in a clamshell with an embedded keyboard, a touch-sensitive screen, and a stylus.

The H/PC is a mobile companion to a Windows-based desktop computer. The programming model and development environment of both are very similar. However, when writing applications for an H/PC, you must carefully consider the unique features of a handheld device. In this chapter, we will discuss in detail H/PC hardware and the H/PC shell, and comment briefly on bundled applications. For other features of the H/PC that you must consider when programming applications, see the chapters identified in the following table.

For information on	See
Power supply	Chapter 28, "Managing Power"
Memory	Chapter 29, "Writing Memory-Efficient Applications"
Communication and connectivity	Chapter 30, "Connecting to the Desktop and Sending and Receiving Data"

Hardware for an H/PC

Because an original equipment manufacturer (OEM) can choose different Windows CE components to include in the H/PC, not all devices have the same features. When programming for the H/PC, you must consider what hardware features the OEM has made available to you. Pay particular attention to the amount of ROM and RAM and the memory page size of the device. In general, H/PCs contain the following hardware:

- Display

    H/PCs have an LCD with a resolution of 480 x 240 or higher in a landscape orientation. The screen can have a color resolution of 2, 4, or 8 bits per pixel color resolution. The pixel arrangement renders the display in black and white, grayscale, or 256 colors.

- Touch panel

    A continuous resistive touch panel covers the LCD. The touch panel, which works similarly to a mouse on a desktop computer, allows a user to directly manipulate objects on the screen. Tapping the screen sends the same kind of messages that are generated by clicking the left button of a mouse that is connected to a Windows-based desktop computer. Because an H/PC has no mouse, cursor support is limited to a spinning hourglass used as a wait cursor. You cannot change the shape of the cursor to indicate an active target, such as a hyperlink.

- Keyboard

    The H/PC keyboard is a QWERTY keyboard with some keys omitted. QWERTY is the standard English-language keyboard layout named for the six leftmost characters in the top row of alphabetic characters. The H/PC keyboard includes a CTRL key, an ALT key, and two SHIFT keys. Infrequently used keys, such as PRINT SCREEN and SCROLL LOCK, are not included. The keyboard supports separate key-down and key-up events.

- Audio hardware

    You use the built-in audio hardware to associate sounds with notification events or to play wave (.wav) files. To reduce code size, you access .wav files stored in ROM.

- Serial port

    H/PCs include a built-in, nine-pin serial port. Applications use the serial port for communication between the H/PC and a desktop computer. H/PCs can connect to desktop computers by using a serial cable or an optional docking cradle that is connected to the desktop computer. The cradle is available from H/PC manufacturers. Some H/PCs support data communications through a modem connected to the serial port. The serial port can be used as a printer port as well.

- Infrared communications serial port

  An infrared communications serial port that conforms to the Infrared Data Association (IrDA) specifications is included. H/PCs can communicate with other H/PCs, desktop computers, or printers through IrDA-compliant infrared ports. Additionally, IR ports support printers that are IR-enabled, as well as printers with parallel interfaces.

- Hardware expansion slot

  Some H/PCs have an internal modem, a built-in, one-way pager, or a PC Card slot for additional communications hardware. Because Windows CE supports only a portion of the Personal Computer Memory Card International Association (PCMCIA) standard, not all modems are supported. However, because Windows CE supports installable device drivers, third-party software and hardware vendors can add support for additional devices by providing device drivers that you can install into an H/PC's RAM. H/PCs also support flash cards as a means of transferring files and adding extra memory.

Using Flash Cards on an H/PC

Flash cards can be a useful method for transferring files and adding extra memory to an H/PC. This section outlines the method for accessing files on flash cards.

A flash card is assigned the folder name Storage Card on the H/PC. To create, copy, or delete files on the storage card, open the Storage Card folder and then create, copy, or delete files on it. A user accesses files on a flash card by double-tapping on the My Handheld PC icon, which brings up the Explorer window, and then selecting the Storage Card folder.

The following code example creates a file named Testfile under \storage card\testdir.

```
HANDLE   hFile;
DWORD    dwFileLen;
char     szText[]="This is a test file.";

if (CreateDirectory(TEXT("\\Storage Card\\testdir"), NULL))
{
   hFile = CreateFile(TEXT("\\Storage Card\\testdir\\test.txt"),
      GENERIC_WRITE|GENERIC_READ,     //we need read and write access
      FILE_SHARE_READ,                //allow read access for others
      NULL,                           //security attributes
      CREATE_ALWAYS,                  //always create new file
      0,                              //file attribute
      NULL);
   WriteFile(hFile, szText, strlen(szText), &dwFileLen, 0);
   CloseHandle(hFile);
}
```

The actual path for the flash card is \Storage Card, but due to the special
character inside the quotes you need to assign the path as \\Storage Card.

H/PC Shell

The H/PC shell is a user interface to the Windows CE operating system. The
shell is based on the Windows 95 shell and provides many features familiar to
Windows users, such as the desktop window, the recycle bin, the taskbar, and
drag-and-drop capability. To program H/PC applications successfully, you must
be aware of the graphical elements of the shell, as well as the shell-supported
functions, structures, and messages. For example, you must program your
application's user interface to work within the constraints of the shell's graphical
user interface. For information on the graphical features of the shell and for
guidelines on designing an interface, see Chapter 6, "Designing a User Interface
for Windows CE," and Chapter 27, "Designing a User Interface for an H/PC."

In addition to its familiar graphical features, the H/PC shell includes some
functions and messages that are unique to Windows CE. These include the
clipboard application programming interface (API), the WM_HIBERNATE
message, and the notification API. For a list of the elements of these APIs,
see the appendix "Lists of Functions and Interfaces."

Clipboard API

The clipboard is the standard Windows method of transferring data between a
source and a destination. Clipboard operations are copy, cut, and paste. Because
all applications have access to the clipboard, a user can easily transfer data within
a single application or between applications.

In most cases, your H/PC application will use the clipboard the same way that it
is used by Windows-based desktop platforms. However, the clipboard API does
not support clipboard viewers and private clipboard formats, and it provides
clipboard functions that are not available to its desktop counterpart, such as
GetClipboardDataAlloc. This function is similar to the **GetClipboardData**
function, except that the memory for the data is allocated and owned by the
calling process, rather than by the clipboard. The **GetClipboardDataAlloc**
function can save you from making an extra memory allocation when clipboard
data is transferred across processes.

WM_HIBERNATE Message

Because it is necessary for applications sharing limited resources to cooperate with one another, Windows CE provides the hibernation message. The H/PC shell sends a WM_HIBERNATE message whenever system resources are low. The hibernation message advises applications to release any resources they do not need to recover their current state when they are reactivated. The release of resources by other applications allows the one currently in the foreground to complete its task. For information on using the WM_HIBERNATE message, see Chapter 29, "Writing Memory-Efficient Applications."

Notification API

A notification is a signal from the operating system that an event has occurred. When an application is registered for a specific event notification, the system generates notification when that event occurs. The H/PC shell uses notifications to communicate with the user and with other Windows CE-based applications. The notification functions and structures are grouped into a notification API that is particularly useful for applications that run on a mobile device.

Windows CE generates two types of notifications, user and application. A *user notification* alerts the user about a timer event. For example, the system might display a dialog box and play a sound before a scheduled appointment. The notification alerts the user so that he or she can perform some action. User notifications are always associated with an application, but the application is not started until the user takes some action.

An *application notification* starts an application when either a timer event or a system event occurs. When the system starts an application as a result of a notification, the system specifies a command-line parameter that identifies the event that has occurred.

User notifications and application notifications have several differences. User notifications alert the user, are generated only by timer events, and are executed entirely by the operating system. The application is started only when the user responds to the notification. In contrast, application notifications may or may not involve the user, can be generated by timer or system events, and always involve the system starting an application.

The two types of events used in notifications are timer events and system events. A timer event indicates that a specified time has arrived. A system event is a system occurrence, such as establishing a network connection or changing a device. A timer event would typically be used for a calendar or a to-do-list application.

User Notifications

You use the **CeSetUserNotification** function to register a user notification. It specifies the time when the notification should occur, the name of the associated application, and the way the notification appears to the user, such as a flashing LED or a sound.

At the specified time, the system places the application icon into the taskbar. If the specified time has already passed, the system places the icon in the taskbar immediately. An icon placed into the taskbar is called a taskbar annunciator. The taskbar can contain multiple annunciator icons at the same time, if they are for different applications. But only one icon for a specified application will be displayed at any time.

When the user taps the annunciator icon, the system starts a new instance of the corresponding application. It also passes a command-line parameter that tells the application why it is being started. If an instance of the application is already running, the new instance must send an application-defined message to the previous instance. The new instance then shuts down.

User notifications exist in either a registered state or an active state. The notification is *registered* from the time you call **CeSetUserNotification** until the time the user is notified. The notification is *active* from the time the user is notified until the event is handled.

Depending on what user notifications an H/PC supports, the operating system notifies the user of an event in one of the following ways:

- Playing a wave (.wav) file

  The user can choose a specific sound for each notification. The user can override sound notifications using the *Volume/Sounds* setup from the Control Panel.

- Flashing the light-emitting diode (LED)

  When a notification causes the LED to flash, the flashing continues until the user handles the notification. If multiple notifications cause the LED to flash, the flashing stops only when the user has handled all notifications.

- Displaying a dialog box

  A notification dialog box contains an application-defined title, application-defined text, an **OK** button, and a **Snooze** button. Clicking the **OK** button handles the notification. If the user clicks the **Snooze** button, the dialog box disappears and is redisplayed after five minutes. Clicking the **Snooze** button does not handle the notification.

- Vibrating the Windows CE-based device

The actions that the system performs for a particular notification should be based on preferences selected by the user. The system obtains a user's preferences by calling **CeGetUserNotificationPreferences**. This function displays a dialog box that contains the options available on the Windows CE-based device. The OEM determines available options. The system places the user's choices into a **CE_USER_NOTIFICATION** structure. The structure's address is specified in the call to **CeSetUserNotification**, which makes the user's preferences available to the system. **CeSetUserNotification** is used both for creating a new user notification and for modifying an existing notification.

User notifications are handled in two ways. For notifications that display a dialog box, clicking the **OK** button handles the notification. For notifications that do not display a dialog box, the application started by the user handles the notification by calling **CeHandleAppNotifications**. This function marks all active notifications for the application as "handled" and also removes the taskbar annunciator icon. **CeHandleAppNotifications** handles only active notifications, not registered notifications.

To delete registered user notifications, use **CeClearUserNotification**. For example, if a user sets a calendar appointment and then deletes the appointment before the specified time, this function removes the notification.

The taskbar annunciator for an active notification remains in the taskbar until the user handles the notification. In cases where an application has multiple active notifications, all of its active notifications must be handled before the annunciator icon is removed.

Application Notifications

The Windows CE operating system uses application notifications to communicate with applications without requiring user intervention. Application notifications are generated when a system event or a timer event occurs. An application does not need to be running when the notification occurs.

The system sends a system-event notification when a specified *system event* occurs. Examples of system events are the completion of data synchronization and the establishment of a network connection. Whenever the specified event occurs, the system starts the application with a command-line parameter.

You register an application for system-event notification by calling the **CeRunAppAtEvent** function. For a complete list of events and command line parameters, see **CeRunAppAtEvent**. Once you have registered a notification for a system event, the notification occurs each time the event occurs. You can delete the registration of an application for all system events by calling **CeRunAppAtEvent** and specifying NULL as the second parameter.

The system sends a timer-event notification at a specified date and time. You register for a timer-event notification using the **CeRunAppAtTime** function. Timer-event notifications are useful when the user notification method does not provide the user with necessary information to handle an event. In a timer event-notification, the system issues the notification at the specified time and the application displays the notification information.

Note Use **CeRunAppAtEvent** and **CeRunAppAtTime** sparingly. Automatically starting an application can confuse the user and cause low-memory conditions on a device with restricted memory. Ideally, the application that starts automatically should be small and non-intrusive.

You must register a separate notification for each instance of a recurring timer event. Typically, an application sets all of the instances for a specified period of time upon startup. To handle cases where the specified time period elapses without the user running the application, register the **CeRunAppAtTime** function to run the application for each desired time during the next time period.

Applications Bundled with an H/PC

Manufacturers bundle software applications with H/PCs. Of the bundled applications, two contain open APIs for manipulating the data used by the bundled applications: Inbox, a mail application, and Contacts, a contacts database application. Such APIs, unique to Windows CE, turn the bundled applications into back-end engines that facilitate rapid application development on H/PCs.

The mail API allows you to build applications that work with Inbox. The address store API allows you to build applications that work with the Contacts information manager. This API exposes functions for adding, sorting, modifying, and deleting records that appear in Contacts.

C H A P T E R   2 7

Designing a User Interface for an H/PC

Because the Handheld PC (H/PC) is designed to be a companion to a Windows-based desktop computer, the shell and the core applications look like their desktop counterparts. This similarity leverages the end user's knowledge of Windows and provides a solid base of potential customers when a new H/PC application is introduced.

On H/PC devices, users will recognize elements made familiar by Windows desktop platforms: a desktop and a taskbar, windows and dialog boxes, menus and controls. These and other elements allow the user to control the H/PC environment.

When designing an H/PC application, all of the principles of good user interface design discussed in previous chapters apply. The information presented here is intended to serve as a supplement, rather than a substitute for, information presented in Chapter 6, "Designing a User Interface for Windows CE."

Working with the Desktop and Taskbar

The desktop forms a visual background for all operations. It provides a familiar interface for accessing documents, launching applications, switching between tasks, browsing the file system, and performing other services. The components of the H/PC desktop include a work area, a taskbar, and application shortcuts or icons, such as the Recycle Bin and Inbox. Though you cannot programmatically control the appearance of the desktop, it is important to understand its specifications, so that you can design your interface accordingly.

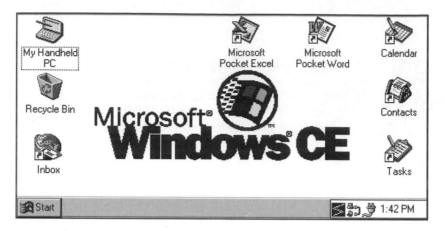

H/PC desktop

The H/PC desktop is similar to other Windows desktops. It contains file, folder, and shortcut icons that can be positioned anywhere on the desktop. Unlike other Windows-based platforms, however, the H/PC has a virtual border around its desktop to prevent icons from being fully obscured by the screen edge or taskbar. The desktop does not permit users to position an icon's (0, 0) point beyond the boundaries defined by the following rectangle coordinates:

(–16, –16), (464, –16), (464, 198), (–16, 198)

Additionally, the browser in the H/PC is integrated with Pocket Internet Explorer, which means that it contains two views: an HTML view to display Internet content and a File view to display a folder's contents. The browser assumes the appropriate view depending on how it was launched. If it is launched by opening a folder, it assumes the File view. If it is launched by pointing to a URL, is assumes the HTML view. Each view in the browser contains it own toolbar. The File view toolbar contains controls similar to the Windows Explorer toolbar. The HTML toolbar contains controls similar to the Internet Explorer toolbar.

The taskbar is used to switch between open windows and to access global commands and other frequently used objects. It contains a **Start** button, window buttons, and a status area. It also contains a **Desktop** button that provides quick access to the desktop from any application. Because H/PC applications do not have title bars, users identify a running application primarily by the icon and text displayed on its taskbar button.

H/PC taskbar

By default, the taskbar is the topmost window in the shell. When fully displayed, the taskbar is 26 pixels tall and either 480 or 640 pixels wide depending on the resolution of the display. The taskbar for the H/PC 2.0 supports autohide functionality. While hidden, the taskbar is 5 pixels tall. When a user hides the taskbar, a notification is sent to all applications that the usable vertical screen is increased by 21 pixels. To reactivate a hidden taskbar, each H/PC touch screen contains a 2.5 mm tap region around all four edges of the display. This, combined with the height of the taskbar, provides a generous tap region for activating the taskbar.

The H/PC taskbar also contains the following elements:

- **Start** menu

    The **Start** menu has two components: the main menu and cascading menus. The main menu has a maximum height equal to 240 pixels, the height of the display. Thus, the menu displays only the number of items that can fit into this region. If the contents exceeds this number, the menu displays as many items as possible in alphabetical order. The width of the main menu cannot exceed 120 pixels. Any menu items wider than 120 pixels are cropped. The cropped text is replaced with ellipses.

    Cascading menus are also displayed in alphabetical order. They have a maximum height of 240 pixels. If the number of items displayed exceeds the height of the screen, the menu adopts a multiple-column mode and shows the remaining menu items in the adjacent column.

    Like other Windows-based platforms, main and cascading menus use the 16 x 16 pixel icon associated with the menu item. Items that cascade to additional menus are appended with a triangular arrow.

- Window buttons

    The H/PC displays window buttons for all open parent windows. Window buttons are 23 pixels tall; button width is equal to the width of the available taskbar tray area divided by the number of buttons. The maximum button width is 1/3 of the available tray area. The minimum button width is 26 pixels. All window buttons display an icon and caption. The icon is 16 x 16 pixels so that the window button is always able to display the entire icon. The caption truncates as the width of the button decreases in size. Activated window buttons do not have bold captions.

- **Desktop** button

  The **Desktop** button provides quick access to the desktop. When the button is pressed, it brings the desktop forward, into focus, effectively hiding the current application. When the desktop is in the foreground, the **Desktop** button appears depressed to denote the desktop is being displayed. Pressing the **Desktop** button while the **Desktop** button appears depressed causes the previously active application to reactivate. The **Desktop** button is 23 x 22 pixels, the size of the standard toolbar button, and is located on the far right edge of the taskbar.

- Notification area

  You can add a status indicator to the notification area of the taskbar. Indicators are represented by graphics supplied by your application. They contain information that is global in nature or needs monitoring by the user when working with other applications. When adding a status indicator to the taskbar, provide a pop-up window that displays additional information or controls for the object when the user taps the indicator icon. Also provide one that displays commands for the object when the user performs an ALT+Tap action on the indicator icon. Carry out the default command defined in the pop-up menu when the user double-taps the indicator icon. Display a ToolTip that indicates what the status indicator represents, and provide the user with an option not to display the status indicator.

  Status indicators are 16 x 16 pixels, except for the clock, which occupies a fixed space. All status indicators are placed 3 pixels to the left of the clock with 0 pixels between each indicator. If you add a status indicator to the taskbar, you must define its access method. The methods supported by the taskbar include Down-Tap, Up-Tap, Double-Tap, and ALT+Tap.

Designing Windows and Dialog Boxes

Windows enable the user to view and interact with data. Consistency in window design is important because it enables users to easily transfer their skills and focus on tasks, rather than learn new conventions.

The H/PC supports most common Win32 application programming interface (API) window functions; however, due to constraints posed by the H/PC screen size, the system is designed for full-screen applications. Windows can be moved around the screen, but they cannot be resized by users. It is possible to create smaller windows for applications, such as a calculator, that can be used while another application is displayed, but most applications should use the entire screen.

While all H/PC devices conform to a hardware specification standard, some manufacturers offer features that extend the functionality of their devices. These additional features include an expanded 640 x 240 pixel LCD screen. The expanded screen allows applications to display up to 80 characters per line at an easily readable character size or half-height VGA graphics resolution. This means the font aspect ratio is similar to a desktop computer and it eliminates the feeling that the characters are squeezed onto the screen.

You can take advantage of the expanded screen size by designing applications capable of displaying a full-width view of documents and images. This minimizes the amount of scrolling and makes applications easier to use. Programming applications for a 640 x 240 screen does not necessarily require that a separate set of code be maintained for H/PCs with standard screens. Create application windows using default values that indicate full screen size regardless of its dimensions. Position objects using relative, as opposed to absolute, coordinates.

Primary windows for the H/PC are similar to all other standard windows. However, unlike other windows, which contain frames or borders, and title bars, H/PC primary windows do not contain title bars. Instead, they contain a command bar. For information on designing command bars, see Chapter 6, "Designing a User Interface for Windows CE."

Dialog boxes differ from primary windows in their behavior and use. For example, dialog boxes do not have taskbar window buttons, so users cannot switch between open dialog boxes by tapping a button on the taskbar. Additionally, dialog boxes obtain or display supplemental information related to objects displayed in a primary window.

Dialog boxes must be smaller than primary windows in order to differentiate between windows. Windows-based desktop platforms use a bold system font when displaying dialog box text. Windows CE uses the non-bold system font when displaying text, except for text on a light gray background. The default system font for Windows CE is Tahoma, 9 point.

Note If you are developing Windows CE-based applications under emulation, and you want to lay out windows and dialog boxes that look the same on your desktop computer as they will look on an H/PC, use Tahoma.fon.

The H/PC supports common dialog boxes, which provide a familiar way for users to perform standard tasks common to many applications. Windows CE supports the **Color**, **Print**, **Open**, and **Save As** common dialog boxes, which function the same on an H/PC as they do in Windows 95, with the following exceptions:

- The H/PC 2.0 **Print** dialog box implements a simple printing interface with one common dialog box that enables the user to choose a printer type, printer port, number of copies, print range, orientation, and margin settings. Windows 95 and Windows NT provide a common **Print** dialog box, a page setup dialog box, and a print setup dialog box to cover these operations.

- The H/PC 2.0 **Font** dialog box is a shared dialog box that contains a default font option and color list.

Common dialog boxes are not movable and are always centered vertically and horizontally on the screen. They always display the **Help** button.

Choosing Menus and Controls

H/PC applications can use all of the standard menus and controls available in Windows CE. For suggestions on choosing a menu or control for your application, see Chapter 6, "Designing a User Interface for Windows CE."

Receiving User Input for an H/PC

The H/PC supports both keyboard and stylus input. It does not support a mouse, and therefore does not have hover capability. The H/PC keyboard layout resembles a standard desktop computer keyboard, but most H/PC keyboard devices do not include the following keys:

> DELETE
> INSERT
> NUM LOCK
> PAUSE
> PRINT SCRN
> SCROLL LOCK
> FUNCTION KEYS

Note Users can use SHIFT+BACKSPACE as a substitute for the DELETE key.

The H/PC supports the Windows key, but Microsoft does not require hardware platforms to include it. Therefore, avoid writing applications that require users to use keys that may not be supported.

When the user presses the stylus to the screen, the input focus moves to the object under the stylus. If the object is a button, it displays its pressed appearance. If the user moves the stylus off the control without lifting the stylus from the screen, the control returns to its original state. Moving the stylus back over the control while the stylus is still touching the screen returns the control to its pressed state. The command associated with the control is only activated if the user lifts the stylus from the screen while the stylus is over the control. If the stylus is not over the control when the user lifts it, no action occurs. If the user presses the stylus to the screen over an object that can be dragged, and then moves the stylus while still touching the screen, the object moves with the stylus.

The H/PC conventions for selection using a stylus are the same as the standard Windows conventions for selection using a pen or mouse. The H/PC supports standard drag-and drop operations using the stylus. It does not support non-default drag-and-drop operations, however, which are the right mouse button drag-and-drop operations on desktop platforms.

The H/PC supports third-party, handwriting-recognition applications. If you support this functionality in your applications, see the *Windows Interface Guidelines for Software Design* for implementation conventions.

Providing Help

Users can access Help in the H/PC either by selecting the **Help** command on the **Start** menu or by tapping a **Help (?)** button included on a window's command bar. This **Help** button looks similar to the **What's This?** button in Windows 95 and Windows NT, but it functions differently. The **What's This?** button activates a Help mode in which the user can select a field about which to receive information. On the H/PC, the **Help (?)** button brings up the Help contents for the current window.

When creating a Help system for an application, follow these guidelines:

- Use ALT+H as the shortcut key for accessing Help.
- Write your application's Help file using HTML.
- Create each topic as a text file with an .htp extension.
- Create your contents page as a text file also, but save it with an .htc extension.

CHAPTER 28

Managing Power

The primary function of power management is to increase the battery life of a Handheld PC (H/PC). This is accomplished by providing accurate estimates of remaining battery life and notifying the user when the batteries are nearing depletion. Power management for an H/PC is based on the following assumptions:

- The computer is used less than two hours per day in bursts from five minutes to one hour.
- The display is powered 100 percent of the time during use.
- The CPU runs less than 10 percent of the time during typical use.
- The computer uses both main batteries and a backup battery.
- The device has no nonvolatile writable memory.
- Maximum battery life is obtained without PC Cards or with PC Cards that require very little power from the computer batteries. PC Cards drawing appreciable power from the internal batteries significantly reduce battery life.

An H/PC manages power by allowing the operating system to automatically select one of three operating states based on user and program activities. These states are:

- Dead

   The computer uses no power. It has no batteries, or all batteries are completely dead. All contents of RAM are lost. The user purchases the device in this state.

- Suspend

   The computer uses minimal power. The CPU internal and external clocks stop and the CPU uses extremely low power. Peripherals and DRAM are usually off. The CPU might take as long as 100 milliseconds to wake up from this state.

- On

  The computer uses more power than in the other two states. Any time the display, keyboard, or touch screen are active, the device is in the on state. When in the on state, the computer can switch between two CPU modes: full speed and idle. In full-speed mode, the CPU runs at normal operating frequency. In idle mode, the CPU internal clock stops and the CPU uses little power. Peripherals and DRAM may be on or off. The CPU can enter and exit this state in approximately 10 milliseconds.

Power Management States

With the exception of the dead state, the computer never completely stops using power. In the suspend state, it uses minimal power to maintain its clock, its applications, and the persistent data stored in RAM. To reduce power requirements, the computer removes power from unneeded circuits and devices, such as the keyboard decoder, display, scratch-pad memory, and processor. A PC Card's driver determines the power that it uses when the computer is in the suspend state.

The computer switches to the suspend state for the following events:

- The user selects the **Suspend** command.
- The computer detects a critical power condition.
- The activity timer performs a time-out.

The operating system uses an activity timer to gauge whether the user is actively using the computer. The timer counts down while the computer is in the on state. When the timer reaches zero, the computer switches to the suspend state. The user can set the maximum value of this timer in seconds. Two events reset the timer to its maximum value: a key press or release and a touch event. When the timer reaches five seconds, the computer sounds a warning to alert the user that it is about to suspend operation. The operating system does not notify an application when it enters the suspend state because most applications are not affected by this transition. When the device resumes operation, applications also resume operation as if they had been continuously running.

Functions that applications can use to reset activity times or to set timers and events that can switch the computer from the suspend state to the on state are described in the following table.

Function	Description
CeRunAppAtTime	Sets a timer or runs an application at a specified time.
WaitCommEvent	Waits for a communications event to occur. Serial, Infrared Data Association (IrDA), or PC Card devices can return EV_POWER when the device resumes operation.

If an application uses the **Sleep** function, it does not increment the elapsed time counter while the computer is in suspend state. It starts counting again when computer operation resumes. The internal clock is not affected when computer operation is suspended. Though an application is not notified when it enters the suspend state, the operating system does notify a device driver by calling a power-handler function. A device driver might use this notification to suspend operation of the device it controls, which may result in a device not being available immediately after the computer switches to the on state. For example, when a file stored on a PC Card is open and the user tries to save the file before the card is turned on, the system returns an error message.

The computer switches to the on state for the following events:

- After the user presses the **On** button.
- After the user triggers an alarm event.
- After the user performs a warm or cold boot.
- After the user changes the battery.

In the on state, the default mode is full-speed. The computer switches from full-speed mode to idle mode when all processes are idle. Switching to idle mode is transparent to the user and most applications, because the system continues to process interrupts, including the time slice interrupt.

When the computer is in the on state, some applications may prevent the operating system from switching the computer to the idle mode. These applications retain control by using idle loops or by using functions that do not let the operating system block operation. All applications can enhance power management by using functions that let the operating system block a return to the application. For example, use the **GetMessage** function rather than the **PeekMessage** function, because **GetMessage** lets the system block a return to the application and **PeekMessage** does not. Letting the operating system retain control allows it to determine when the system is inactive so that it can select the most efficient operating state for the computer.

Resuming Operation, Rebooting, and Resetting

Resuming computer operation from the on state's idle mode or the suspend state does not alter computer memory or change application settings. In contrast, rebooting or resetting the computer does alter memory and affect program operation. The differences between these transitions are described in the following table.

Transition	Description
Wake-up, or resume	Transitions from the suspend state to the on state's full-speed mode. Wake-up does not change memory or application settings.
Cold boot, or cold reset	Resets the device completely. All applications are terminated, the working memory is cleared, and the object store is cleared.
Power-on reset	Transitions from the dead state to the on state. Power-on reset has the same consequences as a cold boot.
Warm boot, or warm reset	Terminates all applications and clears working memory. The object store integrity is maintained.

The cold boot and power-on reset transitions occur when power is first applied to the computer, or when all power is removed from the computer and then reapplied after one minute. Unless the computer uses nonvolatile memory, the user will have to load or reload applications after a power-on reset. Object store data is lost after a cold boot.

A warm boot occurs when the user presses the reset button on the computer. This button is placed in a pin-hole recess or under the battery cover to protect it from accidental activation. Users perform a warm boot only when the computer has stopped responding or has become unstable. A warm boot stops applications that are running and clears the memory used for application execution. Memory used for the object store and file system is preserved.

CHAPTER 29

Writing Memory-Efficient Applications

A Handheld PC (H/PC) application must run in the portion of RAM memory not used for storage memory. Because available memory depends on what applications and data are installed on the device, you cannot predict the amount of memory available for an application. A 350 KB application may seem small by desktop computer standards, but it is large for an H/PC. For maximum portability, applications must be small enough to run on 2 MB devices.

To use available memory efficiently, you must decide what functions are absolutely necessary to the users of your application. Consider reducing or eliminating features that do not meet this criteria. Follow the suggestions in this chapter to write memory-efficient applications for an H/PC.

Memory Pages

In Windows CE, you allocate memory one page at a time. You cannot allocate less than a page, and as a programmer, you have no control over the page size. That is determined by the original equipment manufacturer (OEM). Currently, your choice is either 1 KB or 4 KB. When choosing a page size, the OEM is faced with tradeoffs: A large page size often wastes memory, but a small page size requires more operating system overhead to keep track of pages. When you need to allocate memory for a small object, the larger your page size, the more memory you waste. On the other hand, a small page decreases the amount of memory the translation look-aside buffer (TLB) can address, which can reduce the buffer's effectiveness.

Because RAM is limited on H/PC devices, OEMs generally keep page size small. When you make decisions that affect memory allocation, you should assume that the device you are using has a 1 KB page size. If you need to know the exact page size for your device, check the page specification with the Remote Memory Viewer tool provided with Windows CE.

Types of Memory Allocation

Applications often need to allocate blocks of memory to use while they are executing. There are various memory pools from which the required memory can be allocated.

A primary reason for allocating memory is to store data. When a Windows CE program begins, the system initially allocates 1 KB of memory to the stack. It then adds memory to the stack, as needed, one page at a time up to the fixed limit of 58 KB. To store data, you typically declare it on the stack.

Although the system can shrink a stack when memory is low, it does so only if all other sources of memory pages are exhausted. The stack is a good source of memory for data that changes frequently but is not appropriate for constant data. Neither is the stack the best source of large amounts of memory because the stack does not shrink until all pages are used.

Note Do not allow the stack for a thread to grow larger than 58 KB. Exceeding this threshold results in a system-access violation that causes the program to stop functioning.

Declaring static or global data causes the system to put the data in the read/write (R/W) data section of the application module. This section does not grow or shrink. Its size is set by the operating system when your application initializes. Determining the size of your application's data section allows you to estimate how much memory is available after your program is loaded. To do this, use the standard Win32 DumpBin utility, Dumpbin.exe, or the Remote Memory Viewer.

Use the information you obtain from the Memory Viewer to arrange your declared data to use as little memory as possible. Following are some suggestions for arranging your data:

- Look carefully at everything in the R/W section.
- Declare all constant data items.

  The compiler will move declared constant data into the read-only data section.

- Move other types of data into the R/W section once the system has removed the constant data.

  Removing constant data from the R/W section and moving other data into the section uses space that would otherwise be wasted. This allows you to use less heap space.

- Place a note in your code to remind you to look at your memory use each time you add more data.

  It would be counterproductive to fill the section with additional data, and then have it grow by an entire page just to accommodate an additional variable.

- The loader needs 50 to 75 bytes free in the R/W section.

  Leave space for the loader.

When you declare static or global data objects, the operating system takes care of the memory storage, but you need to explicitly allocate memory. Although Windows CE has various functions for allocating memory, the most-used functions are **VirtualAlloc**, **LocalAlloc**, and **HeapAlloc**. To free the allocated memory, use the companion functions **VirtualFree**, **LocalFree** and **HeapFree**. To create and remove heaps, use **HeapCreate** and **HeapDestroy**. You can use a combination of these functions to minimize wasted RAM.

The **VirtualAlloc** function is the primary tool for allocating virtual memory in the Windows CE operating system. You use **VirtualAlloc** to directly allocate a number of memory pages. Although it is the most efficient tool for allocating a large memory object, you should not use **VirtualAlloc** to allocate small memory objects. Because **VirtualAlloc** can only allocate whole pages, if you need only a partial page, memory is wasted.

One advantage to using **VirtualAlloc** is that the allocated memory is easily returned if the system runs low on memory. When you are finished using the allocated memory, free it by using **VirtualFree**. The system returns the memory to the global virtual memory pool immediately.

Each process has its own default heap from which you can allocate memory. If a process needs memory, call **LocalAlloc** to allocate memory and **LocalFree** to free memory. Whenever you use the function **LocalAlloc**, if there is not enough available memory in the default heap to supply the requested amount of memory, the system adds to the amount of memory in the heap. When the system needs memory and tries to compact a heap, sometimes it cannot because there are partially-filled pages. Even when unused memory exists, if it is fragmented, the system cannot use it. This results in the number of available pages not corresponding to the total amount of free space in the heap. Though the operating system automatically shrinks the heap if it has one or more free memory pages, partially filled pages do not cause the system to shrink the heap.

The **HeapCreate** function creates a new heap for a process that is separate from the default heap for that process. Memory for the new heap is reserved, but it is not committed until needed. To allocate and free memory, use the **HeapAlloc** and **HeapFree** functions. You can free the new heap by using **HeapDestroy**, which returns the memory back to the virtual memory pool.

Creating a separate heap is a good allocation strategy when you need to make a lot of small, temporary memory allocations. For example, you could create a separate heap for an application that works with documents. This heap would allocate all memory for a document. When the user closed the document, the application would free the heap and return the memory to the global virtual memory pool. Using a separate heap keeps the size of the default heap small and avoids generating the numerous partially-filled pages you get when you use **VirtualAlloc**. Because each heap requires approximately 500 bytes of overhead, you should create separate heaps only if you expect to allocate at least 5 KB of memory.

Thread Local Storage

It is often necessary for every thread of a process to have its own copy of read/write data. To provide this data, Windows CE supports thread local storage (TLS). TLS enables each thread to allocate the objects it owns in memory and to manipulate thread-specific data. You can use the **TlsAlloc**, **TlsSetValue**, **TlsGetValue**, and **TlsFree** functions to allocate and free memory for thread storage.

When a dynamic-link library (DLL) attaches to a process, the DLL uses **TlsAlloc** to allocate a TLS index. The DLL then allocates dynamic storage and uses the TLS index in a call to **TlsSetValue** to store the address in the TLS slot. The TLS index is stored in a global or static variable of the DLL. Each time the DLL attaches to a new thread of the process, the DLL allocates dynamic storage for the new thread and uses the TLS index in a call to **TlsSetValue** to store the address in the TLS slot.

Each time an initialized thread makes a DLL call that requires the data in its dynamic storage, the DLL uses the TLS index in a call to **TlsGetValue** to retrieve the address of the dynamic storage for that thread.

TLS functions supported by Windows CE are described in the following table.

Function	Description
TlsAlloc	Allocates a TLS index. The index is available to any thread in the process for storing and retrieving thread-specific values.
TlsFree	Releases the TLS index, making it available for reuse.
TlsGetValue	Retrieves the value pointed to by the TLS index.
TlsSetValue	Stores a value in the slot pointed to by the TLS index.

Use the following criteria to help you decide which memory allocation method is best in particular situations:

- For a single, large data item with multiple pages, use **VirtualAlloc**.

- For a set of small data items that have the same lifetime, allocate memory from a separate heap created by **HeapCreate**.

- For data items that exist for the lifetime of the application, put the items in the R/W static data section, if there is sufficient space.

- For small items that exist for the scope of a function, allocate memory from the stack.

- For small items with random, overlapping lifetimes, allocate memory from the default heap. Try to keep the total size of the heap consistent and predictable.

Monitoring How an Application Uses RAM

Windows CE provides two tools to monitor how much memory your application is currently using: a map file and the Remote Memory Viewer. The two tools are quite different. A map file is a data file produced by the compile and link process and the Remote Memory Viewer is a utility included in the Windows CE integrated development environment (IDE). The Remote Memory Viewer requires that your desktop computer be connected to a remote device to get information about your application's memory use. However, you can get valuable information from a map file without being connected to a remote device. In this section, we briefly discuss making and using a map file, followed by a detailed discussion of Remote Access Viewer.

A memory map file is very helpful to a programmer because it shows how much memory is used in each static section of your application. When you build your application, if you set the map link option, the linker makes a memory map data file and writes it to your hard drive. The length of each static section is provided at the top of the file. In addition to showing the static section lengths, a map file also shows how much data is in the read-only section, .rdata. The R/W data section is composed of two subsections: .data, which contains all initialized global data, and .bss, which contains uninitialized data. R/W data is initialized to zero by the loader. Note the section number, which is typically two for R/W. Then, look in the symbols area of the map file to see what data is in this section and how much space each item uses. For example, to calculate the total memory that is taken up by R/W, add the amount needed by .data and .bss and round up to the next multiple of the page size.

Using the Remote Memory Viewer

The Remote Memory Viewer allows you to view remotely all virtual memory use in the Windows CE system. The Viewer consists of the process information window and two menu commands: the **Kernel Summary** and the **Process Memory Map**, which is located on the Tools menu of the VC++ IDE. The Process Memory Map allows you to examine an application's memory use from a desktop computer.

Process Information Window

The process information window of the Remote Memory Viewer is divided into three sections. The first section provides process information, including the slot assignment and the number of memory pages used. It also describes how much memory the system devotes to aspects of the process, such as R/W memory and the stack.

Process Name	Proc#	PID	Ptr	Slot	Code	R/W	R/O	Stack	Resv	
NK.EXE	8c011b00	20	8c00f870	02	579(8)KB	27KB	51KB	1KB	2681KB	
repllog.exe	8c011b8c	141	8c3acc00	04	125(0)KB	32KB	18KB	15KB	1299KB	
filesys.exe	8c011c18	62	8c3e7800	06	160(0)KB	30KB	9KB	3KB	15528KB	
device.exe	8c011ca4	c3	8c3e0000	08	320(0)KB	22KB	30KB	10KB	1390KB	
gwes.exe	8c011d30	e4	8c3d9c00	0a	371(0)KB	120KB	199KB	18KB	1464KB	
afd.exe	8c011dbc	105	8c3c5c00	0c	294(0)KB	80KB	21KB	13KB	3577KB	
shell32.exe	8c011e48	126	8c3bc800	0e	378(0)KB	11KB	72KB	14KB	1264KB	
rnaapp.exe	8c011ed4	407	8c3a6800	10	67(0)KB	7KB	15KB	5KB	1147KB	
rapisrv.exe	8c011f60	3e8	8c3a5c00	12	94(0)KB	6KB	10KB	7KB	1266KB	
PPPRTSvr.Exe	8c011fec	449	8c37e000	14	258(36)KB	55KB	16KB	6KB	1267KB	

Thread Handle	Owner Name	Running In..	Priority	Status	SchedFlags	▲
8c3fe26c	NK.EXE	NK.EXE	3	00000000	00000003	
8c3fea00	NK.EXE	NK.EXE	1	00000000	00000003	
8c008528	NK.EXE	NK.EXE	3	00000000	00000003	
8c3f03d0	repllog.exe	afd.exe	3	00000000	00000003	
8c3f0304	repllog.exe	afd.exe	3	00000000	00000003	
8c3f2474	repllog.exe	repllog.exe	3	00000100	00000003	
8c3f2c7c	repllog.exe	gwes.exe	3	00000000	00000003	
8c3fe1a0	filesys.exe	filesys.exe	3	00000000	00000003	
8c3fa07c	device.exe	device.exe	0	00000000	00000003	
8c3fa6e8	device.exe	device.exe	3	00000100	00000003	▼

Module Name	In-Use Flags	Handle	Base Ptr	Start IP	▲
PPP.dll	00000020	8c3f5f48	03d40000	01d41a04	
CXPORT.dll	00000020	8c3f6328	03d30000	01d3049c	
AUDIO.dll	00000010	8c3f7c28	03f40000	01f413fc	
KEYBDDR.dll	00000010	8c3f8310	03f90000	01f91c9c	
TOUCH.dll	00000010	8c3f87fc	03f80000	01f81d54	
WINSOCK.dll	0000030a	8c3f9cec	03d10000	01d11954	
IRCOMM.dll	00000008	8c3f9fc0	03d20000	01d204b0	
SERIAL.dll	00000008	8c3fa62c	03f30000	01f31f1c	
PCMCIA.dll	00000008	8c3fb10c	03f70000	01f714a0	
COREDLL.dll	000003ff	8c3fee38	03fe0000	01fe1c88	▼

Ready			Dump 1		10:40:08

Process information window

Process fields included in the process information section of the window are described in the following table.

Field	Description
Process Name	Process name.
Proc #	Process handle.
PID	Process identifier.
Ptr	Address of the slot containing the process.
Slot	Slot number for the process.
Code	The number of ROM-code pages used. RAM use is specified in parentheses.
R/W	The number of read/write data pages.
R/O	The number of read-only data pages.
Stack	The number of stack pages.
Reserved	The number of reserved pages.

The second section of the process information window provides information about the threads running in each process. It identifies the handle of the thread, the name of the process in which the thread is running, and the thread's priority and status.

The third section of the process information window provides information about DLL modules, including each module's name, handle, location in memory, and in-use flag. The in-use flag indicates which processes are currently using the DLL. Because each bit corresponds to a process slot number, an in-use flag with a value of 0x00000006 indicates that the DLL is being used by the processes in slots two and three.

Kernel Summary

The Remote Memory Viewer contains menu commands that help you understand how your application uses memory. The first, the **Kernel Summary** command, opens the **Kernel Summary** dialog box, which describes the resources currently in use by the Windows CE kernel.

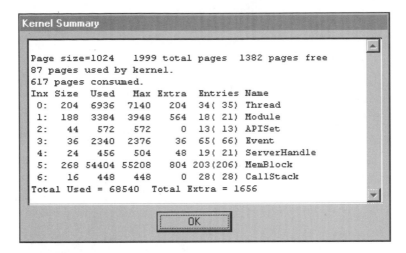

```
Kernel Summary

Page size=1024   1999 total pages   1382 pages free
87 pages used by kernel.
617 pages consumed.
Inx Size  Used   Max Extra   Entries Name
  0:  204  6936  7140    204   34( 35) Thread
  1:  188  3384  3948    564   18( 21) Module
  2:   44   572   572      0   13( 13) APISet
  3:   36  2340  2376     36   65( 66) Event
  4:   24   456   504     48   19( 21) ServerHandle
  5:  268 54404 55208    804  203(206) MemBlock
  6:   16   448   448      0   28( 28) CallStack
Total Used = 68540  Total Extra = 1656

                  OK
```

Kernel Summary dialog box

The top line of text in the **Kernel Summary** dialog box provides the system's page size in bytes. This value, which is determined by the OEM, allows you to convert memory use from pages to bytes. The dialog box also lists the total number of pages, as well as any free pages available. The next two lines of text in the **Kernel Summary** dialog box identify the total pages used and the number of pages used by the kernel.

Below the three lines of text is a table which gives you information about kernel objects. Each row of this table provides information about a different object type. Meanings of each column heading in this **Kernel Summary** dialog box table are described in the following table.

Heading	Description
Inx	The object type number. This is an index number.
Size	The size, in bytes, of an object of this type. The type of object is identified in the last row of this table under the heading **Name**.
Used	The total number of bytes currently used by the kernel to hold all the objects of this type. This number is calculated by multiplying the number of objects by the size of each object.
Max	The number of bytes allocated to hold all the objects of this type.
Extra	The extra memory currently allocated, which is the difference between Max and Used.
Entries	The first item gives the number of objects currently in use. The second, which appears in parentheses, gives the maximum number of objects of this type that the kernel has ever had.
Name	The name of the object type.

Process Memory Map

The second menu command in the Remote Memory Viewer that helps you
understand how your application uses memory is the **Process Memory Map**
command. This command opens the **Process Memory Map** dialog box, which
provides a detailed picture of how a selected process uses memory.

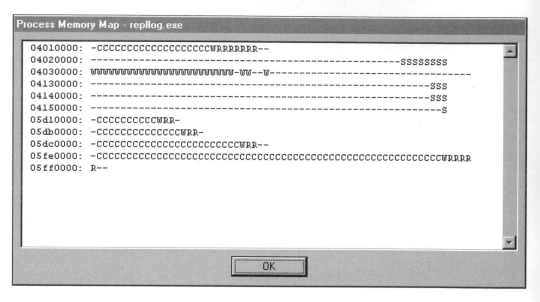

```
Process Memory Map - repllog.exe

04010000:  -CCCCCCCCCCCCCCCCCCCWRRRRRRR--
04020000:  --------------------------------------------------SSSSSSSS
04030000:  wwwwwwwwwwwwwwwwwwwwwwww-ww--w------------------------------------
04130000:  -----------------------------------------------------------sss
04140000:  -----------------------------------------------------------sss
04150000:  -------------------------------------------------------------s
05d10000:  -CCCCCCCCCWRR-
05db0000:  -CCCCCCCCCCCCCWRR-
05dc0000:  -CCCCCCCCCCCCCCCCCCCCCCCWRR--
05fe0000:  -CCCCCCCCCCCCCCCCCCCCCCCCCCCCCCCCCCCCCCCCCCCCCCCCCCCCCCCCCWRRRR
05ff0000:  R--
```

```
OK
```

Process Memory Map dialog box

Each line of text in the **Process Memory Map** dialog box begins with the address
of a 64 KB region of memory. Symbols indicating how a process allocates pages
in this region are described in the following table.

Symbol	Description
S	Stack page
C	Code page in ROM
c	Code page in RAM
W	Read/write data page in RAM
R	Read-only data page in ROM
r	Read-only data page in RAM
O	Object store page
P	Pending commit
-	Reserved page available for commitment

Any white space at the end of a line represents the amount of wasted free space.

Handling Low Memory Situations

No matter how effectively you use the **VirtualAlloc**, **LocalAlloc** and **HeapCreate** functions to allocate memory, and how efficiently your application uses RAM, the system may run low on memory. When memory is low, the **VirtualAlloc** function cannot find any unallocated pages. This can cause your application to stop functioning.

At a programming level, a low-memory situation can manifest itself to the application in the following ways:

- A call to the **VirtualAlloc** function fails.
- The **LocalAlloc** or **HeapAlloc** function attempts to grow a heap, but fails to do so.
- The stack tries to grow, but fails to do so.

The first two failures are returned in an orderly fashion and the user receives warning messages. These failures occur following a call by the application to a function, such as **CreateWindow**. The third manifestation has more serious consequences because it causes the process to wait for a free page, and causes the program to stop responding.

To avoid the problems associated with low memory, the system constantly monitors the amount of memory available and tries to prevent low-memory situations from occurring. It does this in several ways. When an application attempts to allocate memory, the system filters the request. Filtering prevents a single application from using all available memory with one large allocation by lowering the maximum allocation limit. When the system enters a low memory situation, the system lowers the memory limit further.

Another way that the system tries to prevent low-memory situations is by sending warning messages to applications. When available memory falls below a *hibernation threshold*, the system enters the limited-memory regime from which it asynchronously sends a WM_HIBERNATE message to each active application. This message warns the application that available memory is scarce.

Windows CE uses two additional thresholds, low and critical, that define successively more restrictive memory regimes. Values for memory thresholds are described in the following table. The values are based on a 1 KB memory page; values for a 4 KB memory page are provided in parentheses.

Threshold	Value	Description
Hibernation threshold	128 KB (160 KB)	The point at which the system enters a limited-memory state. The system sends a WM_HIBERNATE message when its memory falls below this value.
Low-memory threshold	64 KB (96 KB)	The minimum available memory size that the system must maintain when it is in a low-memory state.
Critical-memory threshold	16 KB (48 KB)	The minimum available memory size that the system must maintain when it is in a critical-memory state.

Maximum memory allocations in limited-memory states are described in the following table.

Maximum allocations in limited-memory conditions	Value	Description
Low Memory	16 KB	The maximum amount of memory that the system allows Virtual Alloc to allocate when the system is in a low-memory state.
Critical Memory	8 KB	The maximum amount of memory that the system allows VirtualAlloc to allocate when the system is in a critical-memory state.

The system must respond to four limited-memory scenarios in Windows CE. These scenarios occur when an application does one of the following:

- Requests less memory than the low-memory maximum
- Requests more memory than the low-memory maximum
- Requests less memory than the critical-memory maximum
- Requests more memory than the critical-memory maximum

If an application calls **VirtualAlloc** and requests less memory than the low-memory maximum, but enough to cause the system to fall below the low-memory threshold, the system displays a **System Out of Memory** dialog box. This dialog box is discussed in more detail in the next section. In this scenario, the user must either select applications for the system to close or allocate more RAM to program memory. If the user chooses to close applications, the system sends WM_CLOSE messages. If an application receives a WM_CLOSE message but does not shut down within eight seconds, the system displays an **End Task/Wait** dialog box. This gives the user the choice of terminating the application or waiting to see if the application closes itself.

Any **VirtualAlloc** call fails if it causes the amount of available memory in the system to fall below the low-memory threshold. The system does not display the **System Out of Memory** dialog box. **LocalAlloc** does not necessarily have the same constraint as **VirtualAlloc**. Depending on the state of the system heap, a function call to **LocalAlloc** can succeed.

If an application calls **VirtualAlloc** to request less memory than the critical-memory maximum, the system displays the **System Out of Memory** dialog box. The user must either select applications for the system to close or increase the amount of RAM allocated to program memory, if there is any available RAM. The system calls **TerminateProcess** to terminate any applications selected by the user.

Applications that call **VirtualAlloc** fail if the function causes the amount of available memory in the system to fall below the critical-memory threshold. Depending on the state of the system heap, a function call to **LocalAlloc** can succeed.

System Out of Memory Dialog Box

As discussed in the previous section, the operating system displays a **System Out of Memory** dialog box in some low-memory scenarios. This dialog box informs the user that memory is critically low on the H/PC and prompts the user either to close applications or to increase the amount of RAM allocated to program memory. This dialog box is a special, *system modal* dialog box that freezes the rest of the system. When it is invoked, socket connections stop functioning and other threads stop running.

After the **System Out of Memory** dialog box closes, any applications selected by the user are shut down just as if the **Close** button was clicked. Applications have eight seconds to close. If more memory is requested after four seconds have passed and memory is still critically low, the dialog box reappears.

Note The success of an approach that sends the WM_CLOSE messages when memory is low depends on the ability of an application to shut down in response while allocating little additional memory in the process. If your application requires a significant amount of memory to shutdown, try caching the needed memory. For example, you could hide a **Do You Want to Save Your Document** dialog box, and then make it visible if you need to close the application unexpectedly.

Application Hibernation

Windows CE uses the WM_HIBERNATE message as its primary mechanism for asking applications to free memory. When freeing memory is required, the system posts the message to one or more applications, beginning with the application that has been inactive the longest. It requests memory from the active application last and does not send WM_HIBERNATE messages to invisible windows.

Note In Windows CE, hibernating is vital. All properly constructed Windows CE-based applications must have a handler for WM_HIBERNATE.

When the system brings an application to the foreground, it sends an WM_ACTIVATE message. If the hibernating application had released memory previously, the system does not restore its memory resources to the pre-hibernation state. Applications should have a WM_ACTIVATE handler that can deal with the restoration of memory resources following hibernation.

An application must take the following actions when it receives a WM_HIBERNATE message:

- Free any large blocks of memory that were allocated by **VirtualAlloc**, for example, a cache.

- Free as many Graphics Windowing and Event Subsystem (GWES) objects as possible, including windows, bitmaps, and device contexts, because they use large amounts of memory.

- Save the state of the heap in order to restore it later, and then free the entire heap.

As the amount of available memory drops, the system posts WM_HIBERNATE messages at an increasing rate. If the system reaches a situation where a call to **VirtualAlloc** is about to fail, it tries to free pages by shrinking stacks. The system shrinks stacks in first-in, first-out order to minimize the risk of a stack fault, which causes an application to fail. If the system cannot free any stack pages, **VirtualAlloc** fails and the function is returned to the application as a failed function call.

Tips for Efficient Memory Use

Writing memory-efficient applications requires practice. Here are some suggestions to guide you while you design and program applications for an H/PC.

- Decide how much memory to allocate to your application.

  Whenever the system attempts to allocate more than 16 KB of memory, it has the potential to fail without displaying the **System Out of Memory** dialog box and without sending a low memory warning to the user.

  Once the system is in a low-memory regime, any memory allocation greater than 8 KB has the potential to fail. Because of this, your application should not allocate large amounts of memory in its shutdown code. The user already knows that a low-memory situation exists.

  Small memory allocations almost never fail. Before this type of allocation fails, the user has been sent both low-memory and critical-memory warnings, in the form of **System Out of Memory** dialog boxes, and has had an opportunity to respond.

- Load only the data that the application needs for the immediate operation, and write the data back to the file when it is no longer needed.

  If you are using large data sets, consider loading only the data that an operation needs immediately, especially if the data will not be modified in the process. When the data is no longer needed, write it back to the file immediately. By loading data on demand, you gain memory, although you lose speed.

- Remove read-only pages when resources are limited.

  If you are not modifying data, declare the data as constant so the kernel can remove it if necessary. The kernel will restore the data the next time it accesses the page.

- Design applications that can modify their use of temporary files or eliminate temporary files completely.

  Many programs use temporary files that are deleted when the program terminates. Though this may be convenient, such files are a burden on memory resources while the temporary files exist.

  Consider not using temporary files. Though eliminating the use of temporary files may decrease speed, simplicity, or perhaps the robustness of the application, the increase in memory efficiency is sufficient to offset the liabilities of this approach. If possible, design applications that can modify their own use of temporary files depending on the state of memory resources.

- Compress text and bitmaps.

  Data stored in text format and as uncompressed bitmaps uses memory inefficiently. Although some compression takes place when files are loaded from a desktop computer to an H/PC, you need to use the memory-saving techniques of compression and decompression fully for maximum benefit.

- Limit your use of bitmaps.

  While one of the most appealing features of Windows-based platforms is the rich graphical environment you can create, graphics use a lot of memory. To conserve memory, you must limit your use of bitmaps and other graphic displays. One approach to conserving memory while retaining bitmaps is to use an algorithm to generate the image on demand, rather than loading the bitmap or other graphics file into memory. Though you gain memory with this approach, you lose speed. Generating images on demand works best for line drawings, though it is practical for other types of graphics as well.

- Include memory management capabilities in your application to supplement those in the system.

  An application that downloads large amounts of data over a modem, such as e-mail or stock quotations, may require more memory than the system has available. Use **GetStoreInformation** to determine the amount of free memory in the object store prior to the download, and then warn the user of potential problems.

- Offer users the option of turning off automatic backups.

  Though an application that automatically creates backup files protects the user from unintentional data loss, the backup files use valuable memory. If your application supports backup files, prompt the user to turn off automatic backups if memory is low.

  If the application has a desktop component, be sure it is sensitive to the memory limitations of the Windows CE-based platform. When downloading an application or data, inform the user if the system has too little memory remaining for the device to operate effectively.

C H A P T E R   3 0

Connecting to the Desktop and Sending and Receiving Data

The Handheld PC (H/PC) is an extension of your desktop computer and allows you to access your critical data when you are away from your desk. By connecting the two computers, you can transfer data from one to the other. You can also perform tasks on the H/PC remotely. For example, you can debug applications or edit the H/PC's registry from your desktop computer. And, by connecting your H/PC to communication devices, such as modems and pagers, you can send and receive e-mail and faxes, and browse the Internet.

Connecting to Other Computers

Being able to share data between your H/PC and a desktop computer extends the functionality of both computers. For example, you can edit the letter you wrote in Pocket Word on your H/PC using Microsoft Word on your desktop computer. Or, in Microsoft Excel on your desktop computer, you can recalculate spreadsheet totals that you generated on your H/PC with Pocket Excel. Although you typically connect an H/PC to a desktop computer, you can also connect it to a variety of other devices. The following list identifies programming considerations for a variety of tasks you can accomplish with your H/PC connected to a desktop computer or another device.

- Synchronizing data

   With Windows CE, you can synchronize databases on an H/PC with a corresponding database on a desktop computer. Windows CE automatically synchronizes the Schedule+ data on the desktop computer with the personal information manager (PIM) data on the H/PC. You can write similar synchronization applications using RAPI functions.

- Converting files

  Windows CE supports an application programming interface (API) for converting files to a different format when they are transferred between the desktop and the H/PC. Converting is necessary because H/PC applications do not incorporate all of the features of their desktop counterparts. For example, Pocket Word does not incorporate all of the features of Word on the desktop computer. Consequently, before a document can be transferred for use on the H/PC, items like unsupported fonts and OLE objects need to be converted or stripped from the file. Altering the files before they are transferred is accomplished with file filters.

  A file filter is a dynamic-link library (DLL) that controls the transfer of files between the H/PC and the desktop computer. Windows CE Explorer automatically adjusts file formats for some types of files and you can extend its file filtering capabilities by defining new application-specific filters of your own. For information about existing filters and how to write new filters, see Chapter 19, "Transferring Files."

- Installing applications

  Because H/PCs do not have floppy disk drives installed, applications that are not loaded in ROM have to be loaded from a desktop computer or other device. Windows CE supports a distinct set of functions and load-file commands for installing applications on the H/PC. You can use these functions to retrieve information about the H/PC, load application files, update the H/PC registry, and create a script for unloading the file App Install.

- Using remote tools

  The Windows CE integrated development environment (IDE) supports remote connections to use debugging applications, such as Spy, Process Viewer, and Heap Walker. You can also perform remote debugging by using either User Datagram Protocol (UDP) or Transmission Control Protocol/Internet Protocol (TCP/IP). UDP is faster than TCP/IP; however, TCP/IP is more reliable.

  In addition to debugging, you can remotely edit an H/PC's registry with the remote registry editor or capture an image from the remote device and display it on the desktop computer.

- Sending and receiving e-mail and faxes, and browsing the Internet

  Because of the portability of the H/PC, it is an excellent tool for sending and receiving e-mail and faxes, and for using Web browsers from remote locations. The H/PC shell and Windows CE Pocket Internet Explorer are fully integrated, which allows you to use either the browser or the Windows CE shell as your interface for manipulating files and shortcuts on the H/PC.

- Printing data

  Because Windows CE includes printing support, H/PC applications may enable printing. Use the **PrintDlg** function to provide printing capability in your applications. The **PrintDlg** function in Windows CE is the same as it is on Windows desktop platforms with one exception. Because Windows CE does not support the **Print Setup** dialog box, the members associated with it do not exist in the Windows CE **PRINTDLG** structure.

  Because the **Print Setup** dialog box is not supported in Windows CE, you cannot set page ranges or specify the number of copies to print. You must print the entire document, or the currently selected portion of the document, and you can print only one copy at a time. However, Windows CE does support some page setup functionality. In Windows CE, two new members have been added to the **PRINTDLG** structure: **rcMargin** and **rcMinMargin**. The **rcMargin** member specifies the widths of the left, top, right, and bottom margins; the **rcMinMargin** member specifies the minimum allowable widths for those margins.

Communications and Connectivity Hardware for an H/PC

Windows CE provides support for a number of standard and optional communications and connectivity hardware. With the right combination of hardware and software, you can accomplish the tasks described above with ease.

All H/PCs are equipped with the following communications hardware:

- An RS-232C nine-pin serial communications port
- An infrared (IR) port that complies with the Infrared Data Association (IrDA) specification

H/PC manufacturers may provide other communication and connectivity hardware, such as internal modems and one-way pagers. One device that is often included is a PC Card slot.

Using the Built-In Serial Port

The built-in, nine-pin serial port on an H/PC operates identically to the RS232-compliant serial port on a desktop computer. Windows CE provides support for applications that communicate over the built-in serial port by exposing many of the serial functions, file functions, and Windows Socket functions that are used by Windows communications applications.

Unlike Windows desktop platforms, the Windows CE **CreateFile** function requires a colon appended to the device name. In most cases, "COM1:" designates the built-in serial port on an H/PC.

Using the Built-In Infrared Serial Port

The H/PC IR port supports point-to-point serial connections with any IrDA-compliant device. IR links are an ideal method for exchanging data between two H/PCs. You can establish connections between two IrDA-compliant devices whose ports are aligned within 15 degrees of each other. They must also be no more than three feet apart. IrDA specifications provide for serial IR links operating at speeds up to 115.2 KBps.

Some manufacturers supply only one universal asynchronous receiver transmitter (UART) to control the built-in serial port and the IR port. To access the IR port on H/PCs with a shared UART, you must redirect communications by using the **EscapeCommFunction**.

▶   **To open and use the IR port on H/PCs with one UART for both ports**

1. Call **CreateFile** to open the built-in, nine-pin serial port, usually "COM1:."

2. Call **EscapeCommFunction** with the handle obtained from **CreateFile** as the *hFile* parameter, and SETIR as the *dwFunc* parameter.

   The SETIR flag indicates the serial port is to be set to IR mode. **EscapeCommFunction** will return TRUE if an IR capable port has been selected.

3. Fill the device control block structure **DCB** with the existing communication port settings by calling the **GetCommState** function.

4. Configure the communication port by assigning values to the members of the **DCB** and calling the **SetCommState** function.

5. Set the timeout values for read/write operations on the port with a call to the **SetCommTimeouts** function.

6. Perform **ReadFile** and **WriteFile** operations on the device handle returned from **CreateFile**.

Windows CE supports Windows Sockets (Winsock) and the IR extensions to Winsock (IrSock) for developing communications applications for the H/PC.

Using a PC Card Serial Device

Windows CE detects PC Cards when they are inserted or if they are in place when the user starts the H/PC. The system automatically loads the device drivers needed to use the card when it detects a supported card.

All active, top-level windows receive a WM_DEVICECHANGE message from the system when a card is first inserted. To determine if a card was inserted before the application started running, call the **EnumPnpIds** function. It returns a double-zero-terminated list of zero-terminated plug and play IDs of all active PC Cards. In most cases, the list returned from **EnumPnpIds** contains only one member because most H/PCs come equipped with only one PC Card slot.

Alternatively, TAPI applications can call the **LineGetDevCaps** function to determine if a particular modem is inserted into the H/PCs PCMCIA slot. The **devSpecific** member of the **LineDevCaps** structure returned from **LineGetDevCaps** contains the device type and indicates whether or not it is active.

Communication and Connectivity Software for an H/PC

As mentioned earlier, the right combination of hardware and software is essential for you to accomplish communication and connectivity tasks. The communication applications that are bundled with the H/PC reside in ROM. They are described in the following list:

- Remote Networking, which combines the functionality of two Windows-based applications.

    - Windows CE uses dial-up networking for connecting to a Remote Access Service (RAS) server. Unlike Dial-Up Networking on Windows-based desktop platforms, Remote Networking allows the H/PC to be a dial-up client, but not a server. The H/PC supports connections to RAS servers using Point-to-Point Protocol (PPP) with TCP/IP as the underlying network protocol.

    - Windows CE uses direct cable connection (DCC) for establishing a direct serial connection between the H/PC client and a Windows-based desktop computer host. Direct cable connection allows the client to share the resources of the host computer. DCC uses PPP to establish a data-link-level connection to run network protocols and transport layer protocols. You can determine the state of the DCC connection by using the RAS API set.

- Terminal

    The Windows CE Terminal application uses a serial cable or modem connection to connect the H/PC with a desktop computer to transfer files or act as a remote terminal. You can also use Terminal to connect to a remote Bulletin Board System (BBS). Although Terminal does not support file transfer protocols, you can use it to cut and paste information from a BBS.

You can use Terminal to configure modems and set up dialing properties. It also allows the following terminal emulation:

- Generic TTY
- VT-100/ANSI
- PC Link

In addition to the bundled applications, some manufactures may include software that allows the user to connect a modem to the device's serial port.

Palm PC

C H A P T E R   3 1

Programming for a Palm PC

The Palm PC is a mobile personal information manager (PIM) that is based on the Windows CE operating system. With the Palm PC, the user can capture and receive data rapidly in real-time situations. And the Palm PC is convenient to use—it fits easily in a pocket and can be used with one hand.

As an electronic organizer, the Palm PC manages contacts, appointments, and other personal and business information. As a voice recorder, it can capture ideas and thoughts as you speak them. As electronic paper, the Palm PC can store telephone numbers and short messages. As an Internet device, it can send and receive e-mail messages. As an information appliance, the Palm PC can receive personal information and news broadcast from a wireless network or a broadcast feed when integrated paging capability is enacted.

Palm PCs support the Windows CE kernel and include many familiar graphical user interface elements found in Windows-based desktop platforms. A typical Palm PC is equipped with 4 MB of ROM and at least 1 MB of RAM. The device may have a CompactFlash Type II Card slot built in for storage expansion and wireless connectivity. In addition, all Palm PCs have a RS232 serial port and an Infrared Data Association (IrDA) port. Some Palm PCs come with a docking cradle that provides a connection to the desktop computer by means of a serial port. The cradle also provides AC power for downloading bulk data overnight by means of a one-way pager.

This chapter describes these features of the Palm PC:

- Shell and user interface (UI)
- Input panel and input methods
- File input and output
- Desktop connectivity

Application Guidelines

Applications for the Palm PC must be carefully designed to enhance the user experience. This means a simple approach to applications and fast access to data. Because of the size of the Palm PC device, an application designer must be conscientious to organize the functionality appropriately to conserve the screen resources and to provide the optimal usability. In the user interface design, this means exposing the critical functions in the most explicit manner possible, and hiding more advanced or less-frequently used functions in places such as pop-up menus.

In general, you should follow these guidelines when you design your Palm PC application:

- An application can have only a single instance. If necessary, multiple-instance features, such as the multiple document interface (MDI) functionality, must be supported from within the application.

- An application must not show the file system. This means that **Open**, **Save**, **Browse**, and other functionality may not expose any path information.

- An application must be able to close and start up immediately to ensure fast user access to applications. If startup performance is slower than desired, the user interfaces should be displayed before the data is processed.

- Applications must offer the Infrared Send/Infrared Receive functionality because Palm PC does not support Windows CE Explorer that could otherwise carry out the functions. They should use **File/Send** and **File/Receive**, or **File/Send To/IR Recipient** and **File/Receive** commands.

- Top-level application windows must be accessible from the **Start** menu or its **Programs** submenus, because any running application does not get an icon on its taskbar. However, top-level dialog boxes without parents will be adopted by the Desktop application. This ensures that the user can bring such dialog boxes to the foreground by tapping the desktop icon on the taskbar. Any owned pop-up window will appear when its owner is brought from the background.

- Design your application to display data in a single-column format to suit the narrow screen of a Palm PC, unless crucial circumstances dictate otherwise.

- Avoid using numerous navigation controls to leave as much screen space as possible for data, rather than controls.

- Do not provide a **Close** button on the application's toolbar. The Palm PC shell automatically shuts down idle applications in the background when an active application requests more memory than is available. Similarly, an application should not enable the **File->Exit** menu item. Applications must handle state and data persistence gracefully.

- Palm PC employs the Coolbar model to display both the menus and the toolbar buttons. Coolbar is a command bar with toolbar buttons and, possibly, a retractable menu field. If you use Coolbar in your application, you should group its functionality into frequently used and infrequently used features. The user should access frequently used features by means of the toolbar buttons and infrequently used options from a pop-up menu.

Installing Applications

The Palm PC is different than Windows-based desktop platforms in two ways that affect how you install applications. First, the file structure is different. Second, because there is no Windows CE Explorer, the user cannot search for executable files or data files.

The following table shows the subset of the Windows CE application installation macros that you can use for a Palm PC. Use these macros in the DestinationDirs section of the CAB Wizard setup .inf file.

Macro string	Windows CE directory	Palm PC directory
%CE1%	\Program Files	\Program Files
%CE2%	\Windows	\Windows
%CE3%	\Windows\Desktop	
%CE4%	\Windows\StartUp	\Windows\StartUp
%CE5%	\My Documents	\My Documents
%CE6%	\Program Files\Accessories	\Program Files\Accessories
%CE7%	\Program Files\Communication	\Program Files\Communication
%CE8%	\Program Files\Games	\Program Files\Games
%CE9%	\Program Files\Pocket Outlook	
%CE10%	\Program Files\Office	
%CE11%	\Windows\Programs	\Windows\Start Menu\Programs
%CE12%	\Windows\Programs\Accessories	\Windows\Start Menu\Programs\Accessories
%CE13%	\Windows\Programs\Communications	\Windows\Start Menu\Programs\Communications
%CE14%	\Windows\Programs\Games	\Windows\Start Menu\Programs\Games
%CE15%	\Windows\Fonts	\Windows\Fonts
%CE16%	\Windows\Recent	
%CE17%	\Windows\Favorites	\Windows\Start Menu

As you can see in the table, several Windows CE directory locations are not included in the Palm PC file structure. These correspond to macro strings %CE3%, %CE9%, %CE10%, and %CE16%. Also, the locations corresponding to %CE11% through %CE14%, and %CE17%, are different than they are on other Windows CE-based platforms.

Because the Palm PC has no Windows CE Explorer, you need to install a link in the **Start** menu to access your executable files. You should install this link in \Windows\Start Menu\Programs and its subfolders. Place data files in projects under the **\My Documents** folder. The **File Open** and **File Save** dialog boxes automatically place data files in **\My Documents** under a project folder that the user chooses. Use the Win32 functions **GetSaveFileName** and **GetOpenFileName** to display these dialog boxes.

Note For the Palm PC, the user will only be able to view shortcuts created in \Windows\Start Menu and its subfolders.

Interfacing with the Shell

The Palm PC shell is the user interface to the Palm PC's operating system. From the shell, a user gains access to the Palm PC file system. The shell lets a user start applications from the desktop or use hardware control buttons. It cooperates with the input panel to enable a user to select an input method. The shell also makes it possible for a user to receive system notifications. With the Palm PC shell application programming interface (API), you can make all these features available in applications. For more information on using the shell API, see Chapter 32, "Palm PC Shell."

File Input and Output

The Palm PC does not expose its file system to the user. Users access the file system by specifying file attributes for a file in the **Projects** dialog box. In this dialog box, a user can open or save a file and organize files by folders and properties. You can incorporate these features into your own applications using the exposed API.

In the Palm PC, all files are stored in the **\My Documents** folder, which is accessible by all applications. Items in the folder can be documents or subfolders for a project. The top-level folder has a default name, **All**. A user cannot delete or rename this folder, but can create subfolders in it for projects. However, the subfolders can only be one level deep. The user places files related to a project in a subfolder. The name of this subfolder is the name of the project.

The Palm PC uses Projects to carry out file input and output. Projects consists of four dialog boxes and a few APIs. You use the functions to manipulate files. The dialog boxes provide a user with a set of user interface elements for opening and saving documents. The documents, including voice and ink notes, are organized by projects. A file is associated with its project folder and identified by its file name. It has a set of editable attributes that describes various file properties, such as the location, type, size, and date of the last modification. The four dialog boxes in Projects are:

- **Folder**

  Manages all project folders. It allows the user to create a new folder, and rename or delete existing ones. In addition, the user can use it to select the current folder.

- **Properties**

  Displays the file properties, including the name of a file; the number of multiple files; the folder name; and the type, location, and size of a file.

- **Open**

  Allows the user to select from all the files on the device. Files can be selected and sorted by folder or file type.

- **Save As**

  Allows the user to save one file at a time with specified properties, such as project, file name, type, size, location, and modification date.

You can enable these system-defined dialog boxes by calling the **GetOpenFileName** and **GetSaveFileName** functions. The two functions take an **OPENFILENAME** structure as input. Depending on the input, the **GetOpenFileName** function creates either a **Folder** or an **Open** dialog box. To open a **Folder** dialog box, you must set the **Flags** member of the input structure to the OFN_PROJECT value. Otherwise, the user will get an **Open** dialog box. Similarly, the **GetSaveFileName** function creates **Properties** and **Save As** dialog boxes. If you set the **Flags** member to the OFN_PROPERTY value, the function creates a **Properties** dialog box. Otherwise, it opens a **Save As** dialog box. You would use such dialog boxes in applications like Voice Recorder and Note Taker.

Because Palm PC applications must not expose the file system in any way, Projects does not make available any file manager view. Instead, the **Folder** and **Properties** dialog boxes allow users to specify the folder and location of files. The location can be the main memory or a CompactFlash card.

Using Flash Cards on a Palm PC

Flash cards can be a useful method for transferring files and adding extra memory to a Palm PC. This section outlines the method for accessing files on flash cards.

You must create a folder called **My Documents** on the flash card to mimic the file structure on the Palm PC. Files can be placed directly in this folder or under one of its immediate subdirectories.

The two ways to access files on a Palm PC flash card are through code in your applications and through a desktop computer connected to a Palm PC.

For coding purposes, the path of the flash card is \Storage Card. On the desktop, after synchronizing with the Palm PC, you click the Storage Card icon. This brings you to the root directory of the Storage Card. You can then create, copy, and delete directories and files on the flash card.

The following code example shows how to create a file named Test.txt under \Storage Card\My Documents\testdir.

```
HANDLE    hFile;
DWORD     dwFileLen;
char      szText[]="This is a test file.";

if (CreateDirectory(TEXT("\\Storage Card\\My Documents\\testdir"),
NULL))
{
   hFile = CreateFile(TEXT("\\Storage Card\\My Documents\\testdir
\\test.txt"),
       GENERIC_WRITE|GENERIC_READ,    //we need read and write access
       FILE_SHARE_READ,               //allow read access for others
       NULL,                          //security attributes
       CREATE_ALWAYS,                 //always create new file
       0,                             //file attribute
       NULL);
   WriteFile(hFile, szText, strlen(szText), &dwFileLen, 0);
   CloseHandle(hFile);
}
```

The path for the flash card is \Storage Card, but due to the special character inside the quotes you need to assign the path as \\Storage Card.

Before opening and processing a document, an application performs certain file operations to ascertain whether an item, such as a file or folder, exists in a specified location and whether it is of the appropriate file type for processing. For this, Windows CE exposes other Projects functions to perform the following three classes of file operations:

- Enumeration of folders and files
- Checking for CompactFlash cards
- Searching for files in a folder

Projects functions are described in the following table.

Function	Description
GetOpenFileName	Creates a system-defined dialog box for opening a file.
GetSaveFileName	Creates a system-defined dialog box for saving a file.
EnumProjects	Enumerates all folders on the requested mountable file system.
EnumProjectFiles	Enumerates all files within a folder or all folders on the requested mountable file system.
FindFirstFlashCard	Searches for and returns the first mountable file system.
FindNextFlashCard	Finds the next mountable file system.
FindFirstProjectFile	Finds the first file in a folder on the requested mountable file system.
FindNextProjectFile	Finds the next file in a folder.

User Input and Output

A Palm PC has a touch-sensitive screen with a resolution of 240 x 320 pixels in a portrait orientation. The screen handles both input and output. A user can use a stylus to type, write, or sketch on the touch screen. A Palm PC has no physical keyboard attached to it. Instead, it uses the input panel to emulate typing on a QWERTY keyboard. The input panel is bundled as the default means for alphanumeric input. A user chooses among the input methods (IMs) installed in the system. With the built-in microphone and speaker, a Palm PC is capable of voice input and output of speech quality. As such, audio is a built-in notification mechanism. Other notification options include a flashing LED and mechanical vibrations.

A Palm PC has various hardware navigation control buttons for fast data access and application switching. These include:

- **Action** and **Exit** buttons for application control without using the touch screen.
- Two rocker switches for up and down navigation, **RockUp** and **RockDown**.
- Application-switching buttons, for example, **App1** through **App16**.

You should map at least one application-switching button to the Voice Recorder application; the limit is 16. The exact number you have available depends on the original equipment manufacturer (OEM). The OEM typically specifies a default behavior for each button. For example, the **App1** button may be assigned to launch the Voice Recorder application. However, you can overide the default mapping by using the Palm PC Buttons control panel. For more information on user input and output, see Chapter 32, "Palm PC Shell."

The Palm PC allows users to take handwritten notes. The underlying technology is known as Rich Ink. The Microsoft Note Taker application is the built-in word processor for Palm PC that accepts handwritten input. It lets a user write and draw on the touch screen with a stylus. The user can edit a handwritten note with **Cut** and **Paste** menu items, open a saved ink file, and read it from the screen. You can enable note taking in your applications that take textual or graphical inputs. For more information, see the documentation for the Microsoft Platform SDK.

Communications and Connectivity Hardware for a Palm PC

Desktop connectivity refers to the services for connecting a Palm PC to a Windows-based desktop platform to perform file synchronization and convert documents automatically from one format to another during data transfer. The exposed API for desktop connectivity includes the remote API (RAPI) and the connection notification API.

Applications Bundled with a Palm PC

Many Windows CE PIM applications, such as Inbox and Contacts, are implemented for and bundled with Palm PCs. In porting to the Palm PC platform, these applications undergo some changes, mostly in their user interfaces, to meet the requirements of a Palm PC.

The PIM and productivity applications implemented for a Palm PC support open APIs to allow an application programmer to take advantage of Windows CE address and message stores. You can use these open APIs to enable and enhance the existing functionality of the bundled PIM applications.

Web Services for a Palm PC

A Palm PC is a mobile Web station that connects the user with the Web. It supports the Mobile Channels technology, which defines a standard compliant with Microsoft® Internet Explorer 4.0 for creating mobile channels on a Windows-based desktop platform and viewing them on a Palm PC or a desktop computer. For more information, see Chapter 22, "Mobile Channels."

Voice Recorder Control for a Palm PC

The Voice Recorder control is designed to enable, with minimal effort, voice recording and playback functionality in its container applications. For example, the Inbox application can incorporate the control to record a voice mail message in a file and attach the voice note to a regular e-mail message. It is a simple task to program with the Voice Recorder control because the exposed API elements are minimal.

Working with the Voice Recorder control involves using only one function, two data structures, and a small number of messages. First you must create and initialize the control. You may do so after the owner window is created. The control is represented by a data structure of the **CM_VOICE_RECORDER** type and must be properly initialized. The following code example illustrates this process of initiation and initialization.

```
// be sure that the owner window exists
if (!IsWindow(hwndMain)) return FALSE;

// initialize the control's data structure.
CM_VOICE_RECORDER cmvr;
memset( &cmvr, 0, sizeof(cmvr));
cmvr.cb = sizeof(CM_VOICE_RECORDER);
cmvr.dwStyle = VRS_NO_MOVE;
cmvr.xPos = 100;  // use -1 to center the control relative to owner
cmvr.yPos = 160;
cmvr.hwndParent = hwndMain;
cmvr.lpszRecordFileName = TEXT("\\My Documents\VoiceRec.wav");

// returns the handle to the control
hwndVoice = VoiceRecorder_Create(&cmvr);
```

The Voice Recorder control offers a user-interface element that provides the user with the Record, Playback and Stop functionality commonly found in an audio recorder. Pressing the **Record** button on this UI element starts the Voice Recorder engine. Pressing the **Stop** button terminates the recording or playback session. Other features exposed through the UI element include **Grip**, **Cancel** (**X**), and **OK** buttons for moving the control, interrupting the recording process, and exiting the control. To move the control around the screen, the user presses and holds the **Grip** button on the left side and drags it to the desired location. Applications can use the **SetWindowPos** function to accomplish the same task programmatically. Currently, it is not possible to use the **Grip** button to manually move the dialog box beyond the area outlined by the boundaries of the owner window. The **Cancel** button, when pressed, discards the recording session and dismisses the dialog box. This button is equivalent to the built-in **Exit** hardware control button for Palm PC. The **OK** button, when pressed, saves the recording in a file before dismissing the dialog box. This button is equivalent to the **Action** hardware control button. Also, in order for **Action** to work, the control, *dwStyle*, must be set with VRS_MODAL, but not VRS_NO_OKCANCEL nor VRS_NO_OK.

The Record, Playback, and Stop features can also be enacted from within the container application. To accomplish this, the application sends the VRM_* messages to the Voice Recorder control. For example,

```
SendMessage(hwndVoice, VRM_RECORD, NULL, NULL);
```

This issues a command (VRM_RECORD) to the Voice Recorder control, *hwndVoice*, to start recording. Similarly, a VRM_PLAY message activates playback, and a VRM_STOP message terminates recording or playback. For more information about these and other VRM_* messages, see the Reference section of this document.

Conversely, the Voice Recorder control, when it is not of the VRS_NO_NOTIFY style, dispatches the VRN_* notification messages to the application's window whenever the control experiences changes in its mode of operation. These messages are sent in the WM_NOTIFY format. The following code example shows how the application can intercept such messages.

```
case WM_NOTIFY
{
   LPNMHDR pnmh = (LPNMHDR) lParam;
   switch (pnmh->code);
      {
         case VRN_ERROR:
            MessageBox(NULL, TEXT("Error…"), NULL, MB_OK);
            break;
         case VRN_RECORD_START:
            MessageBox(NULL, TEXT("Recording…"), NULL, MB_OK);
            break;
         case VRN_RECORD_STOP:
            MessageBox(NULL, TEXT("Stop recording…"), NULL, MB_OK);
            break;
         case VRN_PLAY_START:
            MessageBox(NULL, TEXT("Playing…"), NULL, MB_OK);
            break;
         case VRN_PLAY_STOP:
            MessageBox(NULL, TEXT("Stop playing…"), NULL, MB_OK);
            break;
         case VRN_CANCEL:
            MessageBox(NULL, TEXT("Cancel…"), NULL, MB_OK);
            break;
         case VRN_OK:
            MessageBox(NULL, TEXT("OK…"), NULL, MB_OK);
            break;
         default:
            return DefWindowProc(hwnd, msg, wp,lp);
      }
}
```

The Voice Recorder control is a dialog box of the pop-up window style,
WS_POPUP. It can have an owner window, but not a parent window. As
a pop-up window, the control does not change its state when its owner window
moves or resizes, and it will always appear in Z order above its owner windows
and consequently above the owner's child windows. When the owner window
spawns child windows, each of which in turn creates a Voice Recorder control,
the topmost parent of the children still assumes ownership of the controls. As
such, all the VRN_* notification messages are sent to the topmost owner window,
not its children. Furthermore, closing a child window will not cancel its
associated control.

For more information on Z order and windows, see Chapter 9, "Windows."

C H A P T E R   3 2

Palm PC Shell

The Palm PC shell is optimized for fast application access rather than for managing a large number of documents and applications. Thus, the Palm PC does not support Windows CE Explorer for managing files. Users cannot access the file system from the Palm PC shell.

The Palm PC shell allows users to launch new applications or to reactivate idle applications using the **Start** menu and its **Programs** submenu, or the hardware application switching buttons. The shell includes the following user interface elements: a **Start** menu, an **Input Panel** button, a **Desktop** button, and a date and time annunciator panel, which are all displayed on the taskbar. Running applications are not shown on the taskbar, but they are accessible from the **Start** menu. For this reason, applications can have a single instance only.

The Palm PC desktop is an application-based Active Desktop. For information on Active Desktop, see the Microsoft Platform SDK. Users can configure Active Desktop to display up to five application items, such as Logo, Owner, Appointments, Tasks, and Messages. Tapping on a displayed item launches the associated application. For example, tapping Appointments starts the Calendar application.

Tapping the **Desktop** icon on the taskbar toggles between Desktop and the most-recently active application. As a Palm PC application, Desktop can and will adopt, as its child window, a parentless dialog box of the WS_POPUP style. Thus, tapping the **Desktop** button will bring up such dialog boxes from the background.

The Palm PC shell optimizes memory use for running applications. When the demand for memory is high, the shell sends a WM_CLOSE message to idle applications and closes them to make room for the active one. This automatic shutdown comes without any warning. Therefore, if you need to preserve the application's state from one session to another, you must handle the state persistence within your application. Typically, you archive any persistent state variables to a temporary file after the application receives a WM_CLOSE message, but before the message is passed to the operating system. Every time the application is started, it should check for this temporary file. If the file exists, the application should restore the application state.

The **Input Panel** button consists of two buttons grouped together and serves two purposes: bringing up and retracting the input panel window, and choosing the active input method. Each input method should display an icon on the left side of the **Input Panel** button to indicate the currently active input method. For example, the Palm PC uses a keyboard icon for the keyboard input method. If you provide a custom input method, it should instruct the **Input Panel** button to change the keyboard icon to the one of your design. For more information, see the **IIMCallback::SetImInfo** function.

You can use the Palm PC shell application programming interface (API) to make the system services available to your applications. In this chapter, we will discuss how your applications can do the following:

- Receive notifications
- Work with hardware navigation control buttons
- Access the input panel and manage input methods
- Send and receive infrared transfer

Receiving Notifications

The Palm PC notification system consists of a common dialog box for setting overall preferences, as well as for selecting options for individual items. The common dialog box can be accessed by any application. Notifications can include audio signals, a flashing LED, or interrupted messages on the screen.

Navigation Control Buttons

The Palm PC has four hardware navigation control buttons: **Action**, **Exit**, **Rocker**, and **Apps**. These buttons allow the user to launch applications, navigate lists, activate records, and exit from fields and dialog boxes with one hand. These buttons act similarly to familiar keyboard buttons, as described in the following table.

Navigation control button	Similar key on a keyboard
Action	ENTER
Exit	ESC
Rocker	UP ARROW and DOWN ARROW
App	No keyboard equivalent

The original equipment manufacturer (OEM) decides on the number and the purpose of the **Apps** switches. But every Palm PC must have at least one application-switching button mapped to the Voice Recorder application. If you associate **App1** with the Voice Recorder, the shell launches or reactivates that application when a user presses the application switching button. After that, the user can hold the **Action** button down to start recording and release it to stop recording. **Apps** switches make your applications easily accessible to users.

Pressing and releasing one or more navigation control buttons sends a sequence of virtual key codes to the shell. OEMs are responsible for providing the device driver to map the virtual key codes for the hardware control buttons. The following table lists a sample virtual key mapping. It may not be consistent with the driver installed on your target device.

Operations on buttons	Status message	Functional message
Press the **Action** button	VK_F23 (down)	
Release **Action**	VK_F23 (up)	VK_RETURN (down) and VK_RETURN (up)
Press the **Exit** button	VK_F24 (down)	
Release **Exit**	VK_F24 (up)	VK_ESCAPE (down) and VK_ESCAPE (up)
Press **RockUp**	VK_UP (down)	
Hold **RockUp** down		VK_PRIOR (down) and VK_PRIOR (up) for each auto-repeat
Release **RockUp**	VK_UP (up)	
Press **RockDown**	VK_DOWN (down)	
Hold **RockDown** down		VK_NEXT (down) and VK_NEXT (up) for each auto-repeat
Release **RockDown**	VK_DOWN (down)	

Operations on buttons	Status message	Functional message
Press **App1**	VK_LWIN (down)	0xC1 (down)
Release **App1**	VK_LWIN (up)	0xC1 (up)
Press **App2**	VK_LWIN (down)	0xC2 (down)
Release **App2**	VK_LWIN (up)	0xC2 (up)
Press **App3**	VK_LWIN (down)	0xC3 (down)
Release **App3**	VK_LWIN (up)	0xC3 (up)
Press **App4**	VK_LWIN (down)	0xC4 (down)
Release **App4**	VK_LWIN (up)	0xC4 (up)

For more information on virtual key mapping, see the device driver documentation available from the manufacturer of your target device.

The sample in the table illustrates how you might work with the hardware control buttons. A status message specifies the type and state of a button. **Action** can be pressed or released. The same applies to other buttons. A functional message specifies an intended action. For the application-switching buttons from **App1** through **App16**, it also specifies the identify of the button. The application-switching buttons are registered in the Windows CE registry. Because the functional messages correspond to the associated registry keys, **App1** is associated with **\HKEY_LOCAL_MACHINE\Software\Microsoft \Shell\Keys\40C1**, **App2** is associated with **\HKEY_LOCAL_MACHINE \Software\Microsoft\Shell\Keys\40C2**, and so on. Each key contains a named value that specifies the path of an application that is associated with a chosen button. When a user presses **App1**, for example, the 0xC1 message is sent to the shell. The shell searches the registry for the **40C1** key and launches the application using the information stored in the registry.

A user can use the Palm PC Buttons control panel to associate a navigation control button with any application that is accessible through the **Start** menu or its **Programs** submenu. Therefore, if you intend to use an installation script, install your application in the **Start** menu or **Programs** submenu folder. Do not modify the registry keys to associate your application with a button in the installation unless you notify the user of the change or present him or her with an opportunity to overwrite the suggested mapping.

The separation of status and functional messages gives you flexibility when you use the navigation control buttons in your applications. Because these messages are separate, a custom Note Taker application can start with the most recently saved note when a user presses and releases the associated application-switching button. Alternatively, it can start with a new document, if he or she presses and holds the button down. Furthermore, the user uses multiple buttons together to create chorded actions, in which different combinations of status messages are followed by various functional messages.

The shell includes standard implementation for chorded actions. When a user presses **Action** and **Exit**, the shell is sent a sequence of status messages with no functional messages: VK_23 (down), VK_24 (down), VK_24 (up), and VK_23 (up). The shell turns on the back light of the device. Similarly, when **Exit** and **Action** are chorded, the shell initiates the device calibration upon receiving the following messages: VK_24 (down), VK_23 (down), VK_LCONTROL (down), VK_MENU (down), VK_EQUAL (down), VK_LCONTROL (up), VK_MENU (up), VK_EQUAL (up), VK_23 (up), and VK_24 (up). Other standard implementations of chorded actions are listed in the following table.

Button 1/Button 2	Action sequence	Effects
Action/Exit	Press and hold **Action**, and then press **Exit**.	Turns on back light
Exit/Action	Press and hold **Exit**, and then press **Action**.	Initiates calibration
Exit/RockUp	Press and hold **Exit**, and then press **RockUp**.	Increases contrast
Exit/RockDown	Press and hold **Exit**, and then press **RockDown**.	Decreases contrast
Action/RockUp	Press and hold **Action**, and then press **RockUp**.	Implements Shift/Tab
Action/RockDown	Press and hold **Action**, and then press **RockDown**.	Implements Tab

To minimize potential interference with the standard shell functionality, you should avoid using such combinations of the navigation control buttons in your applications.

When Windows CE dispatches messages generated by the navigation control buttons to the Palm PC shell, the shell acts as a mediator between the hardware control buttons and your applications. This added level of indirection may deteriorate the performance of the application. If performance is critical, you can have these messages sent directly to your applications. Do this by calling the **SHGetAppKeyAssoc** (*szApp*) and **RegisterHotKey** (*hWndApp, keyId, KeyFlag, vkCode*) functions. The first function returns a valid virtual key code, if there is one, of the hardware button associated with the *szApp* application, for example, MyApp.exe. The second function registers the *hWndApp* window, which is your application, to receive the messages when the user presses a hardware button.

Whenever an application-switching button is mapped or remapped to an application, the application receives a WM_WININICHANGE message. If your application processes certain documents, as does Note Taker or Voice Recorder, you can have it call the **SHGetAppKeyAssoc** and **RegisterHotKey** functions, after receiving a WM_WININICHANGE message. This ensures that your application launches itself and creates a new document when the user presses and holds down the associated application-switching button.

Using Hardware Control Buttons

To use the hardware navigation control buttons effectively in your Palm PC application, follow these guidelines:

- Ensure that your application automatically places its focus in the controls that determine various data views when it retrieves a record from a database application, such as an address card in Contacts.

- Use the **RockUp** and **RockDown** buttons for viewing information, not manipulating it. An application should have these buttons associated with those data view controls; thus, the buttons are used to select the desired panel to view the record.

- Expose user interface (UI) elements for common actions in the main application view or directly map common actions to hardware control buttons.

- Ensure that the content of the control buttons does not change when a user tabs between them.

- Keep focus and default focus the same whenever possible, so that the **Action** button activates the control that currently has focus when the user presses it.

Input Panel and Input Methods

The Palm PC uses a touch-sensitive screen, rather than a keyboard, to receive user input, and it uses an input panel to select an input method (IM). The shell and the system cooperate to expose functions and structures, and to send window messages that make Palm PC applications aware of the input panel. Applications can respond to changes in the input panel state either by adjusting themselves or by altering the input panel states.

The Palm PC shell exposes a component object model (COM) interface. This interface allows you to install IMs that work with the input panel to translate user actions and manage input data. An IM is an in-process COM component that implements the **IInputMethod** interface. It manages the input panel window's screen and is responsible for rendering screen output and responding to user input. Typically, an IM converts user input into characters and then sends it to the system by means of exposed input panel functions. Windows CE provides a default QWERTY-keyboard IM to handle alphanumeric input. Another bundled IM is Pen Input.

The choice of IM available to the user is managed by the input panel control panel. The control panel communicates with the shell using the registry and exposes input panel-related API. IMs are added to the system using the COM component installation procedures.

The following illustration describes the interaction between applications, the GWE component of the operating system, the input panel, and IMs.

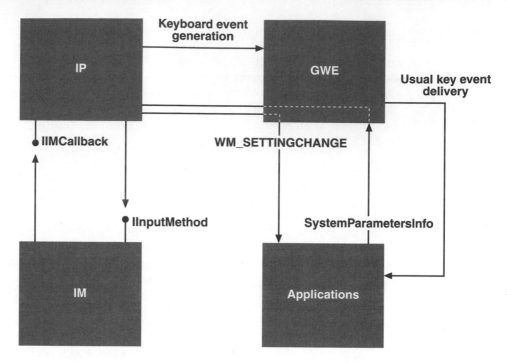

Palm PC interaction

Input Panel

The input panel UI elements include a window, a button on the taskbar, and a control panel. The **Input Panel** button and the control panel let a user change the state of the input panel window and select a favorite IM.

An input panel window is a rectangular area that the user can choose to dock above the taskbar or float in various screen positions. The default input panel window size is 240 pixels wide by 80 pixels high. The user can elect to display or hide the input panel by pressing or releasing the **Input Panel** button on the taskbar. The current state of the input panel is contained in the **SIPINFO** structure. Applications can enable or disable the visible state by setting or clearing the SIP_ON bit in the **fdwFlags** member. The user interacts with the visible input panel window to create system input.

The shell spawns a dedicated thread that registers itself as an input panel thread with the system. The thread creates an input panel window and performs the initialization before it enters a message loop to respond to messages and to the input panel user interface elements. The thread also dispatches messages to the IM's window. The thread calls into the IM object, permitting the IM to create windows that will respond as special input panel windows. The method of input is determined by the currently selected IM. The Palm PC has a default IM installed that displays a keyboard image and converts taps on the keyboard into characters. For more information on thread calls into an IM object, see "Installable Input Methods" later in this chapter.

Windows CE grants the input panel thread a special status. Windows created by the thread are topmost ones that are obscured by other windows. The input panel window, together with its children, will not receive the input focus when a user taps it. Because of this, the system focus remains unchanged when user input takes place using an input panel window. In most cases, the system focus should not change when the IM is called to take input. For example, if an edit control has the focus, the input panel should allow text input into the edit control without changing the focus.

Programming with an Input Panel

An input panel-aware application must know when the input panel changes its state and what the new or current state of the input is. The input panel state consists of its visibility status, its docking or floating status, and its size and position. The current input panel state is contained in the **SIPINFO** structure. A change in the input panel state will generate a WM_SETTINGCHANGE message that is sent to all top-level windows. Applications can determine the input panel information by using the **SHSipInfo** function.

The **rcSipRect** member of **SIPINFO** defines the input panel area of the screen. This area is separate from the working area regardless of application states.

Your application should not raise or lower the input panel on the screen unless you are certain that users want this feature.

Installable Input Methods

An IM is a mechanism for the user to provide text or graphics input by means of a touch screen. The IM occupies space inside an input panel window created by the system. It is responsible for rendering that space and for responding to user interaction in that space. Typically, an IM creates a child window of the input panel window to respond to input from the user. This is because the IM does not have access to the **WndProc** callback function of the input panel windows unless it subclasses that window. The communication between the input panel and an IM is facilitated by the **IInputMethod** and **IIMCallback** interfaces.

An installable IM is a COM component that implements the **IInputMethod** interface. Either you or an OEM may provide an installable IM and the user may change the IM that is selected into an input panel. The input panel dynamically loads the selected IM by invoking the **CoCreateInstance** function. When the user selects a new IM, the input panel frees the old IM by calling **Release** on the interface pointer. The input panel calls **IInputMethod** functions to notify the IM of events related to the input panel and to request information. On the other hand, the input panel implements and exposes the **IIMCallback** interface so that the IM can ask the input panel to send keystrokes and to change the icon displayed in the **Input Panel** button on the taskbar.

An IM is added to the input panel's pool of available IMs when it is installed as an in-process COM server. The input panel and the input panel control panel work in conjunction to present the list of installed IMs available to the user. Together, they allow the user to select the current IM.

In response to the input panel's calls to **IInputMethod**, an IM creates windows in the contexts of the input panel thread. This way, the input panel and the IM belong to the same message loop. Thus, the input panel thread can call into the window procedure of the windows created by IMs. Similarly, all the calls to **IIMCallback** should be made on the input panel thread. That is, an IM should only call the methods in response to a call coming through an **IInputMethod** method.

An IM can create desired worker threads to perform user interface functions. However, be sure that these worker threads do not call into **IIMCallback**. Windows created from worker threads belong to a message queue of a thread that is different from the input panel thread because certain GWE/USER window functions work well only if they are called from the same thread that has created the window.

To avoid mixing threads and the user interface within an IM, your application should not create any threads; rather, it should let the input panel thread do all work in the IM. Alternatively, your application can create worker threads itself, and then it can have the input panel thread work with all UIs for all of the IM windows.

Input Methods Registry Values

IMs are installed in the system as in-process COM servers using the standard COM registry keys. The key **HKEY_CLAS_ROOT\CLSID** contains subkeys representing COM components. The subkeys are textual representation class identifiers (CLSIDs). The CLSID subkeys contain an **InprocServer32** subkey with a default—no name—value specifying the path of the dynamic link library (DLL) that implements the component. The CLSID subkeys also contain an **IsSIPInputMethod** subkey with a default—no name—value equal to the string "**1**." The following is an example of IM registry entries.

Key	Default value
HKEY_CURRENT_USER\CLSID\	
{4a4a96d7-ae04-11d0-a4f8-00aa00a749b9}\	"MS QWERTY IM"
InprocServer32	"\Windows\alphanum.dll"
IsSIInputMethod	"1"

Technically, any COM component that implements **IInputMethod** is an IM capable of being selected into an input panel. The **IsSIPInputMethod** key provides a shortcut to presenting a list of IMs to the user without loading and querying each object for the **IInputMethod** interface.

If you develop your own IM component, you should supply the installation program to perform self-registration of the component by calling **DllRegitsterServer** and **DllUnregisterServer** functions. These functions are to be implemented in the IM server DLL. The input panel control panel provides no user interface for the self-registration service. For more information on COM component registration, see Chapter 2, "Programming Considerations" and the OLE documentation in the Microsoft Platform SDK.

Enabling Infrared Transfer from within an Application

Palm PC applications can transmit data, such as records or files, from one Palm PC device to another by means of the built-in Infrared Data Association (IrDA) port. Such transfers must take place between two compatible devices running the same application. Use **File/Send** or **File/Send To/Infrared Recipient** menu items to initiate the **Infrared Send** command. Similarly, use the **File/Receive** menu items to activate the **Infrared Receive** process. It is your responsibility to declare and implement the equivalent infrared transfer functions by using the standard Windows CE communication API. For more information about the communication API, see Chapter 5, "Using Communications."

The **Infrared Send** command initiates the IR transfer on selected data when the **File/Send** or **File/Send To/Infrared Recipient** menu item is invoked. It also brings up an **Infrared Send** dialog box on the sending device to display the transfer status. To receive the IR transfer, the receiving IR port must be aligned with the sending IR port. Tapping the **File/Receive** menu item activates the **Infrared Receive** command and displays an **Infrared Receive** dialog box. The dialog boxes remain open until the transfer is complete. An application can implement a simultaneous transfer of multiple records or files.

If the transfer fails, the **Infrared Receive** dialog box displays error messages. The whole process must be restarted if subsequent transfers are desired.

C H A P T E R   3 3

Designing a User Interface for a Palm PC

The Palm PC is a mobile companion to a Windows-based desktop computer. It incorporates many of the graphical user interface (UI) elements that are familiar to users of other Windows-based platforms. These elements include a desktop, a taskbar, windows, dialog boxes, menus, and controls. However, unlike other Windows-based platforms, a Palm PC supports voice and ink input; has a small, portrait-oriented touch-sensitive screen; and relies for user input on an input panel and stylus, instead of a traditional keyboard. Though the principles of user interface design discussed in previous chapters also apply to Palm PC applications, this chapter focuses on design considerations specific to the Palm PC.

For more information on general design considerations for all Windows CE-based devices, see Chapter 6, "Designing a User Interface for Windows CE."

Design Guidelines

Palm PCs are designed with simplicity and accessibility in mind. An application that exposes too many functions on its interface risks alienating the user by making the application seem too complex. When you design your application, place commands for critical application features in the most accessible area available, usually on a toolbar, and commands for advanced or infrequently used features in a less accessible area, such as on a menu. Where you place a command item is important because Palm PC applications do not contain separate menu bars and toolbars to help users organize the interface. They contain command bars, a combination toolbar and menu bar, which cannot display toolbar buttons and menus at the same time. To issue a command, users must take an extra step by exposing either the toolbar or the menu bar portion of the command bar before issuing a command. For information on working with command bars, see Chapter 6, "Designing a User Interface for Windows CE."

Other considerations to be aware of when designing a user interface include displaying data and placing controls. Follow these guidelines when you create a Palm PC application:

- Ensure that top-level application windows are accessible from the **Start** menu because running applications do not get a button on the taskbar. However, top-level dialog boxes without parents will be adopted by the desktop. This ensures that a user can bring these dialog boxes to the foreground by tapping the desktop button on the taskbar. Any owned pop-up window appears when its owner is brought to the foreground.

- Display data in a single-column format to suit the narrow screen of a Palm PC.

- Avoid using a large number of controls in windows and dialog boxes, because they require a large amount of screen space. Instead, dedicate as much space as possible to displaying user data.

- Do not provide a **Close** button on the application's command bar. A Palm PC automatically closes idle applications when an active application requests more memory than is available.

Working with the Desktop and Taskbar

The Palm PC desktop provides a user with a familiar interface for launching applications and switching between tasks. The background of the desktop can consist of a wallpaper image, no wallpaper, or an Active Desktop. Active Desktops can be customized by users to contain Web or HTML content supplied by a Mobile Channels content provider. In Active Desktop mode, each desktop component is displayed in its own HTML control, all of which are tiled to share the available screen space. If a user adds or removes a component, the total space is redistributed equally among the remaining components.

The Palm PC desktop includes a taskbar, which contains a **Start** menu, an **Input Panel** button, a **Desktop** button, and date and time annunciator panel. Because taskbars do not contain buttons for running applications, users cannot switch between applications by pressing a taskbar button. Instead, users launch new applications or reactivate idle applications using the **Start** menu, or by pressing application-switching buttons found on the device casing.

The **Start** menu has two components: the main menu and cascading menus. The main menu, which has a maximum height of 320 pixels, contains four standard items: Programs, Settings, Find, and Help. It also has room for 11 additional applications known as Favorites. If there are too few applications on the main menu to use the entire 320 pixels, it shrinks vertically to fit the list of Favorites. The minimum height of the main menu equals the height of the Windows CE banner displayed on the left side of the menu. The width of the main menu is fixed; item names are truncated with ellipses if they are too long.

A cascading menu can accommodate more items than can fit vertically in a single column by displaying a scroll arrow above the top item and below the bottom item. As a menu cascades, it overlaps the previous menu, including the main menu. A cascading menu has a maximum width of 180 pixels, but it truncates to 120 pixels to accommodate three columns of menus on the screen at one time. As on other Windows-based platforms, the main and cascading menus of a Palm PC use an icon associated with the menu item that is 16 by 16 pixels. Items that cascade to additional menus are appended with a triangular arrow. Items on a cascading menu appear in alphabetical order by default. Because users cannot manipulate or view the file system on a Palm PC, directories are not displayed on cascading menus.

The **Input Panel** button displays and hides the input panel, a user interface element that contains a keyboard. Users operate the keyboard using a touch screen and a stylus. When the input panel is displayed, application windows typically resize so that the input panel does not obscure any information. The icon on the **Input Panel** button changes to reflect the current input method. For example, if handwriting recognition is the current input method, the button displays the handwriting icon, and if the keyboard is the selected input method, the button displays the keyboard icon.

The **Desktop** button provides quick access to the desktop. When the button is pressed, it brings the desktop forward, into focus, effectively hiding the current application. When the desktop is in the foreground, the **Desktop** button appears depressed to denote that the desktop is displayed. Pressing the **Desktop** button while it appears depressed causes the previously active application to reactivate. The **Desktop** button is 23 by 22 pixels, the size of a standard toolbar button, and is located on the far right edge of the taskbar.

The date and time annunciator panel provides immediate access to date and time information from any state or application. It also displays icons, called annunciators, which indicate that a user notification is active. Taskbars can contain up to six annunciator icons at once for different applications. However, only one instance of an icon for any application is displayed at a time. If more than six annunciators are displayed, the least recent annunciator is hidden. When you design an application, include an annunciator only when necessary in order to conserve space in the taskbar. If you do include an annunciator, be sure that icons are unambiguous.

Designing and Placing Dialog Boxes

The Palm PC supports most common Win32 application programming interface (API) window and dialog box functions; however, dialog boxes for a Palm PC application must be much more dynamic than dialog boxes for other Windows-based platforms, because the input panel can appear and disappear frequently and unpredictably.

When you design a dialog box, keep the following guidelines in mind to ensure that it will work in conjunction with the input panel:

- Use the entire screen for the dialog box and make it easily resizable when the input panel appears and disappears.

- Place text input and output controls outside the area used by the input panel when you design a full-screen dialog box. This will ensure that the dialog box will not be hidden when the input panel is raised and lowered.

- Design the dialog box to resize, if necessary, to prevent the input panel from obscuring critical data or an area that accepts text. This may require that you move the controls to other panels.

- Size a dialog box to fit, without being cramped, above the screen area occupied by the input panel.

- Center a partial-screen dialog box above the space reserved for the input panel, even if the input panel is not displayed when the dialog box is created. This avoids the possibility that the input panel will obscure the dialog box. However, if the space above the input panel cannot accommodate a partial-screen dialog box, align the top of the dialog box with the top of the screen.

Choosing Menus and Controls

Palm PC applications can use all of the standard menus and controls available in Windows CE. For suggestions on choosing menus and controls for your application, see Chapter 6, "Designing a User Interface for Windows CE."

Receiving User Input for a Palm PC

Palm PCs support several types of user input devices, such as an input panel that emulates a keyboard, a touch screen, a stylus, and an ink-recognition application.

Conventions for implementing various user input devices into your application are described in the *Windows Interface Guidelines for Software Design*.

Appendix

APPENDIX A

Lists of Functions and Interfaces

ActiveSync Functions

The following functions are implemented in the Windows CE-based platform ActiveSync module by the ActiveSync service manager:

InitObjType
GetObjTypeInfo
ObjectNotify
ReportStatus

ActiveSync Interfaces

The following interfaces are implemented on the desktop computer by an ActiveSync service provider and Windows CE Services:

IReplStore
IReplObjHandler
IReplNotify
IEnumReplItem

IReplStore interface methods

ActivateDialog	**BytesToObject**
CompareItem	**CompareStoreIDs**
CopyObject	**FindFirstItem**
FindItemClose	**FindNextItem**
FreeObject	**GetConflictInfo**
GetFolderInfo	**GetObjTypeUIData**
GetStoreInfo	**Initialize**

IsFolderChanged

IsItemReplicated

ObjectToBytes

ReportStatus

IsItemChanged

IsValidObject

RemoveDuplicates

UpdateItem

IReplNotify interface methods

GetWindow

OnItemNotify

SetStatusText

QueryDevice

IReplObjHandler interface methods

DeleteObj

GetPacket

SetPacket

Setup

Reset

IEnumReplItem interface methods

Clone

GetFolderHandle

Next

Reset

Skip

Clipboard Functions

Windows CE supports the following clipboard functions:

CloseClipboard

EmptyClipboard

GetClipboardData

GetClipboardFormatName

GetOpenClipboardWindow

IsClipboardFormatAvailable

SetClipboardData

CountClipboardFormats

EnumClipboardFormats

GetClipboardDataAlloc

GetClipboardOwner

GetPriorityClipboardFormat

RegisterClipboardFormat

OpenClipboard

COM/OLE Functions

Windows CE supports the following COM functions:

CLSIDFromString	CoCreateInstance
CoFreeLibrary	CoFreeUnusedLibraries
CoGetClassObject	CoInitializeEx
CoLoadLibrary	CoTaskMemAlloc
CoTaskMemFree	CoTaskMemRealloc
CoUninitialize	StringFromCLSID
StringFromGUID2	StringFromIID

Windows CE supports the following OLE functions:

CreateOleAdviseHolder

OleCreate

OleDraw

OleIsRunning

OleRun

OleSave

OleSetContainedObject

Windows CE supports the following Automation functions:

SysAllocString	SysReAllocString
SysAllocStringLen	SysReAllocStringLen
SysFreeString	SysStringLen
All variant type functions	All SafeArray functions
DispGetParam	DispGetIDsOfNames
DispInvoke	CreateErrorInfo
SetErrorInfo	CreateTypeLib2
LoadTypeLib	LoadRegTypeLib
RegisterTypeLib	SysAllocStringByteLen
SysStringByteLen	VectorFromBstr
BstrFromVector	All variant utility functions

Windows CE supports the following OLE storage functions:

ReadClassStg

ReadClassStm

StgCreateDocfile

StgOpenStorage

WriteClassStg

WriteClassStm

StgCreateDocfileOnILockBytes

StgOpenStorageOnILockBytes

Windows CE does not support the following functions:

Function	Use instead
OleUninitialize	CoUninitialize
OleInitialize	CoInitializeEx
CoInitialize	CoInitializeEx

Connection Notification Interfaces

The following interfaces are implemented by the application:

IDccManSink	**IDccManSink::QueryInterface**
IDccManSink::AddRef	**IDccManSink::Release**
IDccManSink::OnLogActive	**IDccManSink::OnLogAnswered**
IDccManSink::OnLogDisconnection	**IDccManSink::OnLogError**
IDccManSink::OnLogInactive	**IDccManSink::OnLogIpAddr**
IDccManSink::OnLogListen	**IDccManSink::OnLogTerminated**

The following interfaces are implemented by the Windows CE Services connection manager:

IDccMan

IDccMan::QueryInterface

IDccMan::AddRef

IDccMan::Release

IDccMan::Advise

IDccMan::ShowCommSettings

IDccMan::Unadvise

Contacts Database Functions

Windows CE supports the following functions for using the Contacts database:

AddAddressCard	CloseAddressBook
CreateAddressBook	DeleteAddressCard
FreeAddressCard	GetAddressCardIndex
GetAddressCardOid	GetAddressCardProperties
GetColumnProperties	GetMatchingEntry
GetNumberOfAddressCards	GetPropertyDataStruct
GetSortOrder	ModifyAddressCard
OpenAddressBook	OpenAddressCard
RecountCards	SetColumnProperties
SetMask	SetSortOrder

Control Functions

Windows CE supports the following control functions:

CreateWindow
InitHTMLControl
LoadLibrary

Windows CE supports the following control methods:

IWebBrowser::get_Busy	IWebBrowser::get_LocationURL
IWebBrowser::Navigate	IWebBrowser::Refresh
IWebBrowser::Refresh2	IWebBrowser::Stop
DWebBrowserEvents::NavigateComplete	DWebBrowserEvents::BeforeNavigate
DWebBrowserEvents::FrameBeforeNavigate	DWebBrowserEvents::FrameNavigateComplete
DWebBrowserEvents::FrameNewWindow	DWebBrowserEvents::NewWindow
DWebBrowserEvents::TitleChange	

Windows CE supports the following control messages:

DTM_ADDTEXT	DTM_ADDTEXTW
DTM_ANCHOR	DTM_ANCHORW
DTM_ENABLESHRINK	DTM_ENDOFSOURCE
DTM_IMAGEFAIL	DTM_SELECTALL
DTM_SETIMAGE	NM_BASE
NM_CONTEXTMENU	NM_HOTSPOT
NM_HTMLVIEW	NM_INLINE_IMAGE
NM_INLINE_SOUND	NM_META
NM_TITLE	WM_SETTEXT

Database Management Functions

Windows CE supports the following functions for database management:

CeCreateDatabase	**CeOpenDatabase**
CeFindFirstDatabase	**CeFindNextDatabase**
CeDeleteDatabase	**CeDeleteRecord**
CeSeekDatabase	**CeReadRecordProps**
CeWriteRecordProps	**CeOidGetInfo**
CeSetDatabaseInfo	

Dialog Box Functions

Windows CE supports the following application-defined dialog box functions:

CreateDialog (modeless)	**CreateDialogIndirect (modeless)**
CreateDialogIndirectParam (modeless)	**CreateDialogParam (modeless)**
DialogBox (modal)	**DialogBoxIndirect (modal)**
DialogBoxIndirectParam (modal)	**DialogBoxParam(modal)**
EndDialog(modal)	**GetDlgCtrlID**
GetDialogBaseUnits	**GetDlgItem**
GetDlgItemInt	**SetDlgItemInt**

Windows CE supports the following application-defined dialog box messages:

DM_GETDEFID	**DM_SETDEFID**
EM_SETTABSTOPS	**LB_SETTABSTOPS**
WM_CANCELMODE	**WM_CTLCOLORDLG**
WM_GETDLGCODE	**WM_INITDIALOG**
WM_NEXTDLGCTL	

Windows CE supports the following common dialog box functions:

ChooseColor
CommDlgExtendedError
GetOpenFileName
GetSaveFileName
PrintDlg

Windows CE supports the following common dialog box messages:

CDM_GETFILEPATH	CDM_GETFOLDERIDLIST
CDM_GETFOLDERPATH	CDM_GETSPEC
CDM_HIDECONTROL	CDM_SETCONTROLTEXT
CDM_SETDEFEXT	CDN_TYPECHANGE

File and Scale Control Functions

Windows CE supports the following file and scale control functions:

AddPropSheetPageProc	**CommandBands_AddAdornments**
CommandBands_AddBands	**CommandBands_Create**
CommandBands_GetCommandBar	**CommandBands_GetRestoreInformation**
CommandBands_Height	**CommandBands_IsVisible**
CommandBands_Show	**CommandBar_AddAdornments**
CommandBar_AddBitmap	**CommandBar_AddButtons**
CommandBar_AddTooltips	**CommandBar_Create**
CommandBar_Destroy	**CommandBar_DrawMenuBar**
CommandBar_GetMenu	**CommandBar_Height**
CommandBar_Insert	**CommandBar_InsertButton**
CommandBar_InsertComboBox	**CommandBar_InsertMenubar**
CommandBar_InsertMenubarEx	**CommandBar_IsVisible**
CommandBar_Show	**CreateMappedBitmap**

CreatePropertySheetPage

CreateStatusWindow

CreateToolbarEx

CreateWindowEx

DestroyPropertySheetPage

DrawStatusText

ExtensionPropSheetPageProc

GetClientRect

GetClientRect

GetSubMenu

ImageList_Add

ImageList_AddIcon

ImageList_AddMasked

ImageList_BeginDrag

ImageList_Copy

ImageList_Create

ImageList_Destroy

ImageList_DragEnter

ImageList_DragLeave

ImageList_DragMove

ImageList_DragShowNolock

ImageList_Draw

ImageList_DrawEx

ImageList_DrawIndirect

ImageList_Duplicate

ImageList_EndDrag

ImageList_GetBkColor

ImageList_GetDragImage

ImageList_GetIcon

ImageList_GetIconSize

ImageList_GetImageCount

ImageList_GetImageInfo

ImageList_LoadBitmap

ImageList_LoadImage

ImageList_Merge

ImageList_Remove

ImageList_RemoveAll

ImageList_RemoveAll

ImageList_Replace

ImageList_ReplaceIcon

ImageList_SetBkColor

ImageList_SetDragCursorImage

ImageList_SetIconSize

ImageList_SetImageCount

ImageList_SetOverlayImage

InitCommonControls

InitCommonControlsEx

MoveWindow

PropertySheet

PropSheetPageProc

PropSheetProc

SetWindowPos

SetWindowText

TabCtrl_GetExtendedStyle

TabCtrl_SetExtendedStyle

Windows CE supports the following file and scale macros:

CreateUpDownControl

Header_CreateDragImage

Header_DeleteItem

Header_GetImageList

Header_GetItem

Header_GetItemCount

Header_GetItemRect

Header_GetOrderArray

Header_InsertItem

Header_Layout

Header_OrderToIndex

Header_SetHotDivider

Header_SetItem

ListView_ApproximateViewRect

ListView_CreateDragImage

ListView_DeleteColumn

ListView_EditLabel

ListView_FindItem

ListView_GetCallbackMask

ListView_GetColumn

ListView_GetColumnWidth

ListView_GetEditControl

ListView_GetExtendedListViewStyle

ListView_GetImageList

ListView_GetItem

ListView_GetItemPosition

ListView_GetItemSpacing

ListView_GetItemText

ListView_GetOrigin

ListView_GetSelectionMark

ListView_GetSubItemRect

ListView_GetTextColor

ListView_GetViewRect

ListView_InsertColumn

ListView_RedrawItems

ListView_SetBkColor

ListView_SetColumn

ListView_SetColumnWidth

ListView_SetExtendedListViewStyle

ListView_SetImageList

ListView_SetItemCount

ListView_SetItemPosition

ListView_SetItemState

ListView_SetSelectionMark

ListView_SetTextColor

ListView_SubItemHitTest

MonthCal_GetColor

Header_SetImageList

Header_SetOrderArray

ListView_Arrange

ListView_DeleteAllItems

ListView_DeleteItem

ListView_EnsureVisible

ListView_GetBkColor

ListView_GetCheckState

ListView_GetColumnOrderArray

ListView_GetCountPerPage

ListView_GetExtendedListviewStyle

ListView_GetHeader

ListView_GetISearchString

ListView_GetItemCount

ListView_GetItemRect

ListView_GetItemState

ListView_GetNextItem

ListView_GetSelectedCount

ListView_GetStringWidth

ListView_GetTextBkColor

ListView_GetTopIndex

ListView_HitTest

ListView_InsertItem

ListView_Scroll

ListView_SetCallbackMask

ListView_SetColumnOrderArray

ListView_SetExtendedListViewStyle

ListView_SetIconSpacing

ListView_SetItem

ListView_SetItemCountEx

ListView_SetItemPosition32

ListView_SetItemText

ListView_SetTextBkColor

ListView_SortItems

ListView_Update

MonthCal_GetCurSel

MonthCal_GetFirstDayOfWeek

MonthCal_GetMaxSelCount

MonthCal_GetMaxTodayWidth

MonthCal_GetMinReqRect

MonthCal_GetMonthDelta

MonthCal_GetMonthRange

MonthCal_GetRange

MonthCal_GetSelRange

MonthCal_GetToday

MonthCal_HitTest

MonthCal_SetColor

MonthCal_SetCurSel

MonthCal_SetDayState

MonthCal_SetFirstDayOfWeek

MonthCal_SetMaxSelCount

MonthCal_SetMonthDelta

MonthCal_SetRange

MonthCal_SetSelRange

MonthCal_SetToday

PropSheet_AddPage

PropSheet_Apply

PropSheet_CancelToClose

PropSheet_Changed

PropSheet_GetCurrentPageHwnd

PropSheet_GetTabControl

PropSheet_IsDialogMessage

PropSheet_PressButton

PropSheet_QuerySiblings

PropSheet_RebootSystem

PropSheet_RemovePage

PropSheet_RestartWindows

PropSheet_SetCurSel

PropSheet_SetCurSelByID

PropSheet_SetFinishText

PropSheet_SetTitle

TabCtrl_AdjustRect

TabCtrl_DeleteAllItems

TabCtrl_DeleteItem

TabCtrl_DeselectAll

TabCtrl_GetCurFocus

TabCtrl_GetCurSel

TabCtrl_GetExtendedStyle

TabCtrl_GetImageList

TabCtrl_GetItem

TabCtrl_GetItemCount

TabCtrl_GetItemRect

TabCtrl_GetRowCount

TabCtrl_HighlightItem

TabCtrl_HitTest

TabCtrl_InsertItem

TabCtrl_RemoveImage

TabCtrl_SetCurSel

TabCtrl_SetExtendedStyle

TabCtrl_SetImageList

TabCtrl_SetItem

TabCtrl_SetItemExtra

TabCtrl_SetItemSize

TabCtrl_SetMinTabWidth

TabCtrl_SetPadding

TreeView_CreateDragImage

TreeView_DeleteAllItems

TreeView_DeleteItem

TreeView_EditLabel

TreeView_EndEditLabelNow

TreeView_EnsureVisible

TreeView_Expand

TreeView_GetChild

TreeView_GetCount

TreeView_GetDropHilite

TreeView_GetEditControl

TreeView_GetFirstVisible

TreeView_GetImageList

TreeView_GetIndent

TreeView_GetISearchString

TreeView_GetItem

TreeView_GetItemRect

TreeView_GetNextItem

TreeView_GetNextSibling

TreeView_GetNextVisible

TreeView_GetParent

TreeView_GetPrevSibling

TreeView_GetPrevVisible

TreeView_GetRoot

TreeView_GetSelection

TreeView_GetVisibleCount

TreeView_HitTest

TreeView_InsertItem

TreeView_Select

TreeView_SelectDropTarget

TreeView_SelectItem

TreeView_SelectSetFirstVisible

TreeView_SetImageList

TreeView_SetIndent

TreeView_SetItem

TreeView_SortChildren

TreeView_SortChildrenCB

Windows CE supports the following file and scale control messages:

DTM_GETMCCOLOR

DTM_GETMCFONT

DTM_GETMONTHCAL

DTM_GETRANGE

DTM_GETSYSTEMTIME

DTM_SETFORMAT

DTM_SETMCCOLOR

DTM_SETMCFONT

DTM_SETRANGE

DTM_SETSYSTEMTIME

DTN_CLOSEUP

DTN_DATETIMECHANGE

DTN_DROPDOWN

DTN_FORMAT

DTN_FORMATQUERY

DTN_USERSTRING

DTN_WMKEYDOWN

HDM_CREATEDRAGIMAGE

HDM_DELETEITEM

HDM_GETIMAGELIST

HDM_GETITEM

HDM_GETITEMCOUNT

HDM_GETITEMRECT

HDM_GETORDERARRAY

HDM_HITTEST

HDM_INSERTITEM

HDM_LAYOUT

HDM_ORDERTOINDEX

HDM_SETHOTDIVIDER

HDM_SETIMAGELIST

HDM_SETITEM

HDM_SETORDERARRAY

HDN_BEGINDRAG

HDN_BEGINTRACK

HDN_DIVIDERDBLCLICK

HDN_ENDDRAG

HDN_ENDTRACK

HDN_GETDISPINFO

HDN_ITEMCHANGED

HDN_ITEMCHANGING

HDN_ITEMCLICK

HDN_ITEMDBLCLICK

HDN_TRACK

LVM_APPROXIMATEVIEWRECT

LVM_ARRANGE	LVM_CREATEDRAGIMAGE
LVM_DELETEALLITEMS	LVM_DELETECOLUMN
LVM_DELETEITEM	LVM_EDITLABEL
LVM_ENSUREVISIBLE	LVM_FINDITEM
LVM_GETBKCOLOR	LVM_GETCALLBACKMASK
LVM_GETCOLUMN	LVM_GETCOLUMNORDERARRAY
LVM_GETCOLUMNWIDTH	LVM_GETCOUNTPERPAGE
LVM_GETEDITCONTROL	LVM_GETEXTENDEDLISTVIEWSTYLE
LVM_GETHEADER	LVM_GETIMAGELIST
LVM_GETISEARCHSTRING	LVM_GETITEM
LVM_GETITEMCOUNT	LVM_GETITEMPOSITION
LVM_GETITEMRECT	LVM_GETITEMSPACING
LVM_GETITEMSTATE	LVM_GETITEMTEXT
LVM_GETNEXTITEM	LVM_GETNUMBEROFWORKAREAS
LVM_GETORIGIN	LVM_GETSELECTEDCOUNT
LVM_GETSELECTIONMARK	LVM_GETSTRINGWIDTH
LVM_GETSUBITEMRECT	LVM_GETTEXTBKCOLOR
LVM_GETTEXTCOLOR	LVM_GETTOPINDEX
LVM_GETVIEWRECT	LVM_GETWORKAREAS
LVM_HITTEST	LVM_INSERTCOLUMN
LVM_INSERTITEM	LVM_REDRAWITEMS
LVM_SCROLL	LVM_SETBKCOLOR
LVM_SETCALLBACKMASK	LVM_SETCOLUMN
LVM_SETCOLUMNORDERARRAY	LVM_SETCOLUMNWIDTH
LVM_SETEXTENDEDLISTVIEWSTYLE	LVM_SETICONSPACING
LVM_SETIMAGELIST	LVM_SETITEM
LVM_SETITEMCOUNT	LVM_SETITEMPOSITION
LVM_SETITEMPOSITION32	LVM_SETITEMSTATE
LVM_SETITEMTEXT	LVM_SETSELECTIONMARK
LVM_SETTEXTBKCOLOR	LVM_SETTEXTCOLOR
LVM_SETWORKAREAS	LVM_SORTITEMS
LVM_SUBITEMHITTEST	LVM_UPDATE
LVN_BEGINDRAG	LVN_BEGINLABELEDIT
LVN_COLUMNCLICK	LVN_DELETEALLITEMS
LVN_DELETEITEM	LVN_ENDDRAG
LVN_ENDLABELEDIT	LVN_GETDISPINFO

LVN_INSERTITEM

LVN_ITEMACTIVATE

LVN_ITEMCHANGED

LVN_ITEMCHANGING

LVN_KEYDOWN

LVN_MARQUEEBEGIN

LVN_ODCACHEHINT

LVN_ODFINDITEM

LVN_ODSTATECHANGED

LVN_SETDISPINFO

MCM_GETCOLOR

MCM_GETCURSEL

MCM_GETFIRSTDAYOFWEEK

MCM_GETMAXSELCOUNT

MCM_GETMAXTODAYWIDTH

MCM_GETMINREQRECT

MCM_GETMONTHDELTA

MCM_GETMONTHRANGE

MCM_GETRANGE

MCM_GETSELRANGE

MCM_GETTODAY

MCM_HITTEST

MCM_SETCOLOR

MCM_SETCURSEL

MCM_SETDAYSTATE

MCM_SETFIRSTDAYOFWEEK

MCM_SETMAXSELCOUNT

MCM_SETMONTHDELTA

MCM_SETRANGE

MCM_SETSELRANGE

MCM_SETTODAY

MCN_GETDAYSTATE

MCN_GETDAYSTATE

MCN_SELCHANGE

MCN_SELECT

MCN_SETDAYSTATE

NM_CLICK

NM_CUSTOMDRAW

NM_CUSTOMDRAW

NM_CUSTOMDRAW

NM_KEYDOWN

NM_NCHITTEST

NMCUSTOMDRAW

NMCUSTOMDRAW

NMRBAUTOSIZE

NMREBAR

NMTOOLBAR

PBM_DELTAPOS

PBM_GETPOS

PBM_GETRANGE

PBM_SETPOS

PBM_SETRANGE

PBM_SETRANGE32

PBM_SETSTEP

PBM_STEPIT

PSM_ADDPAGE

PSM_APPLY

PSM_CANCELTOCLOSE

PSM_CHANGED

PSM_GETCURRENTPAGEHWND

PSM_GETTABCONTROL

PSM_ISDIALOGMESSAGE

PSM_PRESSBUTTON

PSM_QUERYSIBLINGS

PSM_REBOOTSYSTEM

PSM_REMOVEPAGE

PSM_RESTARTWINDOWS

PSM_SETCURSEL

PSM_SETCURSELID

PSM_SETFINISHTEXT

PSM_SETTITLE

PSM_UNCHANGED

PSN_APPLY

PSN_HELP

PSN_KILLACTIVE

PSN_QUERYCANCEL

PSN_RESET

PSN_SETACTIVE

RB_DELETEBAND

RB_GETBANDBORDERS

RB_GETBANDCOUNT

RB_GETBANDINFO

RB_GETBARHEIGHT

RB_GETBARINFO

RB_GETBKCOLOR

RB_GETRECT

RB_GETROWCOUNT

RB_GETROWHEIGHT

RB_GETTEXTCOLOR

RB_GETTEXTCOLOR

RB_HITTEST

RB_IDTOINDEX

RB_INSERTBAND

RB_MAXIMIZEBAND

RB_MINIMIZEBAND

RB_SETBANDINFO

RB_SETBARINFO

RB_SETBKCOLOR

RB_SETPARENT

RB_SETTEXTCOLOR

RB_SHOWBAND

RB_SIZETORECT

RBHITTESTINFO

RBN_AUTOSIZE

RBN_BEGINDRAG

RBN_ENDDRAG

RBN_HEIGHTCHANGE

RBN_LAYOUTCHANGED

REBARBANDINFO

REBARINFO

SB_GETBORDERS

SB_GETPARTS

SB_GETRECT

SB_GETTEXT

SB_GETTEXTLENGTH

SB_ISSIMPLE

SB_SETICON

SB_SETMINHEIGHT

SB_SETPARTS

SB_SETTEXT

SB_SIMPLE

SB_SIMPLEMODECHANGE

TB_ADDBITMAP

TB_ADDBUTTONS

TB_ADDSTRING

TB_AUTOSIZE

TB_BUTTONCOUNT

TB_BUTTONSTRUCTSIZE

TB_CHANGEBITMAP

TB_CHECKBUTTON

TB_COMMANDTOINDEX

TB_DELETEBUTTON

TB_ENABLEBUTTON

TB_GETBITMAP

TB_GETBITMAPFLAGS

TB_GETBUTTON

TB_GETBUTTONINFO

TB_GETBUTTONSIZE

TB_GETBUTTONTEXT

TB_GETDISABLEDIMAGELIST

TB_GETDISABLEDIMAGELIST

TB_GETIMAGELIST

TB_GETINSERTMARK

TB_GETITEMRECT

TB_GETMAXSIZE

TB_GETRECT

TB_GETROWS

TB_GETSTATE

TB_GETSTYLE

TB_GETTEXTROWS

TB_GETTOOLTIPS

TB_HIDEBUTTON

TB_HIGHLIGHTBUTTON

TB_INDETERMINATE

TB_INSERTBUTTON

TB_INSERTMARKHITTEST

TB_ISBUTTONCHECKED

TB_ISBUTTONENABLED

TB_ISBUTTONHIDDEN

TB_ISBUTTONHIGHLIGHTED

TB_ISBUTTONINDETERMINATE

TB_ISBUTTONPRESSED

TB_LOADIMAGES

TB_MAPACCELERATOR

TB_MOVEBUTTON

TB_PRESSBUTTON

TB_REPLACEBITMAP

TB_SETBITMAPSIZE

TB_SETBUTTONINFO

TB_SETBUTTONSIZE

TB_SETBUTTONWIDTH

TB_SETCMDID

TB_SETDISABLEDIMAGELIST

TB_SETDISABLEDIMAGELIST

TB_SETDRAWTEXTFLAGS

TB_SETIMAGELIST

TB_SETINDENT

TB_SETINSERTMARK

TB_SETMAXTEXTROWS

TB_SETPARENT

TB_SETROWS

TB_SETSTATE

TB_SETSTYLE

TB_SETTOOLTIPS

TBM_CLEARSEL

TBM_CLEARTICS

TBM_GETBUDDY

TBM_GETCHANNELRECT

TBM_GETLINESIZE

TBM_GETNUMTICS

TBM_GETPAGESIZE

TBM_GETPOS

TBM_GETPTICS

TBM_GETRANGEMAX

TBM_GETRANGEMIN

TBM_GETSELEND

TBM_GETSELSTART

TBM_GETTHUMBLENGTH

TBM_GETTHUMBRECT

TBM_GETTIC

TBM_GETTICPOS

TBM_SETBUDDY

TBM_SETLINESIZE

TBM_SETPAGESIZE

TBM_SETPOS

TBM_SETRANGE

TBM_SETRANGEMAX

TBM_SETRANGEMIN

TBM_SETSEL

TBM_SETSELEND

TBM_SETSELSTART

TBM_SETTHUMBLENGTH

TBM_SETTIC

TBM_SETTICFREQ

TBN_DELETINGBUTTON

TBN_DROPDOWN

TBN_GETBUTTONINFO

TCM_DELETEALLITEMS

TCM_DESELECTALL

TCM_GETCURSEL

TCM_GETIMAGELIST

TCM_GETITEMCOUNT

TCM_GETROWCOUNT

TCM_HIGHLIGHTITEM

TCM_INSERTITEM

TCM_SETCURFOCUS

TCM_SETEXTENDEDSTYLE

TCM_SETITEM

TCM_SETITEMSIZE

TCM_SETPADDING

TCN_KEYDOWN

TCN_SELCHANGING

TVM_DELETEITEM

TVM_ENDEDITLABELNOW

TVM_EXPAND

TVM_GETEDITCONTROL

TVM_GETINDENT

TVM_GETITEM

TVM_GETNEXTITEM

TVM_HITTEST

TVM_SELECTITEM

TVM_SETIMAGELIST

TVM_SETITEM

TVM_SORTCHILDREN

TVN_BEGINDRAG

TVN_DELETEITEM

TVN_GETDISPINFO

TVN_ITEMEXPANDING

TVN_SELCHANGED

TVN_SETDISPINFO

UDM_GETBASE

UDM_GETPOS

TCM_ADJUSTRECT

TCM_DELETEITEM

TCM_GETCURFOCUS

TCM_GETEXTENDEDSTYLE

TCM_GETITEM

TCM_GETITEMRECT

TCM_GETTOOLTIPS

TCM_HITTEST

TCM_REMOVEIMAGE

TCM_SETCURSEL

TCM_SETIMAGELIST

TCM_SETITEMEXTRA

TCM_SETMINTABWIDTH

TCM_SETTOOLTIPS

TCN_SELCHANGE

TVM_CREATEDRAGIMAGE

TVM_EDITLABEL

TVM_ENSUREVISIBLE

TVM_GETCOUNT

TVM_GETIMAGELIST

TVM_GETISEARCHSTRING

TVM_GETITEMRECT

TVM_GETVISIBLECOUNT

TVM_INSERTITEM

TVM_SETIMAGELIST

TVM_SETINDENT

TVM_SETITEM

TVM_SORTCHILDRENCB

TVN_BEGINLABELEDIT

TVN_ENDLABELEDIT

TVN_ITEMEXPANDED

TVN_KEYDOWN

TVN_SELCHANGING

UDM_GETACCEL

UDM_GETBUDDY

UDM_GETRANGE

UDM_SETACCEL   UDM_SETBASE

UDM_SETBUDDY   UDM_SETPOS

UDM_SETRANGE   UDN_DELTAPOS

WM_COMMAND   WM_HSCROLL

WM_NOTIFY   WM_SETREDRAW

WM_VSCROLL

File Filter Interfaces

The following interface and methods are implemented by
Windows CE Services:

ICeFileFilterSite   **ICeFileFilterSite::QueryInterface**

ICeFilcFilterSite::AddRef   **ICeFileFilterSite::Release**

ICeFileFilterSite::OpenSourceFile   **ICeFileFilterSite::OpenDestinationFile**

ICeFileFilterSite::CloseSourceFile   **ICeFileFilterSite::CloseDestinationFile**

ICeFileFilterSite::ReportProgress   **ICeFileFilterSite::ReportLoss**

The following interface and methods are implemented by a vendor-supplied file
converter dynamic-link library (DLL):

ICeFileFilter

ICeFileFilter::QueryInterface

ICeFileFilter::AddRef

ICeFileFilter::Release

ICeFileFilter::NextConvertFile

ICeFileFilter::FilterOptions

ICeFileFilter::FormatMessage

The following interface and methods are optionally implemented by a
vendor-supplied v2 file converter DLL:

ICeFileFilterOptions::QueryInterface

ICeFileFilterOptions::AddRef

ICeFileFilterOptions::Release

ICeFileFilterOptions::SetFilterOptions

File System Functions

Windows CE supports the following functions for file systems:

CreateDirectory	CreateFile
CloseHandle	RemoveDirectory
DeleteFile	ReadFile
WriteFile, FlushFileBuffers	FindClose
FindFirstFile	FindNextFile
SetEndOfFile	SetFilePointer
CopyFile	MoveFile
GetFileAttributes	SetFileAttributes
GetFileInformationByHandle	GetFileSize
GetFileTime	SetFileTime
CeOidGetInfo	

GDI Functions

Windows CE supports the following GDI functions:

AbortDoc	AddFontResource
BitBlt	CombineRgn
CreateBitmap	CreateCompatibleBitmap
CreateCompatibleDC	CreateDC
CreateDIBPatternBrushPt	CreateDIBSection
CreateFontIndirect	CreatePalette
CreatePatternBrush	CreatePen
CreatePenIndirect	CreateRectRgn
CreateRectRgnIndirect	CreateSolidBrush
DeleteDC	DeleteObject
DrawEdge	DrawFocusRect
DrawText	Ellipse
EndDoc	EndPage
EnumFontFamilies	EnumFontFamProc
EnumFonts	EnumFontsProc
EqualRgn	ExcludeClipRect
ExtTextOut	FillRect

FillRgn

GetBkMode

GetClipRgn

GetDeviceCaps

GetNearestPaletteIndex

GetObjectType

GetPixel

GetRgnBox

GetSysColorBrush

GetTextColor

GetTextExtentPoint

GetTextFace

IntersectClipRect

OffsetRgn

Polygon

PtInRegion

Rectangle

RectVisible

RestoreDC

SaveDC

SelectClipRgn

SelectPalette

SetBkColor

SetBrushOrgEx

SetPixel

SetROP2

SetViewportOrgEx

StartPage

TransparentImage

GetBkColor

GetClipBox

GetCurrentObject

GetNearestColor

GetObject

GetPaletteEntries

GetRegionData

GetStockObject

GetSystemPaletteEntries

GetTextExtentExPoint

GetTextExtentPoint32

GetTextMetrics

MaskBlt

PatBlt

Polyline

RealizePalette

RectInRegion

RemoveFontResource

RoundRect

ScrollDC

SelectObject

SetAbortProc

SetBkMode

SetPaletteEntries

SetRectRgn

SetTextColor

StartDoc

StretchBlt

Informational Controls Functions

Windows CE supports the following informational controls functions:

CreateWindow	**CreateWindowEx**
DoFormat	**GetDayNum**
GetSubMenu	**IsLeapYr**
MapWindowPoints	**OnNotify**
PrepCache	**RetrieveItem**
TrackPopupMenuEx	

Windows CE supports the following informational controls messages:

DTM_SETFORMAT	DTN_CLOSEUP
DTN_DATETIMECHANGE	DTN_DROPDOWN
DTN_FORMAT	DTN_FORMATQUERY
DTN_USERSTRING	DTN_WMKEYDOWN
LVM_ARRANGE	LVM_DELETEALLITEMS
LVM_DELETEITEM	LVM_GETITEMSTATE
LVM_GETNEXTITEM	LVM_GETNUMBEROFWORKAREAS
LVM_GETWORKAREAS	LVM_INSERTITEM
LVM_ODCACHEHINT	LVM_ODFINDITEM
LVM_SETITEM	LVM_SETITEMCOUNT
LVM_SETITEMPOSITION	LVM_SETITEMPOSITION32
LVM_SETITEMSTATE	LVM_SETITEMTEXT
LVM_SETWORKAREAS	LVM_SORTITEMS
LVN_GETDISPINFO	LVN_ODCACHEHINT
MCM_GETDAYSTATE	MCM_SETDAYSTATE
MCM_SETMONTHDELTA	MCN_SELCHANGE
MCN_SELECT	NM_CUSTOMDRAW
RB_DELETEBAND	RB_INSERTBAND
RB_SETBANDINFO	RB_SETBARINFO
TB_ADDSTRING	TB_DROPDOWN
TB_GETRECT	TB_LOADIMAGES
WM_NOTIFY	

Infrared Sockets Functions

The subset of Windows Sockets functions used by Infrared Sockets with modifications are described in the following table:

IrSock function	Modification
accept	None.
bind	Must be called before **listen** is called.
closesocket	None.
connect	None.
getsockopt	IRLMP_IAS_GET and IRLMP_ENUMDEVICES options have been added.
listen	None.
recv	None.
send	None.
setsockopt	The IR_LMP_IAS_SET option has been added.
socket	The AF_IRDA value was added for the address format parameter. Only the SOCK_STREAM socket type is supported.

Mail Functions

Windows CE supports the following functions for mail:

To obtain and release resources:

MailOpen

MailClose

MailFree

MailOpenNotify

To manipulate messages:

MailPut

MailGet

MailFirst

MailNext

MailDelete

MailUpdate

MailGetSvcId

To manipulate folders:

MailGetFolderId

MailGetFolderName

MailPutFolder

To manipulate headers in the **pwcHeaders** member of the **MailMsg** structure:

MailHeaderLen

MailGetField

MailSetField

To work with attachments:

MailDeleteAttachment

MailGetAttachment

MailPutAttachment

MailRequestAttachment

MailLocalAttachmentLen

To sort messages:

MailGetSort

MailSetSort

To check error status:

MailError

MailErrorMsg

Menu Functions

Windows CE supports the following menu functions:

AppendMenu	**CheckMenuItem**
CheckMenuRadioItem	**CommandBar_GetMenu**
CommandBar_InsertMenubar	**CreateMenu**
CreatePopupMenu	**DeleteMenu**
DestroyMenu	**DrawMenuBar**
EnableMenuItem	**GetMenuItemInfo**
GetSubMenu	**GetSystemMenu**
InsertMenu	**LoadMenu**
RemoveMenu	**SetMenuItemInfo**
TrackPopupMenu	**TrackPopupMenuEx**

Windows CE supports the following menu messages:

WM_CANCELMODE
WM_COMMAND
WM_ENTERMENULOOP
WM_EXITMENULOOP
WM_INITMENUPOPUP
WM_MEASUREITEM
WM_MENUCHAR

Notification Functions

Windows CE supports the following notification functions:

CeClearUserNotification
CeGetUserNotificationPreferences
CeHandleAppNotifications
CeRunAppAtEvent
CeRunAppAtTime
CeSetUserNotification

Process and Thread Functions

Windows CE supports the following functions for manipulating processes:

CreateProcess
GetCurrentProcess
GetCurrentProcessId
TerminateProcess

Windows CE supports the following functions for manipulating threads:

CreateThread	**ExitThread**
GetCurrentThread	**GetCurrentThreadId**
GetExitCodeThread	**GetThreadPriority**
ResumeThread	**SetThreadPriority**
SuspendThread	**Sleep**

Registry Functions

Windows CE supports the following functions for working with the registry:

RegEnumKeyEx	RegEnumValue
RegCreateKeyEx	**RegOpenKeyEx**
RegCloseKey	**RegQueryInfoKey**
RegQueryValueEx	**RegSetValueEx**
RegDeleteKey	**RegDeleteValue**

RAS Functions

Windows CE supports the following RAS functions:

RasDeleteEntry	**RasDial**
RasEnumConnections	**RasEnumEntries**
RasGetConnectStatus	**RasGetEntryDevConfig**
RasGetEntryDialParams	**RasGetEntryProperties**
RasHangup	**RasRenameEntry**
RasSetEntryDevConfig	**RasSetEntryDialParams**
RasSetEntryProperties	**RasValidateEntryName**

RAPI Functions

Windows CE supports the following RAPI functions:

CeRapiFreeBuffer
CeRapiGetError
CeRapiInit
CeRapiInitEx
CeRapiInvoke
CeRapiUninit

Windows CE supports the following database functions:

CeCreateDatabase	**CeDeleteDatabase**
CeDeleteRecord	**CeFindAllDatabases**
CeFindFirstDatabase	**CeFindNextDatabase**
CeOpenDatabase	**CeRapiFreeBuffer**
CeReadRecordProps	**CeSeekDatabase**
CeSetDatabaseInfo	**CeWriteRecordProps**

Windows CE supports the following file and object store management functions:

CeCloseHandle	**CeCopyFile**
CeCreateDirectory	**CeCreateFile**
CeDeleteFile	**CeFindAllFiles**
CeFindClose	**CeFindFirstFile**
CeFindNextFile	**CeGetFileAttributes**
CeGetFileSize	**CeGetFileTime**
CeGetStoreInformation	**CeGetTempPath**
CeMoveFile	**CeOidGetInfo**
CeRapiFreeBuffer	**CeReadFile**
CeRemoveDirectory	**CeSetEndOfFile**
CeSetFileAttributes	**CeSetFilePointer**
CeSetFileTime	**CeWriteFile**

Windows CE supports the following miscellaneous RAPI functions:

CeCheckPassword	**CeCreateProcess**
CeGetDesktopDeviceCaps	**CeGetLastError**
CeGetSpecialFolderPath	**CeGetSystemInfo**
CeGetSystemMetrics	**CeGetSystemPowerStatusEx**
CeGetVersionEx	**CeGlobalMemoryStatus**
CeSHCreateShortcut	**CeSHGetShortcutTarget**

Windows CE supports the following registry functions:

CeRegCloseKey	**CeRegCreateKeyEx**
CeRegDeleteKey	**CeRegDeleteValue**
CeRegEnumKeyEx	**CeRegEnumValue**
CeRegOpenKeyEx	**CeRegQueryInfoKey**
CeRegQueryValueEx	**CeRegSetValueEx**

Windows CE supports the following window management functions:

CeGetClassName
CeGetWindow
CeGetWindowLong
CeGetWindowText

Resource Functions

Windows CE supports the following resource functions:

ClipCursor	**CreateAcceleratorTable**
CreateCaret	**CreateCursor**
CreateIconIndirect	**DestroyAcceleratorTable**
DestroyCaret	**DestroyCursor**
DestroyIcon	**DrawIconEx**
ExtractIconEx	**FindResource**
GetCaretBlinkTime	**GetCaretPos**
GetClipCursor	**GetCursor**
GetCursorPos	**HideCaret**
LoadAccelerators	**LoadBitmap**
LoadCursor	**LoadImage**
LoadIcon	**LoadResource**
LoadString	**LockResource**
SetCaretBlinkTime	**SetCaretPos**
SetCursor	**SetCursorPos**
ShowCaret	**ShowCursor**
TranslateAccelerator	

Windows CE supports the following resource messages:

WM_GETICON

Serial Communications Functions

Windows CE supports the following serial communications functions:

CreateFile

CloseHandle

ReadFile

WriteFile

DeviceIoControl

Windows CE supports the following functions for setting up and using serial devices:

ClearCommBreak	**ClearCommError**
EscapeCommFunction	**GetCommMask**
GetCommModemStatus	**GetCommProperties**
GetCommState	**GetCommTimeouts**
PurgeComm	**SetCommBreak**
SetCommMask	**SetCommState**
SetCommTimeouts	**SetupComm**
TransmitCommChar	**WaitCommEvent**

Shell Functions

Windows CE supports the following shell functions:

SHAddToRecentDocs	**SHCreateShortcut**
Shell_NotifyIcon	**ShellExecuteEx**
SHGetFileInfo	**SHGetMalloc**
SHGetPathFromIDList	**SHGetShortcutTarget**
SHGetSpecialFolderLocation	**SHLoadDIBitmap**
SHShowOutOfMemory	

TAPI Functions

TAPI functions are identified as asynchronous if they can return before making a call to the application's callback function; otherwise, they are considered synchronous.

Windows CE supports the following TAPI functions:

lineClose	lineConfigDialogEdit
lineDeallocateCall	lineDrop
lineGetDevCaps	lineGetDevConfig
lineGetID	lineGetTranslateCaps
lineInitialize	lineMakeCall
lineNegotiateAPIVersion	lineOpen
lineSetDevConfig	lineSetStatusMessages
lineShutdown	lineTranslateAddress
lineTranslateDialog	

Transport Service Functions

Inbox expects a set of functions that are exported by the transport service DLL. To create a transport service you must export and provide an implementation for each of the transport interface functions listed in the table below.

The following functions are used by Inbox and must be exported by a transport service DLL. These functions are identified by the prefix **Transport**.

TransportConnect	TransportCount
TransportDel	TransportDisconnect
TransportError	TransportErrorMsg
TransportFreeMsg	TransportInit
TransportNonIpm	TransportProps
TransportRecv	TransportRelease
TransportSend	TransportSetPassword
TransportView	

User Input Functions

Windows CE supports the following user input functions:

EnableHardwareKeyboard	GetKeyboardStatus
GetAsyncKeyState	GetDoubleClickTime
GetKeyState	GetMouseMovePoints
keybd_event	MapVirtualKey
mouse_event	RegisterHotKey
SendInput	UnregisterHotKey

Windows CE supports the following messages:

WM_CAPTURECHANGED	WM_CHAR
WM_DEADCHAR	WM_HOTKEY
WM_KEYDOWN	WM_KEYFIRST
WM_KEYLAST	WM_KEYUP
WM_LBUTTONDBLCLK	WM_LBUTTONDOWN
WM_LBUTTONUP	WM_MOUSEMOVE
WM_SYSCHAR	WM_SYSDEADCHAR
WM_SYSKEYDOWN	WM_SYSKEYUP

Windows Functions

Windows CE supports the following windows functions:

BeginPaint	BringWindowToTop
CallWindowProc	ChildWindowFromPoint
ClientToScreen	CopyRect
CreateWindow	CreateWindowEx
DefWindowProc	DispatchMessage
DrawFrameControl	EnableWindow
EndPaint	EnumWindows
EqualRect	FormatMessage
GetActiveWindow	GetCapture
GetClassName	GetDC
GetFocus	GetForegroundWindow
GetMessage	GetMessagePos
GetMessageSource	GetParent

GetScrollInfo	GetUpdateRect
GetWindow	GetWindowDC
GetWindowRect	GetWindowText
GetWindowTextLength	GetWindowThreadProcessId
InflateRect	IntersectRect
IsChild	IsRectEmpty
IsWindow	IsWindowEnabled
IsWindowVisible	KillTimer
MapWindowPoints	MsgWaitForMultipleObjects
OffsetRect	PeekMessage
PostMessage	PostQuitMessage
PostThreadMessage	PtInRect
RegisterWindowMessage	ReleaseCapture
ReleaseDC	ScreenToClient
ScrollDC	SendMessage
SendNotifyMessage	SetActiveWindow
SetCapture	SetFocus
SetForegroundWindow	SetParent
SetRect	SetRectEmpty
SetScrollInfo	SetScrollPos
SetScrollRange	SetTimer
SetWindowPos	SetWindowText
SubtractRect	TimerProc
TranslateMessage	UnionRect
UnregisterClass	UpdateWindow
WindowFromPoint	

Windows CE supports the following windows messages:

WM_ACTIVATE	WM_CANCELMODE
WM_CHAR	WM_CLOSE
WM_COMMAND	WM_COMPAREITEM
WM_COPYDATA	WM_CREATE
WM_DELETEITEM	WM_DRAWITEM
WM_ENABLE	WM_ERASEBKGND
WM_FONTCHANGE	WM_GETFONT
WM_GETTEXT	WM_GETTEXTLENGTH

WM_HELP	WM_HSCROLL
WM_KILLFOCUS	WM_MEASUREITEM
WM_MOVE	WM_NOTIFY
WM_PAINT	WM_QUIT
WM_SETFOCUS	WM_SETFONT
WM_SETREDRAW	WM_SETTEXT
WM_SHOWWINDOW	WM_STYLECHANGED
WM_SYSCOLORCHANGE	WM_SYSCOMMAND
WM_TIMER	WM_VSCROLL
WM_WINDOWPOSCHANGED	

Windows CE supports the following windows macros:

FORWARD_WM_NOTIFY

HANDLE_WM_NOTIFY

MAKELPARAM

MAKELRESULT

MAKEWPARAM

MAPWINDOWRECT

CEUTIL Functions

CEUTIL API functions are described in the following table.

Note In order to use these APIs you must include *ceutil.h* and link with *ceutil.lib*.

Function	Description
CeSvcOpen	Opens and returns a handle to the registry root for a specified logical position.
CeSvcOpenEx	Opens a nested subkey underneath an already open registry handle.
CeSvcClose	Closes a handle previously returned by **CeSvcOpen** or **CeSvcOpenEx**.
CeSvcGetString	Reads a string value from a registry subkey and copies the data into a buffer.
CeSvcSetString	Writes a string value to a registry subkey.
CeSvcGetDword	Reads a DWORD value from a registry key and copies the data into a buffer.

Function	Description
CeSvcSetDword	Writes a DWORD value to a registry subkey.
CeSvcGetBinary	Reads a binary value from a registry subkey and copies the data into a buffer.
CeSvcSetBinary	Writes a binary value to a registry subkey.
CeSvcDeleteVal	Removes a named value from the specified registry key.
CeGetDeviceId	Returns a device ID for the currently connected device.
CeGetSelectedId	Returns a device ID for the currently selected device.
CeSvcEnumProfiles	Enumerates all subkeys underneath a given subkey.

NLS Functions

Windows CE supports the following National Language Support (NLS) functions. Because the OS supports only Unicode, be sure you call the functions with wide character variables.

CharLower	GetSystemDefaultLCID
CharLowerBuff	GetTimeFormat
CharNext	GetUserDefaultLangID
CharPrev	GetUserDefaultLCID
CharUpper	IsDBCSLeadByte
CharUpperBuff	IsDBCSLeadByteEx
CompareString	IsValidCodePage
ConvertDefaultLocale	IsValidLocale
EnumCalendarInfo	iswctype
EnumDateFormats	LCMapString
EnumSystemCodePages	lstrcat
EnumSystemLocales	lstrcmp
EnumTimeFormats	lstrcmpi
FoldString	lstrcpy
GetACP	lstrlen
GetCPInfo	MultiByteToWideChar
GetCurrencyFormat	SetLocaleInfo
GetDateFormat	tolower
GetLocaleInfo	toupper
GetNumberFormat	_wcsicmp
GetOEMCP	_wcsnicmp

GetStringType	_wcslwr
GetStringTypeEx	_wcsupr
GetSystemDefaultLangID	**WideCharToMultiByte**

The following debugging functions and structures are supported by Windows CE:

Supported debugging functions

ContinueDebugEvent

DebugActiveProcess

DebugBreak

FlushInstructionCache

GetThreadContext

OutputDebugString

ReadProcessMemory

SetThreadContext

WaitForDebugEvent

WriteProcessMemory

Supported debugging structures

CREATE_PROCESS_DEBUG_INFO

CONTEXT

CREATE_THREAD_DEBUG_INFO

DEBUG_EVENT

EXCEPTION_DEBUG_INFO

EXIT_PROCESS_DEBUG_INFO

EXIT_THREAD_DEBUG_INFO

LOAD_DLL_DEBUG_INFO

OUTPUT_DEBUG_STRING_INFO

UNLOAD_DLL_DEBUG_INFO

Windows CE does not support the following debugging functions and structures that are common to Windows-based desktop platforms:

Unsupported debugging functions

IsDebuggerPresent

GetThreadSelectorEntry

FatalExit

FatalAppExit

SetDebugErrorLevel

Unsupported debugging structures
LDT_ENTRY
RIP_INFO

Windows Controls Functions

Windows CE supports the following windows controls functions:

CheckRadioButton	CommandBar_InsertComboBox
CreateWindow	CreateWindowEx
EditWordBreakProc	EnagleWindow
GetScrollInfo	GetWindowText
ScrollWindowEx	SendMessage
SetScrollInfo	SetScrollPos
SetScrollRange	SetWindowText

Windows CE supports the following windows controls macros:

Button_Enable	Button_GetCheck
Button_GetState	Button_GetText
Button_GetTextLength	Button_SetCheck
Button_SetState	Button_SetStyle
Button_SetText	ComboBox_AddItemData
ComboBox_AddString	ComboBox_DeleteString
ComboBox_Enable	ComboBox_FindItemData
ComboBox_FindString	ComboBox_FindStringExact
ComboBox_GetCount	ComboBox_GetCurSel
ComboBox_GetDroppedControlRect	ComboBox_GetDroppedState
ComboBox_GetEditSel	ComboBox_GetExtendedUI
ComboBox_GetItemData	ComboBox_GetItemHeight
ComboBox_GetLBText	ComboBox_GetLBTextLen
ComboBox_GetText	ComboBox_GetTextLength
ComboBox_InsertItemData	ComboBox_InsertString
ComboBox_LimitText	ComboBox_ResetContent
ComboBox_SelectItemData	ComboBox_SelectString
ComboBox_SetCurSel	ComboBox_SetEditSel
ComboBox_SetExtendedUI)	ComboBox_SetItemData
ComboBox_SetItemHeight	ComboBox_SetText

ComboBox_ShowDropdown

Edit_CanUndo

Edit_EmptyUndoBuffer

Edit_Enable

Edit_FmtLines

Edit_GetFirstVisibleLine

Edit_GetLine

Edit_GetLineCount

Edit_GetModify

Edit_GetPasswordChar

Edit_GetRect

Edit_GetSel

Edit_GetText

Edit_GetTextLength

Edit_LimitText

Edit_LineFromChar

Edit_LineIndex

Edit_LineLength

Edit_ReplaceSel

Edit_Scroll

Edit_ScrollCaret

Edit_SetModify

Edit_SetPasswordChar

Edit_SetReadOnly

Edit_SetRect

Edit_SetRectNoPaint

Edit_SetSel

Edit_SetTabStops

Edit_SetText

Edit_Undo

EnableWindow

ListBox_AddItemData

ListBox_AddString

ListBox_DeleteString

ListBox_Enable

ListBox_FindItemData

ListBox_FindString

ListBox_FindStringExact

ListBox_GetCaretIndex

ListBox_GetCount

ListBox_GetCurSel

ListBox_GetHorizontalExtent

ListBox_GetItemData

ListBox_GetItemHeight

ListBox_GetItemRect

ListBox_GetSel

ListBox_GetSelCount

ListBox_GetSelItems

ListBox_GetText

ListBox_GetTextLength

ListBox_GetTopIndex

ListBox_InsertItemData

ListBox_InsertString

ListBox_ResetContent

ListBox_SelectItemData

ListBox_SelectString

ListBox_SelItemRange

ListBox_SetCaretIndex

ListBox_SetColumnWidth

ListBox_SetCurSel

ListBox_SetHorizontalExtent

ListBox_SetItemData

ListBox_SetItemHeight

ListBox_SetSel

ListBox_SetTabStops

ListBox_SetTopIndex

ScrollBar_Enable

ScrollBar_GetPos

ScrollBar_GetRange

ScrollBar_SetPos

ScrollBar_SetRange

ScrollBar_Show

ShowWindow

Static_Enable

Static_GetText

Static_GetTextLength

Static_SetText

Windows CE supports the following windows controls messages:

BM_CLICK	BM_GETCHECK
BM_GETSTATE	BM_SETCHECK
BM_SETSTATE	BM_SETSTYLE
BN_CLICKED	BN_DBLCLK
BN_DISABLE	BN_DOUBLECLICKED
BN_HILITE	BN_KILLFOCUS
BN_PAINT	BN_SETFOCUS
BN_UNHILITE	BN_UNPUSHED
CB_ADDSTRING	CB_DELETESTRING
CB_FINDSTRING	CB_FINDSTRINGEXACT
CB_GETCOUNT	CB_GETCURSEL
CB_GETDROPPEDCONTROLRECT	CB_GETDROPPEDSTATE
CB_GETDROPPEDWIDTH	CB_GETEDITSEL
CB_GETEXTENDEDUI	CB_GETHORIZONTALEXTENT
CB_GETITEMDATA	CB_GETITEMHEIGHT
CB_GETLBTEXT	CB_GETLBTEXTLEN
CB_GETLOCALE	CB_GETTOPINDEX
CB_INITSTORAGE	CB_INSERTSTRING
CB_LIMITTEXT	CB_RESETCONTENT
CB_SELECTSTRING	CB_SETCURSEL
CB_SETDROPPEDWIDTH	CB_SETEDITSEL
CB_SETEXTENDEDUI	CB_SETHORIZONTALEXTENT
CB_SETITEMDATA	CB_SETITEMHEIGHT
CB_SETLOCALE	CB_SETTOPINDEX
CB_SHOWDROPDOWN	CBN_CLOSEUP
CBN_DBLCLK	CBN_DROPDOWN
CBN_EDITCHANGE	CBN_EDITUPDATE
CBN_ERRSPACE	CBN_KILLFOCUS
CBN_SELCHANGE	CBN_SELENDCANCEL
CBN_SELENDOK	CBN_SETFOCUS
EM_CANUNDO	EM_CHARFROMPOS

EM_EMPTYUNDOBUFFER	EM_FMTLINES
EM_GETFIRSTVISIBLELINE	EM_GETLIMITTEXT
EM_GETLINE	EM_GETLINECOUNT
EM_GETMARGINS	EM_GETMODIFY
EM_GETPASSWORDCHAR	EM_GETRECT
EM_GETSEL	EM_LIMITTEXT
EM_LINEFROMCHAR	EM_LINEINDEX
EM_LINELENGTH	EM_LINESCROLL
EM_POSFROMCHAR	EM_REPLACESEL
EM_SCROLL	EM_SCROLLCARET
EM_SETLIMITTEXT	EM_SETMARGINS
EM_SETMODIFY	EM_SETPASSWORDCHAR
EM_SETREADONLY	EM_SETRECT
EM_SETRECTNP	EM_SETSEL
EM_SETTABSTOPS	EM_UNDO
EN_CHANGE	EN_ERRSPACE
EN_HSCROLL	EN_KILLFOCUS
EN_MAXTEXT	EN_SETFOCUS
EN_UPDATE	EN_VSCROLL
LB_ADDSTRING	LB_DELETESTRING
LB_FINDSTRING	LB_FINDSTRINGEXACT
LB_GETANCHORINDEX	LB_GETCARETINDEX
LB_GETCOUNT	LB_GETCURSEL
LB_GETHORIZONTALEXTENT	LB_GETITEMDATA
LB_GETITEMHEIGHT	LB_GETITEMRECT
LB_GETLOCALE	LB_GETSEL
LB_GETSELCOUNT	LB_GETSELITEMS
LB_GETTEXT	LB_GETTEXTLEN
LB_GETTOPINDEX	LB_INITSTORAGE
LB_INSERTSTRING	LB_ITEMFROMPOINT
LB_RESETCONTENT	LB_SELECTSTRING
LB_SELITEMRANGE	LB_SELITEMRANGEEX
LB_SETANCHORINDEX	LB_SETCARETINDEX
LB_SETCOLUMNWIDTH	LB_SETCURSEL
LB_SETHORIZONTALEXTENT	LB_SETITEMDATA
LB_SETITEMHEIGHT	LB_SETLOCALE

LB_SETSEL	LB_SETTABSTOPS
LB_SETTOPINDEX	LBN_DBLCLK
LBN_ERRSPACE	LBN_KILLFOCUS
LBN_SELCANCEL	LBN_SELCHANGE
LBN_SETFOCUS	SBM_SETSCROLLINFO
SET_GETPOS	SET_GETRANGE
SET_GETSCROLLINFO	SET_SETPOS
SET_SETRANGE	SET_SETRANGEREDRAW
STM_GETIMAGE	STM_SETIMAGE
STN_CLICKED	STN_DISABLE
STN_ENABLE	WM_CANCELMODE
WM_CHARTOITEM	WM_CLEAR
WM_COMMAND	WM_COMPAREITEM
WM_COMPAREITEM	WM_COPY
WM_CTLCOLORBTN	WM_CTLCOLOREDIT
WM_CTLCOLORLISTBOX	WM_CTLCOLORSCROLLBAR
WM_CTLCOLORSTATIC	WM_CUT
WM_DELETEITEM	WM_DELETEITEM
WM_DRAWITEM	WM_ENABLE
WM_GETFONT	WM_GETTEXT
WM_GETTEXTLENGTH	WM_HSCROLL
WM_PAINT	WM_PASTE
WM_SETFONT	WM_SETREDRAW
WM_SETTEXT	WM_UNDO
WM_VKEYTOITEM	WM_VSCROLL

Windows Networking Functions

Windows CE supports the following Windows networking functions:

WNetCloseEnum	**WNetEnumResource**
WNetOpenEnum	**WNetAddConnection3**
WNetCancelConnection2	**WNetConnectionDialog1**
WNetDisconnectDialog	**WNetDisconnectDialog1**
WNetGetConnection	**WNetGetUser**
WNetGetUniversalName	

Windows Sockets Functions

Windows CE supports the following Windows Sockets functions:

accept	bind
closesocket	connect
gethostbyaddr	gethostbyname
gethostname	getpeername
getsockname	getsockopt
htonl	htons
inet_addr	inet_ntoa
ioctlsocket	listen
ntohl	ntohs
recv	recvfrom
select	send
sendto	setsockopt
shutdown	socket
WSACleanup	WSAGetLastError
WSAStartup	WSAIoctl

WinInet Functions

Windows CE supports the following WinInet functions:

InternetOpen	InternetConnect
InternetCloseHandle	InternetQueryOption
InternetSetOption	InternetSetStatusCallback
InternetStatusCallback	InternetTimeFromSystemTime
InternetTimeToSystemTime	InternetReadFile
InternetFindNextFile	InternetQueryDataAvailable
InternetGetLastResponseInfo	InternetCrackUrl
InternetCreateUrl	InternetCanonicalizeUrl
InternetCombineUrl	InternetOpenUrl

Glossary

A

ACCEL data structure A structure that defines an accelerator key used in an accelerator table.

accelerator table An array of ACCEL data structures, each of which defines an accelerator.

Action button A hardware navigation control that replaces the ENTER key on a keyboard.

Active Channel A Web site that has been enabled for Webcasting to information-receiving programs.

Active Desktop A new technology delivered in Microsoft Pocket Internet Explorer that allows you to include HTML documents, ActiveX controls, and Java applets on your desktop.

active notification The state of a user notification from the time the user is notified until the user handles the event.

Active Server Pages (ASP) An open application environment in which HTML pages, scripts, and ActiveX components are combined to create Web-based applications.

active window In an environment capable of displaying multiple on-screen windows, the window containing the display or document that will be affected by current cursor movements, commands, and text entry. Windows CE identifies the active window by positioning it at the top of the Z order and highlighting its title bar and border.

ActiveX All component technologies, other than OLE, that are built on the Microsoft Component Object Model (COM).

ActiveX client An application or tool that calls an ActiveX object.

ActiveX object An exposed object of the Component Object Model (COM).

ADC *See* **analog-to-digital converter**.

address card The fundamental unit of record in the Contacts database. Each address card contains information about an individual. The information consists of a set of data fields called properties.

Address Resolution Protocol (ARP)
A set of programs that are part of the Internet Protocol (IP). Used to determine the hardware or physical address of a node on a local area network connected to the Internet when only the IP address or logical address is known. When an ARP request is sent to the network, the node that has the IP address responds with its hardware address.

AFD *See* **auxiliary function driver**.

American National Standards Institute (ANSI)
An organization of American industry and business groups dedicated to the development of trade and communication standards. ANSI sets standards for programming languages to use when porting programs. Internationally, ANSI is the American representative to the International Organization for Standardization.

American Standard Code for Information Exchange (ASCII)
A coding scheme using 7 or 8 bits that assigns numeric values to up to 256 characters, including letters, numerals, punctuation marks, control characters, and other symbols.

analog-to-digital converter (ADC)
A device that converts an analog signal, such as sound or voltage, to binary code for use by a computer.

annunciator An icon placed onto the taskbar to indicate that a user notification is active. Although taskbars can contain multiple annunciator icons for different applications, only one instance of an icon for any given application is displayed at one time.

ANSI *See* **American National Standards Institute**.

apartment model A threading model that can be used only on the thread that created it. *See* **free threading model** and **single threading model**.

API *See* **application programming interface**.

application-defined message A message created by an application to be used by its own windows or to communicate with windows in other processes. If an application creates its own messages, the window procedure that receives the message must interpret it and provide the appropriate processing.

application notification An application notification starts an application at a specified time or when a system event occurs. When an application starts as the result of a notification, the system specifies a command line parameter that identifies the event that has occurred.

application programming interface (API)
A set of routines used by an application to direct the performance of procedures by a computer's operating system. For computers running a graphical user interface, an API manages an application's windows, icons, menus, and dialog boxes.

application-specific integrated circuit (ASIC)
An integrated circuit designed to perform a particular function by defining the interconnection of a set of basic circuit-building blocks drawn from a library provided by the circuit manufacturer.

application switch A hardware navigation control intended to launch or reactivate software applications.

ASCII *See* **American Standard Code for Information Interchange**.

ASIC *See* **application-specific integrated circuit**.

ASP *See* **Active Server Pages**.

asynchronous operation **1.** A process in a multitasking system whose execution can proceed independently, or in the background. Other processes may be started before the asynchronous process has finished. **2.** A data transmission method that allows characters to be sent at irregular intervals over a line by preceding each character with a start bit and following it with a stop bit. *Compare* **synchronous operation**.

authentication **1.** The process of verifying that a message comes from its stated source. **2.** The process of verifying the identity or access level of a user, computer, and program.

Automation A technology based on the Component Object Model (COM), which enables interoperability among ActiveX components, including OLE components. Formerly referred to as OLE Automation.

auxiliary function driver The Windows CE communication protocol manager.

B

bandwidth 1. The difference between the highest and lowest frequencies that an analog communications system can pass. For example, a telephone accommodates a bandwidth of 3000 Hz, which is the difference between the lowest (300 Hz) and highest (3300 Hz) frequencies it can carry. **2.** The data transfer capacity of a digital communications system.

bi-directional parallel port An interface that supports two-way parallel communications between a device and a computer.

binary image builder file (.bib) A file used by the Windows CE ROM image builder tool to determine which modules and files to combine when forming the ROM image, and where to place the modules in memory.

Binary Large Object (BLOB) 1. A large piece of data, such as a bitmap, characterized by large field values, an unpredictable table size, and data that is formless from the perspective of a program. **2.** A keyword designating the BLOB structure, which contains information about a block of data.

bit block transfer (BLT, Bitblt) The process of copying the bits that constitute a bitmap from one device context to another. For example, a bit block transfer can be used to move a bitmap stored in memory to the screen for display. The bits can also be altered during a bit block transfer. As a result, light and dark portions of an image can be reversed. Successive displays can thus be used to change the appearance of an image or to move it around on the screen.

bitmap A computer graphic represented as an array of bits in memory that represent the attributes of the individual pixels in an image (1 bit per pixel in a black-and-white display, multiple bits per pixel in a color or grayscale display).

blink time The elapsed time, in milliseconds, required to invert the caret display. This value is half of the flash time.

BLOB *See* **Binary Large Object**.

block mode A synchronous method of calling the **CeRapiInvoke** function by storing input parameters and output data in a single buffer.

boot loader A program that is automatically run when a computer is switched on (booted). After first performing a few basic hardware tests, the bootstrap loader loads and passes control to a larger loader program, which then typically loads the operating system. The bootstrap loader normally resides in the computer's read-only memory (ROM).

brush A tool used in paint programs to sketch or fill in areas of a drawing with the color and pattern currently in use. Paint programs that offer a variety of brush shapes can produce brushstrokes of varying width and, in some cases, shadowing or calligraphic effects.

build environment The state of the development workstation and the directory structure at the time a program build is begun.

build window *See* **command prompt window**.

built-in device driver A software component that permits a computer system to communicate with a device. In Windows CE, it is linked with the GWE component. The Windows CE built-in driver consists of a model device driver (MDD) layer and a platform dependent driver (PDD) layer. Together, these layers make it possible for applications to access physically different, but functionally equivalent, hardware resources in the same way on all Windows CE platforms.

C

cabinet file A self-contained file with a .cab extension used for application installation and setup. In a cabinet file, multiple files are compressed into one file. They are commonly found on Microsoft software distribution disks.

cache A special memory subsystem in which frequently used data values are duplicated for quick access. A memory cache stores the contents of frequently accessed RAM locations and the addresses where this data is stored. When the processor references an address in memory, the cache checks to see whether it holds that address. If it does hold the address, the data is returned to the processor; if it does not hold the address, a regular memory access occurs. A cache is useful when RAM accesses are slow compared with the microprocessor speed, because cache memory is always faster than main RAM memory.

callback function A function that receives messages from the operating system. Callback functions are application-defined.

caret A flashing line, block, or bitmap that marks the location of the insertion point in a window's client area.

cascading menu A hierarchical graphical menu system in which a side menu of subcategories is displayed when the pointer is placed on the main category.

CDF *See* **Channel Definition Format**.

central processing unit (CPU)   The computational and control unit of a computer. The CPU is the device that interprets and executes instructions. It has the ability to fetch, decode, and execute instructions and to transfer information to and from other resources over the computer's main data-transfer path, the bus. By definition, the CPU is the chip that functions as the "brain" of a computer. In some instances, however, the term encompasses both the processor and the computer's memory or, even more broadly, the main computer console, as opposed to peripheral equipment.

Certificate Authority (CA)   An entity that attests to the identity of a person or an organization. The Certificate Authority's chief function is to verify the identity of entities and issue digital certificates attesting to that identity.

channel   A subscription to a Web site that conforms to the Channel Definition Format.

Channel Definition Format (CDF)   A specification developed by Microsoft and presented to the World Wide Web Consortium (W3C) that allows applications to send Web pages to users. Once a user subscribes to a CDF channel, any software that supports the CDF format automatically receives any new content posted on the channel's Web server. The default client subscription application for Internet channel broadcasting in Broadcast Architecture stores subscription information as CDF files.

channel script   A program written in HTML and Visual Basic Script, JScript, Java Script, and other scripting languages to specify the layout and behavior of a channel.

channel synchronization   The process of first downloading Mobile Channels content into a cache using the standard Internet Explorer 4.0 channel retrieval mechanism and then transferring it onto a Windows CE-based device. Channel synchronization makes it possible for users to access Mobile Channels using either a Windows CE-based device without a radio module or a Windows-based desktop computer when the device is not readily available.

check box   An interactive control found in graphical user interfaces. Check boxes are used to enable or disable one or more features or options from a set. When an option is selected, an X or a check mark appears in the box.

child window   A window that has the WS_CHILD style. A child window always appears within the client area of its parent window.

CIFS   *See* **Common Internet File System**.

CIFS redirector   A module through which one computer gains access to another. Its function is to reestablish disrupted connections and to package and send remote file-system requests to host targets.

class identifier (CLSID)   A universally unique identifier (UUID) that identifies a type of Component Object Model (COM) object. Each type of COM object item has its CLSID in the registry so that it can be loaded and used by other applications. For example, a spreadsheet may create worksheet items, chart items, and macrosheet items. Each of these item types has its own CLSID that uniquely identifies it to the system.

client **1.** In object-oriented programming, a member of a class (group) that uses the services of another class to which it is not related. **2.** A process, such as a program or task, that requests a service provided by another program—for example, a word processor that calls on a sort routine built into another program. The client process uses the requested service without having to know any working details about the other program or the service itself. **3.** On a local area network or the Internet, a computer that accesses shared network resources provided by another computer, called a *server*.

client area The client area is the portion of a window where the application displays output, such as text or graphics. *Also called* a client rectangle.

client coordinate A coordinate that is relative to the upper-left corner of a window's client area.

Client Device Driver *See* **Installable Device Driver**.

clipping region A subregion of the client area to which output is restricted. Clipping is used in Windows CE in a variety of ways. For example, word processing and spreadsheet applications clip keyboard input to keep it from appearing in the margins of a page or spreadsheet.

CLSID *See* **class identifier**.

cold boot A startup process that begins with turning on the computer's power. Typically, a cold boot involves some basic hardware checking by the system, after which the operating system is loaded from disk into memory. *Compare* **warm boot**.

COM *See* **Component Object Model**.

COM class The definition of an object in code. In COM, class refers to the general object definition, whereas in C++, the class of an object is a data type.

COM object A programming structure that includes both data and functionality. A COM object is defined and allocated as a single unit. The only public access to a COM object is through the programming structure's interfaces. At a minimum, a COM object must support the **IUnknown** interface, which maintains the object's existence while it is being used and provides access to the object's other interfaces.

COM port Short for communications port, the logical address assigned by MS-DOS (versions 3.3 and later), and Microsoft Windows to each of the four serial ports on an IBM personal computer or a PC-compatible. COM ports also have come to be known as the actual serial ports on a computer's CPU where peripherals, such as printers, scanners, and external modems, are plugged in.

combo box A control that combines an edit control with a list box. This allows the user to type in an entry or choose one from the list.

command band A rebar control with a fixed band at the top that contains a toolbar with a **Close (X)** button, an **OK** button, and optionally, a **Help (?)** button in the upper-right corner.

command bar A control window that can contain buttons, combo boxes, and menu bars. Windows CE-based applications can use a command bar rather than a separate menu and toolbar to efficiently utilize available screen space.

command prompt window   A development workstation command prompt window from which the EDK user has run the Wince.bat tool. *Also called* build window.

common control   A standardized child window that an application uses in conjunction with another window to perform input/output tasks. A common control enables users to view and organize information and to set or change attributes and properties. Most common controls send the WM_NOTIFY message.

Common Internet File System (CIFS)
A standard proposed by Microsoft that would compete directly with Sun Microsystems' Web Network File System.

component   A subset of the Windows CE operating system. Windows CE is structured as a collection of modules that are subdivided into smaller components. Each module and component is a self-contained subset of the Windows CE operating system that can be used to construct a customized operating system for a particular device.

Component Object Model (COM)   An open architecture for cross-platform development of client/server applications. It is based on object-oriented technology as agreed upon by Digital Equipment Corporation and Microsoft Corporation. COM defines the interface (similar to an abstract base class), **IUnknown**, from which all COM-compatible classes are derived.

compound file   A number of individual files bound together in one physical file where each individual file can be accessed as if it were a single physical file.

Contacts database   A collection of names, addresses, telephone numbers, and other information stored on a Handheld PC (H/PC) by the Contacts application. The database is divided into a set of records called address cards. The database contains any number of address cards, limited only by the amount of memory available on the H/PC.

continuous resistive touch panel
See **touch screen**.

control   A standardized child window on the screen that can be manipulated by the user to perform an action or display information. The most common controls are buttons, which allow the user to select options, and scroll bars, which allow the user to move through a document or position text in a window.

control identifier   A value that uniquely identifies a control.

control style   A value, similar to a window style, that specifies the appearance and behavior of a control. The window procedure for the control uses the style to determine how to draw the control and process input.

CPU   *See* **central processing unit**.

critical section object   A segment of code that is not reentrant and therefore does not support concurrent access by multiple threads. Often, a critical section object is used to protect shared resources.

cursor   A small bitmap whose location on the screen is controlled by a pointing device, such as a mouse, pen, or trackball. Some Windows CE-based platforms only support the wait cursor (the spinning hourglass).

D

database synchronization The process of bringing two separate copies of a database into agreement.

database system application programming interface
A set of functions that enable you to create and manipulate Windows CE databases. Each database consists of an arbitrary number of records, and each record consists of at least one *property*.

data link A connection that passes values between two objects or locations.

date and time picker control A control that displays information about dates and times, and provides users with an easy way to modify this information.

DCC *See* **direct cable connection**.

DDB *See* **device-dependent bitmap**.

DDE *See* **dynamic data exchange**.

DDI *See* **device driver interface**.

DDK *See* **device driver kit**.

dead key A key used with another key to create an accented character. A dead key, when pressed, produces no visible character, but indicates that the accent mark it represents is to be combined with the character produced by the next letter key pressed.

demonstration project A set of directories, code, and environment variables that help users to understand the EDK tools.

deserialize The process of converting a series of bytes back into an object. *See* **serialize**.

desktop An on-screen work area that uses icons and menus to simulate the top of a desk.. Its intent is to make a computer easier to use by enabling users to move pictures of objects and to start and stop tasks in much the same way as they would if they were working on a physical desktop.

desktop connectivity The services required to connect a Windows CE-based device to a desktop computer.

development workstation The computer workstation running the EDK development tools.

device **1.** A generic term for a computer subsystem. Printers, serial ports, and disk drives are often referred to as devices; such subsystems frequently require their own controlling software, called device drivers. **2.** A hardware feature that can—or must—be part of the target platform. For example, a built-in device could be a low-battery notification LED, while a PC Card modem is an installable device.

device context A GDI structure containing information that governs the display of text and graphics on a particular output device. A device context stores, retrieves, and modifies the attributes of graphic objects and specifies graphic modes. The graphic objects stored in a device context include a pen for line drawing, a brush for painting and filling, a font for text output, a bitmap for copying or scrolling, a palette for defining the available colors, and a region for clipping.

device-dependent bitmap (DDB)
An array of bits that can only be used with a particular display or printer.

device driver Software that provides control over hardware devices. Device drivers are treated like applications. In the Windows CE environment, they are simply user-level dynamic-link libraries.

device driver interface (DDI) 1. The interface between applications and the device drivers. **2.** A set of functions implemented in the model device driver and called by the Graphics, Windowing, and Events Subsystem (GWES).

device driver kit (DDK) A set of tools and libraries that enable programmers to write Windows-based software used to run hardware devices such as printers.

device driver test kit (DDTK) A set of tools and libraries that enable you to test the porting of your device drivers to the Windows CE operating system.

device-independent bitmap (DIB)
An array of bits combined with several structures that specify the width and height of the bitmap image (in pixels), the color format of the device where the image was created, and the resolution of the device used to create that image. A DIB generally has its own color table, and can therefore be displayed on a variety of devices.

device manager A program, included on all Windows CE-based platforms, that manages installable device drivers. The device manager handles loading and unloading installable device drivers, identifying the correct driver for plug-and-play devices, managing running device drivers, and notifying installable device drivers of power-up and power-down events.

DHCP *See* **Dynamic Host Configuration Protocol.**

dialog box A temporary window that contains controls. You can use it to display status information and to get user input.

dialog box procedure An application-defined callback function that the system calls when it has input for a dialog box or has tasks for a dialog box to carry out.

dialog box template A binary description of a dialog box and the controls it contains. You can create this template as a resource to be loaded from the application's executable file, or created in memory while the application runs.

DIB *See* **device-independent bitmap.**

direct cable connection (DCC) A RAS networking connection between two computers or between a computer and a Windows CE-based device, which uses a serial or parallel cable directly connected between the systems instead of a modem and a phone line.

direct memory access (DMA) Memory access that does not involve the microprocessor and is frequently used for data transfer directly between memory and an "intelligent" peripheral device, such as a disk drive.

DLL *See* **dynamic-link library.**

drag-and-drop A technique for moving or copying data between applications, between windows within an application, or within a single window in an application. The user selects the data to be transferred and drags the data to the desired destination. Windows CE supports drag-and-drop operations. However, non-default drag-and-drop operations, equivalent to right mouse button drag-and-drop operations, are not supported.

drop-down menu A menu that drops from the menu bar when requested and remains open without further action until the user closes it or chooses a menu item.

dummy file filter A means for transferring files of nonstandard or possibly unknown extensions for which no translation is necessary. Passing the file through the dummy filter keeps the **No Convertor Selected** dialog box from being issued to the user.

dynamic data exchange (DDE) An interprocess communication method that allows two or more programs running simultaneously to exchange data and commands.

Dynamic Host Configuration Protocol (DHCP) A Transmission Control Protocol/Internet Protocol (TCP/IP) that enables a network connected to the Internet to automatically assign a temporary Internet protocol (IP) address to a host when the host connects to the network.

dynamic-link library (DLL) A set of autonomous functions that any application can use. DLLs are a set of source code modules with each module containing a set of functions.

E

edit control A rectangular window in which a user can enter and edit text from the keyboard. An edit control is also referred to as a text box.

embedded Software code or commands built into their carriers. For example, application programs insert embedded printing commands into a document to control printing and formatting. Low-level assembly is embedded in higher-level languages, such as C, to provide more capabilities or better efficiency.

Embedded Developers Kit (EDK) A set of tools and libraries for creating a custom Windows CE embedded operating systems. The EDK is part of the Windows CE Embedded Toolkit for Visual C++ 5.0.

environment variable An element of the operating system environment, such as a path, a directory name, or a configuration string. Environment variables are typically set within batch files.

Ethernet A widely used LAN developed by Xerox, Digital, and Intel. Ethernet networks connect up to 1,024 nodes at 10 megabits per second over twisted pair, coax, and optical fiber.

event An event is an occurrence that triggers a notification. Windows CE supports timer and system events.

event-driven operating system An operating system that constantly evaluates and responds to sets of events, such as key presses or mouse movements.

event object A synchronization object that enables one thread to notify another that an event has occurred. Event objects are useful when a thread needs to know when to perform its task. For example, a thread that copies data to an archive needs to be notified when new data is available. By using an event object to notify the copying thread of the availability of new data, the thread can perform its task as soon as possible.

exception handling The process of dealing with exceptions, or errors, as they arise during program execution. Exceptions occur when a program executes abnormally due to conditions outside the program's control. Windows CE does not support C++ exception handling.

execute in place (XIP) The process of executing code directly from read-only memory (ROM), rather than loading it from random access memory (RAM) first. Executing the code in place, instead of copying the code into RAM for execution, saves system resources. Applications in other file systems, such as PC Cards, cannot be executed in this way.

Exit button A hardware navigation control that functions as the ESC key on a keyboard.

extension key An entry in the registry, corresponding to the extension of a given file, that specifies which file filter will handle conversions for that file type.

F

FAT *See* **file allocation table.**

file allocation table (FAT) A table that contains the status of various segments of disk space used for file storage. Also, the file system that maintains the table.

file filter A Windows CE dynamic-link library (DLL) that controls the transfer of data between a desktop computer and a Windows CE-based device.

file system In an operating system, the overall structure in which files are named, stored, and organized. A file system consists of files, directories, and the information needed to locate and access these items. The term can also refer to the portion of an operating system that translates requests for file operations from an application program into low-level, sector-oriented tasks that can be understood by the drivers controlling the disk drives.

file system application interface A subset of the standard Win32 file system functions. These functions let you create directories and data files, read and write file data, and retrieve file and directory information.

File Transfer Protocol (FTP) The protocol used for copying files to and from remote computer systems on a network using a Transmission Control Protocol/Internet Protocol (TCP/IP), such as the Internet. This protocol also allows users to use FTP commands to work with files, such as listing files and directories on the remote system.

firmware A computer program that is saved in hardware (such as a semiconductor ROM) as contrasted with programs stored in volatile RAM.

flash memory Semiconductor memory that can operate as ROM but, on an activating signal, can rewrite its contents as though it were RAM.

flash time The elapsed time, in milliseconds, required to display, invert, and restore the caret display. This value is twice as much as the blink time.

focus window The window that is currently receiving keyboard input. The focus window is always the active window, a descendent of the active window, or NULL.

foreground thread The thread used to create the window with which the user is currently working.

foreground window The window with which the user is currently working. The system assigns a slightly higher priority to the thread used to create the foreground window than it does to other threads.

free threading model A model in which an object can be used on any thread at any time. *See* **apartment model threading** and **single threading model**.

FTP *See* **File Transfer Protocol**.

G

GDI *See* **graphics device interface**.

globalization The process of developing a program core whose feature and code designs do not make assumptions based on a single language or locale, and whose source code simplifies the creation of different language editions of a program.

global variable A variable whose value can be accessed and modified by any statement in a program, not merely within a single routine in which it is defined.

graphics object The pen, brush, bitmap, palette, region, font, and path associated with a device context. Windows CE does not support paths.

graphics device interface (GDI) The Windows CE subsystem responsible for displaying text and images on display devices and printers. The GDI processes graphical function calls from a Windows-based application. It then passes those calls to the appropriate device driver, which generates the output on the display hardware. By acting as a buffer between applications and output devices, the GDI presents a device-independent view of the world for the application while interacting in a device-dependent format with the device. Because of the smaller memory footprint of Windows CE-based devices, Windows CE supports only a subset of the standard Win32 GDI.

Graphics, Windowing, and Events Subsystem (GWES)
The Windows CE module that contains the graphics and windowing functionality needed to display text and images and to receive user input. It includes all the functionality needed to create and manage windows, controls, dialog boxes, and resources such as icons and menus. It also processes all user input. GWES includes the graphics device interface, which displays text and images on display devices and printers.

grayscale A sequence of shades ranging from black through white, used in computer graphics to add detail to images or to represent a color image on a monochrome output device. Like the number of colors in a color image, the number of shades of gray depends on the number of bits stored per pixel. Grays may be represented by actual gray shades, by halftone dots, or by dithering.

gripper bar A gripper bar is a tall, thin rectangle with a dark stripe running through it that appears on a rebar or a command band control. By touching and dragging a gripper bar with a stylus, a user can repostion a rebar or command bar. Gripper bars are especially useful for bringing off-screen rebar or command bar controls into view.

group box A rectangular area within a dialog box in which you can group together other controls that are semantically related. The controls are grouped by drawing a rectangular border around them. Any text associated with the group box is displayed in its upper-left hand corner.

GUID A globally unique identifier. *See* **Universally Unique Identifier**.

GWES *See* **Graphics, Windowing, and Events Subsystem**.

H

handle A variable that identifies an object; an indirect reference to an operating system resource.

H/PC A Handheld PC.

header control A horizontal window that is usually positioned above columns of data. It is divided into partitions that correspond to the columns, and each partition contains the title for the column below it.

heap A portion of memory reserved for a program to use for the temporary storage of data structures whose existence or size cannot be determined until the program is running. The program can request free memory from the heap to hold such elements, use it as necessary, and later free the memory.

hibernation The way in which a Windows CE-based device manages a memory shortage by requesting applications free memory that is not currently needed.

hibernation threshold The point at which the system enters a limited memory state.

high-resolution performance counter
Hardware that provides high-resolution timing useful in improving the performance of applications.

hook A point in the Windows message-handling mechanism where an application can install a subroutine to monitor the message traffic in the system and process certain types of messages before they reach the target window procedure. Windows CE does not support hooking.

hot key A keystroke or combination of keystrokes that switches the user to a different program, often a terminate-and-stay-resident (TSR) program or the operating system user interface. Hot keys generate a WM_HOTKEY message.

hot spot The pixel in a cursor that marks the exact screen location affected by a mouse or pen action, such as a button click. Messages include the coordinates of a hot spot.

HTML *See* **Hypertext Markup Language**.

Hypertext Markup Language (HTML) viewer control
A control that provides programmers with the ability to implement the Windows CE Pocket Internet Explorer and the Help engine. It also provides independent software vendors (ISVs) with the ability to implement additional viewers based on the HTML viewer control.

HTTP *See* **Hypertext Transfer Protocol**.

Hypertext Markup Language (HTML)
A markup language derived from the Standard Generalized Markup Language (SGML). Used to create a text document with formatting specifications that tells a software browser how to display the page or pages included in the document.

Hypertext Transfer Protocol (HTTP)
The client/server protocol used to access information on the Web.

I

IAS *See* **Information Access Service**.

ICMP *See* **Internet Control Message Protocol**.

icon A small bitmap that usually represents a minimized application. Icons may also serve as symbols in warning messages or other windows.

idle priority One of three thread priority groups. Idle priority indicates that a thread's processing can wait until all other threads have finished running.

IEEE *See* **Institute of Electrical and Electronics Engineers**.

IHV *See* **independent hardware vendor**.

IM *See* **input method**.

image list A collection of images that are all the same size, such as bitmaps or icons.

Inbox A mail client application provided with Windows CE.

independent hardware vendor (IHV)
A company that manufactures devices that connect to Windows CE-based platforms, such as PC Cards. IHVs must also produce Installable Device Drivers for their devices. *See* **Installable Device Driver**.

.inf file A CAB Wizard input file that specifies information about the application.

Information Access Service (IAS)
A part of an IrDA infrared communication protocol used so that devices can learn about the services offered by another device.

infrared Of or relating to the range of invisible radiation wavelengths from about 750 nanometers, just longer than red in the visible spectrum, to 1 millimeter, on the border of the microwave region.

Infrared Data Association (IrDA) The industry organization of computer, component, and telecommunications vendors who have established the standards for infrared communication between computers and peripheral devices such as printers. Windows CE supports the IrDA standard through the Winsock Application Programming Interface (API). Windows CE-based applications that communicate over serial cables using the Winsock API will communicate over IrDA-compliant IR links with only minimal reprogramming.

Infrared Link Access Protocol (IrLAP)
A data link layer protocol providing a reliable point-to-point link, which effectively replaces a three-wire serial cable connection.

Infrared Link Management Protocol (IrLMP)
A service multiplexing protocol that provides for multiple sessions over a single point-to-point link.

.ini file An initialization file that registers an application with an application manager. It contains information such as the location of .cab files, icon files, and the installation directory.

input method A mechanism that allows the user to input text by means of a touch-sensitive display screen. For example, the Palm PC supports two input methods: a keyboard and a character recognizer used for ink input.

input panel A user interface element that contains a keyboard, operated by using a touch-sensitive display screen and a stylus.

Installable Device Driver (IDD) A user-level DLL that drives devices connected to a Windows CE-based platform. It presents the functionality of such a device to applications in terms of standard Win32 file input/output functions. Some devices built into a Windows CE-based platform may also be driven by installable device drivers, depending on the software architecture for those devices' drivers.

Institute of Electrical and Electronics Engineers (IEEE)
A organization formed in 1963 by electrical engineering prefessionals from the United States and other countries. The institute develops electrical and communications standards, many affecting aspects of computer technology, such as network connectivity, and formats for representing floating-point numbers.

interface 1. The point at which a connection is made between two elements so that they can work with one another. **2.** Software that enables a program to work with the user (the user interface, which can be a command-line interface, menu-driven, or a graphical user interface), with another program such as the operating system, or with the computer's hardware. **3.** A card, plug, or other device that connects pieces of hardware with the computer so that information can be moved from place to place. For example, standardized interfaces such as RS-232-C standard and SCSI enable communications between computers and printers or disks. **4.** A networking or communications standard, such as the ISO/OSI model, that defines ways for different systems to connect and communicate.

Internet Control Message Protocol (ICMP)
A network-layer Internet protocol that provides error correction and other information relevant to Internet Protocol (IP) packet processing, such as testing whether a particular computer is connected to the Internet ("pinging"), by sending a packet to its IP address and waiting for a response. For example, it can let the IP software on one machine inform another machine about an unreachable destination. *See* **ping**.

Internet Information Server (IIS) A Web server integrated into a Windows NT server.

Internet Protocol (IP) Provides the protocol for connecting hosts over a network, breaking messages into packets, addressing the packets, routing them from the sender to the destination network, and reassembling the packets into the original message at the destination. IP corresponds to the network layer in the International Organization for Standardization Open Systems Interconnection (ISO/OSI) model.

Internet Protocol (IP) address A 32-bit (4-byte) binary number that uniquely identifies a host computer connected to the Internet to other Internet hosts, for the purposes of communication through the transfer of packets. An IP address is expressed in "dotted quad" format, consisting of the decimal values of its four bytes, separated with periods; for example, 127.0.0.1. The first one, two, or three bytes of the IP address, assigned by InterNIC Registration Services, identify the network the host is connected to; the remaining bits identify the host itself.

interrupt A request for attention from the processor. When the processor receives an interrupt, it suspends its current operations, saves the status of its work, and transfers control to a special routine known as an interrupt handler, which contains the instructions for dealing with the particular situation that caused the interrupt. Interrupts can be generated by various hardware devices to request service or report problems, or by the processor itself in response to program errors or requests for operating-system services. Interrupts are the processor's way of communicating with the other elements that make up a computer system. A hierarchy of interrupt priorities determines which interrupt request will be handled first if more than one request is made. A program can temporarily disable some interrupts if it needs the full attention of the processor to complete a particular task.

interrupt identifier (interrupt ID) A unique value used by the kernel to identify the device that raised the interrupt and that requires more processing. The kernel then uses the interrupt ID to indicate whether all handling is complete, or whether to launch an interrupt service thread that handles further processing by the device driver.

interrupt priority One of three thread priority groups. Interrupt priority is reserved for operating system threads.

interrupt request line (IRQ) A hardware line over which a device, such as an input/output port, keyboard, or disk drive, can send interrupt requests to the central processing unit (CPU). Interrupt request lines are built into the computer's internal hardware and are assigned different levels of priority so that the CPU can determine the sources and relative importance of incoming service requests.

interrupt service routine (ISR) A small subroutine that resides in the OEM Adaptation Layer. The ISR executes in kernel mode and has direct access to the hardware registers. Its sole job is to determine what interrupt ID to return to the interrupt support handler. Essentially, ISRs map physical interrupts onto logical interrupts.

interrupt service thread (IST) A thread created by a device driver to wait on an event.

interrupt support handler A routine that registers a driver so that it can handle a particular interrupt and unregister it later. It also enables communication between the interrupt service routine, interrupt service thread, and subroutines within the OEM Adaptation Layer (OAL).

I/O Input/Output.

IP *See* **Internet Protocol**.

IrCOMM An infrared implementation of the serial line communication driver. IrCOMM is supported by Windows CE.

IrDA *See* **Infrared Data Association**.

IrLAP *See* **Infrared Link Access Protocol**.

IrLMP *See* **Infrared Link Management Protocol**.

IrLPT A protocol for printing through a serial infrared connection.

IRQ *See* **interrupt request line**.

IrSOCK Short for Infrared Sockets, IrSock is an implementation of the Winsock protocol.

ISR *See* **interrupt service routine**.

ISV Independent software vendor.

item script A program written in HTML and Visual Basic Script, JScript, Java Script, or other scripting languages that specifies the behavior of an item within a channel.

K

kernel The main module of the Windows CE operating system. The kernel provides system services for managing threads, memory, and resources.

Key A field or expression used to identify a record; often used as the index field for a database table.

keyboard accelerator A keystroke or combination of keystrokes that invokes a command. *Also called* an accelerator, shortcut key, and keyboard shortcut.

L

LAN *See* **local area network.**

launch entry A registry entry that specifies the order in which applications launch.

layered device driver A sample device driver that comes with the Embedded Toolkit. It contains two layers: a model device driver (MDD) layer and a platform-dependent driver (PDD) layer. *See* **model device driver** and **platform-dependent driver.**

list box A window that displays a list of character strings. The user selects a string from the list by tapping it with the stylus. When a string is selected, it appears highlighted. You can use a vertical or horizontal scroll bar with a list box to scroll lists that are too long for the control window. The list box automatically hides or shows the scroll bar, as needed.

list view A common control that displays a collection of items, such as files or folders. Each item has an icon and a label.

load file A file that contains a list of commands for the **Load** function to process. You use load file commands to direct Ppcload.dll to create directories on a Windows CE-based device, copy files into the directories, edit registry entries, execute programs on the Windows CE-based device, and add items to the unload script. The fully qualified path name of the load file is given as a command line argument to Load.

local area network (LAN) A group of computers and other devices dispersed over a relatively limited area and connected by a communications link that enables any device to interact with any other on the network. LANs commonly include microcomputers and shared resources such as laser printers and large hard disks. The devices on a LAN are known as nodes, and the nodes are connected by cables through which messages are transmitted.

localization The process of adapting a program for a specific international market, which includes translating the user interface, resizing dialog boxes, customizing features if necessary, and testing results to ensure that the program still functions properly.

logical palette An array of colors, or color palette, that an application creates and associates with a device context and uses for graphics output.

M

main priority One of three thread priority groups. Main is the default priority.

main window The window that serves as the primary interface between the user and an application.

MDD *See* **model device driver**.

MDI *See* **multiple-document interface**.

menu A list of items that represent an application's commands. A menu item can be either a string or a bitmap.

menu handle A unique value of type **HMENU** used to identify a menu.

menu item A string or bitmap displayed in a menu. Choosing a menu item either sends a command message or activates a pop-up menu.

menu template A menu template defines a menu, including the items on a menu bar and all submenus.

message A structure or set of parameters used for communicating information or a request. Messages can be passed between the operating system and an application, different applications, threads within an application, and windows within an application.

message box A secondary window that is displayed to inform a user about a particular condition.

message identifier (message ID) A unique value that identifies a message. System-defined messages use named constants, such as WM_PAINT, as message identifiers. Windows CE reserves message-identifier values in the range 0x0400 through 0x7FFF for application-defined messages.

message queue An ordered list of messages awaiting transmission, from which they are taken up on a first-in, first-out (FIFO) basis.

message store The database in the object store for storing mail messages.

MFC *See* **Microsoft Foundation Classes**.

Microsoft Foundation Classes The C++ class library that Microsoft provides with its C++ compiler to assist programmers in creating Windows-based applications. MFC hides the fundamental Windows API in class hierarchies so that programmers can write a Windows-based application without needing to know the details of the native Windows API.

Mobile Channels A Windows CE technology that represents a fourth type of IE4 channel to allow the user to access the Web with great mobility.

modal dialog box A modal dialog box requires the user to supply information or cancel the dialog box before allowing the application to continue.

model device driver (MDD) The platform-neutral layer of a built-in device driver supplied by Microsoft. *See* **built-in device driver**.

modeless dialog box A modeless dialog box allows the user to supply information and return to a previous task without closing the dialog box.

module A subset of the Windows CE operating system. Windows CE is structured as a collection of modules. Each module is a self-contained subset of the Windows CE operating system that can be used to construct a customized operating system for a particular device.

monolithic device driver A sample device driver that comes with the Windows CE Embedded Toolkit for Visual C++ 5.0.

month calendar control A child window that displays a monthly calendar. The calendar can display one or more months at a time.

multiple-document interface (MDI)
A user interface in an application that allows the user to have more than one document open at the same time. MDI is not supported by Windows CE.

mutex object An interprocess synchronization object whose state is set to signaled when it is not owned by any thread, and nonsignaled when it is owned. Only one thread at a time can own a mutex.

N

NaN Not a number.

national language support (NLS) A function which enables you to specify system and user locale information.

NDIS A programming interface for different protocols sharing the same network hardware.

network stack An operating system component responsible for processing data that is transmitted or received over a network.

node **1.** In local area networks, a device that is connected to the network and is capable of communicating with other network devices. **2.** In tree structures, a location on the tree that can have links to one or more nodes below it. Some authors make a distinction between node and element, with an element being a given data type and a node comprising one or more elements as well as any supporting data structures.

nonclient area The parts of a window that are not a part of the client area. A window's nonclient area consists of the border, menu bar, title bar, and scroll bar.

nonqueued message A message sent directly to a window procedure.

nonsignaled *See* **synchronization object**.

notification A signal from the operating system that an event has occurred. This could be a timer event or a system event such as establishing a network connection. An application registers a notification for an event and the system generates a notification when the event occurs. Windows CE provides an application programming interface (API) that can be used to register events and select options that determine the type of notification.

notification function A Windows CE function that allows an application to register its name and an event with the system. When the event occurs the kernel automatically starts the named application.

notification message A message a control sends to its parent window when events, such as input from the user, occur.

O

object A file, directory, database, or database record that resides in an object store.

object ID *See* **object identifier**.

object identifier (object ID) **1.** A unique value which identifies each object in the object store. **2.** In reference to the Contacts database, an object identifier is a unique value that the system assigns to each address card when it is added. An application uses the object identifier when querying an address card's properties or when modifying or deleting an address card.

object store   The persistent storage that Windows CE makes available to applications. For example, Windows CE reserves part of its available random access memory (RAM) for the operating system and uses the rest for the object store. This data can be stored in files, registry entries, or in Windows CE databases.

OEM   *See* **original equipment manufacturer**.

OEM adaptation layer (OAL)   That portion of Windows CE that must be provided by the hardware manufacture to adapt Windows CE to their platform.

OLE   Object Linking and Embedding. *See* **Automation**.

option button   A small round button with a label next to it. The label may be text, an icon, or a bitmap. Option buttons, also known as radio buttons, are usually grouped together in a group box, representing a set of related, but mutually exclusive options. When a user selects an option button, all other option buttons in the same group are automatically unselected.

original equipment manufacturer (OEM)
For Windows CE, an OEM is a company that manufacturers a hardware platform and ports Windows CE to that platform.

overlapped communication operation
The performance of two distinct communication operations simultaneously, for example, a simultaneous read and write operation. Windows CE does not support overlapped communication operation, but does support multiple reads/writes pending on a device.

overlapped window   A window with the WS_OVERLAPPED style. Overlapped Windows are top-level windows designed to serve as an application's main window.

P

packet   A unit of information transmitted as a whole from one device to another on a network.

parallel port   The input/output connector for a parallel interface device.

parent window   A window that has one or more child windows.

parser   An application that breaks data into smaller chunks so that a program can act upon the information. For example, Mobile Channels uses a Channel Definition Format parser to parse a channel.

pASP   *See* **pocket Active Server Pages**.

path   **1.** In communications, a link between two nodes in a network. **2.** A route through a structured collection of information, as in a database, a program, or files stored on disk. **3.** In programming, the sequence of instructions a computer carries out in executing a routine. **4.** In file storage, the route followed by the operating system in finding, sorting, and retrieving files on a disk. **5.** In graphics, an accumulation of line segments or curves to be filled or overwritten with text.

PC Card   A trademark of the Personal Computer Memory Card International Association (PCMCIA) that is used to describe add-in cards that conform to the PCMCIA specification. A PC Card is a removable device approximately the same size as a credit card that is designed to plug into a PCMCIA slot. Type I cards are primarily used as memory-related peripherals. Type II cards accommodate devices such as modem, fax, and network cards. Type III cards accommodate devices that require more space, such as wireless communications devices and rotating storage media, including hard disks.

PCT   *See* **Program Comprehension Tool**.

PDD *See* **platform dependent driver**.

pen A drawing tool used to draw lines and curves.

persistent object The Component Object Model (COM) defines standards through which clients can request objects to be initialized, loaded, and saved to and from a data store, such as a flat file, structured storage, or memory. COM objects that adhere to these standards are called persistent objects.

personal information manager (PIM)
A category of software applications such as Lotus Notes or Microsoft Exchange that allow the user to manage scheduling, tasks, and contact information.

phone-book Entries in the Remote Access Service (RAS) phone-book contain the information necessary to establish a RAS connection. Unlike Windows NT, which keeps the phone-book entries in a file, Windows CE stores these entries in the registry.

PIM *See* **personal information manager**.

ping A protocol for testing whether a particular computer is connected to the Internet by sending a packet to its Internet Protocol (IP) address and waiting for a response.

platform **1.** The foundation technology of a computer system. Because computers are layered devices composed of a chip-level hardware layer, a firmware and operating-system layer, and an applications program layer, the bottommost layer of a machine is often called a platform. **2.** In everyday usage, the type of computer or operating system being used. **3.** The hardware upon which an implementation of Windows CE will run. **4.** The directory structure containing the hardware-specific files needed to build an implementation of Windows CE.

Platform Dependent Driver (PDD)
The platform-specific layer of built-in device drivers that is supplied by an original equipment manufacturer. *See* **built-in device driver**.

platform directory The root of the directory structure where platform-specific files are stored. Each subdirectory in the platform directory specifies the name of a development workstation.

pocket Active Server Pages (pASP)
A scaled-down version of the Active Server Pages optimized for server-side Mobile Channels scripting.

Point-to-Point Protocol (PPP) An advanced serial packet protocol commonly used for dial-up connections.

POP *See* **Post Office Protocol**.

POP3 *See* **Post Office Protocol 3**.

pop-up menu A menu that appears on the screen when a user selects a certain item. Pop-up menus can appear anywhere on the screen, and they generally disappear when the user selects an item in the menu.

pop-up window A special type of overlapped window typically used for dialog boxes, message boxes, and other temporary windows that appear outside an application's main window.

position index An identifier associated with each address card in the Contacts database. The position index indicates the address card's position relative to the other address cards in the database. A position index is distinct from an object identifier.

POSIX *See* **Portable Operating System Interface for Computer Environments**.

Portable Operating System Interface for Computer Environments (POSIX)
An IEEE standard that defines the open systems environment standards for system interfaces, shells, tools, testing, verification, real-time processing, security, system administration, networking, and transaction processing. The standard is based on UNIX system services, but it allows implementation on other operating systems.

Post Office Protocol (POP) A standard protocol for transferring mail messages on demand from a mail server.

Post Office Protocol 3 (POP3) A standard protocol for transferring mail messages on demand from a mail server.

PPP *See* **Point-to-Point Protocol**.

Ppsh A parallel port shell utility that enables you to download a binary image from the development workstation to the target platform and gives you access to debugging processes running on the development platform.

predefined control A control belonging to a window class supplied by Windows CE.

preemptive multitasking The ability of the operating system to schedule execution time for multiple processes and threads by periodically suspending the execution of the currently executing thread and switching to another high-priority thread.

priority class A range of thread priority levels. Whereas Win32 utilizes four priority classes with seven base priority levels per class, Windows CE has only eight base priority levels. Hence, for processes running under Windows CE, preemption is based solely on the thread's priority.

priority inheritance A process by which a thread that is blocking a shared resource needed by a higher priority thread inherits the priority of that higher priority thread in order to free the resource for use by the higher priority thread, thus preventing *priority inversion*.

priority inversion Priority inversion is a situation in which a higher priority thread A spawns lower-priority thread B to access a shared resource that is already in use by lower-priority thread C with greater priority than thread B, blocking higher-priority thread A. This situation can be averted by a process of *priority inheritance*.

process An executing application that consists of a private virtual address space, code, data, and other operating-system resources, such as files, pipes, and synchronization objects that are visible to the process. A process also contains one or more threads that run in the context of the process.

program comprehension tool (PCT) A software engineering tool that facilitates the process of understanding the structure and/or functionality of computer programs.

program memory Program memory is used for stack and heap storage for both system and non-system programs. Non-system applications are taken from storage memory, uncompressed, and loaded into program memory for execution.

progress bar A common control that indicates the progress of a lengthy operation by displaying a colored bar inside a horizontal rectangle. The length of the bar in relation to the length of the rectangle corresponds to the percentage of the operation that is complete.

project 1. The implementation of an instance of Windows CE. **2.** The directory structure—under Public—containing files that define which components will be included in an implementation of Windows CE.

property With respect to the database application programming interface, a property refers to a data item that consists of a property identifier, data type, and value. Windows CE supports several data types such as integer, string, time, and binary large object (BLOB).

property sheet A type of dialog box that lists the attributes or settings of an object, such as a file, application, or hardware device. A property sheet presents the user with a tabbed, index card–like selection of property pages, each of which features standard dialog box-style controls for customizing parameters.

public-key encryption An asymmetric scheme that uses a pair of keys for encryption: The public key encrypts data, and a corresponding secret key decrypts it. For digital signatures, the process is reversed: The sender uses the secret key to create a unique electronic number that can be read by anyone possessing the corresponding public key, which verifies that the message is truly from the sender.

push button A small rectangular control that a user can turn on or off. A push button, also known as a command button, has a raised appearance in its default off state and a depressed appearance when it is turned on.

Q

queued message A message in a message queue.

QWERTY keyboard A keyboard layout named for the six leftmost characters in the top row of alphabetic characters on most keyboards—the standard layout of most typewriters and computer keyboards.

R

radio button *See* **option button**.

RAM *See* **Random Access Memory**.

Random Access Memory Semiconductor-based memory that can be read and written by the CPU or other hardware devices.

RAPI *See* **Remote Application Programming Interface**.

RAS *See* **remote access server**.

raster font A font in which each glyph (character or symbol) is of a particular size and style, designed for a specific resolution of device and described as a unique bitmap. There are seven system raster fonts available in several sizes stored in the Windows CE read-only memory (ROM). The built-in fonts are built into the Windows CE operating system. Raster fonts are also known as bitmap fonts and non-scalable fonts.

raw infrared (raw IR) A method of receiving data through an infrared transceiver. Raw IR treats the IR transceiver like a serial cable and does not process data in any way. The application is responsible for handling collision detection and other potential problems.

read-only memory (ROM) Any semiconductor circuit serving as a memory that contains instructions or data that can be read but not modified, regardless of whether it was placed there by a manufacturer or by a programming process.

rebar control A rebar control acts as a container for child windows. A rebar control contains one or more bands. Each band can contain one child window, which can be a toolbar or any other control.

record A data structure that is a collection of elements, each with its own name and type. The elements of a record represent different types of information and are accessed by name. A record can be accessed as a collective unit of elements, or the elements can be accessed individually. A collection of records is a database. A Windows CE database consists of an arbitrary number of records, where each record consists of one or more properties. Each of the records in a specific database typically contain a similar set of properties. A Windows CE database should not be confused with a full-fledged relational database. It is simply a general-purpose, flexible, structured collection of data.

rectangle A function that draws a rectangular image.

reentrant code Code written so that it can be shared by several programs or threads within a single process simultaneously. When code is reentrant, one thread can safely interrupt the execution of another thread, execute its own code, and then return control to the first thread in such a way that the first thread does not fail or behave in an unexpected way.

region A rectangle, polygon, ellipse, or a combination of two or more of these shapes used by Windows-based applications to define a part of the client area to be painted, inverted, filled with output, framed, or used for hit testing.

registered notification The state of a user notification from the time **CeSetUserNotification** is called until the time the user is notified.

registry A central hierarchical database used to store information necessary to configure the system for applications and hardware devices. The registry contains information—such as the applications installed on the computer and the types of documents each can create, property sheet settings for folders and application icons, what hardware exists on the system, and which ports are being used—which the operating system continually references during operation.

remote access server (RAS) A Windows NT feature by which a single serial connection provides a remote workstation with host connectivity, Windows NT file services, or Novell file and printing services (NWLink). Windows CE supports the standard Win32 RAS functions; however it allows only one connection at a time. RAS functions can be implemented for direct serial connections or dial-up modem connections.

Remote Application Programming Interface (RAPI) Enables applications running on a desktop computer—the RAPI client—the ability to make function calls on a Windows CE-based device— the RAPI server. RAPI runs over Winsock and TCP/IP.

resource Binary data the resource compiler or programmer adds to an application's executable file. Windows resources include icons, cursors, menus, dialog boxes, bitmaps, fonts, keyboard accelerator tables, message table entries, string table entries, version data, and user defined data.

Rich Ink The underlying technology that enables a user to write and draw on a touch-sensitive screen with a stylus.

rocker switch A hardware navigation control designed to perform spatial navigation, much like the UP ARROW key and the DOWN ARROW key.

ROM *See* **read-only memory**.

ROM image Files and binaries as they appear in physical memory as defined by the binary image builder (.bib) file.

router An intermediary device on a communications network that expedites message delivery. On a single network linking many computers through a mesh of possible connections, a router receives transmitted messages and forwards them to their correct destinations over the most efficient available route. On an interconnected set of local area networks using the same communications protocols, a router serves the somewhat different function of acting as a link between these local area networks, enabling messages to be sent from one network to another.

S

scan code A code number transmitted to a computer whenever a key is pressed or released. Each key on the keyboard has a unique scan code. This code is not the same as the ASCII code for the letter, number, or symbol shown on the key; it is a special identifier for the key itself and is always the same for a particular key. When a key is pressed, the scan code is transmitted to the computer, where a portion of the read-only memory basic input/output system (ROM BIOS) dedicated to the keyboard translates the scan code into its ASCII equivalent. Because a single key can generate more than one character (lowercase "a" and uppercase "A," for example), the ROM BIOS also keeps track of the status of keys that change the keyboard state, such as the SHIFT key, and takes them into account when translating a scan code.

script A program consisting of a set of instructions to an application or utility program. The instructions usually use the rules and syntax of the application or utility.

scripting language A simple programming language designed to perform special or limited tasks, sometimes associated with a particular application or function. An example of a scripting language is Visual Basic Script.

scroll bar In some graphical user interfaces, a vertical or horizontal bar at the side or bottom of a display area that can be used with a mouse for moving around in that area. Scroll bars often have four active areas: two scroll arrows for moving line by line, a sliding scroll box for moving to an arbitrary location in the display area, and the gray areas in the scroll bar for moving in one-window increments.

scrolling menu A menu with top arrows used to scroll menu items up and down.

SDK *See* **Software Development Kit**.

secure socket layer (SSL) A proposed open standard developed by Netscape Communications for establishing a secure communication channel to prevent the interception of critical information, such as credit card numbers. The primary purpose of the SSL is to enable secure electronic financial transactions on the Web, although it is designed to work with other Internet services as well.

Serial Infrared (SIR) Part of the basic Infrared Data Association (IrDA) communication protocol, a Serial Infrared physical layer provides for serial infrared links.

serial cable A cable that connects to a serial port. It is used to transfer information between two devices. *See* **serial port**.

serial input/output (serial I/O) A communications channel that transmits data one bit at a time.

serialize The process of converting an object to a series of bytes for transmission to another device. *See* **deserialize**.

serial line Internet protocol (SLIP) A data link protocol that allows transmission of Internet Protocol (IP) data packets over dial-up telephone connections, thus enabling a computer or a local area network to be connected to the Internet or some other network.

serial port An input/output location (channel) that sends and receives data to and from a computer's central processing unit or a communications device one bit at a time. Serial ports are used for serial data communication and as interfaces to peripheral devices, such as mice and printers.

server **1.** On a local area network (LAN), a computer running administrative software that controls access to the network and its resources, such as printers and disk drives, and provides resources to computers functioning as workstations on the network. **2.** A program that responds to requests from another program or task. *See* **client**.

service identifier (service ID) An identifier used by a service to uniquely identify messages. This value should be changed only by the service library.

session identifier (session ID) An identifier generated by a mail transport service. Each time a Post Office Protocol 3 (POP3) connection is made to the server, the server looks at all of the currently stored messages and assigns a session ID to each message, numbered 1 through the total number of messages. This makes it easier to reference a particular message without having to use its long unique ID. The session ID can be trusted only during a single connection to the mail server.

SGML *See* **Standard Generalized Markup Language**.

shared directory On a local area network, a directory on a disk that is located on a computer other than the one the user is operating. A shared directory differs from a network drive in that the user has access to only that directory.

shared library Any code module that can be accessed and used by many programs. Shared libraries are used primarily for sharing common code between different executable files or for breaking an application into separate components, thus allowing easy upgrades. In Windows CE, shared libraries are usually referred to as dynamic-link libraries (DLLs).

shell A program that enables the user to connect with the kernel and, thus, the system, usually providing some basic services in addition to facilitating the loading and executing of programs.

sibling window A child window that has the same parent window as one or more other child windows.

signaled *See* **synchronization object**.

Simple Mail Transfer Protocol (SMTP) A standard Internet Protocol (IP) for sending e-mail documents, discussed in RFC821. The format of SMTP messages is discussed in RFC822.

single threading model A model in which all objects are executed on a single thread. *Contrast* **multithreaded application**; *see* **free threading model**, **apartment model threading**.

SIR *See* **Serial Infrared**.

SLIP *See* **Serial Line Internet Protocol**.

SMTP *See* **Simple Mail Transfer Protocol**.

spin button A control containing a pair of arrow buttons that a user can tap with the stylus to increment or decrement a value. A spin button control is most often used with a companion control, called a buddy window, in which a current value is displayed. *Also called* up-down control.

socket An object that represents an endpoint for communication between processes across a network transport. Sockets have a datagram or stream type and can be bound to a specific network address. Windows Sockets provides an application programming interface (API) for handling all types of socket connections in Windows.

Software Development Kit (SDK) A set of tools and libraries for creating software applications for Windows operating systems.

sort order The order in which a set of records or other data objects are to be sorted, or the function that defines this order. Possible sort orders for an array of strings, for example, could include alphabetical order or ascending order by length.

SSL *See* **secure socket layer**.

stack A region of reserved memory in which programs store status data such as procedure and function call addresses, passed parameters, and sometimes local variables.

Standard Generalized Markup Language (SGML)
An information-management standard adopted by the International Organization for Standardization (ISO) in 1986 as a means of providing platform- and application-independent documents that retain formatting, indexing, and linked information. SGML provides a grammar-like mechanism for users to define the structure of their documents, and the tags they will use to denote the structure in individual documents.

static control A control used to display text, to draw frames or lines separating other controls, or to display icons. A static control does not accept user input.

status bar A horizontal window positioned at the bottom of a parent window. A status bar, also known as a status window, displays status information defined by the application.

storage memory Storage memory is similar to a RAM disk on a desktop computer. It is used to store data and non-system applications.

stream mode An asynchronous method of calling **CeRapiInvoke** by using an **IStream** type interface to exchange arbitrary-sized data in any order and direction.

stylus A pointing device used on a touch-sensitive surface.

subfolder A directory, or logical grouping of related files, within another directory.

submenu A menu that appears as the result of the selection of an item on another higher-level menu.

symbol A name that represents a register, an absolute value, or a memory address (relative or absolute).

sysgen phase Refers to the process of defining and building the selected modules and components, as governed by the Makefile located in the directory %_PUBLICROOT%\Common\Cesysgen.

system-defined message A message the system uses to control the operations of an application and to provide input and other information for an application to process. An application can also send or post a system-defined message. An application generally uses this message to control the operation of control windows created by using preregistered window classes.

system registry functions The functions used to manipulate keys and values in the registry. A Windows CE-based application uses the standard Win32 registry functions.

synchronization The process of updating information between the desktop computer and a Windows CE-based device to ensure that data is the same on both computers.

synchronization object An object whose handle can be specified in one of the wait functions to coordinate the execution of multiple threads. A synchronization object will be a member of one of the synchronization classes. Synchronization classes are used when access to a resource must be controlled to ensure integrity of the resource. The state of a synchronization object is either signaled, which can allow the wait function to return, or nonsignaled, which can prevent the function from returning. More than one process can have a handle of the same synchronization object, making interprocess synchronization possible. There are four types of synchronization objects: mutex, semaphore, event and critical section. Of these, Windows CE supports only event and critical section.

synchronous operation **1.** Two or more processes that depend upon the occurrences of specific events such as common timing signals. **2.** Data transmission method in which there is constant time between successive bits, characters, or events. The timing is achieved by the sharing of a single clock. Each end of the transmission synchronizes itself with the use of clocks and information sent along with the transmitted data. Characters are spaced by time, not by start and stop bits. **3.** A function call that blocks execution of a process until it returns. *Compare* **asynchronous operation**.

T

tab control A control that is analogous to a set of dividers in a notebook or labels in a file cabinet. A tab control is used in a property sheet to provide a way for a user to move from one property page to another.

TAPI *See* **Telephony Application Programming Interface**.

target platform The system for which Windows CE is being adapted.

TCP/IP *See* **Transmission Control Protocol/Internet Protocol**.

telephony Telephone technology; the conversion of sound into electrical signals, its transmission to another location, and its reconversion to sound, with or without the use of connecting wires.

Telephony Application Programming Interface (TAPI)
A set of functions in the Win32 API that lets a computer communicate directly with telephone systems. Windows CE supports TAPI version 1.5. It provides the basic functions, structures, and messages for establishing outgoing calls and controlling modems from a Windows CE-based device.

Telephony Service Provider Interface (TSPI)
The Windows CE TSPI defines the external interface of a service provider to be implemented by vendors of telephony equipment. A telephony service provider accesses vendor-specific equipment through a standard device driver interface. Installing a service provider allows Windows CE applications that use elements of telephony to access the corresponding telephony equipment.

TEXT A Win32 macro that exists so that code can be compiled either as American National Standards Institute (ANSI) text or as Unicode. For Windows CE, which supports only Unicode, the macro forces the compiler to convert ANSI characters to Unicode characters. For example, passing the ANSI string "Hello Windows CE!" through the **TEXT** macro converts all characters in the string to 16-bit wide characters.

thread A process that is part of a larger process or program. A thread can execute any part of an application's code, including code that is currently being executed by another thread. All threads share the virtual address space, global variables, and operating-system resources of their respective processes.

thread identifier The unique identifier associated with a specific thread. Note that thread identification numbers are reused; they identify a thread only for the lifetime of that thread.

thread local storage (TLS) A Win32 mechanism that allows multiple threads of a process to store data that is unique for each thread. For example, a spreadsheet application can create a new instance of the same thread each time the user opens a new spreadsheet. A dynamic-link library that provides the functions for various spreadsheet operations can use thread local storage to save information about the current state of each spreadsheet.

thread synchronization The method used to coordinate the execution of two or more threads. There are two states in synchronization, signaled and non-signaled. Threads can either modify the state of the synchronization object or wait for the object to reach a signaled state.

time-out value A specified time interval used by a timer. Each time the time-out value elapses, Windows CE sends a WM_TIMER message to the window associated with the timer.

timer An internal routine that causes the system to send a WM_TIMER message whenever a specified interval elapses.

TLB *See* **Translation Look-aside Buffer**.

TLS *See* **thread local storage**.

toolbar A row, column, or block of on-screen buttons or icons. When these buttons or icons are depressed, macros or certain functions of the application are activated.

ToolTip A small rectangular pop-up window that displays a brief description of a command bar button's purpose.

top-level window A window that has no parent window.

topmost window A window with the WS_EX_TOPMOST style. A topmost window overlaps all other non-topmost windows.

touchpad An input device that functions like a mouse to control cursor movements.

touch panel *See* **touch screen**.

Touch screen A computer screen designed to recognize the location of a touch on its surface. For example, by touching the screen the user can make a selection. Touch screens often serve in place of a mouse or other pointing device.

trackbar A common control, also known as a slider control, that consists of a bar with tick marks on it and a slider, also known as a thumb. When a user drags the slider or clicks on either side of it, the slider moves in the appropriate direction, tick by tick.

Translation Look-aside Buffer (TLB) A table used in a virtual memory system, which lists the physical address page number associated with each virtual address page number. A TLB is used in conjunction with a cache whose tags are based on virtual addresses. The virtual address is presented simultaneously to the TLB and to the cache so that cache access and virtual-to-physical address translation can occur simultaneously.

Transmission Control Protocol/Internet Protocol (TCP/IP)
Transport and address protocols; TCP is used to establish a connection for data transmission, and IP defines the method for sending the data in packets. TCP/IP is the fundamental basis of the Internet.

transport functions A set of functions, exported by a mail transport service dynamic-link library, that are used to transfer mail messages from one location to another.

tree view control A hierarchical display of labeled items. The top item in the hierarchy is called the root. If an item has other items below it in the hierarchy, it is also referred to as a parent. Items subordinate to parents are called children. Child items, when displayed, are indented below their parent item. The hierarchy may be expanded or collapsed at any level to display or hide child items.

TrueType Fonts A scalable outline font whose glyphs are stored as a collection of line and curve commands, plus a collection of hints.

TSP A telephony service provider.

TSPI *See* **Telephony Service Provider Interface**.

U

UNC *See* **universal naming convention**.

Unicode A 16-bit character set capable of encoding almost all known characters and is used as a worldwide character-encoding standard. Windows CE uses Unicode exclusively at the system level.

Uniform Resource Locator (URL)
The address of a resource on the Internet. URL syntax is in the form *protocol://host/localinfo*, where protocol specifies the means of returning the object, such as Hypertext Transfer Protocol (HTTP) or File Transfer Protocol (FTP). Host specifies the remote location where the object resides, and localinfo is a string (often a file name) passed to the protocol handler at the remote location. *Also called* Universal Resource Locator, Uniform Resource Identifier (URI).

Unimodem 1. The universal modem driver, provided with Windows CE, that translates Telephony Service Provider Interface (TSPI) calls into AT commands, and sends the commands to a virtual device driver that talks to the modem. **2.** A universal modem that supports standard modem AT commands. Windows CE currently supports only PCMCIA modems.

universal naming convention (UNC)
The system of naming files among computers on a local area network so that a file has the same path when accessed from any of the computers on the network. For example, if the *directory c*: on computer *servern* is shared under the name *pathdirs*, a user on another computer would open *\servern.ext* to access the file *c:.ext* on *servern*.

Universally Unique Identifier (UUID)
A 128-bit value that uniquely identifies objects such as OLE servers, interfaces, manager entry-point vectors, and client objects. Universally unique identifiers are used in cross-process communication, such as remote procedure calling (RPC) and OLE. *Also called* globally unique identifier (GUID).

up-down control *See* **spin button**.

URL *See* **Uniform Resource Locator**.

user level driver *See* **installable device driver**.

user notification A warning to the user that a timer event has occurred. The notification may require the user to perform some action to handle the notification or may generate a sound to alert the user. For example, the system may display a dialog box and play a sound or icon before a scheduled appointment. The user would tap the dialog box **OK** button to acknowledge the appointment. User notifications are always associated with an application.

UUID *See* **universally unique identifier**.

V

virtual key code A device-independent value that identifies the purpose of a keystroke as interpreted by the Windows keyboard device driver.

W

wait function Allows a thread to block its own execution. Wait functions do not return until the specified criteria have been met. The type of wait function determines the set of criteria used. When a wait function is called, it checks whether the wait criteria have been met. If the criteria have not been met, the calling thread enters an efficient wait state, consuming very little processor time while waiting for the criteria to be met. Windows CE supports only single object wait functions.

warm boot The restarting of a running computer without first turning off the power. *Also called* soft boot, warm start. *Compare* **cold boot**.

wave file A file format in which Windows stores sounds as waveforms. Such files have the extension .wav.

Web Browser ActiveX control An ActiveX control that programmers can use to add Internet browsing capabilities to applications.

Win32 The application programming interface in Windows 95, Windows NT, and Windows CE that enables applications to use the 32-bit instructions available on 80386 and higher processors.

window A rectangular area on the screen where an application displays output and receives user input. On a Windows CE-based device that supports a graphical display, a window, rather than the screen itself, is the primary output device. Windows are also the means by which applications send and receive messages to the operating system. Therefore, all Windows CE-based applications—even those that lack a visual interface—need to create and manage windows.

window class A set of attributes that Windows CE uses as a template to create a window. Each window class has a window procedure that processes messages for all windows of that class. Every window in a Windows CE-based application is a member of a window class.

window control A predefined child window used in conjunction with another application window to provide a standardized way for users to make selections, carry out commands, and perform input and output tasks. Windows controls typically send WM_COMMAND messages.

window coordinate The position of a window in relation to the upper-left corner of the screen or, for a child window, the upper-left corner of the parent window's client area.

window handle A 32-bit value, assigned by Windows CE, that uniquely identifies a window.

window procedure A function, called by the operating system, that controls the appearance and behavior of its associated windows. The procedure receives and processes all messages to these windows.

window style A named constant that defines an aspect of the window's appearance and behavior not specified by the window's class.

Windows CE Services The software supplied with Windows CE that provides ready-made services to aid the applications developer. These services generally deal with interactions between the desktop computer and the Windows CE-based device, and include the Explorer window, file filters, RAPI, ActiveSync, and the Applications Manager.

WinInet function Win32 Internet functions (WinInet) that assist you in adding Internet access to your applications using Hypertext Transfer Protocol (HTTP), File Transfer Protocol (FTP), and gopher.

Winsock Name commonly used for the Windows Sockets programming interface, used to provide a protocol independent transport interface. Windows CE supports most of the common Winsock functions.

X

X.509 An international message-handling standard for message authentication and encryption. X.509 is published by the Internal Telecommunications Union (ITU), formerly the International Telegraph and Telephone Consultative Committee (CCITT) standards body.

XIP *See* **execute in place**.

Z

Z order A stack of overlapping windows. Each window has a unique position in the Z order.

Index

I

Get grounded in the art of Visual C++.

U.S.A. **$39.99**
U.K. £37.49 [V.A.T. included]
Canada $53.99
ISBN 1-57231-510-5

For a solid guide to everything from Developer Studio® fundamentals to compiler optimization, this is the book you're searching for. It's a complete look at Visual C++®—including the redesigned development environment of version 5.0. You'll find guidance on:

- Getting started in Developer Studio and using AppWizard
- Working with the text editor, the graphics editor, and the dialog editor
- Using ClassWizard for creating and maintaining classes and using the Gallery to add ready-made components
- Using and writing ActiveX® controls
- Using the debugger, optimizing your programs, and customizing Developer Studio

Appendixes include tables of ASCII and ANSI characters, descriptions of MFC classes supported by ClassWizard, and an introduction to Visual Basic® Scripting Edition. The enclosed CD-ROM includes sample code to help you get started quickly. In short, this volume is invaluable for anyone who wants to master the powerful development tools in Visual C++ version 5.

***Microsoft*®*Press**

Write
faster Windows applications
with MFC!

U.S.A. $39.99
U.K. £37.49 [V.A.T. included]
Canada $53.99
ISBN 1-57231-511-3

MFC DEVELOPER'S WORKSHOP is the first book to
provide developer-driven, task-oriented relief for
those using the MFC library to program for Windows®.
It targets troublesome, frequently encountered
tasks—and provides solutions for them. In addition,
carefully selected articles from Microsoft's huge
Knowledge Base supplement the main text and
amplify the topics being discussed. Intended for
those with at least one year of experience developing
MFC applications for Windows, MFC DEVELOPER'S
WORKSHOP covers:

- The functionality of AppWizard and the modularity
  of the class library
- Frame window architecture
- Document templates
- Dialog boxes—techniques for modifying their
  attributes and behavior
- Using Windows common controls
- Using ActiveX® controls and implementing OLE
  features such as drag and drop
- Resource-only DLLs and saving the state of MFC
  applications

Microsoft Press

Build
great programs
for 32-bit Windows platforms with
Visual C++!

Building on the solid achievements of three previous editions, INSIDE VISUAL C++®, Fourth Edition, presents detailed and comprehensive coverage of Visual C++ and the intricacies of 32-bit programming in Windows®. This book is loaded with inside information and real-world examples to help you fully exploit the capabilities of Microsoft's powerful and complex development tool.

U.S.A.	**$49.99**
U.K.	£46.99 [V.A.T. included]
Canada	$66.99
ISBN 1-57231-565-2	

Microsoft ®*Press*

Grasp
the power of
Microsoft
Visual C++
in both hands.

This four-volume collection is the complete printed product documentation for Microsoft Visual C++ version 5.0, *the* development system for Win32®. In book form, this information is portable, easy to access and browse, and a comprehensive alternative to the substantial online help system in Visual C++. The volumes are numbered as a set—but you can buy any or all of the volumes, any time you need them. So take hold of all the power. Get the MICROSOFT VISUAL C++ 5.0 PROGRAMMER'S REFERENCE SET.

Microsoft® Visual C++® MFC Library Reference, Part 1

U.S.A.	**$39.99**
U.K.	£36.99
Canada	$53.99
ISBN	1-57231-518-0

Microsoft® Visual C++® MFC Library Reference, Part 2

U.S.A.	**$39.99**
U.K.	£36.99
Canada	$53.99
ISBN	1-57231-519-9

Microsoft® Visual C++® Run-Time Library Reference

U.S.A.	**$39.99**
U.K.	£36.99
Canada	$53.99
ISBN	1-57231-520-2

Microsoft® Visual C++® Language Reference

U.S.A.	**$29.99**
U.K.	£27.49
Canada	$39.99
ISBN	1-57231-521-0

Microsoft Press® products are available worldwide wherever quality computer books are sold. For more information, contact your book or computer retailer, software reseller, or local Microsoft Sales Office, or visit our Web site at mspress.microsoft.com. To locate your nearest source for Microsoft Press products, or to order directly, call 1-800-MSPRESS in the U.S. (in Canada, call 1-800-268-2222).

Prices and availability dates are subject to change.

Microsoft Press

IMPORTANT—READ CAREFULLY BEFORE OPENING SOFTWARE PACKET(S). By opening the sealed packet(s) containing the software, you indicate your acceptance of the following Microsoft License Agreement.

MICROSOFT LICENSE AGREEMENT

(Microsoft Windows CE Programmer's Guide – Book Companion CD)

IMPORTANT—READ CAREFULLY: This Microsoft End User License Agreement ("EULA") is a legal agreement between you (either an individual or a single entity) and Microsoft Corporation for the Microsoft software product identified above, which includes computer software and may include associated media, printed materials, and "online" or electronic documentation ("SOFTWARE PRODUCT"). By installing, copying, or otherwise using the SOFTWARE PRODUCT, you agree to be bound by the terms of this EULA. If you do not agree to the terms of this EULA, you may not use the SOFTWARE PRODUCT; you may, however, return it to your place of purchase for a full refund; or if you received the SOFTWARE PRODUCT as part of a subscription or other service from Microsoft, you may cancel the subscription and receive a pro rated portion of the subscription price.

SOFTWARE PRODUCT LICENSE

The SOFTWARE PRODUCT is protected by copyright laws and international copyright treaties, as well as other intellectual property laws and treaties. The SOFTWARE PRODUCT is licensed, not sold.

1. GRANT OF LICENSE. This EULA grants you the following rights:

a. Software Product. Microsoft grants to you as an individual, a personal, non-exclusive and limited license to make and use copies of the SOFTWARE PRODUCT for the sole purposes of designing, developing and testing your software application product(s) for use with the Microsoft Windows CE operating system ("Application"). You may install copies of the SOFTWARE PRODUCT on an unlimited number of computers provided that you are the only individual using the SOFTWARE PRODUCT. If you are an entity, Microsoft grants you the right to designate one individual within your organization to have the right to use the SOFTWARE PRODUCT in the manner provided above.

b. Electronic Documents. Solely with respect to electronic documents included with the SOFTWARE PRODUCT, you may make an unlimited number of copies (either in hardcopy or electronic form), provided that such copies shall be used only for internal purposes and are not republished or distributed to any third party.

c. Sample Code. In addition to the rights granted in Section 1(a), Microsoft grants you the non-exclusive and limited right to use and modify the source code version of those portions of the SOFTWARE PRODUCT that are identified as "sample code" in the documentation and/or listed in the subdirectory \wce\samples ("SAMPLE CODE") for the sole purposes of designing, developing, and testing your Application(s), provided that you comply with Section 1(e), below.

d. Redistributable Files. Provided that you comply with Section 1(e), Microsoft also grants you the non-exclusive and limited right to reproduce and distribute only the object code versions of the SAMPLE CODE (including any modifications you have made thereto) ("REDISTRIBUTABLES").

e. Redistribution Requirements. If you redistribute the REDISTRIBUTABLES, you agree to: (i) distribute the REDISTRIBUTABLES only in conjunction with and as part of your Application(s) developed by you that adds significant and primary functionality to the REDISTRIBUTABLES; (ii) not use Microsoft's name, logo, or trademarks to market your Application(s); (iii) include a valid copyright notice on your Application(s); (iv) indemnify, hold harmless, and defend Microsoft from and against any claims or lawsuits, including attorney's fees, that arise or result from the use or distribution of your Application(s); and (v) not permit further distribution of the REDISTRIBUTABLES by your end users. The following exception applies to subsection (e)(v), above: You may permit further redistribution of the REDISTRIBUTABLES by your distributors to your end user customers if your distributors only distribute the REDISTRIBUTABLES in conjunction with, and as part of, your Application(s) and you and your distributors comply with all other terms of this EULA.

2. COPYRIGHT. All rights, title, and copyrights in and to the SOFTWARE PRODUCT (including, but not limited to, any images, photographs, animations, video, audio, music, text, and "applets" incorporated into the SOFTWARE PRODUCT) and any copies of the SOFTWARE PRODUCT are owned by Microsoft or its suppliers. The SOFTWARE PRODUCT is protected by copyright laws and international treaty provisions. Therefore, you must treat the SOFTWARE PRODUCT like any other copyrighted material, except that you may either (a) make one copy of the SOFTWARE PRODUCT solely for backup or archival purposes, or (b) install the SOFTWARE PRODUCT on a single computer, provided you keep the original solely for backup or archival purposes. You may not copy the printed materials accompanying the SOFTWARE PRODUCT.

3. PRERELEASE CODE. The SOFTWARE PRODUCT may contain PRERELEASE CODE that is not at the level of performance and compatibility of the final, generally available, product offering. These portions of the SOFTWARE PRODUCT may not operate correctly and may be substantially modified prior to first commercial shipment. Microsoft is not obligated to make this or any later version of the SOFTWARE PRODUCT commercially available. Microsoft grants you the right to distribute test versions of your Application(s) created using the PRERELEASE CODE provided you comply with the Distribution Requirements described in Section 1 and the following additional provisions: (a) you must mark the test version of your Application "BETA" and (b) you are solely responsible for updating your customers with versions of your Application that operate satisfactorily with the final commercial release of the PRERELEASE CODE. In order to determine what constitutes PRERELEASE CODE, consult the SOFTWARE PRODUCT documentation.

4. DESCRIPTION OF OTHER RIGHTS AND LIMITATIONS.

a. Limitations on Reverse Engineering, Decompilation, and Disassembly. You may not reverse engineer, decompile, or disassemble the SOFTWARE PRODUCT, except and only to the extent that such activity is expressly permitted by applicable law notwithstanding this limitation.

b. Rental. You may not rent, lease, or lend the SOFTWARE PRODUCT.

c. Software Transfer. You may permanently transfer all of your rights under this EULA, provided you retain no copies, you transfer all of the SOFTWARE PRODUCT (including all component parts, the media and printed materials, any upgrades, this EULA, and, if applicable, the Certificate of Authenticity), and the recipient agrees to the terms of this EULA. If the SOFTWARE PRODUCT is an upgrade, any transfer must include all prior versions of the SOFTWARE PRODUCT.

d. Termination. Without prejudice to any other rights, Microsoft may terminate this EULA if you fail to comply with the terms and conditions of this EULA. In such event, you must destroy all copies of the SOFTWARE PRODUCT and all of its component parts.

5. EXPORT RESTRICTIONS. You agree that neither you nor your customers intend to or will, directly or indirectly, export or transmit (a) the SOFTWARE PRODUCT or related documentation and technical data, or (b) your Application as described in Section 1 of this EULA (or any part thereof), or process, or service that is the direct product of the SOFTWARE PRODUCT to any country to which such export or transmission is restricted by any applicable U.S. regulation or statute, without the prior written consent, if required, of the Bureau of Export Administration of the U.S. Department of Commerce, or such other governmental entity as may have jurisdiction over such export or transmission.

6. U.S. GOVERNMENT RESTRICTED RIGHTS. The SOFTWARE PRODUCT and documentation are provided with RESTRICTED RIGHTS. Use, duplication, or disclosure by the Government is subject to restrictions as set forth in subparagraph (c)(1)(ii) of The Rights in Technical Data and Computer Software clause at DFARS 252.227-7013 or subparagraphs (c)(1) and (2) of the Commercial Computer Software - Restricted Rights at 48 CFR 52.227-19, as applicable. Manufacturer is Microsoft Corporation/One Microsoft Way/Redmond, WA 98052-6399.

MISCELLANEOUS

If you acquired this product in the United States, this EULA is governed by the laws of the State of Washington.

If this product was acquired outside the United States, then local law may apply.

Should you have any questions concerning this EULA, or if you desire to contact Microsoft for any reason, please contact the Microsoft subsidiary serving your country, or write: Microsoft Sales Information Center/One Microsoft Way/Redmond, WA 98052-6399.

LIMITED WARRANTY

NO WARRANTIES. TO THE MAXIMUM EXTENT PERMITTED BY APPLICABLE LAW, MICROSOFT EXPRESSLY DISCLAIMS ANY WARRANTY FOR THE SOFTWARE PRODUCT. THE SOFTWARE PRODUCT AND ANY RELATED DOCUMENTATION ARE PROVIDED "AS IS" WITHOUT WARRANTY OF ANY KIND, EITHER EXPRESS OR IMPLIED, INCLUDING, WITHOUT LIMITATION, THE IMPLIED WARRANTIES OF MERCHANTABILITY OR FITNESS FOR A PARTICULAR PURPOSE. THE ENTIRE RISK ARISING OUT OF USE OR PERFORMANCE OF THE SOFTWARE PRODUCT REMAINS WITH YOU.

LIMITATION OF LIABILITY. MICROSOFT'S ENTIRE LIABILITY AND YOUR EXCLUSIVE REMEDY UNDER THIS EULA SHALL NOT EXCEED FIVE DOLLARS (US$5.00).

NO LIABILITY FOR CONSEQUENTIAL DAMAGES. TO THE MAXIMUM EXTENT PERMITTED BY APPLICABLE LAW, IN NO EVENT SHALL MICROSOFT OR ITS SUPPLIERS BE LIABLE FOR ANY DAMAGES WHATSOEVER (INCLUDING, WITHOUT LIMITATION, DAMAGES FOR LOSS OF BUSINESS PROFIT, BUSINESS INTERRUPTION, LOSS OF BUSINESS INFORMATION, OR ANY OTHER PECUNIARY LOSS) ARISING OUT OF THE USE OF, OR INABILITY TO USE, THIS MICROSOFT PRODUCT, EVEN IF MICROSOFT HAS BEEN ADVISED OF THE POSSIBILITY OF SUCH DAMAGES. BECAUSE SOME STATES/JURISDICTIONS DO NOT ALLOW THE EXCLUSION OR LIMITATION OF LIABILITY FOR CONSEQUENTIAL OR INCIDENTAL DAMAGES, THE ABOVE LIMITATION MAY NOT APPLY TO YOU.

Si vous avez acquis votre produit Microsoft au CANADA, la garantie limitée suivante vous concerne:

GARANTIE LIMITÉE

EXCLUSION DE GARANTIES. Microsoft renonce entièrement à toute garantie pour le LOGICIEL. Le LOGICIEL et toute autre documentation s'y rapportant sont fournis « comme tels » sans aucune garantie quelle qu'elle soit, expresse ou implicite, y compris, mais ne se limitant pas aux garanties implicites de la qualité marchande ou un usage particulier. Le risque total découlant de l'utilisation ou de la performance du LOGICIEL est entre vos mains.

RESPONSABILITÉ LIMITÉE. La seule obligation de Microsoft et votre recours exclusif concernant ce contrat n'excèderont pas cinq dollars (US$5.00).

ABSENCE DE RESPONSABILITÉ POUR LES DOMMAGES INDIRECTS. Microsoft ou ses fournisseurs ne pourront être tenus responsables en aucune circonstance de tout dommage quel qu'il soit (y compris mais non de façon limitative les dommages directs ou indirects causés par la perte de bénéfices commerciaux, l'interruption des affaires, la perte d'information commerciale ou toute autre perte pécuniaire) résultant de l'utilisation ou de l'impossibilité d'utilisation de ce produit, et ce, même si la société Microsoft a été avisée de l'éventualité de tels dommages. Certains états/juridictions ne permettent pas l'exclusion ou la limitation de responsabilité relative aux dommages indirects ou consécutifs, et la limitation ci-dessus peut ne pas s'appliquer à votre égard.

La présente Convention est régie par les lois de la province d'Ontario, Canada. Chacune des parties à la Convention reconnaît irrévocablement la compétence des tribunaux de la province d'Ontario et consent à instituer tout litige qui pourrait découler de la Convention auprès des tribunaux situés dans le district judiciaire de York, province d'Ontario.

Au cas où vous auriez des questions concernant cette licence ou que vous désiriez vous mettre en rapport avec Microsoft pour quelque raison que ce soit, veuillez contacter la succursale Microsoft desservant votre pays, dont l'adresse est fournie dans ce produit, ou écrire à: Microsoft Customer Sales and Service, One Microsoft Way, Redmond, Washington 98052-6399.

Register Today!

Return this
Microsoft® Windows® CE Programmer's Guide
registration card for
a Microsoft Press® catalog

1-57231-643-8   *MICROSOFT® WINDOWS® CE*   *Owner Registration Card*
                         PROGRAMMER'S GUIDE

_____

NAME

_____

INSTITUTION OR COMPANY NAME

_____

ADDRESS

_____

CITY   STATE   ZIP

Microsoft®Press
Quality Computer Books

For a free catalog of
Microsoft Press® products, call
1-800-MSPRESS